UK INVESTMENT GUIDE

3RD EDITION

UK INVESTMENT GUIDE
3RD EDITION

David Berger &
James Carlisle

WITH AN INTRODUCTION BY DAVID AND TOM GARDNER

NEW INTRODUCTION TO THE THIRD EDITION BY DAVID BERGER

B🌿XTREE

First published 2000 by Boxtree
This updated and revised edition with new introduction by
David Berger and new appendices published 2002 by Boxtree,
an imprint of Pan Macmillan Ltd
Pan Macmillan, 20 New Wharf Road, London N1 9RR
Basingstoke and Oxford
Associated companies throughout the world
www.panmacmillan.com

ISBN 0 7522 6539 3

3 5 7 9 8 6 4 2

A CIP catalogue record for this book is available from the British Library.

Designed and typeset by seagulls
Printed by Mackays of Chatham plc

Contents

What You've (Maybe) Already Got

Bits 'n' Bobs

Rounding Up

Appendices

Introduction to the Third Edition

And the World Kept on Turning

Talk about rapid. Just five years ago when the Motley Fool UK was established, the Internet had yet to hit Great Britain. Since then, it has shot to enormous prominence, that new frontier which was going to change all our lives (and make lots of people rich). Subsequently, it plummeted even more rapidly into a position of popular contempt, as a result of what history will know as 'The Great Dotcom Crash of 2000'.

So how do we make sense of it all? How do we integrate this experience into our lives, file it away as something interesting and noteworthy and move on? Particularly for investors, this has been a tumultuous time, with a lot of fingers getting badly burned and it would be understandable if many people decided they'd had enough of this investing lark and gave it up entirely.

Understandable, but wrong. The past several years have provided a seductive vision of riches to be made for little effort and in an unreasonably short period of time. The Motley Fool, and other voices too, have preached against following an investing path which history has told us is very clearly a fantasy. Investing can bring extraordinary riches, but it takes time, a modicum of endeavour and some reasonable expectations.

In this third edition of our Investment Guide, you'll find much brought up to date, some new chapters, some old ones thrown out or extensively reworked and even a chapter of lessons learned from the dotcom boom. The interesting thing for us, though, as we've looked at what needed to be done for the third edition, was how little of real substance needed to be changed.

The basic message of long-term, steady investing in the stockmarket as the most effective means to build wealth stands. The ways to do it are fundamentally the same, the basic information, the pitfalls and wrinkles, are the same as those we highlighted in the first edition of this guide back in 1998, that Jurassic age of pre-dotcom innocence, as it now feels.

It's reassuring in this investing world where so much seems to happen of such apparently earth-shattering novelty, that much of it is froth. Little that is truly new genuinely occurs and cutting through the froth to the fundamental assumptions underlying the process of investing bring us back to the age-old common sense ideas behind the Motley Fool philosophy. That doesn't mean we don't learn lessons and then build on that experience – all of us at the Fool have learned many lessons in the past five years and you'll find many of those here – just that common sense never goes out of fashion.

I hope, then, you'll enjoy this third edition of our common sense view on the world of investing and, even more, that you'll take the opportunity to put its principles into practice to help you build a more solid financial future for yourself. I also hope you'll come and join us at the Motley Fool website (www.fool.co.uk) where, as we have been doing daily for the last five years, we continue to try to make investing easy, painless and profitable for you.

Here's to wealth!

DAVID BERGER
LANGTREE, DEVON
SUMMER 2002

Introduction to the Second Edition
Of Books and Web Sites

There's something paradoxical about writing a book at the same time as running an Internet publishing operation like the Motley Fool. In the one, the content is updated many times daily, errors corrected in seconds and much of the written content on the Web site is submitted, not by the staff, but by the users, posting their thoughts, ideas, questions and analyses twenty-four hours a day. That gives it an immediacy and vibrancy it's impossible to match in any other medium. With a book, on the other hand, content is submitted once, it takes two years (in this case) to update it, no immediate user input is possible and, in contrast to the Web site, *it costs money to read it.*

Looking at the bare facts of the matter, you'd conclude both that we were insane to continue publishing books and you were insane to continue buying them. As ever in life, though, bare facts are less than half the story. We're creatures of habit. Books have been hallowed objects for thousands of years, even more so before the widespread adoption of printing in the fifteenth century. We could wonder for hours why this is and it's the kind of lazy speculation that goes so well with a fridge full of ice-cold beers or a bottle of Chardonnay on a sun-drenched terrace, somewhere where English isn't the native tongue. (*Mmmm* ...) For now, though, we can probably wrap it up by saying that, for whatever reason, books are wonderful things to own, read and behold. A much-loved book encapsulates a body of knowledge or an experience that we would love to call our own, even for just a short time; and it's much easier to assimilate large bodies of information from a book, which we read as, when and where we want to, than it is from a screen. The Internet is not going to replace books any time soon (let's remember that Amazon, the best-known Internet retailer, started life as a bookstore) and that's why I'm writing this introduction to the second edition of the *Motley Fool UK Investment Guide* and you're reading it.

While the Internet can't replace books, however, it can and does complement them. In the case of the Motley Fool, the Internet provides a forum for discussion and an opportunity to plug into the corpus of information and ideas that has generated the book in the first place – to tap into the energy source. In this, the Internet offers another, entirely new dimension to the experience of reading a book. Just how revolutionary this is is brought home to us here at the Fool every day as we take part in and observe the daily interchange of ideas and information that unites a community of investors on the Internet.

A lot has changed since this book was published back in November 1998 and even more has changed since the inception of the Fool UK in September 1997. From small beginnings and a tiny public awareness of the potential of the Internet, the Motley Fool UK now has hundreds of thousands of visitors each month. This growth in the Internet, which really started with the launch of Freeserve as a free Internet Service Provider in 1998, has proved phenomenal, and the advent of the wireless Internet in the next five years could prove even more far-reaching. A short-lived boom in the prices of Internet and other technology shares in the early part of 2000 resulted in a spate of British press headlines like 'DOT COM MANIA', 'DOT COM FRENZY', 'DOT BOMB', 'DOT GONE?' As ever, the British press was taking a short-term, sensationalist viewpoint, something we talk about later in the book in relation to investing. Well, the 'dot' hasn't 'gone' and it's here to stay. It always takes a while to view new developments in a mature light, particularly when they threaten to upset a comfortable and long-lived status quo, and the wild swings in press opinion and in the stock market in recent times are probably a reflection of that.

Viewing the Internet as a threat, though, just isn't helpful and taking that attitude carries within itself the seeds of one's own destruction. In our experience here at the Motley Fool, the Internet is a tremendous leveller. That is to say it is an extraordinary discriminator of value, in whatever terms, financial or personal, one cares to define it. If someone or something is not providing value – and the traditional practices of the financial services industry are a graphic example – the Internet will blow the whole game wide open.

Similarly, the Internet can also be a tremendous provider of value in its own right and also a complement to traditional sources of value. All those people who say that the Internet is a poor substitute for books are right. They're also right when they say sitting in front of a computer screen is a poor substitute for life. Of course they are. But what the Internet can do is provide a complement to them. The Motley Fool UK Web site provides a complement to this book. A newly struck-up e-mail correspondence with long-lost cousin Edward in the Australian outback provides a tremendous complement to the life of your family. (Well, it may do, depending on why you decided to ship him out there in the first place.)

Having spent all this time musing on why we're still writing books – basically cos we love 'em and think they're great – what have we actually changed in this second edition? In some ways quite a lot and in some ways not so much. The basic ethos of the Fool remains unchanged, many individual passages and indeed some whole chapters remain fundamentally unchanged, but much of the treatment of individual investing issues in this book represents, we think, a more solid approach, and some chapters have been entirely transformed, incorporated into others or dropped as being no longer relevant.

We've updated numbers, updated our thinking where it needed it, beefed up some of the most important bits and inserted secret Masonic catchphrases where we think they'll be most effective.[1] In short, the world has moved on, the Fool has moved on and we've tried hard to reflect that.

In terms of specifics, readers of the first edition will notice the most major changes in:

● The Obviously Great Investments chapter, where we've looked at what went well with our companies from the first edition and what went badly, and thrown in some more companies for consideration. We've also made a couple of changes to the Obviously Great Investment criteria. The old 'Repeat purchase' criterion has been folded into 'Have They Built a Strong Brand?', and a new criterion, 'Is Their Position Easily Defended?', has been added.

---

1 Not actually true.

- Our treatment of pensions, endowments and ISAs. These have all been updated to reflect the current situation and current thinking.
- The Mechanical Investing chapter (formerly Beating the Footsie). It's become apparent that mechanical investing, while attractive for some, requires a greater diligence and commitment than it's possible to instil in a single chapter of a book. We've therefore broadened the chapter out, making it much more about mechanical investing in general than a single strategy, and pointing the interested reader to our Web site where much more in-depth treatment is available.

There's always a fine line to be trodden in any second edition. This is between writing a stand-alone volume in which new readers aren't irritated by constant references to 'In the first edition ... ', while at the same time paying due homage to what went before, both for reasons of intellectual rigour and to give readers of the first edition a sense of continuity. To serve these twin masters, we have therefore adopted a deliberate policy, beloved of generations of British politicians, known as 'fudging it'. Hopefully, though, the fudge has allowed us to achieve a middle ground which will satisfy both camps. I think and hope it has. On the one hand, we hope this edition represents a totally new, stand-alone volume for people who may never have heard of the Motley Fool and on the other it is a worthy successor and inheritor of the first edition, providing a useful refresher and update.

Inestimable thanks are due to the thousands who wrote in and commented on the first edition. We can't say we've incorporated all your suggestions and feedback, but an awful lot has found its way in. We'd love to hear what you thought of this book, too – where we could have made it clearer, bits we should have put in, bits we should have left out and anything else you think of.

Tell us what we ought to do to make personal investment in Britain easier to understand. In fact, tell us how to improve our business – we're always on the look-out for bright ideas and bright people. One thing, though: if you ask us to give you directive, individual advice about what to do with your own money, we'll neatly sidestep the question. Britain already has more than enough financial advisers.

You can send an e-mail with any and all feedback to us at **foolukbook**

@fool.co.uk, or else post a message on the UK Investment Guide discussion board, which you'll find at our Web site – www.fool.co.uk. You can even write:

Motley Fool UK
6th Floor
The Media Centre
3–8 Carburton Street
London W1W 5AJ

And if you're in the area and feel like seeing what goes on in Fool HQ, please drop in.

Viva il Fool!

DAVID BERGER
LANGTREE,DEVON
SUMMER 2000

Introduction to the First Edition

Welcome to the Age
of Foolishness

David B.

Who isn't a little anxious about money? Who doesn't worry that they're not saving enough or that their savings aren't growing fast enough? Who has a total and utter, rock solid, unshakeable faith in their financial adviser and in the financial professions as a whole? If none of these questions worries you, then you should probably put this book back on the shelf and leave very quietly the way you came in. Our bet is, though, that most people picking up this strangely named volume have at least some doubt in their mind on one or other or all three of these questions. It's only natural. After all, who amongst us was taught anything whatsoever about personal finance at school? Who amongst us has ever understood, *really* understood, what a financial professional was going on about? Yes, we bet the answers are pretty doubtful to these questions too.

There's a dark void in many people's lives when it comes to finance, a feeling that 'Here be dragons', that it's best not to meddle in what you can never hope to understand. Well, tosh, piffle and rubbish! We don't believe that's so at all and in this book we plan to show why. We'll show you how the financial professionals and the City are out to keep the public as ignorant as possible, how they sell investment plans which eat up 80 per cent or more of the first two years' contributions in charges and take a full seven years to break even, how they sell other plans which perform worse than even the average in over 90 per cent of cases. We'll take you on a tour of all those

TESSAs, PEPs, PPPs, ISAs and BAPs (one of these is a type of filled roll, no prizes for guessing which). We'll show you what they all mean – in very simple, easily understandable terms – and then we'll show you just how you can beat the professionals at their own game. And beat them roundly.

You don't need GCSEs, 'A' levels or a degree for this. Just a smattering of common sense, your feet on moderately firm ground and a willingness to challenge the orthodoxy, to rise against convention. In fact, as usual, Winnie the Pooh puts his finger right on the spot. Here he is summing up his friend Owl:

'Owl hasn't exactly got Brain, but he Knows Things.'

Knowing Things, not very many things, is one of the keys to this whole business.

The final quality you'll need is a sense of humour. In contrast to the financial professionals, we don't believe that learning about investment has to be worthy or turgid or boring. We believe it should be fun. We have got a lot of enjoyment out of writing this book and from working to promote a sound understanding of basic financial principles, both offline and on and we hope you'll come and share in our spirit of lightheartedness. But please don't think us flippant. We understand how deadly serious is the issue of financial security; we, however, simply don't buy into the mock awe and very real pomposity with which it is invested by the ranks of the professionals.

So who are we, these three strange-looking characters in silly hats? For that, we must go back to 1993, when David and Tom Gardner sat down and took a long, hard look at the investing orthodoxy that prevailed in the United States of America. The wisdom seemed to be that Mr Joe Average, as the common punter is termed in the United States, was a hopeless case when it came to understanding anything about investing; one step removed from a flatworm in fact. His only hope lay in finding a benevolent professional who would take over the burden of managing his savings and steer it through the financial minefield which, alone, he had no chance of negotiating without losing a leg at the very least. In return for this limb- and possibly even life-saving help, the professional would take a modest commission. The result? Mr J. Average could go home and sleep at night, secure in the knowledge that his savings were in good hands and the professional would make a fair living, returning to his family every evening and basking in the satisfying glow of an honest job, well done.

It was fairyland, but in this prosperous nation, with its sunstruck coasts, purple mountains, gun-toting crazies and pizzas the size of tractor tyres, all was not quite as it seemed. Mr Average was ignorant all right, but it wasn't because money and finance were impossible, or even difficult to understand. It was because he had never been *taught* anything about them at all. Simple concepts like pensions, price-to-earnings ratios, stock market indices and execution-only brokers were not just unknowns, they were terrifying, shadowy concepts, the very mention of which might unleash malign powers.

Nowhere in the entire educational system was provision made to teach this basic and vital information. Without education, it was true that the average investor (read: 'Everybody who ever hoped to save any money for their future') had no chance of understanding what was going on and had no choice but to hand over his or her hard-earned dollars to the professionals. That was a shame in itself, because actions based on ignorance of any kind cannot be auspicious for the future. But that was far from the end of the story.

You see, the professional money managers of the United States were not stepping into the breach of ignorance and delivering a solid, dependable service as part of a public service commitment. It turned out that it was in their interests to keep the level of ignorance and confusion about money as high as possible, because the foundation of their industry was based on some very unstable bedrock indeed. It was an extraordinary but true fact that 90 per cent of the returns on offer from America's professional money managers were lower than the returns that could be made off simple, low-cost investments, easy to purchase, requiring no skill to pick and with negligible charges attached to them. With a tiny amount of time and even less effort, Joe Average could outperform the professionals, precisely by being average. He just didn't know it yet. Another thing he didn't know was that in itself the stock market is not a dangerous place to invest, but is in fact one of the *safest* kinds of investments. With the financial media constantly harping on potential short-term losses in the stock market, the long-term story of reliable, outperforming growth was totally lost. Of course, short-term panic stories are what sell newspapers and lure television viewers.

America was being duped and neither its financial professionals nor its media had any real interest in the spread of mass education about their subject. They had it very cushy, which was how it had been for a long time and that's how it might have stayed. Then something happened, something which this writer, with characteristic vision, welcomed with open arms:

'What's it called? The Internet? You can talk to other people with your computer? You can get hold of information? Why on *Earth* would you bother to do that?!'

Yes, really, and at about the time that the Oracle of Bournemouth (where David hails from originally) was dismissing the greatest revolution in mass communication since the invention of moveable type, David and Tom Gardner were transferring their print publication *The Motley Fool*, started a year earlier in 1993, onto America Online, otherwise known as AOL. A small, subversive movement had begun.

The name alluded to Shakespeare's Fool – Touchstone in *As You Like It* – who had an unnerving habit of demonstrating that truth often lay beyond the bounds of conventional wisdom. Fools in the olden days were about the only people who could tell the King how it really was without getting their heads lopped off for their pains. In its print incarnation, *The Motley Fool* ('Ye Olde Printed Foole', as it is now fondly remembered) had a terribly small audience, mostly of family friends, we are told, who wanted to support the boys' attempt to make a living. (And about time too, their mum was probably saying.) Things soon took off, though, with the move to the mass medium and by the end of 1995 they were the most popular site on AOL, they had added a website and were publishing a book which went on to become a best-seller. Soon, the Fool was on the lips of everyone in America who had any interest in finance, the Fool's newspaper column was syndicated in over 160 newspapers around the country and the website was registering 20 million visits a month. As the Wise grew more disdainful, so the Fools were growing ever more popular, helping people to help themselves out of financial bondage.

It was about at this time that I, a jobbing British doctor, sometime of Bournemouth as we've heard (Three cheers for Bournemouth! Hello, Mum!), stumbled across the Fool on the Web. Humour? Down-to-Earthness? A willingness to engage with the world and do something novel? And all this in a site about investment? Very strange.

So strange in fact that I got hooked and, well, you know, one thing led to another and while initially I only needed five or ten minutes a day of the Fool online to keep me satisfied, pretty soon I was doing cold turkey without three, four or even more hours plugged in every day. Yes, the Fool had snared another unsuspecting innocent. It was pitiful to see. And then this happened:

One day, after many hours' surfing, I found myself moving through a deep, inner sanctum of the online area, a place I had never visited before. The cavernous walls of the chamber echoed with the clicks of my mouse. It smelt damp and musty and all of a sudden the stillness was broken by the distant sound of breaking glass and a woman's high-pitched scream. Then all was quiet once more. On the muted, darkened screen there was now just one gently flashing icon and it said 'Click here if you wish to become a Fool'. I hesitated, awestruck and barely comprehending the step I was about to take. There was no going back now, that at least I knew. I clicked. A message came up: 'Please Wait.' Then: 'Please be still while we upload your brain. Click here to proceed.' I clicked and sat motionless, as bidden. Suddenly, the screen became busy with activity and it was clear that something extraordinary was about to happen. And then I felt it – as if someone had pulled the plug out of the bath at the base of my skull. My brains were leaving me and being *uploaded to the Motley Fool*! I sat still, a curious sense of ease washing over me. After a few minutes, another dialogue box sprang up through the misty haze of well-being: 'Please click here to download a test version of a Mark 1 Foolish brain.' As the Foolish brain was downloaded, I felt my skull filling up once more and my consciousness returning to clarity. I had become a card-carrying Fool.

All right, it didn't happen *quite* like that, but the brain-sucking, Boris Karloff imagery was too tempting to forgo. What actually happened was that I composed an e-mail one wet Tuesday afternoon in April to David and Tom Gardner. 'It's just the same here, you know,' I said. 'We pay outrageous charges for underperforming investments, just like you,' I said. 'No-one knows anything about this stuff and when the professionals come and sell it to us, we just gawp and nod blindly and believe it, like you do,' I said. 'How about a British Motley Fool? And soon!' I said. To their credit – and this says something about the accessibility this new medium provides, as well as their openness to new ideas and innovation – they didn't do the high-tech equivalent of screwing up my e-mail and lobbing it at the basketball hoop they have poised over the wastepaper bin.

Again, one thing led to another and by the autumn of 1997, five months after the first e-mail, the Motley Fool UK Online was launched on AOL UK (keyword: FOOLUK), followed in February 1998 by the Web site www.fool.co.uk). With what we hoped was a similar blend of humour and irreverence, we set ourselves the same Foolish task of pointing to the Emperor and revealing that those new clothes he thought he was wearing weren't such a bargain after all.

In the very birthplace of Folly, the United Kingdom, the Wise spin doctors had kept the upper hand for more years than anyone could remember: 'It's too complicated for you. Trust us. We'll look after your financial future. We have your *best* interests at heart.'

But as the Emperor paraded the streets on his magnificent charger, collecting tributes and dispensing blessings as he went, already there were rumblings of discontent and not a little merriment: 'That fellow might believe he's wearing a new suit of clothes and he's certainly been telling us that for more years than we can remember, but it looks almost as if he's got nothing on at all, as if he's been having us on all these years! He still believes it, though. Amazing!' With sentiments like this already circling on the peasants' rumour-mill, the soil was ripe for the Fool to sow even more seeds of revolution and, yes, even treason.

The bloke on the horse, you see, really does have nothing on. Not a stitch.

Bombast, bamboozlement, overcharging, investment underperformance, longer words where shorter ones would do: it's all here. The truth, though, is that you don't have to put up with paying through the nose to investment managers, 90 *per cent* of whom, as we've heard, will perform worse than the average. You don't have to smile gratefully as you slip most of your first two years' worth of pension contributions directly into your financial adviser's pocket. You don't have to weep tears of thanks as it takes seven years or more for your endowment policy to even *start* to show a positive return on your money.

None of what we are going to discuss in this book is complicated or intimidating or impenetrable to the average person. It's all totally simple and totally Foolish and it will give you the key to unlock the sinister mystery which investment remains for so many of us. It will also show you how, with no skill whatsoever, you can beat the professionals at their own game. And what's more, it will show you how you can do this with as little as half an hour of effort each year. Or even less.

Does that sound a trifle unrealistic? Really, it shouldn't. You see, your motivation and that of the financial professionals are very different. While your first priority is to make money for you, *their* first priority is to make money *from* you. Their second priority is to make money for you, but it comes a long way down the line. As a savvy individual, you can cut out the middle-man, head straight for the best value, lowest-cost investments bringing in 'average' returns and outperform 90 per cent of the pros. Jim Slater, who has written some excellent books on investment himself with a highly down-to-Earth take on the subject, had this to say about the *Motley Fool Investment Guide* (the US version) in his January 1998 newsletter:

> *One of its main contentions, with which I agree wholeheartedly, is that ordinary private investors are in many ways much better placed to make consistently good returns from shares than highly paid professionals in the City and on Wall Street.*

And if all this is starting to sound just a little too suspiciously easy, rest assured you won't find any get-rich-quick schemes between these pages. You won't even find anything controversial or risky. All you will find is the investment good sense we should all have been learning since we were in secondary school explained in simple terms and without huge amounts of jargon. We hope that by the time you have finished this volume (a weekend of frippery and delight or eighteen weeks of tooth-grinding misery, depending on your constitution) the black cloud of guilt and unease which hangs over you as you contemplate the need to do something for your financial future will have lifted. We hope you'll feel free and light and knowledgeable and ... Foolish.

Before I make way for David and Tom G., I'd like to hark back a few years. Some of you reading this will have spent the early 1980s as enthralled as I was by *The Hitch Hiker's Guide to the Galaxy*, the book, radio and television series that followed the adventures of one Arthur Dent to the ends of the universe after the Earth had, regrettably, been demolished to make way for a hyper-spatial express route. Printed in large, coloured, friendly letters on the snug plastic cover of the *Guide* – the most remarkable book ever to come out of the publishing corporations of Ursa Minor and containing an alarming recipe for the best drink in existence, the Pan-galactic Gargle Blaster (see Appendix 6) – was the most useful piece of advice in the universe:

DON'T PANIC

We can't pretend that *The Motley Fool UK Investment Guide* has even an atom's worth of the brilliance of the *Hitch-Hiker's Guide*. But the advice? Surely, surely no Fool can do without it.

David and Tom G.

Something had to be done about this situation. Ah, but there we go again, starting in *medias res*, 'in the midst of things', as was Homer's inclination in the *Iliad* and the *Odyssey*, and now ours too (in a desperate attempt to appease the Homeric Society we have offended in the past). So we should back-pedal. And be brief.

A few years ago, we two brothers stayed up past midnight for a few months running, in order to pour our souls into a literary product – that's what the book salesman called it, 'product' (had to get used to that) – designed to revolutionize thinking about money in our home country. It needed to be done. Despite the tremendous prosperity of the US stock market, studies showed that the distribution of wealth was growing more and more skewed. Of course, the haves have *always* had, and the have-nots have always had not, but the situation was growing more distressing. We deduced (correctly, we still believe, despite what the haves tell us) that one of the primary reasons for the *status quo* was the almost complete lack of education about money in the United States of America. No standard study of the subject has ever been made mandatory for American ankle-biters, something which would teach them the subtly destructive power of credit card debt, something which would teach them to understand just how much better the stock market had done than any other competing investment over the entire century. It was ironic to us that we had studied quadratic equations and binomial coefficients, and yet our own schools had never taught the far more important facts about compounded financial returns. It was incredible that the example of Anne Scheiber was not shouted from the rooftops of our educational institutions. This humble New Yorker died at an advanced age in 1995, leaving a fortune of over $20 million to charity, a fortune accumulated, from a starting point of $5,000 in the closing years of the Second World War, entirely through investments in common stocks such as Coca-Cola and Gillette.

Swooping in to redress these wrongs, *The Motley Fool Investment Guide* was published in January of 1996 to some critical acclaim, went on to earn that sine qua non label 'best-seller', and continues to sell well several years later ... in the United States. We checked our sales in Great Britain, and discovered we'd sold seventeen copies. That's as best we can tell – there's some question as to whether that seventeenth copy was in fact purchased or used as wrapping at Billingsgate fish market, but we'll leave that to the accountants.

Something – we repeat – *something* had to be done about this situation.

(That one was for you, Homer, and please be more understanding now, gentle Society.)

Enter David Berger. This British junior hospital doctor had been playing the voyeur for several months, peeping into our US website (http://www.fool.com) from his perch in the pastoral setting of North Devon. He grew gradually braver, to the point of contributing occasional scribblings to our communal effort. Indeed, his written stuff was sufficiently sassy that we felt we must meet the fellow. Without really even being able to afford it (we're an 'Internet startup company', after all, a phrase synonymous with 'unprofitable'), we flew David across the Atlantic Ocean to spend a week with us at Fool Global HQ. We discovered among other things that he was far funnier than we, and (as it turned out) more intelligent, and better-looking, too. (He had hair, for instance – hey, why do you think we wear the caps?) We also discovered, with his help, that the lack of education about money in the UK was at least on par with the situation in our own country, if not even a little bit worse (!) ... and that a book speaking in plain and entertaining terms about the subject might be a valued contribution to the British literary scene.

In addition to those revelations, we spied further evidence that he could write, which mattered to us most of all. We then asked him to draw up a series of *Steps to Investing Foolishly* for a proposed UK Fool site. In typical Bergerish (his own language), Step Five began like this:

Editor's Note: Welcome to a short treatise on the importance of shares, which also happens to constitute the Fifth Step in the Ten Steps to Investing Foolishly. You can find the fornicating monkeys about halfway through, but we suggest you read the entire article slowly from the start to allow the suspense to build.

If that doesn't read like winning material to you, return this book to the shelf right now, as you are the proud possessor of better taste than will be on offer here. From our point of view, though, any writer capable of using fornicating monkeys to make an important point about shares was our chap.

Something therefore *has* been done about this situation.

You see, as funny as we once wanted to hope we were in our own country, we were clearly neither amusing, nor useful, nor interesting in even a superficial sense in the United Kingdom. Our answer is thus to tag along with the fellow on the cover photo of this book, figuring that he might be.

In closing, all the blame for the appearance of this subversive text or its contents must fall on David's head (his e-mail address is **foolukbook@ fool.co.uk**). Any spontaneous overflows of emotion, recollected in tranquillity, that tilt toward the 'praise' end of the spectrum are, however, still best addressed to TheGardners@fool.com. Bless you and thank you, Dear Reader.

How to Use This Book

Chaos often breeds life,when order breeds habit.
Henry Brooks Adams, *The Education of Henry Adams* (1907)

Many people reading this book *will* like to start at the beginning and read all the way through and that's fine. It's even how we initially planned it would be. Others, though, will start at the end and read it backwards. Others still will skim back and forth through the text, eyes alighting here and there on a different spot of interest on each pass. Yet others will read only the one or two chapters that interest them and a few, a very few, will be so aghast at what they read in the first few pages that they will fling themselves in front of a bus in protest against the unfair practices of the financial professionals before they even get to any of the really juicy bits. While it doesn't really matter how you come at the book, we'd prefer you not to plump for the latter option as the liability implications make our jumpy lawyer even jumpier.

Most of the chapters in the book can more or less stand on their own, although we do think they add up to a coherent story in which the total is greater than the mere sum of the parts. The way you tot up that total is down to you, but above all we hope your journey to understanding the basics of investment will be not only liberating, but fun. Please promise us, therefore, that as soon as you find yourself glazing over, and certainly as soon as you find yourself re-reading paragraphs in a desperate and increasingly frantic attempt to understand just what we're banging on about, that you'll take a break. Make a sandwich, listen to some music, hitchhike to the South of France, do anything as long as you're not breaking your head over something you don't understand. We don't actually think there's anything very complex in here – indeed, there is very little in this book a twelve-year-old couldn't understand; in fact, we hope there *are* a few twelve-year-olds read-ing this – but eventually any brain which has dealt with a single subject for too long seizes up. When that happens to your brain, be kind to it and give it a rest. When you come back, things will seem much clearer.

How the Book is Structured

In the first section, we look at how and why you should invest for your future and how to go about it simply and Foolishly. Then we have a short interlude where we depart on a couple of tangents for light relief before embarking on the second section which gets into the juicy stuff about investing in shares. The third section, 'What You've (Maybe) Already Got', dishes the dirt on pensions and endowments. The last main section, 'Bits 'n' Bobs', is where we've stuck all the, er, bits and bobs and this is followed by a summary (of sorts) and a glossary. Oh *yeah*, a *glossary*, you say. Well, don't! We went to a bit of trouble putting it together and we think it's a useful reference.

At the end are a number of useful appendices.

In fact, that's enough of an introduction. Now it's up to you to read this book and decide if it's any use or not.

Starting Out

Why You Should Invest

I am a Millionaire. That is my religion.

George Bernard Shaw, *Major Barbara*

Think about it: Monday matinées, Saga holidays to Scarborough, trips to the shops in a Mini Metro at 18 miles an hour. You're going to have to finance all these somehow. The money that you are earning today is going to have to pay for what you hope will be – and is increasingly likely to be – a long retirement. Whether it will be happy or not is down to you and will depend at least partly on whether you have to worry about where the next box of teabags is coming from.

That's one very important reason to think deeply about investment.

Maybe you're a bit ashamed about the other reason. Maybe you want to make some money, some *real* money, by investing. That's OK, you can admit that here and, yes, you've come to the right place. It is possible, genuinely possible for you, Arthur Smallridge of Chorlton-cum-Hardy, to take a portion of your regular income, invest it and watch it grow to monumental proportions. We've already seen how Anne Scheiber did it in the United States, but just the same is possible here. You don't have to know exactly what you'll do with the financial freedom you are going to buy for yourself in years to come, but our guess is that something will come to you. As we see it, money is like fuel. Most of us have to work fairly hard to bring in enough logs to feed the fire we need to keep us warm in our daily lives. And the curious thing is, the fire just seems to get hotter the more fuel you throw at it. One day, though, with a stockpile of enough logs to feed a reasonable-sized fire, perhaps you'll have the time to turn your creative attentions elsewhere. Jean-Jacques

Rousseau, the Swiss philosopher, and incredibly enough one of the first people to point out in the eighteenth century that the Alps were in fact beautiful, had this to say of money:

Money in one's possession is the instrument of liberty.

Even today in Britain, with all the hoo-hah that surrounds the Lottery, many of us feel that setting our caps in pursuit of a large sum of money is at the very least a trifle vulgar and at worst obscene. Seeing money as opportunity, however, we don't subscribe to this view at all. Things have changed a lot in the last fifty years and the idea of a secure job for life isn't with us any more.

Since we're all likely to change jobs and careers many times in our lives, we don't see anything wrong with earning yourself the opportunity to do what moves you. You might want to write the history of the Darlington marshalling yards, compose a masterpiece, devote your entrepreneurial skills and your fortune to working on behalf of others or maybe you'd just like to take the time to walk in the woods and hear, really hear, the wind rustling the leaves and the birds calling to each other in the upper branches. Whichever you choose, you're going to need the resources to sustain yourself while you do it.

By picking up this book, buying it and reading this far you are soaring ahead of most of your contemporaries, the majority of whom are already guaranteed to know less about investment than you do. Your future wealth is assured. So sit back, relax, make yourself another cup of tea and have a biccy – you've broken the back of it.

What Investing Means

Investment is something we do every day, consciously and unconsciously. We invest in our relationships, our jobs, our hobbies, and our lives. (We hope you've just invested £12.99 in this book and if you haven't, if you've stolen it, put it back this instant.) If we didn't invest in these things, we wouldn't get anything back, or at least nothing back of very much worth. And investment is all about 'getting back'. We invest something, whatever that may be, in the hope of a return over and above the original input. It seems so pathetically simple that you're probably wondering why we're going on about it at such length. What is interesting, however, is that while we put a lot of effort and time into, say, investing in our relationship with our partner – flowers, surprise weekends away, not screaming and stamping our feet when they smash Grandma Flo's prize fruit bowl – so often we put pitifully little thought or effort into investing for something as vital as our financial future. Oh yes, many of us are paying into some plan or other, sold to us by some adviser or other, but *time, effort, interest, energy*? 'Fraid not. There are quite a few reasons for this and we'll look at some of them later on, but the purpose of this book is not to turn you into an investment geek, an anorak who is barely able to converse with their fellow human beings except in terms of earnings per share and cash flow analysis. No, instead we hope to awaken more than a spark of excitement in this thrilling and very Foolish business of investing. The business of managing your own money and guiding your financial ship towards its ultimate destination is as fulfilling as it can be simple and as enjoyable as it can be lucrative.

A Very Crafty Move and a Little Bit of History

Time was when you could expect to work all your life, retire at sixty-five and drop dead shortly after. The advantage of this system was that it meant there was no need for investment by the state to provide a wage for the country's pensioners. The number of people in work so far exceeded the number of OAPs that incoming taxes were more than able to cover the outgoings, a reasonable-ish pension was provided and everyone was happy. Pensioners marvelled at the enlightened, beneficent nature of the newborn welfare state, while looking back on a hard life, well lived. The welfare state paid up every week with a smile, while at the same time crossing its fingers and counting on the pensioners' imminent demise.

Now, though, the population is becoming less and less obliging and not only are people living longer and longer, they are retiring earlier and earlier. Whereas there were around five employees per pensioner in the 1950s, there are likely to be closer to two per pensioner in the second decade of the twenty-first century. 'Not much dosh coming in to pay for all those pensions,' you whistle. Yes, but Mrs Thatcher was there before you. In 1981 or thereabouts.

In 1981 a crafty thing was done. We don't want to get into politics here, but whatever you think of the Lady Who Was Not For Turning, this was a crafty thing, a very crafty thing, to do. Up until 1981, the old age pension was linked to average earnings. This meant that as average earnings went up each year, so the pension increased by the same percentage amount, an arrangement which seems equitable enough. The only problem was that this was costing an awful lot of money, more money in fact than the Government could afford. There was no investment fund out of which pensions were paid, a fund that was growing with time. Instead, pensions were paid – and are still paid – out of the National Insurance contributions of people in employment, and those in the know could see that one day soon it was all going to prove just a dash too expensive. The solution? Clearly it was impossible to simply cut pension payments – there would have been an outcry and this, you will remember, was a Britain still smarting from the deprivations of the 1970s. No, there had to be a better way and it was this: instead of linking the pension to average earnings, link it to the Retail Price Index ('the rate of inflation' to the rest of us). This sounded all right in principle, but the fact is that the Retail Price Index appreciates on average at around 2 per cent less per year than average earnings. Effectively, this means that the state old age pension is now depreciating at 2 per cent per year in relation to average earnings. This is great news for the Treasury, but at the time of writing, the single person's basic state pension is £3,926 per year and average earnings currently stand at about £24,000. Taking the one as a percentage of the other, we end up with ... not very much.

Something, then, had to be done about the future destitution of the nation's pensioners and, you will not be surprised to hear, the onus was put on to the individual to save for themselves. This took the form of savings incentives like the Personal Equity Plan, introduced in the late 1980s and now replaced by the Individual Savings Account or ISA, and the Personal Pension Plan, introduced shortly after. We won't go into detail here about just what these consist of – that comes later – but they are tax-efficient means of saving that have had quite a degree of success. This success, however, has only really been among those who could afford to pay, and that includes paying for the charges they carry. A report by the Association of British Insurers reveals that even people who pay personal pension contributions for thirty years can see a quarter of their final investment fund eaten up by charges.

Cough! Splutter! Gasp!

Please excuse us, tales of Wisdom always have this effect on us, but – pass the smelling salts, will you? – we are feeling better now.

This is loadsamoney and someone, somewhere, is laughing all the way to the proverbial bank. Just how hard they're laughing will be revealed later in the book.

It is fair to say – whatever pups the financial services industry has sold us to date – that governments now and in the future will have to continue to encourage personal saving in a big way, because pictures of pensioners in soup queues don't do much for the image of 'Cool Britannia'. All this, of course, is splendid news for investors.

A Foolish Investor

We hope that having read this far you realize not only how much of an investor you already are, but how much of an investor it is necessary to be in modern Britain. Some people reading this will already know a fair amount about the basics of personal finance, while others will not. Whichever is the case, most people who have a pension plan or investment plan of one sort or another do not think of themselves as 'Investors'. They just think of them-selves as someone who has a pension plan or investment plan.

'So what, Fool?! You're nit-picking!'

Well, we beg to differ. If you consider yourself an Investor, rather than just simply someone who pays into a pension plan, this changes the mind-set, broadens the outlook and, crucially, it puts a level of responsibility on you to look after your investments. 'Looking after your investments' means ensuring maximum return with minimum cost in terms of charges and tax and within the limits set by your own attitude towards risk. By calling your-self an Investor, whichever investment vehicle you choose to use is simply that – a vehicle. Whereas in the other case, investments are potentially frag-mented into a pension plan, ISA and a host of other things, each in its own encapsulated world. The Investor, or rather the Foolish Investor, is able to take an overview and to think in terms of Total Return and Risk. As long as an investment is pulling its weight in the Total Return scheme of things with an acceptable level of Risk, then that's fine. If it isn't, then Out It Goes.

By 'Total Return' we are talking about the total gain on the sum of an individual's investments, after all taxes and charges have been accounted for. By Risk, we mean the chances of the investment not doing what you want or need it to. Very little else is relevant. Whether an investment is sold as a School Fees Plan, a Personal Pension Plan or a Put Your Dog Through Obedience Training Plan is irrelevant. Does it bring in the rate of return you expect, at a risk you are prepared to bear? It's very simple, but it involves being prepared to sweep through the suffocating layers of humbug that envelop much of what the financial services industry (hereinafter known as 'the Wise') is busy peddling to the British public. By doing this, you will soon find it simple to distinguish between contributing to the Send A Pension Fund Manager To The Bahamas Plan, and the Retire At A Young Age And Breed Racing Pigeons/Collect Stamps/Take Up Freefall Parachuting Plan (delete as appropriate). Sadly, many more people are contributing to the former than the latter types of plan.

Think of yourself, then, as an Investor. Look[2] you're a person, you have thoughts and ideas and opinions about all kinds of things. You can have them about investing too. Once you've been through this book (and perhaps visited the Fool online), you will have the basic knowledge necessary to cut away the confusion and hype of so many of the investment products being marketed in Britain today. We will even make a promise. Before you are halfway through this book you will know how to beat most of the financial professionals (that's the Wise, again), with the expenditure of just a few minutes each year.

The world has never looked better for Foolish Investors. Despite the occassional wobble, as we've seen recently, the stock markets of the Western world continue to provide the same *long-term* returns as they have done so faithfully for the last hundred years or more, standards of financial reporting and regulation have never been higher and the UK Government is firmly committed to principles of tax-efficient investing for the reasons already

---

2 Look, we borrowed this habit of saying 'Look' from Tony Blair. It worked for him, didn't it?

outlined. Most importantly of all, perhaps, the Internet is in the process of bringing information and opportunity to the average citizen which was previously the province of only the professionals. Anyone who has ever kept hold of the remote control in the typical British family's Saturday night telly scrummage will testify to the fact that:

(S)he who controls the flow of information controls the flow of life itself.

Increasingly, it is the common person who controls the flow of life and boy, do the Wise not like it.

The Miracle of Compound Interest

Oh wonderful, wonderful, and most wonderful wonderful! and yet again wonderful, and after that, out of all whooping!

William Shakespeare, *As You Like It*

Not all investment years are created equal. The strange thing is that people who really ought to know this often don't. The *Financial Times* has a 'write in and ask the expert for advice' section in its weekend Money Supplement. In one edition, a question was asked by two parents about their daughter, who was aged thirty and living in the USA and had no pension provision. They wanted to start her off with a gift of £6,000 (what marvellous people!), but where should they invest it on her behalf? A reasonable question from two savvy and obviously loving parents. It is clear from the answer, however, that the expert in question had not the first appreciation of the Miracle of Compound Interest, for he started his answer by saying: 'The age of thirty is not very old, particularly if your daughter is getting valuable qualifications which could lead to high earnings as her career progresses. So, do not worry too much.'

Do not worry too much?! Do not worry too much?! Eeek! The age of thirty is definitely not very old in life-years, but we're not talking life-years here, we're talking investment-years. You calculate dog-years by multiplying human-years by seven (although why Yorkshire terriers and Great Danes have the same exchange rate, we've never quite figured out), but investment-years are altogether more complicated. To investment-years must be applied a complex formula, integrating expected lifespan with current age, shoe size and favourite Sixties rock group into a fractal geometry-based, chaos-driven equation. This is all then fried and served with a sprig of basil and a drizzle of olive oil on a bed of financial advisers. For lesser minds this can be summarized as signifying that, early on, investment years are worth a great deal more than they are later on. A huge amount more, in fact.

Welcome to the Miracle of Compounding! It is the bread, the water, the mead of the investor. It sustains and nurtures in times of famine and exalts in times of plenty. It is the carrot and the stick; it keeps us Playing the Game. Without a firm faith in this particular miracle, Fools are lost souls, doomed forever to bang at the oaken gates of Investment Plenitude, but never to pass those self-same, hallowed portals.

Let us turn back the clock, back to an era you may, or may not, prefer to forget. Already the focus is dissolving, the camera pans to the round window, a trill of gurgling music escorts us through and we burst into ... into the past!

You are thirteen years old and sitting in Miss Doublebottom's classroom. It is late May, almost lunchtime and you are coming to the end of a double maths lesson. Through the open window wafts not only the gentle scent of spring flowers and the embracing warmth of an almost summer afternoon, but the lazy drone of a lawnmower and occasional disembodied snatches of the groundsmen's conversation. It all seems so peaceful and the soporific voice of Miss Doublebottom so comforting as she rambles on and on and on, that very soon ... ZZZZzzzzzzzzz

And that, unfortunately, was your big mistake (and quite possibly also the mistake made by the *Financial Times* expert). In the twenty minutes between your falling asleep and the bell going for lunchtime, Miss Doublebottom dealt with and dismissed the crucial topic of compound interest. Oh, go on, why don't you? Why not blame Miss Doublebottom for it? You can if you want, but it was not entirely her fault. Perhaps she should have stressed it a little more. Perhaps she should have gone over it again, but the truth is that even teachers aren't all that clued up about personal finance and investment and, like the rest of us, they are just a teensy bit frightened of it. Now, this is understandable and the astonishing implications of compound interest are so far-reaching that it is not surprising she wished to gloss over the whole affair. In maths textbooks, interest in general is always looked at in terms of debt: *Johnny buys a motorbike and borrows X amount of money at Y rate of interest, to be repaid over Z years. How much must he repay in total? Answers to be given in the* *form of X x 10^y* . We find questions of this sort are at once tedious and terrifying and it's only natural to want to shy away from the subject as much as possible.

Don't be too hard, then, on Miss Doublebottom. Instead, start to assume some Foolish responsibility – after all, it was you that fell asleep, wasn't it? And, by coincidence, that's just what you're doing: having reached the age of majority you are about to put right the ignorances of the past, a Foolish course of action indeed. You are going to embark on a voyage of mathematical discovery, one of wonderment and awe. You are poised to change the way you look at life and, quite possibly, you are about to become a party bore on the subject of compound interest.

The brave, the foolhardy and the frankly obsessive will find the full ins and outs of the sums involved in compound interest covered in Appendix 1 on page 322. For now, we shall merely derive a few basic principles. So sit back and enjoy the Foolish Laws of Compounding, with inspiration from Mr Hilaire Belloc. Yes, the *Cautionary Tales* of Hilaire Belloc were the moral guides of generations of British children. Who cannot nod sagely at such instructional verses as 'Sarah Byng, Who could not read and was tossed into a thorny hedge by a Bull', 'Charles Augustus Fortescue, Who always Did what was Right, and so accumulated an Immense Fortune' and 'Jim, Who ran away from his nurse and was Eaten by a Lion'. Now we shall hear some modern cautionary tales ...

The First Foolish Law of Compounding, or Ferdinand, Who Frittered Away His Twenties and Suffered Dreadful Agonies

Fay, a Foolish young woman of twenty, decides to save £100 per month from her secretarial salary. She puts this into an investment plan that gives her an average return of 10 per cent per year on her money. She does not give this another thought, but presses on contributing throughout her twenties, year in and year out, all the while living a life of independence, modest excitement and everyday pleasures. At the age of thirty, she meets Ferdinand, a rake who has frittered away his twenties, but who nevertheless captures her heart. Shortly after meeting, the two decide to have children (whether they marry or not in this modern tale we do not know – that is left up to you, the reader, to decide). Fay decides to stop working and bring up the children (again, fearing accusations of prejudice, we would like to affirm that this is a decision she felt free and happy to make). With no income, she must now stop contributing to the investment plan, something she does with a heavy heart. Ferdinand, however, now takes his responsibilities seriously and starts to contribute £100 per month into a similar plan of his own, something he continues until the age of sixty. For the numbers, see the table below.

Ouch! Extraordinary, isn't it? Ferdie thought so too. By the age of sixty, Fay has almost twice as much as Ferdinand, although she has not contributed anything for thirty years. Now, Ferdinand retires and they both let their nest eggs grow for the sake of their grandchildren. At the age of one hundred, Ferdinand is worth the staggering sum of £9,410,712, but Fay is still worth getting on for twice as much: £15,910,348. And all because she started a paltry ten years earlier, and yet she contributed only a third as much.

	Fay (£100 per month age 20 –29)	Ferdinand (£100 per month age 30 –59)
Age 20	0	0
Age 30	£20,146	0
Age 40	£52,254	£20,146
Age 50	£135,533	£72,399
Age 60	£351,538	£207,929

We were going to continue this model for another few hundred years, but the numbers became too huge. There was an ear-splitting explosion and smoke started pouring from the Foolomatic supercomputer's overheated main processor. Seconds later, the ground outside Fool headquarters was littered with the groaning, writhing forms of baled-out Fools, begging for mercy from the God of Compounding.

Anyway, this sacrifice was not in vain and neither were Ferdinand's squandered twenties, for from them we derive the **First Foolish Law of Compounding**:

Start early, Fool!

The Second Foolish Law of Compounding, or A Foolish Female Who Learnt Too Late about the Building Society and Was Burned to Death as a Result

In this next Foolish example, we follow the fortunes of a Frippery of Foolish *Femmes*, five in all. They all, at the age of twenty, agree on the importance of regular, long-term investment, but they disagree as to which type of investment is the best. Each opts for a different one, ranging in long-term return from a building society deposit account, to a volatile, yet lucrative, share-buying strategy. For the sake of argument, the returns range as follows: 4, 7, 10, 12, 15 per cent per year. They each contribute £100 per month from the ages of twenty to sixty – for the numbers, see the table below.

What interests us most here is the last line. Look how the return increases at each stage. Now, these women are only sixty and have only been contributing £100 per month, yet some of them have managed to accrue seriously alarming amounts of cash. What has made some of their piles double or treble the size of their nearest neighbours is a paltry difference in return of a few per cent.

	Fennella 4%	Felicity 7%	Freda 10%	Faith 12%	Florence 15%
After 10 Years	£14,718	£17,202	£20,146	£22,404	£26,302
After 20 Years	£36,503	£51,041	£72,399	£91,986	£132,707
After 30 Years	£68,751	£117,606	£207,929	£308,097	£563,177
After 40 Years	£116,486	£248,552	£559,461	£979,307	£2,304,667

This leads us, inescapably, inexorably and ineluctably to **The Second Foolish Law of Compounding:**

Small differences in investment return matter. A lot.

They matter far, far more than the uninitiated could possibly think. Two to three per cent simply does not sound like it could matter very much, but it does. It matters so much it hurts. It matters so much that Fools have been known to cut off vital body organs in anguish at the investment return they have lost through heavy investment charges. That's how much it matters.

And while we're on the subject, the Second Foolish Law of Compounding also allows us to conclude that the British Government of 1981 was familiar with the ins and outs of compound interest (well, you'd hope they would be – they were the Government, after all). A lower relative increase of 2 per cent per year in the state pension doesn't sound like much, but as we can now see, over time it most surely adds up.

You will be wondering when we are going to get round to the 'Burned to Death' bit. It's only natural and, go on, be honest, that's what's kept you reading this far, isn't it? Aye, 'tis a sad tale, that's for certain and it concerns 'Fennella Four-per-cent'. Labouring under the sad misapprehension that the building society was the place to save her hard-earned cash, poor old Fennella entered retirement ill prepared for what was to come. She found herself with little more to live on than – *frisson* of horror! – the **state old age pension** ! Unable to pay her electricity bills, she was forced to live in a single room, huddled up to a one-bar electric fire. One cold day she fell asleep, slipped forward and *whoof!* Within minutes there was nothing left but the charred remnants of a flowery housecoat, some pink, fluffy slippers and the uneasy, cordite-like tang of burnt human flesh.

And that, Dear Fool, is what happens to those who put their faith in the building society.

The Third Foolish Law of Compounding, or Ffyona, Who Squandered Her Inheritance and Came to Grief

Now, one final example. Let's take our Foolish gals again, debs one and all, and add another, Ffyona. At the age of twenty, each of them has come into £50,000 from an aged great aunt. They are still a sensible crew and each of them decides to invest all the money in their chosen investment vehicle, choosing to continue with their jobs and live off the small salaries they provide. All, that is, except Ffyona, who has decided she is going to live what used to be called, so quaintly, the 'High Life'. Within six months, yes, you've guessed it, there is nothing left. With no money and now no job, poor old Ffyona finds herself a Fallen Woman, earning her living in a way Too Terrible for the ears of Young Children. For the rest of our Foolish friends, however, the future looks like this:

	Fennella	Felicity	Freda	Faith	Florence
	4%	7%	10%	12%	15%
After 10 Years	£74,012	£98,358	£129,687	£155,292	£202,278
After 20 Years	£109,556	£193,484	£336,375	£482,315	£818,327
After 30 Years	£162,170	£380,613	£872,470	£1,497,996	£3,310,589
After 40 Years	£240,051	£748,723	£2,262,963	£4,652,549	£13,393,177

Look at the last line again. Ooooh, doesn't it make your eyes water? From this last table we progress naturally and seamlessly to **The Third Foolish Law of Compounding**:

Don't squander your inheritance on sex, drugs and rock 'n' roll. (Unless you want to, that is.)

The Rule of 72

Now consider, dear Fool, the 'rule of 72'.Consider it a labour-saving, convenience aid to modern living. If the Fool is the food processor of investing, then the Rule of 72 is the natty little attachment which grinds the coffee beans. The Rule of 72 lets you estimate with a fair degree of accuracy how long it will take your lump sum investment to double at a given rate of interest, and it couldn't be simpler. Divide 72 by the rate of interest and you have approximately the number of years to doubling your investment:

$$72 \, /x\% = \text{years to doubling}$$

Like any rule of thumb this one has its limitations and in this case it is increasingly inaccurate once you get much above 15%, but actually even then it's pretty good. Frankly, if your investments are regularly above 15%, the minor errors here are irrelevant anyway.

Here's an example:

£10,000 invested at 11.4% will take 72/11.4 years to double = 6.3 years

The Fourth and Fifth Foolish Laws of Compounding, or David and James Skimp on the Numbers, but Are Saved by the Benevolence of a Foolish Public

Lavish numbers and spreadsheet Foolery were the order of the day for the first three Foolish Laws of Compounding, but now it may seem as if there's precious little to support the final two. A swizzle, says you! Quite possibly, says we, but we hope you will see that the essence of these final two Foolish Laws is encapsulated within the previous three and that by now you will have us down for an honest couple of fellows. Here, then, without further ado, are our two final Foolish Laws of Compounding, every bit as vital as their predecessors, even if a little shorter on the padding:

The Fourth Foolish Law of Compounding

Over time, regular saving of quite small amounts can build up to an astonishing sum of money.

The Fifth Foolish Law of Compounding

Time and patience are the friends of compounding and, therefore, of investing.

Coming Soon to a Fridge near YOU!

We hope that with the Foolish Laws of Compounding rattling around in your head, you are starting to settle into the mindset of Foolish investing. Maybe you are starting to dream, to realize that you do not need a huge sum of money to begin investing profitably for the future. In short, you're limbering up for what is to come. The key, though, to successful investing is regular saving and keeping your investment objectives in mind. It can be tough to maintain that sort of resolve over a long period, but to aid you in your Foolish quest, you will see that on the next page we have duplicated the Laws of Compounding in a super-deluxe, easily digestible form and we've also thrown in the Rule of 72 as a free gift. You can cut it out and stick it up somewhere visible, somewhere where its elegant simplicity and timeless beauty will be a lasting complement to your home. Why not the fridge door? From now on, every time you reach for a pint of milk or the liquefying remains of last Thursday's quiche, the Miracle of Compound Interest will enfold your grey cells with a most gentle and wondrous awe, inspiring you to new heights of saving and investing.

The Motley Fool UK's Laws of Compound Interest

The First Foolish Law of Compounding
Start early, Fool!

The Second Foolish Law of Compounding
Small differences in investment return matter. A lot.

The Third Foolish Law of Compounding
Don't squander your inheritance on sex, drugs and rock 'n' roll. (Unless you want to, that is.)

The Fourth Foolish Law of Compounding
Over time, regular saving of quite small amounts can build up an astonishing sum of money.

The Fifth Foolish Law of Compounding
Time and patience are the friends of compounding and, therefore, of investing.

The Rule of 72
72 / x% = years to doubling

All That Glitters
Is Not Gold

It is not that pearls fetch a high price because men have dived for them; but on the contrary men dive for them because they fetch a high price.
Richard Whateley, *Introductory Lectures on Political Economy*

We're moving on, slowly but Foolishly. In the introduction we learnt what the Motley Fool was all about and whence it sprung. In Chapter 1 we learnt why we need to be investors and in Chapter 2 we were thrilled and awestruck by the Miracle of Compound Interest. Now, we're raring to go and, er, invest.

But in what? If you're like most people, you'll have already flicked through the Table of Contents and a few of the later chapters and have figured out that the Fool loves shares. No, it doesn't just love shares, it eats them, it breathes them, it savours them, it caresses their smooth, yielding ...

OK! OK! That's enough! (Sorry about this, Dear Readers, but some of us get a little carried away at times. Normal service will now be resumed.) No, shares aren't the only possible investments in this wonderful world of markets and market makers and we'd like to take just a little time now to examine some of the other investment options facing us, before devoting the rest of this book to shares.

Invest in Yourself

Why not? You are your best potential money-making asset. Take the time and the money to invest in yourself. New skills or a new outlook could well propel you into a newer, more highly paying job and one that is more rewarding. If you are running your own business, then investment in that, an enterprise whose value and potential you are uniquely placed to assess, could be your best move. Don't neglect yourself or your talents – it won't pay off in the long run. Of course, if you don't have any talents or you don't think you have much scope to increase your money-making potential, then don't throw good money after bad. Concentrate instead on saving as much as you reasonably can and developing your sense and knowledge of Foolishness as far as you reasonably want to take it. Looked at in that way, your purchase of this book is one of the best investments in yourself you've ever made. Now, who says you don't have any talents?

Britain's Favourite Investment

Is it the chance to watch Dale Winton, Carol Smillie and heavens knows who else on the telly on Saturday and Wednesday nights? Is it the desire to contribute to the good causes? Or is it the opportunity to dally with fate and perhaps, just perhaps find ourselves the grinning subjects of a News of the World spread: 'I'll still be going in to work on Monday, honest. It won't change nuffink!'? Sadly for the Lottery good causes and the egos of Dale and Carol et al, we play the National Lottery because we want to win. No matter that the chances against are 14 million to 1, it could, it just could be us.

Ever made acquaintance with Schrödinger's cat? This unfortunate feline has spent the last sixty years since his invention in a sealed box. Inside with him is one bowl containing cat food and one containing poison. Until we open the box and see which one the moggy has chosen to eat, we cannot know whether the cat is alive or dead. It exists in an indeterminate, multi-potential state, neither dead nor alive. Herr Schrödinger invented his cat to illustrate some fairly way-out concepts in quantum mechanics, but he could just as well have been talking about the Lottery. Until the balls start to roll out on Saturday night, each of us who has bought a ticket is neither a winner nor a loser. And it's a thrill!

It's also an investment, just not a very good one. You can tell it's not a very good investment because of what happens to your stake money. Only half of it actually gets paid out in prizes, the other half gets split between the Government, good causes, retailers and Camelot. So, every pound staked generates an average of just 50p in prizes.

However you look at it, with odds of fourteen million to one against winning (and frankly who cares about anything else?), money put on the lottery is not smart money. Granted, the stake is only a pound, but we'd be fools (note the small 'f ') indeed to dream too long or hard of what we'll do with the cash when we win. No, if you just want a delicious shiver at the other-worldly possibility that you may win, then play – there aren't many thrills you can get for a pound these days. But if things have gotten out of hand and you spend the second half of every Saturday night punching holes in doors with the soggy remnants of a Lottery ticket protruding from a contorted, foam-spattered mouth, then maybe you need to think again and almost certainly you need to get out a little more often for some fresh air.

History's Favourite Investment

In the last section a poor feline explained, with reference to quantum mechanical theory, why we play the Lottery. In this section, we will be looking at the philosophy of value. Heavy stuff, hey? But don't worry, this isn't going to be too intense. We're just going to wonder why we value one of our oldest commodities as highly as we do. Or did. For gold, store of value since before the Phoenicians were plying the Mediterranean and mincing through the Hanging Gardens, is looking a little tarnished these days.

Since the beginning of recorded history, gold has been the 'gold standard' of value (you see – it's so enshrined in our language that it is now totally synonymous with value). As a mediaeval merchant, you would have taken gold coins with you on your travels. Gold was the universal currency and was prized for its beauty, malleability and, above all, its quality of remaining untarnished down the years. None of this would have meant much, of course, if the stuff hadn't been scarce as well, but with all these qualities gold was set to be the US dollar – the 'greenback' – of its age, universally convertible and universally valued. Unlike the greenback it's not so easily forged, but that didn't stop a lot of people trying, including our own Sir Isaac Newton who incidentally spent far more time on alchemy than he ever did on classical physics. Tsk, tsk, Sir Isaac.

Over the years, though, people have lost faith in gold. The gold price has fallen from $850 per ounce in 1980 to around $300 today while most other things have gone up. Some of the world's central banks, the national banks of each country, have even been selling portions of their huge gold stores. They reason that they can hold US Government bonds (Treasury Bills) instead and earn interest on them. The problem with gold is that it doesn't pay interest.

Well that's not quite true. The banks can earn interest on gold bullion too – by lending it out – but it's only a tiny amount. As long as the gold price has been falling, it has paid speculators to borrow gold, sell it for dollars and invest those dollars in Treasury Bills. Then, when the time came to give back the gold, they were able to buy the required amount at a cheaper price than they had sold it, making a profit on the deal in that way too. The low rate of interest they received wasn't too much of a bother for the banks, as they didn't have to pay the cost of storing and guarding it. Neat, hey? As long as the gold price keeps falling, that is ... Recently, though, even the Australians, one of the world's gold-producing nations, had had enough of this horse trading and sold a large proportion of their gold reserves. The Swiss, too, and our very own Bank of England have been selling off large wedges of their gold reserves. This kind of trading based solely on price speculation obviously worries them. It worries us too.

There we have it then. We say:

1. If the world's central banks want to put their faith in them good ol' boys in the US Government rather than an off-yellow metal of indeterminate value, then we'd be fools to argue.
2. If you're after a store of value when the nuclear winter finally draws in, invest one third in tinned food, one third in petrol and the final third in guns to protect the first two thirds. If things are that desperate, Mad Max probably won't be interested in your gold.
3. No gold bars for these Fools.

The Gee-gees

Got a tip for the 2.30 at Newmarket? No? Oh well, never mind. Like the Lottery, this business is too uncertain for Fools interested in the business of wealth accumulation. Again, you can think about what happens to the stake money. It's not as bad as the Lottery, because with the horses the average punter gets back something like 90p for every £1 staked, but the odds are still stacked against you. It can be fun though and if you're looking for an excuse to wear a dickie bow or a silly hat, this could be your answer.

Cash

The bank was Fennella Four-Per-Cent's investment option in the last Chapter and you saw where it got her. Over the long term, the returns (interest to you and me) from cash hidden away in banks and building societies just about beats inflation, but not by very much. This means that creaming the interest off and using it to buy a new frock occasionally actually shrinks the real value of your money.

Banks and building societies are good as a store of money you actually need for spending in the next few years and for an emergency reserve. It's better than stuffing fivers into your mattress, but not by much. As far as the long-term accumulation of wealth is concerned, it's pretty useless. What's next?

Gilts

Gilts you say. What the heck are they? Fair enough, we're beginning to get technical. We dismiss gilts pretty roundly in the next chapter so you can skip this bit here if you like. For the keen ones, though, we'd better explain what they are and how they work. They're called gilts because they're said to be 'gilt-edged'. They represent a slice of the UK's national debt and, if you invest in them, then you're effecitvely lending money to the Government. On the face of it, this isn't a bad idea, since they're as safe a bet as bets go. The UK Government has never failed to repay money on a gilt, which is hardly a surprise since they do print the stuff.

A typical gilt might be called something like 'Treas. 7% 2008' and will be sold in slices of £100. The word 'Treas.' just stands for Treasury. Occasionally you might find something else like 'Conv', which stands for 'Conversion', but these have funny rules, so it's best to steer clear! The '7%' is called the 'coupon' and means that, on £100 of gilt, you'd get paid £7 every year, split into two payments of £3.50. Finally, the 2008 tells you when the thing comes to an end and the Government will repay your £100.

If you're really on the ball, then you might notice that the 7% 'coupon' on this particular gilt is somewhat higher than current interest rates. This means that the gilt is slightly more valuable than the £100 it will repay because for the next six years, it will be paying you 7 per cent. interest instead of 5 per cent. So, the price of the gilt will be a few pounds higher than £100. So, although gilts are rock solid in terms of paying you back, between now and then their prices will move around along with interest rate movements. For this reason, if you buy a gilt, it generally makes sense to try to match its repayment date with when you think you'll want the money back.

Even if you do wait until the Government pays you back, it may no longer be worth as much as you invested, in real terms, because of the effect of inflation and changes in interest rates. One way to avoid this problem is to invest in index-linked gilts, where the twice-yearly interest payments and the final capital repayment are adjusted to account for inflation. Unfortunately, though, you'll have to accept a lower rate of interest for the privilege.

The problem with gilts is that you have to pay for their absolute safety by accepting a pretty low rate of interest. In fact, we'll see in the next chapter that, over the years, the returns from gilts have been little better than what you could get in a high-interest deposit account. On that basis, it's hard to make an argument for them, since you might as well just find a decent deposit account. That way you avoid transaction charges and you needn't worry about losing money if you need it sooner than expected. Really gilts are more suited to institutions like pension funds that know they need to make certain payments to their pensioners on certain dates. For the rest of us, though, it's hard to find much room for them in between our short-term cash in the bank and long-term investments.

Corporate Bonds

Corporate bonds are a little bit like gilts. Instead of representing a loan to the Government, they represent a loan to a company. So instead of 'Treas 7% 2008', you might have 'Tesco 7% 2008'. There is a big difference between the two things, though. Much as they'd probably like to, Tesco doesn't print money. So, while the Government is sure to pay you back, Tesco is merely very likely to. That might sound like nit-picking, but if we're investing in this sort of thing for extra safety, because we might need the money soon, it makes quite a big difference.

As a result of the added risk, the Tesco bond will pay you perhaps 0.5 per cent more interest than a gilt. A more flighty company, on the other hand, might pay you 3 or 4 per cent more than the gilt, but then that's because it's more likely to go bust. So is it worth it? It might be if you could buy lots of them, minimising the impact of one company going bust, but otherwise, if you might be needing the money, then you're probably better to stick with gilts. And, if you might as well stick with gilts, then it's probably best to stick with cash in a high-interest account.

Another way of investing in corporate bonds is to buy units in a 'corporate bond fund'. That way you get to spread your investments across loads of different companies. There are a couple of problems with this, though. First of all, the bonds will all have different dates when they repay money and, in any case, the fund manager will be buying and selling them before then. So more risk is added by the prices changing along with interest rates. They'll also charge about 1.25 per cent per year for the privilege of managing your money. So you have to be invested in bonds that are a fair bit riskier than Tesco, with its 0.5 per cent extra return over a gilt, just to earn what you'd get from a gilt.

All in all, corporate bonds are niether one thing nor the other. They're not safe like gilts and cash and they don't provide the long-term returns that we can expect shares to so, as with gilts, it's hard to see much room for them in between the short-term cash we need in the bank and our long-term investments.

Property

Property as an investment? Well, yes. It's a special case, complicated by the irksome need imposed by the British climate for Fools to keep a roof over their heads. We'll talk about this in much more detail in Chapter 18, 'Be Your Own Landlord'. For now, let's just say that it's pretty good, but a bit awkward.

The Bible of the Long-distance Investor

Steady, boys, steady; We'll fight and we 'll conquer again and again.
— David Garrick, 'Heart of Oak '

Welcome to this, the fourth chapter. It may not sound like much to you, but to us it means a great deal, for this fourth chapter isn't just any old fourth chapter. It's more thrilling than *The Compleat Taxidermist's* Chapter 4, 'Dealing with the Entrails', it's a dimension beyond *A Guide to Icelandic Nightlife's* Chapter 4, 'Thorvald Sigmundsson's Friday Night Country Music Hoedown' and it has more surprises than *Banking's* Chapter 4, 'The Cheque Book'. Chapter 4 in the *Motley Fool UK Investment Guide* is the reason we are here and it reveals the truth about shares. It is the heart of our humble book and we can't help but get rather excited about it.

What Many People Think about Shares

Stocks and shares. Equities.[3] The stock market. The Footsie. Wall Street. The Dow-Jones. It sounds impressive, but what does it all mean? What image does it conjure up? For many people who are not familiar with investing in shares (and some who are), it probably looks a little like this:

---

3 Stocks = shares = equities. You can pretty well use them interchangeably.

A skyscraper in the City of London with mirrored windows. Black Jaguars swishing back and forth. An immaculate receptionist with razor-red nails and shoulder pads jutting out as far as the Essex end of the District Line. Somewhere in the depths of the building, men in shirt sleeves (stripy ones) and red braces screaming into telephones and tearing out tufts of hair by the handful as they peer intently into television screens: 'BUY!!! SELL!!! Is that Tokyo? Get me Higginbotham, dammit! I'll flay him within an inch of his life!' With year-end bonuses of hundreds of thousands of pounds, the Wise never, ever leave their desks at Arrow, Gant and Lowd (motto: 'Profit or Die!') before ten at night. When they do get home to their trophy houses and spouses, they crack open the champagne as they celebrate another evil day in the service of Mammon, before spending the rest of the night torturing small, furry animals on a shrine specially dedicated to the purpose.

If this is how you imagine investing in shares, and it would not be entirely unreasonable, then odds-on you probably don't think it is something in which you should be dabbling. 'Best leave it to the experts', you've probably told yourself for so many years.

But investing in shares does not have to be like that. It is possible, for Fools, to make a great deal of money in shares without performing regular human sacrifices. Not even when the value of your investments goes for a Burton, as it will do occasionally. Let's examine some of the evidence, and pretty stunning evidence it is, too.

The CSFB Equity-Gilt Study

Despite being one of the most thrilling reads in Britain today, most people have never even heard of the CSFB Equity-Gilt Study, but they should not fret, for this is a good thing and means the delight and frippery of this tome still awaits them. Although the study runs to around 80 pages, it's well worth every little pixel. It comes out every year and looks into the returns to be had from shares, cash and gilts (remember these from the last chapter?) since 1869.

You would be forgiven for thinking we had temporarily taken leave of our senses. There is nothing interesting in the movement of share prices over the last 130 odd years. OK then, punks, tell us that after you've rolled your eyeballs across this graph:

Total Returns From UK Shares 1869-2001

This graph shows the total return of shares on the London Stock Exchange from 1869 to 2001. Look at it again and notice four things.

1. The scale of returns, which represents what would have happened to £100, is logarithmically compressed. If it were not, we wouldn't be able to fit it on the page.
2. Notice the direction it goes.
3. Notice that it doesn't proceed in a straight line of perfect algebraic proportions.
4. Notice once again the direction it goes.

You know, if the financial media and commentators would simply apply this basic 1-to-4 approach to thinking about the stock market, the world would be a much better place. Some of the most experienced financial-journalists do their readers a constant, ongoing disservice by causing them to focus on the short term. The way some have been going on, you might have been forgiven for thinking that there had been a major catastrophe in the stock market over the last couple of years. In fact, when you look at the long-term graph, it's barely a wiggle. If you want a catastrophe, then look at 1974, but even then the recovery was swift. Talk about not seeing the wood for the trees. This is what we refer to as 'the journalistic approach to the financial markets'.

The CSFB Study tells us that, since 1869, shares have, on average, returned 9.5 per cent per year, equivalent to 6.4 per cent after taking inflation into account. Gilts, which you will remember are slices of Government debt, and cash have returned just 4.7 per cent over the same period. After inflation it's 1.7 per cent for gilts and 1.8 per cent for cash (the difference is simply because gilts round down from 1.74% while cash rounds up from 1.76%).

All roads lead us back to compound interest. If we had had a solvent ancestor with sufficient foresight and compassion to invest for his grandchildren back in 1869 and he had decided to invest £100 in the various available options, how would he (or rather we) have fared? The table below reveals all:

	Dec 1869	Dec 2001	Dec 2001 (after accounting for inflation)
Cash	£100	£42,294	£996
Gilts	£100	£41,285	£972
Equities	£100	£15,965,856	£376,068

Source: CSFB E–G Study

There is no competition. If only great-grandfather had had a spare thousand or two back in 1869, we can hear you sighing, but let's flip back to reality: hardly anyone in 1869 had a thousand pounds to spare. The victorians were too busy using any spare lolly to expand the Empire. It's no good wishing: we're going to have to create our wealth for ourselves, but the example of history gives us strength for the future.

People – misguided people – often say that a building society account or gilts are safer than shares. Long term, very long term, we've just seen that that isn't so. In fact, it isn't just not so, but it's very resoundingly not so. What about the shorter term? You won't be surprised to hear that it isn't really so there, either...

If you take every single five-year period since 1869 (that's 1869-1874, 1870-1875, 1871-1876 and so on...you get the picture), shares have done better than cash in 78 per cent of cases. For 'rolling' ten-year periods, shares did better than cash 93 per cent of the time. For twenty-year periods shares did better in all but 6, or 95 per cent, of the 113 periods. Of these six twenty-year periods where shares lost out, five of them ended between 1916 and 1921 (the other was the period ending in 1974) and in none of these periods did cash outperform by more than 1 per cent per year. Once you get up to 30-year periods, then you find that cash has never outperformed shares since CSFB's data began in 1869. And this, of course, is a period that includes two World Wars, a couple of major market crashes, a 'great' depression and a spell of hyperinflation. Wow! They didn't teach you that at school, did they?

The evidence, the incontrovertible evidence, is that the stock market per se is not a risky place to put your money. In fact, the evidence is that for long-term savings, the biggest risk is to have too much money in cash. Yet ask most people in Britain whether their cash is 'safer' in a bank deposit account or the stock market and you'll almost be able to see visions of the sort we described earlier (power-dressing secretaries, the torture of small, furry creatures etc.) flashing through their minds. These will be followed by the instinctual memory of the 1929 Crash and investment bankers falling from skyscrapers like tiles off a roof in a high wind and then they'll come out with the supposedly 'obvious' answer: 'A bank deposit account – what do you think I am? Stupid, or something?'

Why is this? Well, take a look at the first line of an article entitled 'A quick guide to market basics' in the Weekend Money section of the Financial Times of the weekend 11–12 April 1998: 'The stock market is a dangerous place and small investors may be confused.' If no less a body than the Financial Times is telling you the stock market is a dangerous and confusing place, you'd have to be a fool to argue, wouldn't you? Nope, you'd have to be a Fool. Oh, there's danger a-plenty in the stock market alright, if you're going to approach it in a reckless and impulsive manner, but the same goes for the M25 on a Friday night. The thing is that the media, that self-same media that is unable to follow our simple 1-to-4 approach, doesn't find the true story behind the stock market newsworthy. What the financial media wants you to think about is fear and change and specifically what happens NEXT (and 'next' here refers to any time period of up to six weeks). What happens NEXT is what sells newspapers, but the unfortunate result is that many adults are turned off the thought of investing in the stock market because it is so risky and so volatile and so treacherous that they feel they couldn't ever keep up with it.

Look back at the stock market graph. There are groups of several years where it zags more than it zigs. If it zags for deep enough and long enough, (1973–4 springs to mind) then that is called a 'bear' market. Those who sell out during these times, losing large amounts and swearing off the market forever, in most cases deserve what they get. If they're going to take that sort of approach, they're fools, not Fools. Anyone who invests in the stock market with short-term horizons – less than ten years and definitely less than five years – is spinning a roulette wheel. Which brings us to a point we want to be extremely clear about:

We have no idea where the stock market is heading over the next few years. Neither does anyone else. DO NOT LISTEN TO ANYONE ON TV, ON RADIO, OR IN THE PAPERS WHO PRESUMES TO BE ABLE TO FORETELL THE SHORT-TERM MARKET DIRECTION. THIS PERSON IS MOST LIKELY AN IDIOT. If you're convinced otherwise, research all his or her previous market predictions. Compare those to the actual moves in the market and you will discover we're right. If you discover we're wrong, immediately e-mail us at FoolUKBook@fool.co.uk. We'll probably try to hire this oracle, even though we will almost certainly have lost out to a large City firm first.

Interestingly, even if this person were fairly consistently right about the market's short-term direction, it wouldn't be a good move for you to follow along. To play the short-term game involves jumping in and out of a lot of shares. The amount you'd pay in commissions, stamp duty and, potentially, Capital Gains Tax as you jumped hither and thither would most likely leave you with fewer profits (and more headaches) than just buying and holding good companies.

Nope, trying to time the market's short-term movements is definitely not

Foolish. In fact, you can cut down on any of the possible dangers of a sudden sharp downturn by saving steadily and regularly, because you will be taking advantage of the downturn by investing your next chunk of savings at the new lower prices.

This point is amply demonstrated if we go back to a section in the 2000 version of the CSFB Study called 'Consistent investing and market timing'. They only went back 30 years in this section, covering the period from 1970 to 2000, but bless them for that, because the sums are quite a lot harder. First of all, they work out what would have happened if, instead of just investing a lump sum at the beginning, you had invested £100 at the start of every year since 1st Jan 1970. Quite predictably, they find that by the start of 2000, investing this money in shares would have generated the biggest pot, worth a healthy £88,315. In contrast, gilts would have got you to £30,328 and cash would have got you to £17,644. As always, after knocking off inflation the figures are even more startling, with equities producing £21,236, gilts £8,693 and cash only £5,376.

It gets even better, though. Consider the same scenario, of saving £100 per year from 1970, but this time, instead of simply investing it on the first day of each year, imagine that you actually invested it on the worst possible day in each year. In other words, you found the peak of the market in each year and, for some sad and obscure reason, you chose that day to invest your £100. Pretty damn unlucky but, even in this scenario, equities win hands down over the long term. After five years (ending with the nasty crash in 1974), your equity fund would have stood at £246, with gilts at £407 and cash at £650. After an excellent year six, though, equities never looked back. From the sixth year onwards, the equity fund would have always been ahead of cash and gilts and, after the full 30 years, the equity fund would be worth £74,302, the gilt fund £22,921 and the cash fund £17,644. After taking away the effects of inflation, you'd have £17,196, £6,709 and £5,376 respectively. And this is from investing only once a year. Think what little effect any attempted market timing would have had if you were investing, say, every month.

So, Fools, this shows the power of making regular savings into a broad spread of shares. We'll talk about it again in Chapter 7, 'A Tale of Two Professions', in which we learn how to buy into the market as a whole, follow its ebbs and flows and beat the vast majority of professional investors. For many, this type of investment – an index tracker, which aims to 'track' the market's growth over time – will be the beginning and end of your investment career. Nothing further is necessary to ensure a lifetime of Foolish and profitable investment.

Some of you, though, want to beat the average, beat the index trackers, beat that zig-zagging line, and we think we know some ways to do just that. In fact, we take it as a personal challenge to beat the market average, because we believe it can be done by people like you and us.

But let's close with a question, one that is often asked. How far can it go? When will it stop? Is 'growth' eternal? Will the market continue to rise on and on and on, until the ultimate cessation of the human race?

Good question. Please let us know if you have a definitive answer to this. For ourselves, we have a few thoughts on the subject, but which ultimately lead to no firm conclusion, except that we keep coming back and throwing our money into shares anyway.

Over the long term, the market reflects the growth of business. (Over the short term the market moves for an assortment of other, usually far less consequential, reasons.) So, the first question is, will business always grow? Now, obviously it doesn't always grow, because there are bad years and good years, but what this question means is could there ever be a prolonged period – say, as long as a human lifetime – in which business and thus the stock market fails to grow, or even shrinks?

Well, what sustains business? A large number of factors, primarily things like population growth, environmental conditions and government stability (and, since we're out-and-out capitalists, we'll also add here 'lack of excessive government interference'). Increasingly, advances in science and technology that are changing the way we live are also fuelling the growth of business productivity. The question now becomes, do you at present perceive conditions that would lead to fifty or so years of stagnation or decline?

It is very easy to create scenarios in which that would happen, but most of those scenarios involve catastrophic events (nuclear war, asteroid impact, alien invasion, lethal airborne flesh-eating viruses – or all four at once). We put it to you that, in each of these situations, gilts and cash are still very unlikely to do any better than shares and, in any event, the investment returns of your portfolio would be the least of your worries. Each of these situations could bring about the end of civilization.

Thus, our own best guess is that as long as our civilization is still around, you will continue to see long-term growth in business and in the world's stock markets.

5

You Have More Than You Think

Now is not the time to misuse money.
> Advertising slogan for an Indian insurance company painted
> on a rock on the mountain road to Darjeeling, 1993.

Now, we're ready to invest. No holds barred, we are *serious*. Stand back, the City of London, this is Darren Normal-Bloke of Scrimthorpe and he's coming through.

But what, Darren, have you got going for you? Who are you, anyway? And where is Scrimthorpe?

Brain

This may come as a surprise to you, but you're pretty well stacked in the grey matter department. You've picked this book off the shelf, after all. Somewhere in the depths of your psyche, filed in the 'Dread Department' between cancer, AIDS, a comet striking the Earth and Mrs Tucker, your moustachioed form teacher when you were in Class 1A, is the topic of your financial future. Most people have elected to shut out what they perceive as a far distant era and the financial demands that may be made on them when the cash flow has dwindled to zero. Yet you, Fool, have identified the questions of how you're going to pay the electricity bill and/or the grandkids' bail money in 2030 as issues of not a little importance and have elected to educate yourself. This is the act of a supremely rational human being.

'All men by nature desire knowledge', wrote Aristotle. How remarkable it is, though, that we can elect to cast our essential nature aside when it comes to something as basic as money. This stuff is important. We do not live in a barter economy. Trading half a dozen leeks for a knitted woolly hat is not an option outside of a couple of communes in the west of Wales, and even the British winter can be distressingly chilly without suitable headgear, as we all know. We need money and we use money and we think about money many times a day. Why do we allow a steel curtain of despair and panic to drop down (*clang!*) every time we need to think rationally about it? Fear. Gut-wrenching fear. It's only human to want to shut out the unpleasant, but the consequences can be disastrous.

You, reading this, with your Mark 1 Foolish brain, are now going to do a simple sum:

16 – 10 = ?

Now, let's see …

This little piggy went to market, this little piggy … No, that's not it.

One banana, two banana, three banana, four … Nope, not that either.

If you have 16 Motley Fools in a row and you take one away and you do that 10 times, that leaves you with …

13?

No.

5?

Warmer.

6?

Now you're talking! Move over, Stephen Hawking, we have a Brain here. Yes, 6 is the answer we've been grappling for. Six is the amount left when you take 10 away from 16. For want of the ability to perform this simple calculation (or else wilful and shameful ignorance), large swathes of the British population have cast themselves into bondage, the bondage of irre-deemable debt.

Sixteen is the number of per cent you might typically pay back every year on the running total of your credit card debt. This is already far more than you pay on your house (around 6 per cent at the moment) or on a personal loan (say, 10-12 per cent). As we saw – nay, as we had rammed down our throats in the previous chapter – the average return from the stock market has been 10 per cent per year since 1869. Now remember that shares are the highest returning of all investments, and then consider that people who are carrying credit card debt, who nevertheless decide to invest in the stock market, are effectively borrowing at 16 per cent to invest at 10 per cent.

We'll come back to credit card debt later, but you don't have to be the winner of Mastermind to realize that the credit card companies have hit on a great money-making scheme. We'll call it the Mushroom Plan because it involves keeping the herd in the dark and feeding them ... well, you know what mushrooms get fed. The thing about the Mushroom Plan, though, is that it relies on the herd staying in the dark because they like it there and it's warm and it's cosy and it smells right good!

The thing is, we've made up our minds that finance and investments are things that we are not capable of being involved with. We think it's boring, or too complicated, or too much of a gamble and as a result we try not to think too much about it. It's an awe-inspiring prospect. *Moi?* Making decisions on investment? *Mais non*, Sire! Many people with these kinds of feelings turn to the financial advisers we've already mentioned, people who work in an industry in which their bread and butter depends on fostering a climate of uncertainty and despair and replacing it with a fug of comforting 'Come to Daddy' warmth. Part of growing up is learning that Mum and Dad don't always have all the answers, and so it is here.

We will see in Chapter 6 'Be Your Own Financial Adviser' how some of the professionals who advise us operate, and this question should always be in our minds: 'How do *you* make money?' Once we've asked that, we should then move on to the follow-up: 'How do you make *more* money than that?' Most of us have a sense of fair play that does not object to people earning a living if they do a good job on our behalf, but the scales are so stacked in the direction of the finance professional that it is only natural to be uneasy at the business relationship involved.

If nothing else, walk away from these Foolish pages with the simple understanding that:

● Financial advisers working on commission earn their daily bread by selling you endowments, ISAs, Personal Pension Plans and Free-Standing AVCs, and they make more money by selling you the investment plan that pays them the highest kickback.
● Stockbrokers earn commission every time a share is bought or sold on

your account and then make more money by trading on your behalf more often.

● Unit trusts take a portion of the funds you give them to manage, and then make more money by attracting as many other people's money as possible.

'Nothing astonishes men more than common sense and plain dealing', wrote Ralph Waldo Emerson. Employ this common sense, this quality so integral to the survival of the human race, and astonish yourself as you reflect on how each of the ways that the entities listed above make *more* money is ultimately by taking as much as possible of it away from you. So, the best way to invest effectively is to give as little of your money away to advisers as possible. Every penny that you pay to an adviser is a penny that you haven't invested. Some-times the advice might be worth it, but be very careful to remember how these guys make their money. We will talk later and in more detail about financial advisers and stockbrokers, but the conflict of interest is obvious. Briefly, though, let's talk about 'discretionary' stockbrokers. If you have discretionary stockbroking account, this means that you have deposited a sum of money with a stockbroking company and entrusted them with the task of rendering you wealthy. Their aim and your aim, of course, is for them to buy good investments on your behalf. But while simply buying and holding good investments may make money for you, it won't make money for them. The incentive to trade and trade and trade again, earning healthy commissions each time, is hard to resist. Further, this frenetic activity is likely to make the customer think that this is a horribly complicated business which only a *stockbroker* could understand and aren't I lucky to have such a nice man working on my behalf? *Au contraire!*

Unit trusts spend the 5 per cent or so you give them upfront to promote themselves and invite more people to the party, thus giving them more money to manage. It's a bit like one of those backpacker's guide books. No sooner have they written about João DaSilva and his family who run the nicest little guest house on the beach in Goa where three months' stay costs 50p, including three delicious meals and free use of João's motor-scooter, than the place is overrun by hordes of hippie wannabees and the party is spoiled for ever. To put that in financial terms, the more money a unit trust has to invest, the less nimble it becomes; the clumsier it is, the less likely it is to outperform the stock market.

The easiest way to understand things is to ask very simple questions, very slowly and then wait for the answers. Unfortunately, many of us feel afraid to do so, because we worry we may look stupid. In reality, we only look stupid when we try to hide behind presumed knowledge. By contrast, thinking we ought to be able to understand these things, even though we've never really given them much of our attention before – now that *is* stupid!

To return to our theme: we have more than we think. We have the power of reason, our mundane, everyday common sense, and the capability to bring it to bear on what may seem at first to be an intimidatingly complex subject. Reason's simplest tool is the asking of questions, something many financial professionals don't want you to do.

To understand the power of simple reasoning, try this game. There are 128 people entered for this year's men's championship at Wimbledon. How many matches have to be played to find the winner?

Hmmm …

OK, so there's 64 matches in round one, plus 32, plus 16 …

Stop! There's a much easier way than that. We know that each match produces precisely one loser and we know that, by the end of the two weeks, all but one of the 128 entrants must become a loser. So, there must be 127 matches to play. One less than the total number of players because there has to be one left over at the end (sadly not our Timmy). So, what if we had a simple knockout darts competition with 587 entrants? Easy, we need 586 losers, so we need 586 matches. And so it is with finance. None of it is very hard, it's just a question of thinking about things in the right way. Faced with this sort of question, the darts promoting equivalent of a financial adviser would probably launch into a Wise discussion about how many rounds would be necessary, how many byes you'd need in round one and the pros and cons of various different seeding structures. You could be left bemused and happy to take his word for it but, by thinking around the problem a bit and using some common sense, you can reach the right answer for yourself in less than a second.

Finally, the very act of sitting down to read this book already demonstrates you have taken the decision to move from servitude to freedom. The heart of Foolishness is a fundamental belief in rationalism, in the idea that we can and should bring our powers of reason to bear on financial matters. In fact, the application of reason is the only way to succeed with finance and your employment of your reasoning faculties will mark you out from the majority of other people in the marketplace. If you're not using your brain, you're using something else: someone else's advice, the daily horoscope, or just plain luck. Don't let yourself down. Instead, use your most powerful asset and the cheapest aid to investing yet invented: your brain.

Time

You also have more of this than you think. Even if you don't think you have very much of it, you have more than you think.

In this context 'time' means a couple of things. Firstly, it means the seconds and minutes and hours we cobble together into the daily hullabaloo we call life. We can squander these through precipitate action, or we can husband them and cherish them and use them – Aha, you think we're going to say 'wisely', don't you? – Foolishly. Use time to your advantage. Do not, ever, agree to anything immediately, particularly if it's an investment that someone else wants you to buy. Stall, stammer, feign an epileptic fit if you must, but don't get bullied into signing anything the first time around. This also goes for people who are allegedly on your side, like your financial adviser. Use time to your advantage by deferring any decision and research-ing it and any possible alternatives. If you do that, you may find yourself calling your financial adviser back and saying: 'Felicity, I see the unit trust ISA you want me to buy has a 5 per cent initial charge and has significantly underperformed the market average over the last ten years. Now tell me why I should buy it.'

It was George Bernard Shaw who referred to the UK and the US as 'two nations separated by a common language' and, as a company that operates in both countries, we can attest that it is true. Only, the difference isn't just in language, it's in approach and style as well. Here in Britain, we nurture a reti-cence, a desire not to rock the boat and above all not to create a scene, which seems to be lacking across the water. Cultural stereotypes are a dangerous thing to bandy about as we enter the new millennium, but what we're trying to say here is that this kind of challenging approach seems to us far less natural for a British person than an American. A friend of one of us, a doctor, was on the verge of being sold a clutch of high-commission products by a financial adviser. Following some discussions of the type you have read here, she returned to the adviser fully armed with a series of questions concerning the performance of these investments as compared to the stock market index, their flexibility, alternatives at lower cost, etc. Unfortunately, she was not able to get past the adviser's secretary. On hearing the kind of thing our newly Foolish doctor was going to be asking, she rolled her eyes and said, 'Oh, he's going to love talking to you. I'll get him to phone you with an appointment.' And that was it. She never heard from him again. The point is that this kind of approach was not something she felt comfortable with and she had to steel herself to do it. When she finally got over that hurdle, her attitude cut through the layers of obfuscation and blather like a knife through warm butter. It is so important to train yourself to take a hard-headed and firm line. Practise polite but emphatic refusal and delaying tactics in front of the mirror. This is your future you're dealing with, after all.

There are also other ways to use time when you decide to start investing on your own, as we hope you will by the time you have finished this book. At all costs, do not rush headlong into the stock market, convinced you are going to make a killing. That kind of attitude leads to large stakes in aggressive shares and big gambles. It is far more likely that *you* will be killed, lose a significant amount of money and be turned off investing forever, with sad consequences for your financial future.

Instead, practise. Just practise. Create a paper portfolio (or a practice online portfolio at one of the many sites offering this facility) which you go on to track, leaving your stack of crisp fivers safe and sound in the bottom drawer of the freezer (you didn't know we knew, did you?). Follow the ups and downs of the shares you would have invested in. Rejoice as they plummet and groan as they rocket skywards – it's the exact opposite of what you'd be doing if you'd staked real money in them and it's all the more useful for that. Do it for a year if you like, or longer. This may sound like it contravenes the First Foolish Law of Compounding ('Start early, Fool!'), but it doesn't. Compound interest is your friend and it's an especially good friend if you hug it to your bosom early enough, but compound depreciation can have as devastating an effect on your investments as compound interest a miraculous one. So, start early on the Foolish investing ladder and don't squander time with unFoolish investments. Use that time instead to set up the habits for a lifetime of savvy investing. You have years and years to invest – don't spoil it all right at the beginning.

The other obvious thing 'time' means is the years (hopefully) you have left before the band starts to play and St Peter's asking if you'll be taking the full board or demi-pension option. We touched on this in Chapter 2, where we saw the effect of time and compound interest demonstrated before our very eyes. It was inspiring, was it not? Salt away your stash, make a regular contribution to it and turn up in thirty years to collect the abundant proceeds. But time alone isn't enough – you need to combine it with patience. And faith.

Over the years, the stock market produces a reliable return, but there are times, such as the last couple of years and, further back, in 1973–74, when it loses ground: sometimes quite a lot of ground. If you lose faith at times like this, you will scupper all the hard work and patient effort you have put into your investments thus far. One person who had patience was Anne Scheiber who we mentioned in the introduction. This was the humble New Yorker whose $5000 investment in shares on the New York stock exchange in 1944 grew, by the time of her death in 1995, to $22 million. She left all her money to Yeshiva University, also in New York, and the resulting media splash was the only reason we ever heard about her. Through good times and bad, Ms Scheiber plugged away, her investments growing all the while at a steady 18.3 per cent per annum, far above the average of 11 per cent per annum for the US stock market as a whole during that period. Some years, the value of her portfolio doubled. Others, it halved. When she woke up in the morning and, we presume, read headlines in the newspapers about doom and gloom and bursting bubbles, she just plugged on regardless. What was running through her mind as she left the Wall Street professionals gasping in the far distance behind her? We will never know, but we can hope that she spent many of those years bathed in a quiet satisfaction. The reasons for her ascent to such heights were that she had patience a-plenty, she bought common, well-known shares, she held onto them and held onto them and she had confidence in her approach. If anyone knew the value of time, it was Anne Scheiber.

What about the eighty-year-olds reading this? All this talk of time means this can't be a party they're invited to, surely? No, we think the points we're making apply to everyone. These days, you probably *do* have more time left than you think. Even if you don't, you will likely be looking to pass your invested pile on to your descendants in your bid to obtain Most Favoured Ancestor status. Of course, if you really want to leave them a worthwhile legacy, you will not only be investing Foolishly on your and their behalf, but encouraging them to learn about the subject for themselves. As we see it, if you get up in the morning and despite careful scrutiny of the obituaries column fail to find your name, you are set for another day of Foolish investment.

Other People

As with our brain power and the time we have, so we often overlook the value of other people to us.

Sadly, not all people are valuable to us all the time. When your flatmate throws out your twenty-year (*twenty-year!*) collection of *Motor Sport* magazine, because he thought those were the recycling boxes, he loses value to you pretty quickly. (I've been waiting over ten years to make this confession in a national medium. Sorry, Kirk. D.B.) Or how about when your toddler pours Ribena into your computer keyboard? Or you discover years later that your financial adviser has sold you one of the worst-performing, highest-charging pensions there is? Sometimes it's enough to make you want to declare the Republic of MacFool on a rocky Hebridean outcrop and repel all invaders with clods of peat and solidified porridge.

But don't do it.

Turn the tables. *Learn* from other people. Learn from older brother Arthur's venture into Venezuelan coffee futures. Profit from Aunt Dora's experience with the cowboy plumbers (£800 for an hour's work on a blocked pipe at a weekend – it got a full page spread in the *Sun*). Reflect on the poor financial planning of your friend Ted ('Lend us fifty quid till the weather breaks'). If you lecture them from a tone of high financial rectitude, you'll get the come-uppance you deserve, but try showing them some of the numbers from this book.

There will be other people in your life who you can turn to for positive lessons in how to look after money and make it grow. Perhaps another friend has negotiated a cheap mortgage deal or you have an uncle who has always been a sound investor. Take him out to dinner, pump him for information – it's an investment that may repay itself many times over. (It may not, but you'll have healed the rift in the family dating back to when your dad pushed him down the stairs for pinching his tricycle.)

You can't make use of any of this huge repository of financial experience, though, unless you and they are prepared to talk about the subject. It's strange how in our age when just about anything else is fair game for general conversation, money and investment is still a taboo topic. Loosen up and try and get your immediate circle to do so too. The professionals are out there to profit from our ignorance and the best weapon we have is ourselves and our pooled experience. Let's use it.

If you like, we'll help you. Start a dining club of half-a-dozen friends or so who meet once a month to discuss money and investment strategies. Put on jester caps, call yourselves the Motley Fool UK Dining Club (Hartlepool Chapter) – we're always on the lookout for licensing deals.

You might want to go even further and start an actual investment club. These are groups of friends, neighbours, business partners and a sprinkling of very smart gerbils, who invest a pooled sum of money in shares and track their performance over time, buying and selling according to the conclusions of the regular group meetings. Some clubs seriously outperform the professionals and many investment club members actually find the club's investments outperform the ones they hold on their own. It's something to do with the centring effect of a group of Foolish people discussing investment, or the effect of rhubarb crumble and custard on the decision-making centres of the hypothalamus – scientific opinion remains divided. Whatever the explanation, it's a real effect and an organization called ProShare, whose aim is to promote share ownership in Britain, has a sheaf of information on the subject. Details of how to contact them are in our Foolish Glossary under 'Investment Club'. We've even written a cheap, short book ourselves on the subject, the *Fool's Guide to Investment Clubs*, available from a good bookshop near you (or the book bin of your local charity shop if you're reading this in 2010).

The universe of investing knowledge does not end, though, with friends and family. There are other people out there who have something useful to say and some of them are people who write books on investing. Naturally, we think you've bought the most important book on investing already, but there are many other books on finance and investment worth reading. Authors such as Graham, Buffett, Lynch and Fisher all have useful things to say and of course there are a number of other Motley Fool books too (you'll find these listed at the end of the book).

Finally, we would not be Fools if we left this section without mentioning our online world. Without it, the Motley Fool could never exist. It's people who have made the Motley Fool and who continue to make it what it is. Out there, on the Web, is a community of people who are interested in the same subject as you are: how to increase their savings and have an enjoyable time doing it. Only, this isn't one or two people getting together for a chat occasionally, this is hundreds of thousands of people, all with specialist knowledge of one sort or another, stopping by regularly and helping each other out with advice and suggestions. Any mistake you're about to make, someone else will have made before you and will be prepared to give you the benefit of their experience. It's a community like no other. If you like what we've been saying here, then come and visit – it could be the most profitable and enjoyable free thing you've ever done.

That you're prepared to mention in public, anyway.

Money

We reckon that the people reading this book are perfectly capable of deducing that if they give up smoking forty cigarettes a day they'll have plenty of money left over for investment, or that if they cycle instead of taking the bus the pennies saved will soon add up. Mrs Thatcher told poor people not to go shopping when they were hungry and obviously thought she was dispensing pearls, but the fact is we all have to figure out for ourselves where we can make economies in our lives. Most of us, if we look hard enough, will have some cash-draining activity or other we could happily live without and may even be the better for it.

A lot of this money thing is down to priorities. Investment isn't such a priority for most of us, because it's not something we *want* to do. It's something we have to do, something we feel compelled to do. As long as investing isn't fun, as long as it remains a remote, incomprehensible business, then figuring out how to save more money to put away isn't going to be high on the List of Enjoyable Things to Do This Month. Simply having a little knowledge about the basics of investing, though, and knowing the awesome might of compound interest can alter the whole way you look at investment and make it a lot more real.

We all need targets of some sort and quite a good one to start with is to aim to save 10 per cent of your income. This may be way too much or way too little for your personal circumstances. It doesn't matter – it's just a tool. Take a look at your finances, ask yourself if you're saving 10 per cent of what you make and if you aren't, look at the reasons why. It might be illuminating.

We won't present you with a series of money-saving ideas here, but we are going to mention just one. Consider very carefully whether you want to spend fistfuls of cash on a brand new car. A friend of one of us bought a new MG sports car with borrowed money. Within a year it had depreciated to just over half its initial value and she was now carrying more in debt than the car was even worth. Spending large amounts – and, worse, borrowing large amounts – on a new car is one of the surest ways to savings penury for the majority of us who don't have unlimited incomes. These things are expensive! There are some out there whose life aim since the age of twelve has been a Ferrari sports car with leather seats and the acceleration of a Saturn V rocket. That's fine, but to the rest of you, we say: take a critical look at what you're paying for your wheels and you may find you want to spend some of that money more fruitfully elsewhere.

6

Be Your Own Financial Adviser

Never give a sucker an even break.   W.C. Fields

'Wait a minute!' you're saying, 'this is getting out of hand. You people – Fools, you call yourselves – are making some pretty outrageous claims here and you tell me there are more to come. I'd like to hear what the professionals have to say about you upstarts.'

Look, this is fine with us, it really is. In fact, the urge to seek independent, impartial advice could hardly be considered anything but Foolish. Entering the world of investment is an intimidating step. It is intimidating because, firstly, the Wise like to make it so. There is seemingly a large amount of information to be digested, jargon to be deciphered and swish brochures with impressive-looking graphs to be waded through. The Wise like it this way because it gives them the drop on the punter. (That's you.) Secondly, it is intimidating because it quite obviously is, dummy! Look, you're taking on the sole responsibility for investing for your and your family's future. You are effectively saying that you will invest your available funds more effectively than a highly trained professional. By your own efforts your retirement will be spent either living on bread and dripping in the one room you can afford to heat, or snapping your fingers at the waiters in the Grand Hotel in Cannes. Scary stuff, indeed.

By reading this far, though, you have proved yourself to have some Foolish mettle. You're not the run-of-the-mill punter, you like to ask questions and are prepared to engage with life. You'll take on responsibility, but are also aware that by doing so you may reap benefits and satisfaction far higher than if you hand over this most important aspect of your life to someone else. Watch out, you're turning into a Fool!

Now where are you, a Fool, going to go for impartial, independent advice? It's a good question because, as things stand at the moment, there doesn't seem to be too much of it around. The current regime for finanical advice, which is regulated by the Financial Services Authority (FSA), is known as 'polarisation'. It sounds more like something out of Star Trek, but it refers to an attempt to split, or polarise, the different advisers into two categories.

First of all, there are the 'tied advisers', known as such because they are tied to one particular company and can only sell the products of that partic-ular company. Within that company's range of products, they're supposed to find something that's suitable for you, but they don't have to go off investi-gating, much less recommending, the products of different companies. They are there, as best they can within the regulations, to flog the products offered by the company they're tied to. It's about as far away from impartial, inde-pendent advice as you can get.

The second type of adviser is styled the 'independent financial adviser' or 'IFA' for short. The idea is that they sit you down, find out your needs and wants, and then find something suitable for you from across the whole range of products on the market. So there you go, impartial, independent advice. Thank goodness for that. Unfortunately, there is one very large fly in the oint-ment. IFAs typically get paid by commissions on the products they sell you and those commissions come out of the money that you're putting into the product. As we shall see later, there are significant differences between the sizes of commissions that the various types of investments pay IFAs and it is a fact, a not very surprising fact, that those charging the highest commission tend to do the worst. After all, the more commission that goes to the IFA, the less money you have working for you from the start and if we cast our minds back to the Miracle of Compound Interest, we'll remember what a difference that can make. With IFAs only being human and us being suspicious Fools, we reckon there's a teensy conflict of interest going on here.

Stop the book! Fade the focus! We're going on a fantasy journey ...

You're an IFA. A client, Mr Alan Average, sits in front of you. You lean back, feet resting on your imitation mahogany desk with leather writing pad and muse that two types of investment might be suitable for him, both of which you can justify as being appropriate. One pays pitiful commission, the other a hefty whack over the first two years, followed by a healthy trailing commission over the next twenty. They're much of a muchness, you think, so you'll sting him with the heavy commission, you think. He won't be too disadvantaged and I have to make a living. Is this so wrong? Well, is it?!

Change the scene slightly. The hefty commission-paying investment isn't quite as good as the other one (which, in fact, is almost certainly going to be the case for similar products). The trouble is you've got the Child Support Agency on your tail for maintenance payments for your children, Doris and Edna. Also, Edna wants a pony in the way only a twelve-year-old can and Doris wants to go on the school ski trip this winter. Which are you going to choose now, given that you're only a human being?

The potential for conflicts of interest is obvious and people started getting rather suspicious about it, particularly after the 'mis-selling' debacles involving pensions, endowments and free-standing AVCs (we'll say more about these in Chapters 14 and 15). Finally, the FSA has decided to investigate the root of the problem and it asked Charles River Associates, an independent market research company, to look into the situation. We're a website recovering from the travails of the dotcom boom and bust, so you'll forgive us if there are no prizes for working out what they found…

> We found evidence that commission influences advisers' recommendations in two dimensions, namely at the product level and the provider level.

In other words, there was bias towards high-commission products both in selecting the product and in selecting the provider of that product. Most scary of all, though, is that they found more cause for concern among the so-called 'independent' financial advisers than among their 'tied' brethren. About IFAs, they said:

> In the single-premium investment market, in around 4 out of 5 cases we do not find any concern regarding commission bias. However, in the remainder, we find that commission influences the decision to recommend non-ISA products and in particular, unit-linked bonds and with-profit bonds.

Unit-linked and with-profit bonds are the things that tend to pay the largest up front commissions to advisers – certainly more than your typcial, common or garden, ISA. Now we don't want to cause too much hysteria. After all, in four out of five cases, there was no concern. But, if you turn it around, then there are problems 20 per cent of the time. Those aren't good odds when you're dealing with your future financial wellbeing.

At the time of writing the FSA is still mulling over it all and plans to say more later in 2002, but the indications are that there will be a major overhaul of the way that advice is delivered. The key proposals, as they stand, are that the existing regime, or 'polarisation', be removed and that only advisers that are remunerated by a fixed fee rather than a commission, regardless of the products they recommend, should be permitted to describe themselves as independent.

We see the second part of this as being the most important. It's something we've been banging on about for years, including in previous editions of this book. As we hope we've made clear, it's just not possible to be confident of the independence and impartiality of advice where there are commissions involved. In some cases, IFAs already offer customers the opportunity to choose between a commission-based or fee-paying service, but there are problems even with this. After all, if an IFA is recommending one product to their commission-paying customers, they they'll potentially have a lot of explaining to do if they then offer a different product to a fee-paying customer in a similar posistion. As we see it, wherever an adviser accepts commissions, even if it's not from you, then the advice is necessarily suspect. So it's excellent news that the FSA plans to permit only pure fee-paying advisers to style themselves as independent. Of course, it remains to be seen whether this is actually what happens but, at the very least, it's a great start that the conflicts of interest that have dogged the industry for years are now being recognised for what they are.

Now we don't want to give you the idea that we're a hard to please grouchy lot – it ain't true, we promise (well we are perhaps a little fussy, but be fair, this stuff is important) – but there are problems even when you do find a truly independent, purely fee-based, good IFA. It stems from the paradoxical disadvantage of their being accountable.

If you are given misleading advice, or sold a totally inappropriate product, you have redress. You can go to the Financial Services Authority (FSA) and complain and are likely to get a satisfactory result. Isn't Britain an enlightened place, compared with, say, Chechnya or Sierra Leone? How can this be a disadvantage? Well, we might be being a little picky here, but it can. For the majority who wish to place their trust entirely in another's hands, it is obviously crucial that the people in whom they place that trust are highly regulated. The effect, however, on those who are being watched over, is to make them conservative and conformist, prepared to choose between the stale clutch of products on offer by the Wise, but not prepared to step outside those narrow confines into a wider world. They may be impartial themselves, but their thoughts are affected by an industry that is influenced by commissions and a desire to promote certain types of product. By offering the control of your finances to someone whose horizons are already limited, you are closing down the spectrum of your investment universe before you've even started. As a Fool, you are accountable to no one but yourself. That sets you apart from the teeming masses, giving you independence of action and an invaluable edge. Take advantage of it.

While we will make the point once more that there *are* good independent financial advisers out there, given the situation, and the fact that its changing as we write, we're reluctant to use the term independent financial adviser in this book. You see, 'adviser' somehow implies impartiality, and what we've seen is that the nature of the business means that it is extremely hard for them to be that. For the rest of this book, we will refer to them as independent financial advisers (salespeople) or IFAs (salespeople). We don't mean to cause any offence, but since that's clearly what they are, let's call a spade a spade.

So, if you wish, seek independent, impartial advice and do your utmost to verify that it really is. Do so, however, in the awareness that the only person who truly shares your aims, hopes and aspirations is yourself. By reading this book and devoting just a small amount of time to learning about Foolish investment, you are setting the scene for a lifetime of fulfilment, Folly and wealth. In short, get educated, get Foolish and be your *own* financial adviser!

7

A Tale of Two Professions and Basic Foolish Investment

All professions are conspiracies against the laity.
George Bernard Shaw, *The Doctor's Dilemma*

Tales of Amateurism

In the nineteenth and early twentieth centuries, there was a strong tradition of amateurism in Britain. It was generally reckoned that being a professional was somehow underhand, that it was a trifle vulgar and that there was really nothing a professional could do that an amateur couldn't do better and with more aplomb. Sometimes this was true. The early Everest mountaineers thought training was for cissies and that smoking cigarettes was a cure for the altitude sickness caused by the lack of oxygen at great heights. In 1924 Mallory and Irvine puffed their way to the stupendous height of 28,000 feet and were last seen alive going strong for the summit. Maybe they reached it. Nobody knows for certain, because they never returned and the discovery of Mallory's frozen body in May 1999 seems only to have added to the confusion. It wasn't for another thirty years that Everest was finally climbed, a stunning testament to the stamina and endeavour of these amateurs.

In the nineteenth century, many of the greatest linguistic works were compiled by amateurs. One of the major contributors to the forerunner of the *Oxford English Dictionary* was a Dr W. C. Minor, an inmate at Broadmoor with a persecution complex and a conviction for murder. When you look up a word in the *OED* today, you may well be reading an entry penned by an insane, Victorian murderer.

So, don't knock amateurs because they can sometimes turn in surprising performances.

Let's see how amateurs fare against a couple of professions in the late twentieth century – the heart surgeon and the investment fund manager. How well can the 'know-nothing' hope to perform against these two groups of professionals, each of whose jobs is highly skilled and requires years of training? The answers may surprise you.

A Tale of Two Professions

The heart surgeon

You gasp at *Your Life in Their Hands*. You're a *Casualty* and *ER* groupie. You've been studying these programmes for a long time now, you've picked up the terminology and you're starting to say to yourself that it really doesn't look that difficult. Thoughts like this are starting to arise more and more frequently in your mind: 'I've got a 'C' in biology O level. I could do that.'

Come up close and we'll let you into a secret – it isn't that difficult and you don't even have to be very good-looking or drive a red sports car. Heart surgery is a hobby you can develop in your own garage, at your own pace. If it takes off – and there's no reason why it shouldn't – you could find your-self with a part-time job that is more lucrative than selling water filters door to door and so much more satisfying. Interested? We think you should be. Here, let's show you how to get started.

First, clear out the accumulated junk of lifetimes from the back of your garage and take it down to the car boot sale. The proceeds from the sale of jam jars full of nuts and bolts with Imperial threads and Great Aunt Doris's collection of Victorian thimbles will fund the next stage of your self-improve-ment programme. Next, scrub down the inside of your garage with a hard bristled broom and a bottle of Domestos. (We consider the importance of antisepsis in surgical procedures to have been overplayed, so this is not strictly necessary, but the smell does impress future customers, er, sorry, 'patients'.) Next, cover over the inspection pit with some planks, borrow your neighbour's Black and Decker Workmate and, with your own, place them together end to end on the planks. The operating theatre and operating table are now ready for use. Some Fellows of the Amateur Cardiothoracic Society of the Royal College of Surgeons (FACSRCS) do advocate sound-proofing the garage to mask the screams of ungrateful clients, but we have found Radio 1 played at full volume works just as well and is much cheaper.

Now you are ready for a trip to the DIY Superstore. Load the kids in the car, leave the dog in the garden and off you go. You're looking for a pair of garden shears (go for a good make, as these do tend to work loose other-wise), a large cool box (the purpose of which will become clear), a length of garden hose (five metres should do it) and a pair of bellows (you may have to make a side trip to the ironmonger's for these). Oh yes, and you'll need a pig, a bucket, some bailer twine and a pair of jump leads (you may have these already, in which case, so much the better).

Back home again, turn the pig loose in the garden and cut your hose up into two equal lengths, one of which you now insert into a hole you have cut in the side of an empty, plastic lemonade bottle. Now, make a hole in the bottom of the bottle and plug your other length of hose into that. This can be a bit fiddly, but do make sure the seal is tight, as otherwise you will have blood running all over the garage floor and seeping down into the inspection pit, which is a nuisance. Into the top of the bottle, insert the bellows. Your basic, but functional, cardiopulmonary bypass machine is now ready.

It remains only to fill the cool box with six packets of frozen peas and tether the pig to a convenient spot and you are ready for action.

If no prospective patient has turned up by word of mouth, then an advert in your local paper will usually bring in a number of possible punters. Be sure to peg your rates at around half of what the local private hospital is offering to ensure a good response.

Greet your client at the front door and offer them a glass of sherry. This always breaks the ice as they may be feeling a little nervous. After some small talk to put them at their ease, escort them through to the operating theatre and invite them to lie down on the operating table, all the while keeping up the flow of chit-chat. If you think you may be disturbed by screams and wild flailings as you operate, take the opportunity at this point to disable your patient with a swift but clean blow to the head with a trolley jack.

The scene is now set for operation. Open the chest with the shears directly through the sternum. This should be the work of just a few moments and now part the ribs to expose the heart (you can identify this as it is the only thing moving). Identify the inflow and outflow tracts of the heart – it's worth mugging up on this beforehand – and, cutting small holes in them, insert the lengths of garden hose. Again, make sure the seals are tight. Now, instruct your youngest child to commence pumping the bellows. The patient is on cardio-pulmonary bypass.

You will have noticed that there is a fair amount of space within the thoracic cavity and into this you empty the frozen peas, thus slowing the heart down and eventually stopping it.

At this point, send your next youngest child out to slaughter the pig and get them to bring back the heart in the bucket, while you open the patient's own heart and extract the diseased heart valve. Then, exchange the pig valve for the patient's valve, sewing it in with the bailer twine.

You are now ready to restart the heart. Disconnect the patient from the bypass machine, sew up the holes and, connecting one end of the jump leads to the battery of your car which your teenage child has started in the driveway, apply the other end to the heart. This should, usually, start it beating again.

Finally, scoop out the peas and sew up the chest wall. (If you don't manage to locate all the peas, it doesn't matter too much.) The operation is now over and by this time the patient should be waking up from the blow on the head and a strong cup of coffee is indicated.

It is only courteous to call a taxi to take the patient home, as they do not generally feel like taking the bus. We usually pay for this from our own funds and add it to the bill later.

Some budding amateur heart surgeons worry about the legality of garage cardiac surgery, but we can genuinely assure you after enquiring at the Royal College of Surgeons of London that it is entirely legal. As long as you do not label yourself as something you're not and the patient gives their consent, the law of the land takes no position on operations carried out by people without officially recognized qualifications. The same is not true for animals, however, and since, in this instance, a licence from the Home Office will be required for the pig, we suggest you consider starting off with coronary artery bypass surgery instead. Simply become competent at sewing together two pieces of soggy macaroni without any leaks and you should be all set.

Having mastered the intricacies of DIY heart surgery, you are now set to become your own investment fund manager.

The investment fund manager

While we have to admit that you will be doing well at amateur heart surgery to outperform the majority of professional cardiac surgeons, we are confident that as an amateur fund manager you will be able to achieve this level of expertise. Not only that, but the degree of preparation required is less, as is the clearing up afterwards.

How so? How can the amateur, 'no brain' (no offence intended) investor hope to outperform the majority of the professional unit trust fund managers who have spent years training for their jobs and spend twelve hours a day or more living, eating and breathing shares? They earn hundreds of thousands of pounds, drive fast cars and wear flashy suits. It is hard to imagine how Alan and Cynthia Average in their suburban semi in Middlesex are going to better them. This is a complicated business, after all, and not one the lay person should really get involved in. Not unless they want to lose their shirts, that is! (Guffaw! Guffaw! Guffaw!)

Not.

To understand the true situation, you need to understand, just a little, about how the stock market works. First of all, consider that almost all of the share trading in the stock market involves one highly paid fund manager buying shares from another highly paid fund manager. At a given price, one of them is buying and the other is selling. They can't both be right, yet they are paid lots of money to be right. Let's imagine two of our fast-car-driving, flashy-suited fund managers. One is called Ingrid, and the other, Dexter. They both manage standard UK equity unit trusts with an initial charge of 5 per cent and annual management charges of 1.5 per cent per annum. They have both taken the same investment exams and read the same newspapers. They also both speak to the same stockbrokers' analysts (and get taken on the same freebie jaunts). They are both supported by huge marketing organizations telling everyone how Wise they are, yet they both spend their days buying and selling shares from and to each other and others like them. They just can't both be right. In fact, overall, for every decision that is made, someone is right and someone is wrong. Therefore, there are as many wrong decisions being made as right ones. Despite this, the fund managers are all being paid highly to get it right more often than not. It is not possible, *on average*, for this to be achieved. Just in the same way that it is not possible for people, *on average*, to be above *average* height. *On average*, people must, of course, be the *average* height and weight and, *on average*, fund managers must provide *average* returns (that is, *average* returns **before we take away their charges**).

Both Ingrid and Dexter will try to convince you that they will be right more often than each other. They will each have plenty of apparently good reasons why this might be the case. So, who do we believe? If they're so Wise and they disagree about the best approach to selecting shares, what chance do we have of deciding which of their approaches is best? Well, we can do something rather sneaky. Since we know that the performance of all the Ingrids and Dexters will average out between them over time, we may as well simply buy the market average. That is, a sort of combination of all the Ingrids and Dexters mushed together. OK, you know it's been coming: we'll buy the 'index'. This way, we can let Ingrid and Dexter fight it out between themselves, knowing that it doesn't matter to us which of them is right. Effectively, we hedge our bets between them, so we don't run the risk of picking the wrong one.

But here's the really clever part: by buying the market average (that is, an index tracker), we can significantly reduce our charges. We can entirely dispense with the initial charge so that we've got about 5 per cent more money working for us straight away. On top of this, we can reduce our annual charge by around 1 per cent, so that we have a statistical expectation of doing 1 per cent a year better than Ingrid and Dexter on an ongoing basis. Over the long term, an advantage of 1 per cent a year can make a very big difference. Going back to our height analogy, imagine that we take a group of people who happen to be exactly the same height with their shoes on. Now, we tell everyone to take their shoes off. The people who had the biggest heels on will now be the shortest. In these terms, the highest charging fund managers wear four-inch stilettoes. Index trackers wear flip-flops. When we take away everyone's charges, index trackers will, on average, stand head and shoulders above the crowd.

Be warned, Ingrid and Dexter don't want to be put out of a job, so they will tell you that buying an index tracker is very Foolish. Dexter will tell you how confident he is of outperforming Ingrid and Ingrid will explain how Dexter's style of fund management is past its sell-by date. They will also both tell you that they will be able to outperform an index tracker in 'difficult market conditions', because they will see it coming and move some investments into cash. **Don 't believe it, it 's absolute twaddle.** They might see the crash coming, but they might not: and who's to say that they will switch the cash back into shares in time for the upswing? *On average*, they just can't do it. Whatever they tell you, there is one inescapable fact. Their charges are like a leak in the portfolio. Money is dripping out of it year after year and, over the long term, this will make a big difference to performance. They are both going to have to do **extremely** well to overcome their high charges and beat the index over the years and, quite frankly, it's very unlikely that either of them will manage it. In fact, the longer the time period that you take, the harder it becomes.

Research conducted by the WM Company in 1999 backs this theory up. They analysed data from managed funds and index trackers over twenty years to the end of 1998. The basic conclusions that they reached were as follows ('active funds' means the funds managed by people like Ingrid and Dexter, 'passive funds' means index trackers):

Active and passive funds compared
- Active funds naturally had a much greater range of returns than passive funds.
- Passive trusts performed in line with the index but slightly below it due to management costs.
- Over three-year periods, the average passive fund was in the second quartile of overall performance.
- Over longer periods, passive funds maintained their performance relative to the index while that of active funds fell away.

Consistency of performance
- Over five years, the chance of an active fund beating a passive fund is around one in four. The issue is how much this can be used to predict the fund's future performance.

- Overall, the probability of a trust achieving top quartile performance in a five-year period and repeating this in a subsequent period was no better than random.
- There was stronger evidence that investing in a bottom quartile fund would give a better than random chance of achieving top quartile in the subsequent period.
- The key to benefiting from active management is the identification of superior managers before their superiority shows. Past performance figures would appear to have a limited role in this process.

The first bit, 'Active and passive funds compared', stands to reason – it simply flows from what we've been saying about averages and charges. We think the really interesting bit is the 'Consistency of performance'. After all, if there was a way of picking the funds that would perform above average, then we'd be laughing. The WM Research shows that this can't be done. Think of the typical fund management company. It has, let's say, ten or fifteen funds in operation. At any one time, most will be underperforming. However, there's always one or two that will be doing OK, perhaps a bit more than OK. Which funds do you think they'll be concentrating their marketing effort on? You've guessed it. But there's no reason at all to think that the decent performance can be sustained. In fact, there's every reason to think that it can't be. To be fair, in the 2001 version of the WM Report it found that 'there was evidence of a shorter-term persistence with a defined top quartile of trusts in any one year continuing to out-perform as a group in the subsequent year *but this information cannot be used as the basis for a profitable trading strategy after costs'* (our italics). What this means is that there is some chance of picking a fund that will keep performing for one more year, but the costs of changing funds frequently to invest in these more than erodes any possible benefit.

Another myth often put about by fund mangers is that they can beat the market when the index is falling. The idea is that they can move some of their money into safer investments or cash, thereby avoiding the worst of the falls. It sounds logical but, when you look at it more closely, it doesn't stack up. The reason is that the stock market doesn't have a predictable direction (at least in the short-term). It is never *going* upwards and it is never *going* downwards. It has only ever *gone* somewhere. Imagine what would happen if all the fund managers in the City decided that we were about to move into a 'bear market' and that they should switch assets into cash. Bosh! We'd not so much have a bear market, as a full-on crash. What's more, it would be impossible for them all to reach the exit in time. Since it's their selling that actually causes the fall in prices, it must be the case that the *average* active fund manager (or, to be pedantic, their average pound invested) just follows the market downwards. In 2001, a very definite down year in stock market terms, only 36 per cent of the actively managed unit trusts in the UK All Companies sector managed to outperform the FTSE All Share Index. So much for beating the market when the index is falling.

All we have to do, then, is invest in the market average. Is that complicated? Nope. It's very simple.

Index-tracking unit trusts have as their sole aim the mimicking of the stock market index, the market average. The index in question may be the FTSE 100 or the FTSE All Share Index, but it doesn't make too much difference as they return similar rates over the longer term. In Appendix 2, in which we explain how they work in a bit more detail, we try to zap them up a bit, but it's an uphill struggle and it hasn't really worked, because index trackers are dull things. There is no flair to them. Their sole *raison d'être* is to be average, to be unremarkable. In fact, the more unremarkable they are, the better they are. You don't want an index tracker to post returns *greater* than the index, as this shows a high degree of error in following the average and implies they may be *under* in future. By the very fact of being unremarkable, index trackers shine as beacons to the investor who wants to outperform the professionals with the expenditure of precisely no cerebral calories and almost as little effort.

Average is best? Run-of-the-mill rules? Standing out from the crowd ain't chic? Yup, it's a topsy-turvy world.

Below, you'll see what the return of an index tracker looks like, as compared to the average return of the market, for which we've used the FTSE All Share Index, and the return of the average actively managed unit trust, for which we've used the average of the unit trusts in the UK All Companies sector. This is the sector that most closely reflects unit trusts investing in UK shares. It actually includes the index trackers, but there are only a few of them so it doesn't affect the results much. For the index tracker we've used the Gartmore UK index fund as an example. It was first started in February 1989 and it charges 0.5% per year.

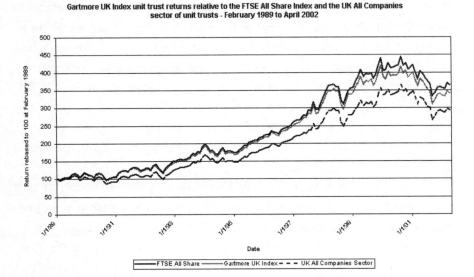

Gartmore UK Index unit trust returns relative to the FTSE All Share Index and the UK All Companies sector of unit trusts - February 1989 to April 2002

The first thing to notice is that all three lines look the same. This demonstrates the point that we were making earlier – that actively managed unit trusts, no matter what their managers will try to tell you, on average just reflect the overall market. In fact, they actually are, of course, the overall market. Rather than the UK All Companies sector following the FTSE All Share, it's the FTSE All Share that follows their average performance. Except that it does so without any of their costs, so it's that much higher up the page. The line representing our index tracker comes in between the other two, as you'd expect, because it's charges are in between.

To us, this graph is one of the most remarkable sets of statistics in modern investing. We have to keep pinching ourselves to make sure it's real. It is so hard to believe that all that fire and fury which goes into active fund management really counts for less than nothing. The Emperor's shivering in nothing but a pair of shoes here as we reflect that the average return of UK All Companies unit trusts over this period was 8.5 per cent. This was just more than 1 *per cent* behind the index tracker. How much more does the average unit trust charge than the Gartmore index tracker? Well, funnily enough, it's pretty close to 1 per cent. Think back now to the Second Foolish Law of Compounding: *Small differences in investment return matter. A lot.*

Let's have a look at how being average in performance (but lower than average in costs) works out in terms of real money. We'll look at the performance of the average fund in the UK All Companies sector, the Gartmore UK Index Tracker and the FTSE All Share. The figures show the effect of investing £1000 (with income reinvested in each case). Going backwards from December 2001 for five and ten years looks like this:

	Five-year performance		**Ten-year performance**	
	(Total of 204 funds)		**(Total of 152 funds)**	
	Value of £1,000 invested in Dec 1996	Annual growth rate	Value of £1,000 invested in Dec 1991	Annual growth rate
Average Fund	£1,348	6.15%	£2,655	10.26%
Gartmore UK Index Tracker	£1,388	6.78%	£2,799	10.84%
FTSE All Share	£1,441	7.58%	£2,909	11.27%

FIGURES FOR DECEMBER 2001

Notice that there are more funds that have been around for five years than there are that have been around for ten years (204 against 152). It's interesting to think about why this is. Naturally funds that are doing well tend to stay around. The ones that do badly tend not to. They tend to get closed down or absorbed into other funds. So to a large extent, these figures, especially the ones for ten years, exclude the performance of the very worst funds. That might explain why the annual growth rate for the average fund is only 1.0% behind the index over ten years, while it's 1.4% behind the index over five years.

Anyway, the Gartmore tracker is comfortably ahead of the average fund over both periods, while being a little behind the FTSE All Share (it has charges too, though they are of course less than for the average fund). Overall, this performance puts the tracker in 39th place out of 152 funds over ten years and in 63rd place out of 204 funds over five years.

Interestingly enough, in the second edition of this book, which looked at figures up to April 2000 (near the peak of the stock market), the equivalent figures were 34th out of 157 funds and 51st place out of 193 funds. That seems like remarkable consistency, but it's nothing more than we should expect. The tracker will come in a little below the market average due to its costs. The various funds that make up the market average will be spread around that, but with a bias to the downside because of their costs. The amount of that downside bias is dependent on the level of costs and that's not something that changes much in the investment industry, no matter how loudly we Fools shout about it. The Gartmore Index Tracker that we've been looking at charges 0.5 per cent per year and that looks like being enough to keep it ahead of about three quarters of actively-managed funds over five and ten year periods and you'd expect it to do relatively better as you look at longer periods. Remember also that there's no reliable way of picking, in advance, the few funds that actually manage to outperform. There can't be, else we'd all do it and the particular method would stop working.

These seem like amazing findings – probably sufficient in themselves to fill a whole investment book (we tried to pull that one on our publishers, but they insisted we pad it out a bit, hence the other three hundred-odd pages). Yet, if you think about it a bit, it's not at all surprising and the fact is that the Wise fund managers don't like it when we think about it a bit. They'd be much happier if we continued to pay for their lavish lifestyles without batting an eyelid. Well, sorry, guys and gals, but we have batted an eyelid and we're not too happy with what we see. All the effort and money that goes into running your underperforming unit trusts is totally wasted. You could have done a better job by not having tried to beat the market at all and merely put your efforts into mimicking it. All your snazzy offices, with their complimentary coffee and tea dispensers, hordes of staff and latest computer systems, expensive research materials and daily meetings – it's all a complete waste of money.

No, we had better correct ourselves here. The money is not totally wasted, it is only wasted from the point of view of the hapless investor who is paying through the nose for a service which he or she could get better and more cheaply elsewhere. You see, it doesn't really matter to the unit trusts how well they perform as long as the money keeps rolling in. Of course, they all want to do well, because that's a draw to new investors, but as long as people can be bedazzled by glittering prospectuses and cleverly reported statistics, then just how well isn't crucially important. It is a fact that few unit trusts report their results as compared to the performance of the market average. You don't have to be a rocket scientist to realize that it sounds much more impressive to say '74 per cent growth over five years' than to say '74 per cent growth over five years, versus market average growth of 125 per cent over the same period'.

So, the Foolish lesson to draw from all this is that the only way that you can give yourself an edge in performance terms is to keep your charges low. On the whole, the cheapest, and therefore the best, funds are index trackers. Index trackers also give you a benefit in terms of risk since their returns necessarily track the growth in the stock market. Remember that the UK stock market has returned, on average, 9.5 per cent per year since 1869. Since 1918 it's been 11.8 per cent, since 1945 it's been 12.8 per cent and over the last ten years its been 11.3 per cent. If we're looking for a nice round number, it wouldn't seem unreasonable to look for around 10 per cent growth in future years, even allowing for half a per cent of tracker charges. Casting your mind back to Chapter 2, you'll remember that this was enough to get Freda's £100 per month up to £560,000 over 40 years and her £50,000 inheritance up to £2.3 million.

Can it really be so simple that all you have to do is to make regular contributions into an index tracker, keep breathing for thirty or forty years and you'll come out at the end with a bulging pile of cash, for which you have paid very little? Yes, indubitably it can be.

It will come as no surprise to learn that others have seen the potential of this kind of investment before you. Richard Branson, the bewhiskered, balloon-piloting, retiring self-publicist of Virgin fame is one. It was he who brought index trackers to the forefront of the public imagination with the launch of his Virgin UK index-tracking unit trust in 1995, although the idea is not new at all. Gartmore have been running their's since 1989 and the Vanguard 500 fund in the US has been in existence since the early 1970s.

To reiterate: there is no catch to this. We're not suggesting you send us five pounds and then write letters on to twenty of your friends telling them you've got a great new money-making scheme and why don't they do the same? (Although, if you do have a spare fiver, you can always send it our way.) No, this is kosher, bona fide, straight up. Anyone can do it. If you stop at this point in the book and read no further, you have set yourself up with the only investment information you will ever need (besides having been pointed in the direction of a lucrative and fulfilling new hobby).

Fear Not a Falling Market

And as if that wasn't enough, there's even more to this amateur exercise. Perhaps you have followed the steps to be outlined in the final section to this chapter and have gone out and started investing in an index tracker. Perhaps you're feeling pretty good about yourself and are even starting to be a bit of a loudmouth at parties: 'Oh yah, I'm in trackers, actually.'

Well, hang on, you don't even know just how clever you are. Take a look at this:

You contribute £100 per month into an index tracker. At the time you start, each unit of the index tracker costs £1, buying you 100 units a month. Then the market falls after six months to half its value, cutting the cost of the units in half to 50p. After twelve months – six with units costing £1 and six with units costing 50p – what is the average price of the units you have bought? Common sense would tell you that half the time you bought the units at £1 and half the time at 50p, so the answer is 75p. Common sense – and why did you know we were going to say this – is leading you up the garden path. The real answer is $66\frac{2}{3}$ p. How?

> For 6 months at £1, £100 will buy 600 units. Total cost £600.
> For 6 months at £0.5, £100 will buy 1200 units. Total cost £600.
> Over 12 months, therefore, 1800 units have been bought at a total cost of £1200.
> Cost per unit = £1200 ÷ 1800 = £0.666666 = $66\frac{2}{3}$ p

By putting a regular pound amount into the index tracker, you have bought into the index over twelve months for an average price of 66$\frac{2}{3}$ p, when the *actual* average price of the units was 75p (half the time at 100p, half at 50p, giving an average of (100 + 50) ÷2 = 75p). Magic? Yes, in a way, and it's called *pound-cost averaging*.

In this example, we assumed that the index dropped in value by half from one six months to the next, but it would have worked just as well if the index had instead been highly *volatile*. If the units of the index tracker had instead fluctuated from £1 to 50p on alternate months, the effect would have been just the same – six months buying at £1 and six months buying at 50p. Pound-cost averaging isn't just relevant in a market that is turning down, but also in a market that is simply volatile. Look back at the first graph of the Gartmore UK Index Tracker against the index to see what we mean. It's volatility – the fluctuations in share price from day to day and thus in the value of the index – which often scares people out of the market. They can't bear the thought of their holdings darting up and down in value from week to week, but as long as they're net purchasers of shares – and most of us are, since we don't yet need to live off our holdings – pound-cost averaging means that they need have no fear of a stock market that either looks like it is falling or which is highly volatile. Radical, very radical.

In fact, all this talk of pound-cost averaging is making us a bit peckish, putting us in mind of hamburgers. How so? Warren Buffett, ace long-term investor, wrote the following on hamburgers in the 1997 Letter to Share-holders of his Berkshire Hathaway investment company in a section entitled 'How We Think About Market Fluctuations':

A short quiz: If you plan to eat hamburgers throughout your life and are not a cattle producer, should you wish for higher or lower prices for beef? Likewise, if you are going to buy a car from time to time but are not an auto manufacturer, should you prefer higher or lower car prices? These questions, of course, answer themselves.

But now for the final exam: if you expect to be a net saver during the next five years, should you hope for a higher or lower stock market during that period? Many investors get this one wrong. Even though they are going to be net buyers of stocks for many years to come, they are elated when stock prices rise and depressed when they fall. In effect, they rejoice because prices have risen for the 'hamburgers' they will soon be buying. This reaction makes no sense. Only those who will be sellers of equities in the near future should be happy at seeing stocks rise. Prospective purchasers should much prefer sinking prices.

It's a funny old world.

Getting Started

But how do you actually go about buying an index tracker? How do you physically do it? Where do you start?

Relax, we're nice guys, we've made it easy for you.

If you're connected to the Internet, then probably the easiest thing to do is pop along to the Trustnet Web site. The address is www.trustnet.com. There you can search a huge range of UK and overseas unit and investment trusts. Go into the unit trusts area and narrow down the field of the search to 'indexed funds', click 'select' and, Bob's your uncle, around fifty UK index trackers pop up from nowhere. It gets better than this, though, since you can get details (including charges) for most of the funds (the bigger ones anyway) just by clicking on their name in the list. If you're not connected to the Internet, then we've included a selection of index trackers in Appendix 3, together with their contact details.

With this in hand, or with your own selection from the Trustnet Web site, sit down in your most comfy chair with a cup of tea, the telephone and a stout heart. Start at the top of the list and dial the number of Company A. The exchange will probably go something like this:

VULTURE FUND MANAGEMENT. Hello, Vulture Fund Management, 'Carrion is our game', how can I help?

YOU. Umm, hello. Can you tell me about your index tracker, please?

VULTURE FUND MANAGEMENT. Ah, you mean our Vulture Index Fund? *(They often have a fancy name for it and you may have to ask a couple of questions to make sure it really is their index tracker you're both talking about.)*

YOU. How long has the 'Vulture Index Fund' been in existence?

(If they give a time less than three years, say 'thank you very much' and hang up. You can't really assess the accuracy with which an index tracker follows the market over such a short period.)

THEY. Five years.

(Excellent.)

YOU. Right, and how much are the annual charges?

(If they're much more than 0.5 per cent and certainly if they're more than 0.75 per cent, think carefully.)

THEY. 0.5 per cent, with no initial charge.

(Fine.)

YOU. Uh-huh. And what about an exit charge?

THEY. No exit charge.

(That's good, because some companies have a sliding scale of exit charges if you withdraw your money in the first five years. We are long-term investors, yes, but we don't tie our hands unnecessarily.)

YOU. Can you give me the annualized total return on an offer to bid basis since it started?

(Hey, impressive, Fool.)

THEY. Certainly. It has returned an average of 9.7 per cent per year.

(Reasonable enough.)

YOU. And can you tell me the annualized total return on the FTSE All Share index, with dividends re-invested, over the same period?

(Now you've got them just where you want them. You need to specify that the FTSE All Share has its dividends re-invested, because it's normally quoted without them. The return on the tracker, however, will normally be given including them. You need to compare apples with apples.)

THEY. Just one moment…Yes, the FTSE All Share has returned, with dividends re-invested, an average of 10.3 per cent per year over the same period.

(Right, now it's time for a quick spot of arithmetic. You need to check that the tracker is lagging the index by about the same amount as its charges. So…10.3 minus 9.7 equals 0.6, which is close enough to the 0.5 per cent charges.)

YOU. That's great. And is it possible to hold this investment within an ISA? If so, how much will it cost me?

(To tell you the truth, they will probably have mentioned this by now but, if they haven't, then now's your moment.)

THEY. Of course and it costs no extra.

(It shouldn't cost extra.)

YOU. Is it possible to make regular monthly savings into it and what is the minimum amount?

THEY. Certainly, you can save upwards of £50 per month.

(Obviously the minimum needs to be below the amount that you're planning to save.)

YOU. Well, that sounds very interesting. I wonder if you'd send me all your bumf?

THEY. Of course, what's your address?

(Etc. etc.)

By the time you've been through the list, you'll have eliminated a goodly proportion of the candidates. Now, sit back and wait for the A4 envelopes to start clogging up your letterbox. (Strike from your candidate list any companies that take more than five days to send you a brochure: if they're not prompt and efficient at responding to potential customers, do they have the acumen to manage your money over the next half-lifetime or so?)

Once you've got all the prospectuses in front of you, draw up a table covering all the points we have talked about and make your selection. If you really have a stomach for detail, there's more on how to pick them in Appendix 2, but we've probably gone a bit over the top (we do like trackers a lot, after all). Also, you could visit our Web site and see the thoughts and selections of other Fools, with their reasoning, on our index trackers discussion board. Once you've made up your mind, it is simply a matter of filling in the form and sending off a cheque (or signing the standing order from your bank) to get the ball rolling.

At this point, you can sit back and breathe a sigh of relief as the nagging guilt that has plagued you – for oh so long! – with the knowledge that you really ought to tidy up your financial affairs and learn something about this whole bally business starts to lift. It is a blissful feeling and one to be savoured.

As you sit and bask in this warm glow of a job well done and an onerous task completed, perhaps you'd also like to give a thought to other Fools around the country. If you'll permit us another plug, why not come along to our Web site and post the information you have gleaned about the various index trackers on our discussion board? That way, others can take advantage of your endeavours and the net sum of Foolishness and co-operation in the world can be increased. A noble aim, we think, and hope you do too.

Finally, you will have noticed that the book does not end here. Far from it. There is still a good half inch to go. What will we be talking about from now on? A hint: we think index trackers are an excellent first step on the path to Foolishness, but Foolish investors with an interest in the subject often want to try to do better than the mere average, impressive though that average may be. Most of the Foolish activity you'll find online revolves around this aspiration, so read on for a diverting interlude and then an introduction to the exciting and Foolish world of single company investing.

Interlude
(Two, Actually)

8

A Foray into Some Very foolish Futures

Fortune's a right whore: If she give aught she deals it in small parcels, That she may take away all at one swoop.

John Webster, *The White Devil*

You may be thinking that our copy-editor has slipped up and failed to capitalize the 'f' on 'foolish' in the title to our interlude. You know by now what a wealth of difference there is between 'foolishness' and 'Foolishness' and you're thinking we should sack our publishers for doing a sloppy job.

You're wrong, though. This is most definitely a 'foolish Futures Foray' rather than a 'Foolish Futures Foray'. Mark Kelly wrote to us in the early days of the Fool UK with a story which he has courageously offered to the world. We think it shows very eloquently why a Fool turns his back on any sort of trading that involves forecasting of short-term market trends. In this case it was index derivatives that turned Mark's world upside down for a short period, but it could just as easily have been share options or simply day trading in shares – buying and selling on the basis of what you think the share price will do that day, or afternoon, or minute.

Before we let Mark tell his story and once more praise his courage and candour for doing so, we must issue a health warning. This is not for the faint-hearted, those recovering from major operations or psychiatric breakdowns. Have a box of tissues handy and if these do not prove sufficient, trained operatives are on hand twenty-four hours a day at our Web site to provide counselling and trauma support.

Mark, the floor is yours:

The news from the front line of idiocy is that a fool and his money continue to enjoy a short acquaintance. Only a few months ago I was reading a Sunday Times article about spread betting on sports events. A throwaway line there suggested that spread betting on the financial markets was best left to the experts. I recall feeling certain that I knew better. I had, after all, been paper trading the FTSE 100 Index for all of a month, using as my guide the live prices published on the City Index Web site. Out of twenty-five trading days I had shown a profit on all but two. Betting £10 a point, I was already £10,000 ahead. On paper, that is.

I don't know what rush of blood to the head or hormonal imbalance led me to believe that I could turn that notional paper money into the folding, bankable variety. The impulse was strong enough, however, for me to resign a well-paid, if boring, career to risk my Christmas bonus on the pursuit of serious riches.

Equipped with a futures pager and a mobile phone, and with accounts opened with two financial spread betting companies, I was ready to start throwing my money at the market. I had no clear strategy – merely an unshakeable belief that I could spot the trends at an early stage, jump on to their coat tails and ride them to a quick profit. I laughed at the very idea of using the limited risk products offered by both companies, namely traded options and limited risk futures. The cost of the option premiums or additional futures spread looked like so much wasted money.

The outcome was sadly predictable. I could have foreseen it myself had it been anyone else who was approaching the business this way. On Day 1, I was late into the market on the morning of a huge rise in the FTSE 100. I bought near the top, over-committed by betting £20 a point and spent all day sweating it out to come out only £80 in front. A late surge by Wall Street saved my bacon. Even at this stage the numbers were frightening. Around £500 down in the UK market and £580 up in the US. A lot of money had been at risk for the eventual paltry reward.

Day 2 was somewhat better, with another strong finish by Wall Street leaving me up by around £350. Again I had taken a pounding in the FTSE contract and was beginning to doubt my innate ability to read market directions. I was also beginning to see how misleading paper trading could be. Both of the financial spread betting companies set their quotes not at the current level of the index, but rather at where they think the index is heading. The result was that by the time I thought I had spotted a trend, they were ahead of me by 10 or 20 points. Adding that to the normal spread between buying and selling prices of between 6 and 8 points meant that there had to be a substantial market movement just for me to break even.

On Day 3 it all began to come apart, with me giving up almost all of the previous day's gains. Again I was pacing the floor until the close of the US markets at around 9pm. This time Wall Street didn't come to the rescue. Even at this stage it didn't occur to me that maybe I wasn't cut out for the life of a trader, this knife-edge balance between elation and despair. Nor did I think of starting to use limited risk products. Instead I simply thought that tomorrow would be the crunch day and I would have to make up for my dismal performance to date.

I was right that the crunch would come on Day 4. The market was waiting for the latest interest rate pronouncement from the Bank of England and I correctly guessed that it would stay unchanged. As a result, by ten o'clock in the morning I was showing a profit of £580. At this stage I should have gone back to bed. Instead a greedy notion came over me that the London market might be given an extra boost by any early gains in Wall Street, which were indicated by the direction of the futures markets. I hadn't exactly played a cautious game up until this point, but now I really lost the plot. By using up my credit limits with both companies I was able to place a total of £40 a point on both the FTSE 100 and the Wall Street Dow-Jones index. Within minutes of opening, Wall Street had indeed soared to new heights. However, perversely, the London market seemed to be slipping. Unknown to me, Merrill Lynch was taking advantage of the market conditions to offload a large number of March FTSE futures. As the effect of this selloff took hold, first the FTSE, then the Dow began to slide down, with me on the wrong side of the market. At this stage I should have panicked and sold, taking the loss on the chin. Instead I calmed myself down, reassured myself that the market would turn around and watched it plummet for the next five hours. A kind of fear-induced paralysis came over me. I was terrified to close my positions, because it would mean taking the losses. At the same time a residual optimism was telling me that the markets must surely turn around again and that I could still end up with a handsome profit on the day.

Head in hands, I bowed to the inevitable at around 8pm, with just an hour left of trading in the USA. I started ringing around, closing positions and counting the cost. Which was huge. To close out all of my positions left me with a net loss of just over £8000, wiping out a large portion of my bonus and completely annihilating any illusions of my possessing the ability to trade in the futures markets.

Bizarrely, one of the people whom I instructed to close my account, who had just told me that I owed his company £6000, asked me whether there was any particular reason why I was closing the account. I guess they must have people throwing money at them like this on a regular basis. And coming back for more. I told him that I had passed my personal pain threshold by a sizeable margin and didn't want to have the mechanism open for me to repeat the experience.

So four days into my career as a financial speculator, I resigned. I wouldn't say that it's impossible to make money in that way. What it does take is a certain discipline to know when to let your profits ride and when to cut them, when to take an early loss to avoid a later larger loss. A sensible approach to the management of risk, including the use of the range of limited risk products available. And a lack of naïve optimism.

Ah well, back to the grind. Anyone know of any vacancies for an unexpectedly available senior audit manager, with extensive experience in derivatives risk management?

9

This Online World

How much a dunce that has been sent to roam. Excels a dunce that has been kept at home.

William Cowper, *The Progress of Error*

c. 55,000 years ago, Tunbridge Wells, Kent

Hew and his brother, Blok, are out hunting deer in the forest. The forest covers almost the whole of that part of the peninsula that will one day be called 'Angle-land', for no better reason than that 53,000 years later a people from Germany called the Angles would sail up, show themselves to be the most frightful boors and thenceforth behave as if they owned the place. What Hew and Blok called it, history does not record.

Ignorant of the momentous events to come, Hew and Blok were concerned only with catching a deer, but were not having much success. Every time they came close, Blok would sneeze, or stumble, or snap a twig and off the deer would go, tails bobbing through the undergrowth. Hew became increasingly exasperated and Blok, sensing this, grunted and whined in apology, for Hew and Blok did not have the gift of language.

By the third time this had happened, it was starting to get dark and Hew knew if they did not return with meat by nightfall there would be trouble at home. He became more and more angry and frustrated until, instead of the enraged grunt and blow on the back of the head that he had intended to deliver to Blok, he came out with this: 'Look, dunderhead! If you can't keep quiet, then at least go up to the head of the river, make a noise and drive the deer down towards me. I'll hide behind this tree and spear one as they go past. Now, move!'

Well, Hew was as surprised as Blok and clasped his hand to his still open mouth in horror at what had come out. Blok, by now picking up the general drift of what was required and having been thinking along the same lines himself, decided it might be wiser to absent himself up to the head of the watercourse. In a short time, down came the deer, followed by Blok. Hew took aim at a plump doe and the rest, as they say, is history.

Hew and Blok returned to camp, where they deposited not only a month's worth of deer meat, but also the gift of language. Before long, they had set themselves up as itinerant language teachers, giving lessons in basic and advanced Cro-Magnon and Neanderthal for the price of a week's board and lodging. Their invention was taken up across the whole of Europe and soon people were discussing everything from the state of the market in wild boar futures to the latest fashions in sabre tooth tiger jewellery.

c. 5500 years ago, 42a Hanging Gardens Terrace, Babylon, Mesopotamia

Tetiphet is one of the entrepreneurs of his age. It was he who supplied the pot plants for the Hanging Gardens and he holds the state-wide monopoly on amphora production. Recently, he has started a bread delivery service, running twenty-four hours a day and delivering slabs of unleavened bread, topped with optional olives, tomatoes or curd cheese. An idea that was over 5000 years ahead of its time, it has taken off in a big way among the elite of ancient Babylon. Tetiphet is thinking not only of a new chariot and team for his wife, but perhaps an executive reed boat which he plans to moor on the Euphrates and with which he'll take his more important business clients on cruises.

Things are generally going well, but there is a fly in the ointment. Shrewd businessman that he is, Tetiphet is worried by all the unpaid bills that he fears are eating into his profit margins. Every time he says to one of his more troublesome customers, 'You haven't paid,' they say, 'Yes, I have,' and he has no means of proving it one way or the other.

He goes home and thinks. And thinks and thinks. Finally, he has it. The clay he uses in his factory to make amphoras – when it's wet you can scratch the surface. He will scratch marks in wet clay to show who has paid and who hasn't. Then there'll be no argument.

Tetiphet's scheme is a roaring success and soon all the businesses in Babylon are using a similar system. From there, the news spreads around the known world and it's not long before even the bards and storytellers are writing their stories down so they don't forget them.

c. 500 years ago, Germany

Johannes Gutenberg, a metalworker, has diversified into the Bible-copying business. The hunger for Bibles in Christendom is insatiable and Johannes has twenty-five scribes copying away in his scriptorium, night and day. Yes, Johannes makes reasonable money, but the rate of production is so painfully slow, the scribes have such large, expensive appetites and they make so many mistakes. He tries to hurry them up by increasing the speed at which the head scribe dictates to the rest, but it backfires and first one, then another, and another, leaves. Before long they're all gone, leaving their manuscripts torn into shreds on the desks of the scriptorium. Johannes wanders through the now silent room and, sighing, is about to start scooping them into the bin, when he notices that this is no random pattern. His departing employees have torn the pages up letter by letter and rearranged them into rude messages directed at him and his mother and … what's that … his donkey? (The exact content need worry us no further here; suffice to say that Middle German of that period was rife with choice expletives and insults.)

Hang on, thought Johannes, I'm on to something here. Suppose that instead of wood block printing, which is a time-consuming, irritating business, I was to make letters out of metal and then move them about to make the words I wanted? Just like this shower of no-goodniks has done. Hmm, it could just work …

Soon, Johannes was devoting the entire output of his metalwork shop to moveable type and printing presses and before the decade was out, a Bible wasn't a Bible if it wasn't a printed, *Gutenberg* Bible.

And what of the dissident scribes, without whom the printed word may have been delayed by another hundred years or more? Certainly Johannes never mentions them again.

c. 77 years ago, Edinburgh, Scotland

John Logie Baird has had enough of sitting in the 'three and nines' to watch the British Pathé News every day. It would be all right if the children who were waiting for the main feature would just sit down and be quiet while the adults catch up on what's happening in the world. No discipline these days, that's the problem. In fact, wouldn't it be splendid if you could watch the news in your own home, just as you listen to the wireless? muses Mr. Baird.

Shock! Another aniseed ball thrown by MacDonald minor, the notorious delinquent from 24 Stirling Street, bounces off his balding pate. 'Right, that's enough! I'm going home to sort this out once and for all!'

For weeks he doesn't come in for meals, sometimes working continuously for twenty-four hours at a time. Mrs Baird peeks anxiously through the net curtains. From the garage comes the sound of banging, crashing and curses. Occasionally, the door flies open and aerials, valves, cathodes, rays, tubes are ejected, before it closes again and the ferment continues.

Finally, a dishevelled Baird, red hair in wild disarray, the fire still in his eyes, storms back into the kitchen, sweeps his wife's embroidery to the floor and plonks down in its place a wooden box, with a dirty window at the front and an aerial on top. 'Aye, Morag, this is the answer to those pesky brats!'

And we've been watching the news at home ever since.

1996, Bill Clinton's acceptance speech following re-election to the White House, Washington D.C., US

'When I entered office in 1992, only nuclear physicists were surfing the World Wide Web. Now, my cat Socks has its own Web page.'

The Internet is about Communication

Five pivotal shifts in the way human beings communicate. Five turning points in history, and the last of these we are living through right now. As products of the Internet age ourselves, perhaps you'll forgive us our embarrassing enthusiasm for a few moments and let us show you what we think this astonishing new medium has to offer. (If you're already an Internet enthusiast, whether you're using it for the odd bit of serious research or are spending the wee small hours with your face basking in the blue reflected glow of your computer screen, then please bear with us. By all means, read on for a spirited and light-hearted account of what you already know, or else skip to the next chapter.)

As with many things, Internet usage in the United States has taken off far more rapidly than in the UK, but we are fast catching up. Most people have some idea of what the Internet is in physical terms – a network of computers around the world linked up through the phone lines – but don't necessarily know what it has to offer them personally. Obviously, the best way to find out what it is all about is to go and have a look yourself and if you have a friend or relative who is online, then ask them to budge up and let you have a gander. (One Foolish bit of advice: ask them to let you wield the mouse. Otherwise, they'll zap around all over the place and, apart from feeling a bit sick, you won't quite know what's going on.) We hope that by the time you've finished this book you'll have decided that one place you *must* be is online.

When you hear people talking about the Internet, you often hear them talking about 'information' and the 'Information Superhighway'. You would have thought 'information' was the last thing we would have needed more of in our lives. It sounds so unattractive, doesn't it? What are you going to do with this 'information' you've just received, anyway? File it away in the recycling pile with all the other 'information' that comes through the door? Add it to all the other 'information' that is beamed at you night and day through the television and radio? Perhaps this is the image you have of the Internet: 'Oh, bother! Looks like we're running low on information again, darling. It really is the most terrible nuisance. Hey ho, off to the computer to stock up.'

Banish these thoughts from your mind. The Internet is not just a hypersonic *Encyclopaedia Britannica*, set to come flooding out of your computer screen at the touch of a button. It is first and foremost a means of communicating and is a natural successor to the endeavours of Hew and Blok, Tetiphet, Johannes Gutenberg and John Logie Baird that have so shaped human history.

Words, words, words. What are we actually talking about? Let's have an example, one totally unrelated to investing. (Come to think of it, we're already 1500 words into this chapter and not a word on investing yet. Yikes!)

One of us (D.B.) is an enthusiastic Telemark skier. 'A what?' Indeed. A Telemark skier. Unless you are yourself a Telemark skier, a disciple of the arcane art of skiing in the style of the original skiers from Telemark in Norway, you are unlikely to know much about it and there aren't all that many of them around. Not in North Devon, anyway. But you can find them on the Net and they are talking. Phew, are they talking! It was November

1997 and D.B. had £500 burning a hole in his pocket, one hundred crisp fivers that he was going to spend on a new pair of Telemark skis and bindings. So far, so good, but how on Earth to decide just what equipment to buy?

Bring on – you've guessed it – the Internet. A quick search on the Internet revealed a Web site devoted entirely to Telemark skiing, called Telemarque. com* and describing itself as a 'Resource for the Telemark skier'. Besides articles, listings of Telemark events across the world, listings of suppliers of Telemark equipment and information (Ugh! that word again) about Telemark races, there was a large section devoted to 'Discussion'. This section contained areas where, among other things, people were swapping hints of good places to ski, hair-raising stories of Telemark derring-do and the ins and outs of Telemark gear.

Getting warmer. A click on the Telemark gear discussion folder and D.B. was soon immersed in a world where people were buying, using, testing and manufacturing the very equipment he was thinking of buying. In response to a few initial questions left at the discussion board, replies were received from people who had bought the skis and bindings that D.B. was interested in and were skiing on them every day. Their advice – not always agreeing – was noted, as were the thoughts of people using different equipment, but who felt they had better ideas about what might suit this lonely British Telemarker. Finally, a tentative decision was made to purchase a particular ski and binding combination. Then, in reply to a question about suitable ski length, the very person who had designed the skis replied with what he felt was appropriate and in reply to a technical question about mounting the bindings, the very person who had designed the bindings came up and offered his advice. Finally, another British Telemarker passing by the site dropped off the link to the Web site of the only shop in the UK selling these particular brands of equipment.

Now, that's information!

But that's not all. Over the next few days, D.B. was able to offer advice to

---

* Unfortunately, since the first edition of this book Telemarque.com has mysteriously slunk back into the Internet ether whence it came. However, in the unlikely event you still want to find a Web site on Telemarking with a thriving discussion forum you could try www.telemarktips.com or even www.tele-skiers.co.uk , a UK-based site. RIP, Telemarque.com!

another person on a particular ski boot/binding combination he had experience of, and joined in a useful debate on the prevention of injury among Telemark skiers, directing other respondents to a Web site run by a physician with a special interest in the subject and who was conducting an online survey of Telemark injuries. He also gave advice from his own experience to people coming to the Alps to ski and advanced some rather forceful opinions on the advisability of using safety bindings when Telemarking. There then followed an interesting discussion with a skier in Alaska on Telemark skiing in America's last frontier, which eventually turned into a more private exchange of e-mails and heralded the birth of a friendship.

So, it's not just information we are talking about here: this is interacting and engaging with your fellow human beings for mutual benefit. The group of people congregating at Telemarque.com was a community of people united by a single, great enthusiasm – for Telemark skiing. Only, this wasn't a community that could exist in any other sphere beyond the virtual one. Even if you could have gathered together, say, half-a-dozen people in the whole of Devon who were interested in Telemark skiing, you'd still have been reduced to meeting on the third Thursday of each month at 7.30pm under a single 60-watt light bulb and a leaky roof in the 14th Sea Scouts Meeting Hall in Exeter. Telemarque.com had over *10,000* visitors every day. You were able to join in the comings and goings of the community as and when you wanted and – if you had a laptop computer – from wherever you wanted.

Now are you starting to see where we're heading? Contrary to how it may seem, you have not stumbled on a 'How to' manual for Telemark skiing, cunningly disguised as an investment guide. There is rhyme and reason and rhythm to our musings, for while there may not be many Telemark skiers in the green fields of Devon, there aren't many investors either. Let's put it another way. There are a great number of investors – all those with personal pensions, ISAs, endowments and what-have-you – but relatively few who are actively investing in shares on their own behalf. If you wanted to stage a get-together of these active investors, you'd be looking at a relatively small club which would meet, perhaps on a regular basis, to talk things over. In fact, we favour these sorts of gatherings, whether they are informal dining clubs or actual investment clubs, where the members pool a sum of money and invest it in shares they have researched. However, they still involve relatively small numbers of people – ten or twenty at the most – and can hardly be termed a community.

Enter the Fool!

Ever since its inception in 1994 in the United States, the Motley Fool has been bringing investors together and forging its own, unique online community. Its offshoot, the Motley Fool UK, has been bringing the same spirit of Foolishness to Britain since 1997. If you come and visit the Motley Fool UK, as we hope you will, you will find not only interesting articles, ideas and musings on Foolish investing, but useful reference material and one of the most enjoyable parts of the site – the discussion boards. In the same way as Telemark nuts at sites like Telemarque.com swapped advice and information and knowledge about Telemark skiing, so the Fool UK discussion boards are teeming with Fools jawing about investing.

They're not talking about skis and bindings, but companies, managing directors, whether Laura Ashley has a future or is nothing more than a brand name, the ins and outs of endowments and ISAs, investment strategies, painful (and wonderful) investing experiences they have had, whether Pizza Express's pizzas are really good enough to justify such a phenomenal expansion … the list goes on. Instead of the people who designed the skis and bindings responding to others' queries, it's the people who work in the different industry sectors who are coming on to give the world (or at least Fooldom) the benefit of their unique experience. Instead of ski owners coming on to tell you how they give a 'great ride in the powder, man', you have purchasers and users of companies' services coming online to tell you where they shine and where they need to pull their socks up. You have professional share analysts from the City giving their opinion on a potential investment and steel importers, doctors, accountants, teachers all giving their unique points of view. Independent financial advisers (salespeople) – yes, they grit their teeth and stop by too – will provide useful perspectives on endowments, Personal Pension Plans and tax, among other things. Others will interject pithy comments and witticisms into ongoing discussions and the feel is one of a hurly-burly of ideas and opinions and advice erupting around you. Every level of investing skill and experience is represented, from the total novice asking what 'ISA' stands for, to seasoned investors of many years' standing discussing the sustainability of a company's business model.

Whatever level of investing experience people have, we hope they will feel free to ask or comment on anything they like, or, if they're feeling shy, to lurk awhile, not saying anything and simply lapping up the atmosphere and Foolish good sense.

So, the Internet brings together communities of like-minded people, but is that all? No, not on your nelly. It is the most responsive of all media to individuals' ideas and beliefs. Remember all those science fiction stories from the 1950s and 60s? Some of them were pretty strange, but in any collection of short stories you'd always be able to find one in which there was not only personal transport by aerocar or gyrocopter, but democracy via the television: they were voting every five minutes from their living rooms for something or other. (You don't remember? Believe us – there were loads of these stories.)

Well, it's here. It's the Internet. We've tried it. We've tried putting up articles on our site that weren't entirely correct (for that, read: 'contained stupid errors') and it wasn't a pretty experience. Within minutes the e-mails and discussion board posts started flooding in to tell us just where we'd gone wrong. While this may be momentarily uncomfortable for us at times, we actually welcome it. There is no other sphere in which the relationship between the people doing the writing and the people doing the reading is so equal or so fluid. It's not like a newspaper where there are journalists and readers and the two seem separated by a barrier as impenetrable as the Berlin Wall – before it came down. At our site (ours is by no means unique in this), the readers are writing – on the discussion boards and often formidably well – and the writers are reading what the readers have to say. Confused? You soon will be.

Most of our writers here at the Fool were actually recruited from among active participants on the discussion boards. We are always talent-spotting, because we understand that no one understands this new means of communicating as well as the people who are using it all the time and who are enthusiasts for it. That doesn't mean professionals or journalists, but you, sitting in your bedroom in Accrington Stanley and tapping away on your computer keyboard. The Motley Fool UK itself came into being as the result of an e-mail one wet April afternoon from David B. to David and Tom Gardner, co-founders of the Motley Fool in the United States.

Being connected to the World Wide Web (the part of the Internet most of us use most of the time) brings us all together and puts us all on the same footing. Reading a posting from someone, you cannot tell what they look like, what sort of house they live in, what accent they speak with and often even what part of the world they're in. It's a great leveller, giving everyone the same opportunities to advance themselves on their merits.

Another example of Internet democracy. In the United States, large companies have what they call 'conference calls'. In these calls, companies give briefings to the analysts who monitor them on their current perform-ance and expectations. Mostly, these companies will now allow members of the general public to participate. After all, if the professionals can have a slice of this information, why shouldn't we? The stocks we hold are just as valid as the stocks they hold.

OK, OK, here endeth the lesson on the Internet meritocracy. We'll stop harping on about it lest you think we're a couple of dangerous zealots.

Anyway, having talked about how the Internet isn't about information, it's about communication, we reckon you're now sufficiently indoctrinated to be able to cope with what comes next.

The Internet *Is* about Information

We admit it: it is about information as well. There is loads of it, unimaginable expanses of the stuff, everywhere you look and on every subject you can ever think of. Everything those scaremongers have told you is true: you can over-load yourself with information via the Internet, but equally there are resources available out there that will make you gasp in wonderment.

As an investor connected to the Internet, you'll be able to access company news as it breaks, read company reports, obtain share quotes, buy and sell shares, consult the financial press, set up a portfolio of shares, with their prices updating automatically so that you can keep track of your investments and, of course, have the resources of the Motley Fool at your disposal.

All this information is there on your desktop immediately. There's no penning of letters – 'Dear Sir/Madam, I would be very grateful if you could send me your latest ...' – and no licking of stamps. There's just raw, useful data – as much or as little of it as you like.

Information is often wielded in surprising ways on the Web. Take Amazon.com, for instance. This American company began life as as 'The World's Biggest Bookstore', with literally millions of titles available to order. These days, you can buy anything from cordless drills to porcelain on their Web site. Go and visit them when you get online (the Web addresses of the US and UK sites are in Appendix 5) – it is an extraordinary experience. Not only will you find summaries of the books sold on the site, but readers are encouraged to write reviews of books they have read and to e-mail them in. It works like this. You read *Shares for Dogs: a simple guide to equity investing for the genus Canis*, and you like it, so you write in 'An excellent starter book, although goes into a little too much detail on financial analysis at times. Enjoyed the section on "Buy What Everyone Knows: buy dog food companies". Arf! Arf! John D. Pinscher, Barking, Essex'. This review then appears below the book on the Web site, along with other readers' reviews, which may strike a chord with you or not. Finally, when you decide to buy the book, you are presented with a list of books bought by those other dogs who bought this book: *Rubber balls 1945–95, The History of the Dog Collar, Sniffs and Smells of an Alsatian's Life: a career with the Metropolitan Police,* and so on. Neat marketing trick this may be, but it is also very useful and is another way of narrowing down the amount of information you have to sift through to find something relevant. If you like this book and so do they and they also liked the other books in the list, then there's a good chance you may do so too.

Some people are worried by what they might find out on the Web and it is true there are weirdos out there, but if you don't bother them, they won't generally come and bother you. A few Web sites are pretty nasty, but to be honest the really nasty ones aren't easy to find. If you reckon that 99 per cent of the stuff on the Web is harmless and you have to go out and actively search for the other 1 per cent, you won't be far wrong.

More on Information

Remember the Wright brothers, the two bicycle mechanics who flew the world's first controllable aircraft? Of course you do. Some of you will even remember the name of their aircraft – the Wright Flyer. But do you know the name of their next aircraft, or their next? Chances are you don't.

The Wright brothers first flew in December 1903 and then retreated from the public eye for the next two years. Partly, this was to perfect their invention, but partly it was because they were afraid of others stealing their ideas before they had them adequately patented. The only place they would allow coverage of their machine was in a not surprisingly little-read journal run by a friend of theirs entitled *Gleanings in Bee Culture*. During this time, countless other people around the world were trying to fly, but having very little success. One or two made uncontrolled hops of a few tens of metres, but for the most part they ended up on their noses in ploughed fields, lakes and what have you.

When the Wrights did finally emerge and started giving flying displays in the United States and in Europe, they were still streets ahead of their contemporaries, but they were getting more and more obsessed with their patents. As time went on, they were putting less and less of their creative energy into their machines, and were instead spending a large part of their time fighting lengthy lawsuits. Even as early as 1910 the Wrights' aircraft were practically obsolete.

So what's the point here? The point is that they were on a futile mission from the start. There was no way they were going to be able to patent the process of flying, which was essentially what they wanted to do. By trying to keep a tight hold of information that was so powerful it was destined to change the world irrevocably, they lost their lead. Perhaps, just perhaps, if they had said to the world 'Mimic us if you will, but we don't care for we are the Wrights!' then we would be crossing the Atlantic today on the Wright Flyer Mark 86.

So what's the *real* point here? The real point is that we're seeing a similar phenomenon today with the Internet. For a long time, a lot of people have made a lot of money from hanging on to large masses of information and letting little bits out at a time. (For a handsome consideration, of course.) Now, though, information is losing its value as a commodity, because there is so much of it about and it is so easily accessible. The old guard knows something's up and is looking distinctly anxious, but as yet isn't quite sure exactly what's going on or how to react to it.

Information as a marketable commodity is dying and the people who rely on selling information for their livelihood will have to adapt or watch the world pass them by. *That's* what's meant by the information revolution.

The Written Word: The Sequel

The written word has never left us since Tetiphet decided to rationalize his accounting procedures back at the dawn of civilization. Thanks to the industrial action of his scribes, Johannes Gutenberg gave it quite a boost with his remarkable invention of moveable type. Of late, though, it has lost a little of its impact. The invention of the telephone by Alexander Graham Bell and our very own John Logie Baird's contraption to allow him to watch the news in peace have, let's say, knocked it from the pedestal it once occupied in the life of the Western world. These days, you tend to pick up the phone rather than write a letter. You slip in a video rather than read the latest instalment of the *Pickwick Papers* to the family in the parlour. Imagine telling the kids they can't watch *Terminator 2* tonight and are going to have a sing-song around the piano, followed by reading aloud. They'd drop to the floor and hyperventilate to death.

All that is changing. Now people love to write e-mails, which is a little like writing letters, but not entirely and is almost, but not quite entirely, unlike a telephone conversation. We believe that the Internet signals the resurgence of the written word and that characters, words, sentences and paragraphs are a superior medium for teaching and learning than the moving image. It is less easy to savour and digest and reflect on the moving image. It is hard to refer back to, even with a video, and when you do, it seems curiously lacking in depth and context. There's an adrenalin hit there, that's for sure, but something lasting? Uh-uh.

The written word is an ideal medium for learning and when the Internet combines it with the snappiness and dynamism we've come to expect from the moving image, then that's a winning combination.

Which leaves you wondering why we're writing a book. Well spotted, but you didn't seriously think we were going to leave ourselves wide open on this one, did you? It's down to aesthetics. Books are enjoyable things to wield. When was the last time you saw someone lounging for hours on the sofa with a laptop computer flipped open? You can't take a computer to the beach or to bed, at least we don't recommend it, and there is something pleasing about simply holding a book and knowing that in your hands you have a snug capsule of knowledge. Books are here to stay and it's a jolly good thing, too.

A Final Note

One day soon the Internet will be delivered to people via their mobile phone or a digital television set, or via cable TV or all three. It's all changing so fast that some people say there's no point wasting money on buying a computer at the moment when it's all in such a state of flux; far better to wait until you can see which way things are going.

Ignore these people, for they are dangerous. We say:

One year in Internet time is like seven years in snail time.

Get online!

Now.

Moving On

10

When *Not* to Invest

He that diggeth a pit shall fall into it.

Ecclesiastes 10: 8

That graph of the performance of UK shares over the twentieth century is pretty compelling. The value of public business has forged ahead at a rate of around 10 per cent a year and the companies that have fuelled that growth have poured rewards into the widening pockets of their shareholders. It's a story that passes so many people by. Consider that if, in a given year, shares on average rise 9 per cent, they'll actually have turned in an *under par* year. Yet, that 9 per cent return marks the outperformance of the historical average of every other investment vehicle out there, from unit trusts to property, from gold coins to gilts. Slow years on the stock market are fast ones off it. The enduring direction of the stock market is upward; investments in shares since 1869 have doubled on average every seven or eight years or so.

What does all this say? What have we been saying throughout the book so far? We've been saying 'Invest in the stock market, for it will not disappoint.' And that's quite true, it won't, as long as you are ready for the challenge. If you're not ready for it, on the other hand, and you lose faith at the critical moments which will come upon you in years to come, or else you start to invest when you shouldn't even have been considering it, then things could get to look very ugly indeed.

So, when *shouldn't* you invest in shares, Fool?

When You Owe Money

Harry's in debt. He's already lost a fortune at Honest Ed the Turf Accountant, but he's got some acquaintances who've made a few bob on the stock market.

The light dawns. Why not borrow more money, invest it in shares and pay off the debt in a few months? It's *so* simple!

If the year ahead is like 1993, when shares rose by 28 per cent, or 1999 when they jumped 24 per cent, then it'll be drinks all round at the Dog and Duck and everyone who wanders into range will be regaled with the share-picking prowess of this Buffett of Ilford. 'Mmm, interesting, Harry. And how are the ferrets these days?' yawns the hapless citizen, before slinking off surreptitiously to the other end of the bar.

But, if the market clocks in a year like 1973, always a possibility, those self-same ferrets might just start to look like a succulent substitute for Sunday's roast. In 1973, shares fell by 29 per cent, turning £100,000 into £71,000 in twelve months. Worse, much worse, was to come: 1974 brought a breath-taking 52 per cent decline, shrinking the £71,000 into £34,000. (Excuse us while we pause here for some fresh air and a gallon of hot, strong coffee. Fifty-two per cent – did we say that?! OK, the following year they rose by 152 per cent. That makes us feel a bit better.)

That 1974 was a bad year all right and it puts the recent down years of 2000 and 2001 into some perspective. But while the losses were painful for anyone investing their savings money, they were calamitous for debtors banking on quick profit. Betting against your debt is simply ludicrous *and it doesn't make mathematical sense.*

Fire up your Mark 1 eyeballs, Foolish investor, and spy the numbers with us. Below sits an investor with £2500 in cash and £2500 in credit card debt, who decides not to pay off that debt, but to put that cash into shares:

WHAT HAPPENS WITH £2500 CONCOMITANTLY IN SHARES AND DEBT

	Shares (10%)	Debt (16%)	Difference
At Launch	£2,500	£2,500	£0
Year 1	£2,750	£2,900	−£150
Year 5	£4,026	£5,251	−£1,225
Year 10	£6,484	£11,029	−£4,545

A decade later, his debt has grown to over £11,000, while his investments have only grown to around £6,500. Though he started the experiment with enough money to eliminate the debt, he's now in a £4,500 hole and things are looking mighty black down there. 'Loadsamoney', as a well-known comic of the 1980s used to say. In fact, loadsamoney to the tune of several hundred copies of this book, one restricted view seat for the Men's Final at Wimbledon, or a private hip replacement and half a knee thrown in for luck.

Now, had he capped himself in bells and donned motley, he would have paid down the debt first, and later begun a savings and investment plan. Nobody in their right mind lets debt pile up on their credit cards and nobody in their right mind likes to be lectured to either. Credit card debt isn't Foolish, and long term it will scupper your chances of investing success, sure as too many chip butties are a direct route to the coronary care unit. Anyway (flourish of trumpets, Fool heraldic banner unfurled) …

We promise to largely drop that point for the remainder of this book.

Before moving on to the next situation that would cause you not to put new money into the market, let's digress briefly and ask, 'What sort of debt can you be carrying as a stock market investor?' There are myriad types of debt, but here's a Foolish rule of thumb: Any debt at interest rates greater than about 2 per cent above the Bank of England base rate will prove enduringly unbeatable. What kind of debt do we typically carry at around this level? Yup, mortgage debt, Fools, and we will see in Chapter 18 ('Be Your Own Landlord') how we can get this kind of debt to work in our favour. But those flexible friends, those springy bits of plastic – they will suck your lifeblood if you let them. Oops! We said we'd drop it, but we got carried away, so important is the point. So we're only human, OK? For the last time, the message is: pay down your non-mortgage debt *before* you start investing. That will bring you one giant step closer to building broad and enduring wealth. There, we're finished.

The first time you shouldn't be investing is when you owe money. The second?

When You'll Need to Spend Your Savings

Now that you've bid adieu to the misery of liability, and have squirrelled away, say, £2500 to invest, are you ready to get right into shares? There's a stock-broker two doors down from your office. United Kingdom PLC, power-house of Europe, is waiting to reward you. You've had a few tips from Uncle Sidney. And Russell Grant says your star is in the ascendant: *Now is the time!*

Just a minute.

Not every penny of your savings is created equal. That's especially true when you may need to use some of them to buy a sandwich for lunch tomor-row, another handful for new clothes, a few thousand for car insurance, thou-sands more for travel and entertainment, and a half-million or so for the deposit on your dream house. In fact, much of your savings money will be eaten up by immediate concerns. A little preparation and planning, really, no more than a few hours of thought, will go a long, long way here. You cannot be investing what you'll need shortly, because over the short term the market can get hammered, devastated, annihilated. Remember 1974? If you lose 50 per cent of the money you will need to live on in the year ahead, you may try and put a brave face on it, look at it as an emotional growth experience perhaps, but cornflakes three times a day for a year? Not pretty.

Sadly, far too many 'investors' have been flattened by a marketplace that has no mercy on those who would chance their savings on a single year. Buying shares with money you'll need next month or next year will have you anxiously pacing a moonlit living-room floor. The miracle of compounding takes time to work its magic. So how much time can you give to your latest amount of savings? Answer that question honestly and it will help you decide where to put them.

We don't think you should invest in shares any savings you will need within the next five years. Why five years? Because since 1869 shares have out-performed cash in a bank account in 78 per cent of five-year periods. In fact, the longer you plan to invest in shares, the more likely you are to come out on top: shares outperformed cash in 93 per cent and 100 per cent of ten-year and thirty-year periods respectively. Still, the odds are pretty good for five-year periods and we think that you should think of this as the minimum.

Short-term money, then, should be placed in a high-interest bank account. You are aiming to use this as you or your family need it, whether that's for a replacement car, holiday, dental treatment or any emergencies that crop up. Spend it, don't gamble with it.

When else shouldn't you invest?

When You Don't Yet Know Enough

You 've clawed your way out of debt. You've hived off money you won't need for four or five years. Hi-ho, let's get it into shares!

Brrrrrrrrrrring!

Now just hang on one cotton-pickin' minute. Again. There are two things to think about here: first, do you really, really know what investing in the stock market means and, secondly, does it feel like you're making share selections on the back of a guess and a hope, a wing and a prayer?

You have to be sure you've understood the nature of the stock market beast before you throw money at it. It's a frisky mare and if you're going to take fright every time that it bolts or rears, then you don't yet know enough. Stick outside the market and watch its daily antics a while longer. Similarly, if you're looking at individual companies and can't get over that uneasy feeling that you don't really feel comfortable making a decision about this one or the other one, it's Not Your Time.

Thomas Huxley, described at the time as Charles Darwin's 'Bulldog' and the man who publicized and fought for the theory of evolution against a hostile and sceptical Victorian establishment, had this to say on knowledge: 'If a little knowledge is dangerous, where is the man who has so much as to be out of danger?' Now, none of us can ever be totally out of danger, but we can all achieve a level of knowledge where we feel comfortable with the risks. That level is different for all of us and Foolishness is about finding that level out for ourselves.

Right, so you don't owe anything, you have some money earmarked precisely for stock market investment that you won't have to touch for five years at least and you know what you know, so when *else* can't you invest, for Pete's sake?

When You Are Dead

The fourth and final reason not to invest is if the blood has stopped moving through your veins and your lungs are no longer drawing in oxygen. When the background sopranos strike up, and you see that flash of bright light through a tunnel of clouds, and the Giant Hand reaches down to pull you into the next life, that's about as good a time as any to stop flicking Teletext on and off to check your share prices. Once you're settled at the Gates of Paradise Holiday Inn, you've unpacked your suitcase, tested the bed and the shower and cleared out the mini-bar, we hope you'll spare a thought, just once, for what went before. Raise your Martini and toast yourself as you recall that before your departure, you paid down all your debts, set aside some inheritance for those who would invest after you and even conferred some useful investment principles for your descendants to mimic. The wealth that you have left to trickle down through your family tree – mere earthly riches though they be – will go on to support the scholarship, creativity and daring of your offspring. Certainly, it'll allow a few ne'er-do-wells to flit around the honeypots of Europe, quaffing champagne and cavorting licentiously wherever they go, but your financial gifts will be a big fat positive in the lives of many others and to all your descendants you will be their Most Favoured Ancestor. And while you're in the vicinity, perhaps you'd have an otherworldly whisper in the ear of the management on behalf of all the Fools still toiling down here. We'd all appreciate it.

11

A Share Primer

There is less in this than meets the eye.

Tallulah Bankhead, quoted in Alexander
Woollcott's Shouts and Murmurs

You need never go to the trouble of buying an individual share. If you wish, you can invest directly in the stock market without using a stockbroker by buying into one of the 'collective investments' that we will look at in Chapter 17. These are essentially portfolios of shares bought and sold by a management team into which you can buy a stake. If you have good share-pickers in the team, you'll do well; if not, you won't. Mostly, these collective investments don't do very well and the vast majority of them, as we have already seen, fail to beat the average. We do, however, advocate one particular type of unit trust as a first Foolish investment and that is the index-tracking unit trust we talked about in 'A Tale of Two Professions' (see Chapter 7). These worthy animals aim to mimic the movements of the market as exactly as possible and are the first plank in our investing philosophy. If you think you'll be bored by learning just what shares are about and how they are traded, but still want to become a Foolish investor, then skip the rest of this chapter, fly onward to the next section at Chapter 14 and that's you sorted out. Don't worry, you're not doing your financial prospects irretrievable damage. In fact, you're still setting yourself up to be in far better shape financially than most of your contemporaries, but you may want to come back at a later date and finish off here. Alternatively, if you know all this stuff already, then purse your lips into a long 'Beeep', as you would if you were beeping over the names in a Russian novel, and we'll see *you* later too.

We're going to start with an overview of what companies are all about and how the stock exchange came to be. Incredibly, by the end of this section you will be bandying about terms like 'Articles of Association' and 'PLC' like nobody's business and actually enjoying it. Don't believe it? Read on ...

Companies and Shares

Enterprise is the foundation of the modern economy. By setting up and running businesses, people generate jobs and wealth. It's not surprising, then, that the Government is pretty keen for people to be enterprising. The trouble is that setting up a business and taking on obligations to suppliers and staff can be risky. If you set yourself up as a straightforward trader, then the obligations of your business are yours personally. If the business goes bust, then those people who are owed money can come after you to get it back. Your personal assets are likely to be seized to repay the debts. Not surprisingly, this is not a great incentive for people to be enterprising. Starting way back in the seventeenth century, successive governments have developed the notion of a limited company to try to solve this problem.

As its name suggests, the obligations of a limited company are limited to the company itself, rather than to the people who have invested money in it. This means that if the company goes bust, then those people who are owed money can only get back what there is in the remains of the company. Other than in very unusual circumstances (which needn't concern us here), what they can't do is try to get any money back from the investors. This is fair enough, since when these people (the *creditors*) decided to do business with the company, they were aware that it was the company, and not the individual investors, that they were dealing with. The flip side of all this is that limited companies have to go to the trouble of getting their accounts checked (by *auditors*) and published to the world. That way, the theory goes, everyone can make their own assessment of a company's creditworthiness themselves and decide, for instance, whether (and at what rate of interest) to lend it money.

Companies are therefore created and governed by a long list of statutes. These are now mostly condensed into the Companies Acts of 1985 and 1989. They run to a total of about 600 pages, most of which are written surprisingly clearly. Amongst other things, they set out the basis for a company's constitution. A company has two main constitutional documents called the

Memorandum and Articles of Association. The Memorandum is fairly boring, just setting out a few things like the name, how many shares there are and what the company is going to set out to do. The Articles of Association is a much more interesting read. It goes into how the company is to be managed. This involves giving the directors a series of rights and obligations and, importantly, saying when the shareholders are entitled to call their own meetings to do things like check on the performance of the directors (and, if necessary, to vote them out). The important thing to note is that when you buy a share in a company, you are basically buying the rights to which that share is entitled according to the Articles of Association, a few statutes and a bit of company law.

Private and Public Companies

In the United Kingdom there are two main types of company: private companies and public companies. You can spot private companies because they have the word 'Limited' or 'Ltd' at the end of their names. Public companies are denoted by the words 'Public limited company' or 'PLC' at the end of their name. The difference is that Public companies have to follow a few more rules, designed to show that they are particularly creditworthy. This is supposed to inspire a bit more confidence in those who deal with these companies, and indeed it does.

All the large companies that you see around the UK will tend to be PLCs, because in business you need to inspire confidence in people (such as your bank and your suppliers) and the little extra work that's involved in being a public company is generally well worth it. However, both public and private companies have shares and these shares are owned by individual people, pension funds or financial institutions such as banks. Whenever anyone owns shares, they are in possession of something that can be bought and sold. However, unless a company's shares are 'listed' or 'quoted' on a stock exchange, it is going to be very hard to find buyers for them. Indeed, a buyer of unquoted shares should certainly do things like read the company's Articles of Association, so that they know what they are actually buying. The uncertainty involved in buying into unquoted companies and the difficulties in matching buyers and sellers mean that the buying and selling of unquoted companies is inefficient and there is clearly a need for a more user-friendly way of going about it. Enter, the Stock Exchange.

The Stock Exchange

The London Stock Exchange grew out of informal meetings of investors in the coffee houses of seventeenth-century London. Here, bewigged gentlemen with, incidentally, accents far closer to the contemporary American accent than the English one, would haggle with each other to buy and sell portions of likely-looking companies. As the volume of trading grew, they eventually moved to their own premises in Threadneedle Street, renaming it the Stock Exchange in 1773. The Industrial Revolution of the nineteenth century and the need this created for companies to raise large amounts of capital fuelled the growth of the exchange, and at one point there were about twenty provincial exchanges dotted around the country. Now they are all concentrated into one – the London Stock Exchange.

In 1995 a smaller, subsidiary market was created, the Alternative Investment Market (AIM). This was to give smaller, more speculative companies the opportunity to be listed on the stock market. The requirements for entry to the AIM are not so stringent and the volumes of shares traded much smaller. We're all for opportunity but, for the most part, we don't advocate investing in shares on the AIM. They can be risky, difficult to trade and often not worth the heartache.

Many of us are intimidated by the City and the Stock Exchange, but really it's just a big market. It's bigger than it was when it was an assembly of gents swapping tall stories and shares in East Indies trading concerns over cups of coffee, but that's all. It's a giant shopping centre, offering shoppers the partial ownership of around 2000 British businesses. Instead of buying a jumper from Marks & Spencer, you buy a portion of M&S itself. Instead of filling your car with £20 of BP's petrol, you buy some of BP itself.

As we saw above, buying a share makes you a part-owner of that company. This means that you have a share in the profits and can vote in major company decisions. If the company does well, then the share price will go up as other people start to look interested in buying into this promising enterprise and earning some profits themselves. Conversely, if the

world decides it isn't yet ready for a combined television/microwave/
refrigerator ('Never take your eyes off the telly!'), then your shares in
MicroWatch PLC are likely to decline in value. The people who buy and sell
shares on your behalf are called stockbrokers. Some charge more and some
less for the privilege.

The to-ing and fro-ing of share prices as people value companies differently at different times is what makes up the 'market', and we'll be talking a
little more about this idea of the market later. The major share prices from the
previous day can be found in all the major daily newspapers, and most of the
shares listed on the London Stock Exchange can be found in the *Financial
Times*. If you're hooked up to the Internet (and if you've not been convinced
to do so by the time you finish this book, we've failed), then you can get the
current share prices (delayed by a mere twenty minutes) for free at many
places on the World Wide Web.

Quoted Companies

If a company wants investors to be able to buy and sell its shares on a stock
exchange, then it must apply for its shares to be added to the list of companies whose shares are quoted on that exchange. Not surprisingly, stock
exchanges tend to be a bit sniffy about which companies' shares are added to
its list. This doesn't mean that there aren't any bad companies on any particular stock exchange (anybody who's been investing for a while will probably
have a few to tell you about, ourselves included). What it does mean is that
for a company to be quoted, it must follow the rules of the particular
exchange on top of all the rules of law that we've already mentioned. These
rules cover a range of things like having a reasonably standard set of Articles
of Association (so people know roughly what their rights are without having
to check a company's Articles every time they invest), disclosing a certain
amount of extra information (so that investors can judge how a company is
doing) and giving shareholders extra rights to vote on certain major transactions. Oh, we almost forgot, as far as the London Stock Exchange is
concerned, to be added to its list, you also need to be a PLC.

So, if you want to buy shares in a particular company, you've generally
got to hope that it has its shares listed on a major stock exchange. Do you

own or have you seen advertised a Dyson vacuum cleaner? You might want to buy shares in this company and we couldn't blame you, because it represents one of the most innovative triumphs of British manufacturing industry of recent years (and it's been pretty skilfully marketed too). Here at Fool UK, we'd love to look into grabbing a piece of this action, but this is one business which isn't for sale because it's a privately owned company. At the moment, anyway. Presumably, Mr Dyson is satisfied with the way things are going and he doesn't want thousands of shareholders breathing down his neck, demanding higher profits every six months. Shareholders are just that, part-owners of the business, and often they think they know what's good for the company. In fact, they often think they know better than the management and large shareholders have to be listened to. Sometimes this can be helpful, but if it's not, it'll be distracting or even downright disastrous.

Also, we have to presume he doesn't need the money.

Money?

Yes, companies go public to raise cash. If a company wants to expand its business, it is generally going to need cash to do it and, broadly speaking, there are three routes to new capital. If Rent-a-Family – 'Ready-made families by the hour or day to busy business executives' – wants to go national, it can do any of the following:

1. It can toddle off to the local bank or building society and get a loan, which will demand regular interest payments.
2. As a private company, Rent-a-Family can look for investment from venture capitalists – investors representing large companies, trusts or just wealthy individuals. Venture capitalists make early investments in rapidly growing companies. They aim to strike it rich on start-up businesses with big stories but not enough cash to do more than simply tell those stories.
3. Finally, it may decide to divide itself up into a few million equal-sized bits and flog most of them off to the highest bidder, while keeping a chunk back for themselves. This will give them a huge cash injection, which they won't have to give back, but it will leave them beholden to a crowd of often impatient shareholders.

Just about every quoted company out there will have gone through some variant of these three financing stages. They started by borrowing money, then perhaps they brought in some venture capitalists and then they worked with an investment firm to get their shares listed on the market. In Britain this is called a New Issue (or, often, a flotation) and in the US it's called an Initial Public Offering, or IPO. Once a company has *floated* on the market, its shares will move up and down depending on the demand for them. If investors feel that the company is doing better than before, then there will be more demand for the shares and the price will move upwards. If investors feel that the company is doing worse, then demand will dry up and the shares will fall until they reach a price at which the demand returns. As we've said before, investors can be a funny bunch, and fast-changing opinions of a company's worth can make share prices very volatile in the short term. However, over the long term, a share's performance will match very closely the actual performance of the underlying business. The great American investor Ben Graham expressed this well when he said that in the short term the stock market is a voting machine, while in the long term it is a weighing machine.

Market Capitalization

Despite all the to-ing and fro-ing, at any one time a company's total value (as far as the overall investing public is concerned) can be calculated from its share price and the number of shares that it has. Take the Magic Umbrella Company, Kilmarnock PLC. You haven't heard of them? Never mind, they are listed on the Highland Stock Exchange under the symbol MUCK, and they make umbrellas that will not only keep a Highland downpour at bay, but will retain their shape in anything up to a Force 11. Not surprisingly, sales of this product are going well, with an overseas factory recently opened in Cherrapunji, India, the world's wettest spot. Currently, the shares are trading on the market at 500 pence (that would be £5 to you or us, but in the world of shares, most things happen in pence; just smile and say nothing). It has 100 million shares (sometimes you'll hear this expressed as 100 million *shares in issue or shares outstanding* but it just means that it has 100 million shares). Are you ready for this? Did you pass GCSE maths? If not, fire up your calculator, because the answer is … £500 million. At current prices, MUCK is valued at £500 million. Another way of saying this is that it has a market capitalization of £500 million, often abbreviated to 'market cap.'

If MUCK PLC corners the heavy duty umbrella industry, boosts its sales, cuts down its costs, and as a result its profits soar, then more and more people are going to want shares in this dynamic enterprise. More, more, more. The share price will go up – supply and demand operating here: if you really want what I've got, you'll have to pay more for it – and so will the market cap. Everyone will be happy, except those prevaricators who foresaw the huge potential of this product but could never find *quite* the right moment to make their investment in it.

Now, market cap. is used in Britain to subdivide shares into 'indices'. You'll have heard them on the radio and television every morning and evening, sounding like body parts in some strange jig: 'The Footsie's up, the Footsie's down, shake it all around.' What this really refers to is the FTSE indices. There is the FTSE 100 index, the FTSE 250 index and the FTSE All Share index. The FTSE 100 index is made up of the 100 shares with the highest market cap. (the UK's hundred largest companies), the FTSE 250 is the next 250 and the FTSE All Share is a list of around 800 of the most important shares on the London Stock Exchange and includes those in the FTSE 100 and the FTSE 250. ('FTSE' stands for *Financial Times* – Stock Exchange', the two organizations that established the indices.)

It is useful to subdivide companies according to value in this way because different sizes of companies pose different risks and benefits to the investor. The very largest companies, those in the FTSE 100 and including oil companies like Shell, shops like Marks & Spencer and pharmaceutical companies like GlaxoSmithKline have market caps. in many billions of pounds. These companies all own large amounts of what are called fixed assets – buildings, factories, mineral rights, etc. They employ many people, have very large amounts of sales each year and have strong brand names. In themselves they have a lot of 'value'. If you buy part-ownership in one of these companies you are buying part-ownership of bricks and mortar and of a successful enterprise with a proven track record. It's not quite that simple, because you will also be paying a premium above the sheer monetary value of the company based on its earnings and the projected increase in those earnings over the next few years, but still underlying your investment there is the feel of solidity, of a business which is one of the backbones of the economy. In short, you do not lie awake at night worrying that the company may go bust and you will lose all your money. Far more likely is that you will make a comfortable, steady sum from these sorts of investments. OK, so M&S shares haven't done very well over the last few years (in fact not much has) but the company is still there, it's still selling a huge number of underpants and it is still making a healthy profit from doing so. The company keeps plodding along and, over the long haul, it seems very likely that M&S will continue to participate in the overall growth of the British economy. It is this long-term participation in economic growth that makes shares attractive compared with cash and gilts. By buying into the large companies in the FTSE 100 you buy into businesses that tend to have the strength to continue to participate in this.

Let's contrast this with a small-cap. biotechnology company, which is far off making it into the FTSE 250 and whose total number of shares on the market is worth just £30 million. This company, Flab-o-Zap PLC, has just one avenue of interest and it's called, yup you've guessed it, Flab-o-Zap. Flab-o-Zap, still in the early stages of development, promises to revolutionize the eating patterns of the developed world. One tablet of F-o-Z will cancel out the flab-building effects of up to twelve Big Macs or fifteen Mars Bars, and the company is aiming to market the tablets in sweetie dispensers and at fast-food outlets around the world ('That'll be four Big Macs, three apple pies, a large Coca-Cola not diet and an F-o-Z, please.') If it all comes off, this company is going to be big, but F-o-Z is still very early on in the notoriously fraught drug development process. Anything could happen between now and approval by the drug licensing authorities: tumours in rats, hair in human volunteers turning pink, feet falling off, anything. Flab-o-Zap PLC is probably burning £5 million or more every year as it sinks money into its wonder drug and it has no other income. There is nothing else to this company and if F-o-Z does not make it to the marketplace, then your investment will be worth zilch. The other side of the coin, though, is that if F-o-Z changes the eating patterns of a generation, the share price will double, quintuple, centuple, can you say 'go up a very great deal'?

Midway between large-cap. and small-cap., you will find, wait for it, mid-cap. companies, which behave somewhere between the two and which are also a fertile ground for investors. The FTSE 250 is an index of mid-cap. companies.

As a rule, then, small-cap. companies are riskier investments than large-cap. ones, although they may provide much greater returns. These differences in the character and nature of large- and smaller-cap. companies are sufficiently consistent to make it worthwhile separating them out into distinct groups – the indices we have already heard about.

How to Read the Share Tables

With a cup of coffee on the kitchen table, a piece of bread in the toaster and the children still fast asleep, prop this book up against the cornflakes packet and open up the copy of the *Financial Times* you surreptitiously bought yesterday. We're about to do some work.

As confusing as all those numbers may look, they're quite easy to decipher once you know what to look for. In the *Financial Times*, you'll find the share tables in the 'Companies and Markets' section, just inside the back page. You can find the share prices in other major newspapers and at a number of sites on the Internet too, but the Sporting Pink seems like a good place to start.

Have you found them? Good. What do you notice first? That it's all looking just a teensie bit dull and not at all the kind of thing you want to be bothered with? Wrong! That's not what you notice. Believe it or not, you may be scanning these pages regularly a few months from now and enjoying it. Try again. Aha, you've noticed that the companies aren't arranged alphabetically as one might have thought, but by type of business: Aerospace & Defence, Automobiles & Parts, Banks, Beverages, etc. Fool, we knew you had it in you. Splendid work!

Finding the share you want can be a little trying if you don't know exactly what sector it's classified under, but once you have it figured out, this system actually makes quite a lot of sense, as it makes it simple to compare companies in the same industry. In fact, these sectors are placed together into larger industry groupings. You can see a list of these (with the various sectors listed underneath each group) if you have a quick look at the very back page of the paper. Can you see them? Down at the bottom left? Excellent. If you're good, we'll come back to this bit later on. Anyway, we like this system and are prepared to put up with the minor inconvenience of occasionally having to hunt through a number of industry sectors to find the share we're after. It's actually a far better system than in the US papers, where US shares are listed alphabetically.

Let's take Tesco as an example. This is one of the biggest retail companies in the world and a strong, solid FTSE 100 performer. Where you gonna look, Fool? Under 'Food & Drug Retailers', yup, and there it is. No, hang on, there it is. Wait. Grab your glasses. *There it is*. And it looks like this:

	Notes	Price	+ or −	52-week high	low	Volume '000s	Yield	P/E
Tesco	✠	251xd	+1	270¼	218	54,140	2.2	20.4

OK, so perhaps it doesn't look exactly like this, but it did when this was written on 31 May 2002. How it looks for you shouldn't be that far different. Don't tell us you've got a copy of the Monday FT. If you have, then it might be quite a bit different. As we'll see later, it gives slightly different information about the dividend and, on top of that, it gives the market capitalization, which can be very handy. Anyway, we're going to stick to explaining what happens on the other days. So, starting from left to right, we have the company name. We're OK with that – we found the company, after all. Then come the notes. If you look at the bottom right-hand side of the right-hand of the two share pages, you will see the notes explained and see that this symbol means that Tesco is an 'FT Global 500 Company' for the year 2002. Bully for it. In fact, it's bully for the FT too, since it means that they'll charge you £95 for the FT's own detailed analysis of the world's top 500 companies. Well, you'll know by now what we're likely to think about that, won't you? It seems like an awful lot of money to pay when there is so much data and analysis available free on the Internet, both from the companies' own Web sites (like www.tesco.com) and various financial Web sites. Anyway, back to business …

Now comes the price: 251 xd. '251' is the price in pence at the close of trading (4.30pm) on the previous day. For big companies like Tesco, this will more or less be the last price at which a deal was struck before everyone went home. For other shares (generally the ones that aren't in the FTSE 100), it will be the 'mid-price' of the share, and it falls between the price at which you could have bought it (the 'offer' price, which will be higher than the mid-price) and the price at which you could have sold it (the 'bid' price, which will be lower than the mid-price). It's essentially a fantasy price, used for reference only. Using the mid-price means only one price has to be quoted, saving on time and space. Now, 'xd'. This simply refers to the fact that if you were to buy this share now, you would not be in line for the upcoming dividend payment. This isn't getting any simpler, is it? Think way back to the introduction of this book: DON'T PANIC. Do, however, ask: 'What's a dividend?'

Dividends are simply payments that companies make directly to their shareholders. Companies like Tesco pull some money out of their flow of earnings and use it to encourage shareholders to hold onto their shares for the longer term. They're like a salary to shareholders. The year's dividend is paid in two halves, six months apart. Each dividend payment is payable to people who hold the shares at the close of trading on a certain date (specified by the company when it announces the dividend). This is called the 'ex-dividend date'. As far as Tesco and its next dividend are concerned, that day has passed. If, say, the dividend was for 2p per share then, all things being equal, you would expect Tesco shares to have fallen by 2p in price after 'going ex-divi-dend'. This would be because the shares have lost their entitlement to an extra 2p and are, therefore, worth 2p less. So, by telling you that the shares have already 'gone ex-dividend', the FT is letting you know where you stand. How kind. In truth, though, it's only of much relevance when you're looking at a company that pays a very big dividend relative to its share price – this is measured by dividend yield and we'll come to this in a moment. Onward!

The next column ('+ or –') shows how many pence higher or lower the share price closed compared to the previous day. In this case, it was a mere penny up which, when compared to a share price of 251p, is not very much at all.

The 52-week high and low of the share comes next. We think this is fairly self-explanatory. One point to make is that at some point later on in the year, the FT suddenly switches to giving the highs and lows for the current year, rather than the last 52 weeks. We've never really worked out when it does this, and we're not actually very interested, but it's worth making sure that you know what you're looking at. Over the last year, Tesco shares have fluctuated between 218p and 270¼p. This might sound like a lot but, given the way the share prices of some technology companies have gone recently, it's really very steady. You'd expect this from a large food retailer like Tesco. Whatever the economic conditions, you've got to eat, and opinions about Tesco's valuation change less quickly than for companies with less steady (or even no) profits.

It's easy to think that at 251p, closer to its 52-week high than to its 52-week low, Tesco is looking expensive. Well, fiddlesticks! While many people are leery of buying shares that are near their 52-week highs, you shouldn't make this your instinctive response. You will come to notice that the shares of truly winning companies score new highs fairly consistently from one decade to the next. Oh yes, they may have a bad three-week run, four-month run or even three-year run, but, if sales and earnings grow, more investors will pile in. Don't be scared off by a share hitting new highs unless you can find something else worrying about the company.

Next, on to the volume of shares traded on the Stock Exchange that day. About 54 million. Quite a lot, really. With shares worth just over £2.50, the stock market shifted around £135 million of Tesco shares yesterday. Even so, this only amounts to less than one per cent of the company. That's probably a bit more than usual, but not wildly so.

'Yield' refers to the dividend yield on the shares. Take the dividend that Tesco paid last year, divide it by the current share price and multiply it by 100 to give the percentage. That's the yield, or rather the dividend yield, as it is properly called. If you like formulas, it looks like this:

dividend yield = dividend ÷ share price x 100
or
2.2 = dividend ÷ 251 x 100

Knowing all the other parts of the equation, we can, if we wish, calculate the total annual dividend that was paid on each share. And after a little mathematical jiggery-pokery, the answer is 5.52p. Now, we've shown off and calculated the dividend, but if we'd been patient and waited until the

Monday edition of the newspaper, we would have seen that it includes the actual dividend. For Tesco, this turns out to be 5.6p which still comes to 2.2 per cent (to the nearest 0.1 of a per cent). The Monday *FT* also shows that the 'Last xd' (last ex-dividend date) was '17.4', or 17 April.

Why do we care what the dividend yield is, anyway? It tells us what percentage return we may expect from the share if it does not rise or fall at all in the year. In this case, it is only 2.2 per cent, which isn't a great deal. It loses to gilts, it loses to a deposit account at the Middle Earth building society and loses to just about anything else you can think of. It barely matches inflation, for heaven's sake. Clearly, investors are not going to buy Tesco for the dividend alone. They are hoping instead that Tesco is going to increase its earnings by selling more food next year, hopefully more efficiently, and that as a result its dividend, and share price, will grow. OK, here comes a fast-paced, pub-quiz starter for ten. Which company do you think investors are expecting more earnings and dividend growth from?

Dividend Yield	
Tesco	2.2%
ICI	5.0%

Yes, you're right. They're counting on more growth from Tesco. If neither share price was to move at all in the next year, ICI holders would be happier campers than Tesco holders (assuming ICI managed to keep paying its high dividend, but that's another story). The market is counting on Tesco to achieve more earnings and sales growth over the long term.

Unfortunately, in the wake of a column that demanded some basic calcu-lato-fragilistic expertise, we run into a slightly more complicated beast to its right: the P/E ratio. 'P' stands for the company's share price and 'E' stands for the company's earnings per share. Thus, this ratio compares the company's share price to its last twelve months of earnings per share. Gasp. What's that? Forget it, you're never, ever going to grasp this. (Just kidding. Take a deep breath and read on.)

OK, Tesco has a P/E ratio of 20.4 on the day in question. The current price is 251p, giving us earnings per share over the last twelve months of 12.3p (20.4 = 251 ÷ 12.3). The same numbers for ICI are a P/E ratio of 11.6, a price of 322 3/4p and earnings of 27.8p per share. Investors in Tesco are prepared to pay *twenty* times what each share has earned in the past year for their shares while, in the case of ICI, they are only prepared to pay *twelve* times. The earnings are what the company actually brings home to investors from its forays out into the wide, wild world of commerce. Investors are prepared to pay more for Tesco's earnings, because they believe that it has the potential to make them increase at a faster rate than ICI. In fact even Tesco has a P/E ratio below the market average of 23. This is because there are lots of companies out there from whom investors expect even quicker earnings growth. Pearson, for example, which actually owns the *FT* has a P/E ratio of a shade over 30. Pearson has its work cut out to justify these expectations, but investors clearly think it can do it, because otherwise they wouldn't be prepared to pay this much for the shares.

Going back to ICI, its prospects just aren't that good, as assessed by investors, and all they are prepared to pay is twelve times earnings. If someone came along and tried to sell his shares in ICI at *fifteen* times earnings, he'd be laughed out of court. This company isn't worth that, he'd be told, it's not going to expand its business quickly enough for us to be prepared to pay that kind of price. Now, begone!

We said earlier that, if you were good, we'd come back and make a couple of points about the bit on the very back page of the *FT* and we think you have been, so here goes. Go to the very back of the paper and look at the bottom left-hand corner. There should be a table full of numbers covering about a quarter of the page. Now we're not going to cover this table in quite as much depth, but we want to draw your attention to a couple of the columns: 'Actual Yield %' and 'P/E ratio'. These are the same figures that we've just been talking about. The difference is that here the dividend yield and the P/E ratios are given for all the different FTSE indices and for all the different sectors of the market. If you look at the row for the FTSE All Share (which should be fairly near the top), you see a figure for the average yield for all the companies in that index. In our paper, it says that it is 2.75 per cent. The average P/E ratio for the FTSE All Share is 23.00. If you think that the presence of investment companies (which are just companies with stakes in all the others) distorts the values, then you can look at the row below called 'FTSE All Share ex Inv Co'. The figures are actually only very slightly different.

Since Tesco has a lower P/E ratio than the market average, we can deduce that investors expect Tesco to grow at a slower rate, overall, than the average company. That's not especially surprising, since Tesco is a food retailer and, despite an interesting international growth strategy it's a sector that investors just aren't very excited about. So, instead of comparing Tesco to the average of the whole market, we can have a look at how it compares to the average of the Food & Drug Retailers sector. You can find the row for this listed under 'Non-cyclical services', towards the bottom of the table. The average dividend yield for this sector is 2.45 per cent and the average P/E ratio is 19.06. So, we thought Tesco was a better than average company and that's how it appears. Since its P/E ratio is higher, and its dividend yield lower, than the average of similar companies, we can deduce that investors expect more growth from it.

While we're looking at the 'Non-cyclical services' grouping, we can add a quick warning about how arbitrary the groupings of companies can be. Take a look at the other sector that makes up non-cyclical services. It's 'Telecommunications Services' and it has a whopping P/E of 80. In fact, there is a little sign next to the figure of 80 which indicates that when the *FT* got that far, they stopped counting, so the actual P/E ratio is very likely quite a bit higher. This is probably mostly to do with the fact that many telecommunications companies saw their earnings shrink dramatically last year. Even so, investors must expect those earnings to recover, to a large extent, because otherwise they wouldn't be prepared to pay such a fancy P/E ratio for the shares. Anyway, the retailing of food and drugs and the provision of telecommunications services fall into the same grouping, but they are oceans apart in terms of what investors expect from them. So, beware and always have a thought about what it is that you're actually looking at.

There are all sorts of things that investors will look at when deciding how much they expect a company to grow. Perhaps the prime factor is the estimates of potential growth in earnings provided by the analysts who follow the company. These are the people who are paid by the large financial institutions to live, eat, sleep and breathe the company or companies they follow. They assess what the company is likely to earn in the next several years and investors then decide how much of a premium they are prepared to pay for this projected growth. The limitation here is that these analysts only tend to look two or three years ahead. They're a bit frightened of going further ahead than that because they might end up being way off and looking a bit silly. Also, brokers make their money from people changing their minds about shares (and then buying or selling them as a result) and they find it a bit limiting to set out their stall on a company too far into the future. They want results and action now.

Other things, of course, figure alongside the projected earnings estimates when investors decide how much they are prepared to pay for a company: namely, the past history and the current performance. There is more, though, much more, to the P/E ratio and estimates of earnings growth. To learn more about it, a good starting point might be the *Motley Fool UK Investment Workbook* or you might even want to come along to our Web site, where there are a number of articles and endless discussion about this sort of thing.

When you've had a well-deserved break, you can come back and read the next chapter about Obviously Great Investments with confidence, secure in the knowledge that you already know far more about shares than most of your contemporaries ever will.

12

Obviously Great Investments

Greatness knows itself.

William Shakespeare, *Henry IV*

Buying an index tracker is a sound, Foolish investment and is as far as many people will ever need to go. There are others, though – and we count ourselves amongst this group – who want to be more involved with the growth of their money and who believe that it is possible to actually *beat* the performance of the market as a whole by choosing their own investments. What we're going to consider in this chapter are investments that appear to be such obviously great long-term investments that it is impossible to imagine why in preference anyone would want to invest in an underperforming, overcharging investment scheme such as an endowment policy.

Even so, the jump into investing in individual equities – no matter how 'obviously great' they appear to be – is a big one and not one you should consider making without ample, Foolish preparation. Go back and read Chapter 10, 'When Not to Invest'. Particularly go back and read 'When You Don't Yet Know Enough' (see p. 96). If you invest in individual shares before you're ready, what will happen is what happens to anyone who gets out of their depth: they drown. After a few attempts to stay afloat, fairly soon one 'glug' leads to another and they're asking the fishes why the air's so annoyingly thick and wet down here. If you're in shares and the market starts to drop, as it has over the last couple of years and certainly will again, then you'd better have a sound understanding and faith in the overall tendency of the market to rise as the years goes by. If, when the time comes, you panic and sell out as your shares start to drop along with everyone else's, then

115

we're very, very sorry you ever bought this book. We hope we're giving you the bare bones here with which to frame the understanding that long-term wealth is assuredly yours if you will but think with a long-term perspective, but only you can know how well you have really digested it.

Whether it's a first-day skier enticed to the top of the hill with a 'The best way to learn is to start at the top and fall all the way down', or a tyro parachutist looking down and reflecting that it's all looking awfully high up here, the fact is that any pursuit that requires an appraisal of risks and benefits should be approached with circumspection. Now, if you spend too long circumspecting – or whatever the verb may be – you'll never do anything more positive with your life than switch channels with the remote control and issue dire warnings to all your friends and relations. That's it – just issue dire warnings. As long as you have no other aspirations in life than to spend it ingesting a televisual diet of pap and purveying pessimism to anyone who will listen (there won't be many), then that's all right. But we're presuming that if you have read this far, you're some way towards becoming a Fool and have, let's say, slightly higher aspirations. We're hoping, specifically, that you nurture the aspiration to take hold of your fate with your own two hands and, through your own efforts and endeavours, build a future for yourself.

You do? That's great – read on!

Oh, hang on. You didn't go back and read 'When Not to Invest', did you, you eager beaver Fool? We really think you should. Go back to page 92, read those Foolish guidelines again and we'll see you back here in a few minutes. Don't worry about us, we'll take this opportunity to have a well-earned (well, we think so) cup of tea … Tum tee tum tum …

Schlurrrrrp!

(Sorry, you didn't hear that, did you? It was terribly hot. Sorry.)

Now, moving swiftly back to our thrilling investment plot: you've returned and you're thinking of making a positive decision to invest directly in some of the powerful companies that make up the UK market. Excellent! Our hope is that in years to come this decision will bring you market-beating returns, something an index tracker cannot, of course, provide. However, reflect yet again that there is no shame, no shame whatsoever, in never going any further than investing in the index itself. By doing this, you will beat the vast majority of professionals, leave investments in cash and gilts languishing, assure yourself the most secure future and all this for next to no input or ongoing hassle at all. By stopping at this point and saying to yourself 'I've sorted my finances, I'm not that interested in all this investment stuff, I'd like to devote more time to my family/quilting circle/tired old MG' then you are being a Fool indeed. You are not letting your initial enthusiasm push you into something you may later regret. Well done. We'll see you Fools towards the end of the book in our eloquent closing dissertations. Now go off and enjoy yourselves.

After what seems to have been a lengthy series of disclaimers on our part, but which really represent an attempt to set the right atmosphere, the rest of you are finally deemed to have taken the Fool's shilling. We ask you to spend a moment reading this light-hearted, amusing story of an Old Sea Dog from the Second World War. We think it sets the scene for the kind of contrarian, lateral-thinking mindset we like to use in investing. Look on it as a Foolish limbering-up exercise and a brief respite from this oh-so-serious business of investing:

Commodore 'Monkey' Brand had been hauled out of retirement to try and lick the British trawler fleet into shape as a minesweeping and anti-submarine force …

One of 'Monkey' Brand's favourite tricks was to speed over to a ship in his motorboat, hustle up the ladder on to the assembled quarter-deck, grab off his gold-braided cap and throw it to the deck shouting: 'There's a bomb – what are you going to do about it?' The ruse never failed to create momentary panic. Until one day, when he tried it out on a trawler. As he flung his cap down in front of the startled company and made his challenge, a rating stepped smartly forward and kicked the cap overboard. The surprised Commodore gazed unbelievingly at his cap floating away on the water. But he was not beaten. 'Good work,' he said approvingly, 'splendid.' Then pointing to the cap, he roared: 'Quick, that's a survivor who can't swim – save him!'

Paul Lund and Harry Ludlam, Trawlers Go To War

You see, we're not going to think like ordinary investors: we're going to try and think a little like Commodore Brand. We are not going to think short-term profit, we are not going to be looking at the market and trading our shares twenty times a day and, perhaps most importantly of all, we shall not believe what the financial press says about the market. Think of yourself from now on as deeply contrarian. You are going to buck the trend of our short-term, sound-bite, thirty-second-attention-span culture and think in years, tens of years. You are going to invest in strong world-beating businesses. You are going to invest in things you can't imagine yourself, Great Britain or the world doing without. In fact, you are going to 'Buy what you know'.

We'd love to take the credit for inventing this natty little investment aphorism and, believe us, if we thought we could get away with it, we would. Sadly, though, we must give the credit to another: Peter Lynch. Peter was a highly successful mutual fund manager (there are some!) in the US through the 1980s and penned two excellent books on investing: *One Up on Wall Street and Beating the Street.* 'Buy what you know' is a simple idea and it's an excellent route into investing.

Understanding the company in which you are about to become a part-owner is vital to success. Do you know much about drilling for oil around the Caspian Sea? Do you have a detailed knowledge of geophysics and are you equipped to speculate on the potential geopolitical repercussions of a large oil find in this area? Have you been keeping up to date with the progress of organized crime in the republics of the former Soviet Union and are you ready to factor in how much of a cut the Mafia will take of any profits? What are your thoughts on the effect of the pretty shaky politics of the area on the safety of the new oil pipeline from the Caspian to the Black Sea through Armenia and Georgia? We wouldn't be surprised if one or more of these questions drew a blank. What is so much more surprising is how many people are prepared to invest in small companies in these kinds of fields, which are so distant from their everyday lives. Can a small company really hope to make a go of it in this dodgy area or is it only the likes of BP, ExxonMobil and Shell that have a chance of turning out a healthy profit at the end of the day? We simply don't know and neither, we are sure, do most of the investors in these companies.

The world is full of investors with tales of woe concerning often small companies they bought into without knowing anything about them, other than hearing from a 'friend' that they had to jump on board quick or else they'd miss the boat! Penny shares, companies you've never heard of, commodities, options, Venezuelan bean futures. If you find yourself thinking that you could make a quick 200 per cent profit in one of these, switch into another, clear 300 per cent with that one, switch around like this for a couple of years, retire, buy a floating gin palace on the Côte d'Azur and spend your remaining years mixing ever more lurid cocktails and swapping ' ... and then this old tub of a sailing boat almost rammed me as I pootled out of the harbour at 35 knots, can you believe the cheek of it?' stories, then WHOA! It *is* possible to clear huge profits on dodgy investments which you don't understand in a short period. You are more likely, much more likely, to lose all your money in one fell swoop. Don't believe you will be the one to beat the odds, because Sod's Law of Investment says you won't. There's a place for people like you. It goes by the name of Las Vegas and sits in the desert sucking up water and fools somewhere between Los Angeles and the Grand Canyon. Buy a cheap airline ticket, take a thousand pounds and no means of procuring any more and return when you're broke or you've made a million. Dealing with your gambling habit in this way will cost you less in the long run than thinking you will make outrageous returns from investments about which you know nothing. It is also less likely to annihilate any long-term human relationship you happen to have built up over the years.

Consider: one of the richest men in the United States, and therefore the world, is an unassuming Nebraskan called Warren Buffett. We'd tell you exactly where he stood in the richness league tables, but there seems to be something of a tussle going on with postitions changing on a seemingly daily basis. The 'Sage of Omaha' is worth somewhere around $30 billion. How has he done this? Purely and simply by investing in simple, understandable businesses with favourable long-term prospects and which are already efficient at what they do. Using this somewhat mundane strategy, he has returned around 20 per cent annually since 1964 for investors in his Berkshire Hathaway investment company. Let's repeat that: Warren Buffett, the world's greatest investor, has returned 20 per cent a year over the last thirty-eight years. It is a phenomenal performance and yet one he calls 'remarkably unremarkable'. By sticking to the basics and investing in companies like Coca-Cola, American Express, Disney and Gillette, he is living proof that the huge investment returns claimed by many investment newsletters and investing schemes are total and utter rubbish, garbage or trash, depending on your linguistic preference. If you buy investing magazines, you will find advertising inserts for investment newsletters falling out all over the place, offering you 20 per cent gains a month or more if you follow their advice (which generally involves stumping up a couple of hundred pounds). These sorts of claims are simply fantastic and we find that the flyers offering them are generally the right size to fit neatly over our corporate Motley Fool dartboard. Buffett has 'only' returned 20 per cent over the long term and this has 'only' made him one of the world's richest men. Fool, if you need a goal, a dream, an aspiration, then 20 per cent every year from easily understandable, reputable companies is sitting slap in front of you. Of course, the mighty Buffett has a knack at being very good at picking the right companies, but the strategy is simple and low risk and has very good odds of at least beating the pros. Verily, look ye not to 'Phenomenal profits in just 3 MONTHS!!!!' schemes, lest ye be burned most Horriblie.

When you've been Fooling around for a while, you can start to branch out from just buying what you know. The rule, in fact, can be turned on its head. If you feel sufficiently confident, give yourself some leeway by 'not buying what you don't know'. What we don't understand, after all, is what we're really trying to avoid and this mantra gives you a little more scope to find investments in areas that you know well enough, but not absolutely. So what is knowing enough? Well, really it relates to knowing enough about an investment to be confident that it meets the other important elements of a great investment (which we'll come to in a moment). You don't need to know the precise chemical processes that go into the manufacture of each (or any) of GlaxoSmithKline's drugs. You just need to understand why their business has, for example, a large element of repeat purchasing (drugs are anything but a one-off purchase), why they add value for the end user (just ask an asthmatic the value of a Ventolin puffer) and why it is hard for other companies to break into their market (patents and brand name drugs). Anyway, we're getting slightly ahead of ourselves, but knowing enough means knowing enough. OK?

If you want to be really Foolish, you can try to think about markets that you have reasons for understanding better than the average investor. Perhaps you are a doctor and have good reason to think that the market underestimates the importance of a new drug. Perhaps you are a software engineer and you understand, better than most, why a particular company's software is likely to become an industry standard because it works so much better than this or that. Be careful, though. Apple Computers is generally regarded as having had a superior product to Microsoft, but look where the two of them have ended up. Although Apple has improved its performance in the last few years, Microsoft still rules the world. Whatever the merits of the two products, Microsoft was better at developing its market position and the rest, as they say, is history. Don't forget, though, that your superior knowledge is only useful in so far as it helps you to recognize whether an investment meets the right criteria. Just because you know a great deal about aeroplanes and flying does not mean that you are going to make a killing by investing in airline companies. It may well be (and probably is) the case that there are no Obviously Great Investments among them.

What Makes an Obviously Great Investment?

As we have already said on several occasions in this book, investing in the stock market is about participating in economic growth. What we're going to consider here are investments that, because of almost unbeatable market positions, are so likely to participate in this growth that they are, to our mind, Obviously Great Investments. Over the short term, their share prices may move up and they may move down but, over the long term, continued profitable growth looks almost inevitable. The emphasis here is on the word 'almost'. Unfortunately, we Fools are not in possession of a crystal ball and we can't predict the future. It would be a wonderful thing if we knew which shares would *definitely* do well. Obviously we don't and neither does anyone else. What we can do, though, is build a portfolio of a number of shares that have good chances of doing well. That way, even if we pick a few companies that turn out not to be so obviously great (or even obviously bad), our overall chances of coming up smiling are very good. We'll say more about 'diversifying your portfolio' in Chapter 13, 'The Ten Most Common Investing Mistakes'. For the time being, we just want to be clear that, individually, Obviously Great Investments are not obviously infallible and you need to have plenty of them to be confident of making good long-term returns.

Most invested money is managed by professional fund managers who often have to justify their performance over absurdly short periods. As a result, they are too frequently tempted to throw their money at the latest fashion in the hope of quick profits. The strong and steady performers, frequently rather dull by comparison, often attract rather less interest than they deserve. This tends to keep their share prices at attractive levels. It comes back to that thing about woods and trees and not being able to see the former on account of the latter.

So, Foolish investors are able to use patience, and, in particular, the rest of the market's lack of it, to their advantage. However, to let our friend, the miracle of compounding, do its job, we need to find companies that we can rely on to be around, and still showing steady growth, in twenty years' time (or, preferably, even longer).

Fundamentally, what we are looking for in an investment is growth. Now, by this we don't simply mean a growing share price. What we want is a growing business. Without a growing business, a growing share price is ultimately unsustainable. On the other hand, with a growing business, the share price will ultimately take care of itself. Essentially, a growing business generates an increasingly large amount of surplus cash each year. The trouble with cash, however, is that it is a bit lumpy. A company might be spending an extra amount on investment in any one year to reap future benefits, and that may put a dent in their cash flow. This is why accountants like to talk about profits. Profits are designed to smooth out lumpy cash flows and give an idea, from year to year, how much money a company is making. A standard measure of profits is earnings per share (EPS). Remember this? We talked about it a bit in Chapter 11. Basically, it is the profits of a company, after tax has been taken off, divided by the number of shares that there are in that company. This gives a figure for how much profit is being generated for each share. What we like to see is growth in EPS over the long term, although it's important to note that this is really just a proxy for growth in the generation of surplus cash.

Anyway, let's get back to the importance of growth. Indulge us for a moment, Fools, for it is a subject very dear to our hearts. Take a company with its business growing (by which we mean its EPS) at a rate of, say, 15 per cent per year. After twenty years, it will be 16.4 times bigger. Not bad at all.

Now let's consider a company that grows at a mere 5 per cent per year. After twenty years, it will be just 2.7 times bigger. If the two companies were the same size to start with, the faster growing company will now be more than six times the size (in terms of EPS). To put it another way, we could have paid a P/E ratio (remember these from Chapter 11?) six times higher for our high growth company and, assuming that their P/E ratios end up the same, you'd still have been better off buying it instead of the slower growing company. Things go really crazy if we look at the picture after thirty years. Our Obviously Great Investment (as it clearly would be), growing at 15 per cent per year, would have increased by just over sixty-six times and would be more than fifteen times the size of the now forgotten laggard. We'll let you do the sums for forty years because the results are a bit messy and this is a family book (have a look at Appendix 1, 'Coping With Compound Interest', to learn how to do this sort of sum).

The point of all this is that it is growth, continued sustainable growth, that makes the real difference to an investment over the long term. It clearly matters how much you initially pay for an investment, but the further you look into the future, the less the price paid matters compared to the actual growth achieved. Take the drugs company GlaxoSmithKline. You could have bought shares in this company (or rather in Glaxo) in 1965 for 2.5p.* Since then it has achieved annual EPS growth of 18.1 per cent and its share price is now 1404p, having grown at 18.7 per cent over the last thirty-seven years. The slightly higher share price growth is explained by the increase in Glaxo's P/E ratio from 13.7 to 19.4. We could have paid twice as much for our Glaxo shares in 1965 (a P/E ratio of 27.4) and our rate of share price growth since then would only have fallen to 16.5 per cent. We'll repeat that. Paying twice as much for our Glaxo shares in 1965 would merely have reduced our annual return since then from 18.7 per cent to 16.5 per cent. The world's stockbrokers would almost certainly have greeted such a sudden doubling in Glaxo's share price at the time with advice to sell to 'lock in profits', while the truly Foolish investor would not have given the matter a second glance. Notice also how close both the figures for annual share price growth are to the rate of annual EPS growth (18.7 per cent and 16.5 per cent against 18.1 per cent).

---

* Data supplied by Datastream.

So, if someone comes along and tells you that what matters is how much you pay for a company's shares, then say to them, 'Sure it matters, but what really makes the difference over the long term is how much that company's business actually grows.'

The stock market is full of people who want to make their fortunes here and now. For these poor Wise souls, looking long into the future is a bit of an irrelevance and, not to put too fine a point on it, very frightening. It's like those old maps that, at the edge of the explored world, have pictures of dragons and other unpleasant monsters. Of course, aside from the odd kangaroo, the previously unexplored part of the world (at least it was unexplored by those mapmakers, not the people who actually lived there) has turned out to be pretty much like the explored world. Fools are wary, or rather respectful, of the future too, but we're not frightened of it because as we move forward into it, we're accompanied by our trusty old chaperone, Compound Interest. In short, we expect the stock market to tend to undervalue companies that have very solid prospects of good steady growth long into the future. These companies are what we call Obviously Great Investments.

How to Spot Obviously Great Investments

The two most important things about our chosen investments, then, are that they should show solid growth and that they should be able to sustain this growth long into the future. Over time the economy grows and, as a result, most companies that are around at any one time are growing. Over the long term, what happens is that many companies arrive, grow a bit for a while and then disappear. What we are trying to find are the companies that have arrived, have grown a bit for a while, will grow a bit more and then, after that, will just carry on growing. In other words, while growth in companies is everywhere, what isn't everywhere is *sustained and sustainable* long-term growth and this is therefore the supporting plank of any Obviously Great Investment. It's that sustainability that our criteria are designed to seek out.

Have they built a strong brand?

This is your first filter for an Obviously Great Investment. Find the businesses that have built at least nationwide or, even better, global brands in their industries. The more world-beating brands a company has, the better. A strong brand gives a company an edge because it represents the faith that the company's customers have built up in a product. It gives the company the opportunity to sell more of the product at the same price as less well-branded competitors. Alternatively, it means the company can charge more and still sell the same amount.

Ideally, a brand should be fixed firmly in the minds of consumers, creating a strong mental association between that brand and the particular product. You know the sort of thing: Hoover and vacuum cleaners, Heinz and baked beans, Gillette and razor blades. Once a company has reached the minds of consumers in this way, it is hard for others to replace it. The perfect brand will be one which consumers buy and use regularly. 'Repeat purchasing' is fantastic and not just because it keeps the profits flowing in, but because it means receiving free daily promotion. Companies like Coca-Cola, Gillette and Cadbury Schweppes are getting this promotion gratis millions of times a day. Every time a consumer buys one of their products, it is an opportunity for the company to extend the relationship of trust with that consumer and, without meaning to sound too sinister, an opportunity to get further inside their minds. For this reason, we suggest you study most carefully those businesses that are frequent servants of their global base of customers. These companies aren't just getting their promotion free, they're *making* money as they use the daily sales of their products to promote themselves. Very nifty.

Are they the best in their business?

Once we've found our world-beating brands, we need to ask ourselves whether the company is the best in its business. Does it have competitors that are doing a better job? If it does, then it may be that we're looking at the wrong company.

So what exactly is a company's business? It's worth thinking about this on several different levels. Take Tesco for example. At the nub of it all, its main business is food retailing, which it carries out mainly in the UK. So, first of all, we need to decide whether Tesco is the UK's best food retailer. If a company is not the best there is at its 'core' business, then it is unlikely to qualify for obvious greatness. However, it goes beyond this. Tesco is also involved in a certain amount of non-food retailing and it would be nice, although not vital, to see the company being best at this too. The company is also taking on an increasing amount of business overseas. Again, it would be nice to see them being best at this but, since it's a relatively new market for them, we perhaps shouldn't expect too much.

Beyond all this, what we'd really like to see is a company that dominates its entire industry, not just its direct competitors. Consider whether the company you're looking at is the one that makes its industry tick. Generally this comes down to having the brand that the consumer wants, but not always. It might be the company that has a patented widget, which makes it possible to make something twice as cheaply. Everyone in the industry will be at this company's beck and call. So, look at the industry that a company is in. If you find that another company dominates it so comprehensively (whether it is a competitor, supplier or customer) that it makes all the real profits and everyone else is left picking up the scraps, then you're looking at the wrong company. The dominant company is probably making all the money. Ask yourself questions like does Persil need Tesco or does Tesco need Persil? Persil would lose a lot of sales if Tesco stopped stocking it, but Tesco might lose a lot of Persil-loving customers to Sainsbury if it tried something like this. It's probably a dead heat in this case, in the UK at any rate. We actually looked at Tesco in the second edition of this book but, though we like the company, we felt that it didn't quite qualify as an Obviously Great investment.

More generally, choosing a best over a second best isn't always terribly easy. However, in any given group you can usually distinguish the superior two or three businesses from the rest. We don't think it's a good idea to invest in businesses trying to turn around or trying to become a top-tier competitor after years of slumber. Once you have the top two or three, decide which is the best of the lot, do a few minutes of research into their financial situation (which we'll consider in a bit – honestly, it's not overly complicated) and then buy and hold the strongest among them. Preferably for decades, but at least until they stop matching up to the criteria. If it's too close to call, consider buying the two or three main competitors.

Is their position easily defended?

For a company to sustain its growth over the long term, it needs to have some form of sustainable advantage. Commenting on Coca-Cola and Gillette, Warren Buffett had this to say in his 1993 letter to the shareholders of Berkshire Hathaway:

> *The might of their brand names, the attributes of their products, and the strength of their distribution systems give them an enormous competitive advantage, setting up a protective moat around their economic castles. The average company, in contrast, does battle daily without any such means of protection. As Peter Lynch says, stocks of companies selling commodity-like products should come with a warning label: 'Competition may prove hazardous to human wealth.'*

It's easy to agree with Warren Buffett and we'd agree that a company's brand is about the most important protective moat that a company can build around itself and this is where our criteria began. However, as Buffett also points out, there are other factors that can keep the competition at bay. Take ARM Holdings, a designer of microchips. Many of its designs are patented and this immediately gives it an advantage: if a company wants to make the type of chip that ARM designs, then it needs to pay ARM, and no one else, to use that design. In ARM's case, though, it goes further than this. It has established development partnerships with the majority of the world's large chip manufacturers. This means that it is involved in a daily discourse with these companies about how the designs can be improved upon or used more effectively. For this reason, if anybody is going to improve on the design in the future, the chances are pretty good that it will be ARM itself. As a result, ARM has a series of moats around it which even the most persistent of competitors will find it hard to overcome. We'll talk more about ARM Holdings shortly.

Are they making a lot of money for their efforts?

The above criteria are designed to find companies that should make a steadlily increasing stream of profits. In fact, if a company is doing the above things right, then we'd be very surprised if it wasn't doing this already. So, the best way to check our thinking is to have a look at its accounts and make sure that this is the case (don't worry, this is easier than it sounds, it really is). If we look at the company and it doesn't seem to be making much money, then we need to ask ourselves why. Generally, we'll have missed something which relates to its brand or its industry dominance. If you can't find anything wrong, then go back and keep thinking about what it might be. There may be a good reason for it but, on the whole, an Obviously Great Investment will be making good, steadily increasing profits and will have been doing so for some time.

The bottom line as far as making money is concerned is the return on invested capital. In just the same way as the measure for a savings account is whether you get three per cent per year, or four per cent per year, on the money you put into it (your 'invested capital'), so it is with companies. You want to find a business enterprise that's generating the biggest returns possible on the money that's invested into it. Of course with companies, though, we're looking for rather more than three or four per cent. In fact, any business worth its salt should be producing a 'return on capital' of more than 10 per cent per year and the very best can generate more than 20 per cent.

Each year, a company will, we hope, make a profit. Part of this profit is then, generally speaking, paid out in the form of a dividend, while the remainder is 'retained' in the company to invest for future growth. So, each year, more invested capital is being introduced to the company through the retention of some of its profits. How quickly our company can grow will depend on the return that it can make on its new invested capital and the best guide for that is the return that it's making on it's existing capital.

The capital that a company 'employs' in its business is the amount of its net assets, plus any borrowed money (or less any cash that it has lying around doing nothing in particular). Unfortunately, the figure for net assets on a company's balance sheet is notoriously unreliable, because it involves estimating the value of all the company's assets. Tangible assets (generally speaking the ones that you can touch), like a factory, for example, will be valued at the amount it cost to build, less an amount per year to allow for wear and tear (called 'depreciation'). Computers and office furniture will be valued at what they cost to buy, again less a bit for deprecation. Stocks (that is, things that are ready for sale but not yet sold) should have a fairly predictable value, but you only need the bottom to fall out of the widget market and all of a sudden you only get half as much for your widgets.

Then there are terrible problems with 'intangible' assets (essentially the ones that you can't touch). If you buy another company for more than the value of its net assets, the rules of accounting mean that you have to add the difference to your balance sheet, as something called 'goodwill', to make the books balance. But what's the wear and tear, as it were, on the goodwill?

It gets still worse with things like research and development or advertising expenses. If you spend £100m on advertising your new soft drink, then you could (and indeed should according to the rules of accounting) write it off in your profit and loss account reducing your profit, or increasing a loss, for that year. However, you'll hopefully make nice profits over the coming years partly as a result of those initial advertising expenses. In many senses, the cost of advertising was capital invested in the business and, if we don't put anything on the balance sheet to recognise it, then the return on capital in future years will be flattered. But what figure should you put on the balance sheet and what's the annual wear and tear on that?!

Fancy analysts get paid vast sums of money in the City to argue about just this sort of thing and we say let them get on with it. There are so many uncertainties that you rarely get very close to the truth. Even when you do, it's hard to be sure about it. It's a class one example of obscuring the wood for the sake of looking at the individual trees and it's why we suggest taking a step back and looking at the overall quality of a business. One way or another, if you find a business which passes the earlier tests that we mentioned, then we'd expect it to be making a very nice return on its invested capital.

But now we're going around in circles, because we introduced this test to see if a company was making good money. The answer is to keep it relatively simple and we'll see how we can do that in a few short moments. The reason for introducing the concept of return on capital is that it is, despite the hopeless mess that surrounds it, the bottom line on making money. So when we look at other tests, we should at least be aware that they're simply 'proxies' for the real thing.

The way to keep things simple is to stick to the profit and loss account, since it relies on things that are relatively easy to quantify. It shows us how much profit a company is making relative to its sales (also known as 'turnover' or 'revenue'). This is the money that comes into a company through its front door, as customers pay it for the things it produces. Of course, all the time there is a lot of money leaving through the back door (that is, the company's costs). What we want to know is how much money stays in the company, relative to how much is coming in. This is called the margin.

A company's profit and loss account starts with 'Sales' (or 'Turnover') at the top. It then takes off the 'Cost of Sales'. Cost of Sales basically includes the cost of the things actually used directly to create a particular product: the most obvious example is raw materials. The figure we're left with after taking this off is called 'Gross Profit'. The 'Gross Margin' will be the Gross Profit expressed as a percentage of the Sales. This figure is useful, as it tells you how much value a company is directly adding to the materials it uses in creating its products. The problem is that this can vary hugely depending on what type of business a company is in. For instance, a shop will tend to have low Gross Margins (around 20 per cent) because it only sells things for a little bit more than it costs to buy them. By contrast, a company making something like software, which essentially costs almost nothing, *directly*, to produce, will tend to have very high Gross Margins (perhaps as much as 90 per cent).

The great leveller between these two types of company is what comes in the profit and loss account below the Gross Profit, namely 'Operating Expenses' (or it could be called something else: like 'General and Administrative Costs'). This encompasses all the other costs in a company, things like salaries, wages, paper clips and all those other incidental expenses. It's where most of the costs of a software company will come in, since it has to pay all those clever computer bods large salaries for all the great software that they're creating. By contrast, the extra costs of a retailer at this level are small compared to the Cost of Sales. The figure arrived at by deducting Operating Expenses from Gross Profit is the 'Operating Profit' (sometimes called 'Trading Profit') and you won't be surprised to hear that the Operating Margin is the Operating Profit expressed as a percentage of Sales. So far, so good.

Finally, the cost of paying interest on any debt is taken off to give a figure called Profit Before Tax. You can work out the 'Profit Margin' by dividing this figure by Sales. After this comes the tax, leaving us with, not surprisingly, Profit After Tax (sometimes called 'Earnings'). It is this figure which is divided by the number of shares to leave us with Earnings Per Share. The following is a very basic example of how a company's profit and loss account might look. The company we've chosen is called Leather 'n' Lashes PLC, 'the riding crop of the connoisseur'. Their main line of business is, well, you can guess …

LEATHER 'N' LASHES PLC 2001 PROFIT AND LOSS ACCOUNT

		£ million	
	Sales	10,000	
(less)	Cost of Sales	6,000	
(equals)	Gross Profit	4,000	Gross Margin = 40.0%
(less)	Operating Expenses	2,400	
(equals)	Operating Profit	1,600	Operating Margin = 16.0%
(less)	Net Interest Costs	150	
(equals)	Profit Before Tax	1,450	Profit Margin = 14.5%
(less)	Tax	450	
(equals)	Profit After Tax	1,000	

Wow. Did you spot the amount of sales? £10 billion. Yikes, that's a lot of whips!

Sometimes companies decide to take both cost of sales and operating expenses away from their sales in one fell swoop, going straight to the operating profit. They're quite at liberty to do that, but this means that we only have the operating profit to look at, and as we saw earlier it is worth splitting out cost of sales and operating expenses as they both give useful information about what it's costing a company to get their product into your hands.

Anyway, however we've got there, we've arrived at the operating margin. We like the operating margin because it comes after all of a company's business costs have gone out the back door and therefore, unlike gross margin, it doesn't depend too much on what industry the company's in. On top of this, since it comes before a company has paid out things like interest and tax, the operating margin is an indicator of the business itself rather than the current financing and tax situation. For these reasons, operating margin is the measure that we tend to concentrate on (after giving the others a quick shufti). Generally speaking, we like to see an operating margin of at least 10 per cent, although 15 per cent is preferable. Upwards of 20 per cent is very good.

Margin is a good proxy for a company's return on capital, but it's far from perfect. By comparing companies on the basis of their margin, we're basically assuming that they employ the same amount of capital to generate the same amount of sales. While this is generally not a bad approximation, it can be a long way off for certain types of business. Supermarkets, for example, tend to have very low margins, of as little as five per cent or so, but they make up the slack, in terms of return on capital, because they're able to sell several times as much stuff as most companies, for the same amount of capital. When you buy something from Tesco, for example, there's a very good chance that it hasn't even yet paid its supplier for it. There's therefore less capital tied up in its business. Companies that are very 'capital-intensive', on the other hand, like an engineering business with all its factories and machinery, might need margins up around the 20 per cent level, to be making the same return on capital.

So margins get you a long way, but they're not perfect. Have a look at other companies in the same industry sector to give you an idea of what's normal. More importantly, think about why a particluar sector might need more or less capital than other areas to get an idea whether the typical margins across that sector are acceptable. Over the years, investors keep an eye on the different industries and will generally only give them the capital if they can offer decent returns. At the same time, more capital will get provided to industries that are making good returns, creating more competition and lowering the returns. On that basis, very broadly speaking, things should even out between different industries over the long term. That doesn't mean, though, that there aren't dud industry sectors. Airline companies, for example, have made notoriously poor returns over the years but, for whatever reason, competition remains as tough as ever.

When you're looking at a company's financial performance, all sorts of factors can come into play in any one year. If you're really serious about an investment, then you should take the time to look back at the figures for the last five or ten years and work out the margins for the same year (there should be a five or ten year record somewhere in the accounts). Perhaps also look at similar figures for competitors to see if they had especially good or bad years at the same time. Needless to say, you want your company to be doing slightly better in both the good and bad years.

Ideally we like to see stable and strong margins, but don't worry too much if one year is an aberration. It can be interesting and highly instructive, though, to think about why this might be the case.

Are they up to their eyebrows in debt?

There's good debt and there's bad debt for companies, just as there is for you. Having a mortgage makes sense because the interest rate you pay on that debt is relatively low and is financing a very necessary thing: your home. Having a mountain of high-interest credit card debt because you can't stop buying Armani shirts isn't so clever. What we really don't want is to find a great company that can't then sustain its position because it is having to spend all its cash paying interest on a large pile of debt. Plenty of companies carry a little bit of debt and this is OK. They borrow a comfortable amount to finance investment, because they are confident that the returns that they'll earn from that investment will outweigh the interest they have to pay. The companies *choose* to be in debt and it is called gearing.

Too much gearing can turn sour. Back to mortgages. Remember what happened to some householders in the negative equity saga of the early 1990s in Britain? In the late 80s, people bought houses with massive mortgages (property was booming, right?), only to watch the market crash. They struggled to pay the loan and meanwhile the asset on which it had been taken out was no longer worth that amount. All this would have been OK if they had been able to live through the downturn and take a long-term view of things. The lesson is to make sure that you don't overstretch yourself. You need to be able to live through a period of rising interest rates and falling house prices. If you can do this, everything should turn out rosy but, if you can't, then you might end up having your house repossessed and sold at precisely the wrong time. All this applies equally to companies. A highly geared (that is, highly indebted) company in an industry with highly volatile or cyclical profits like, say, the building industry, could be asking for trouble. Similarly, a company with too much debt might find its profits dipping rapidly if interest rates start to rise.

One of the simplest ways to look at how much a company is in hock is by looking at how many times over a company's operating profit (skip back to the previous section) will pay the interest on the loans it is carrying. This is called the 'Interest Cover' and, if you want to express it as a formula, it looks like this:

$$Interest\ Cover = Operating\ Profit / Net\ interest\ Cost$$

Net interest cost is the total amount of interest paid on any debt, less the interest received on any cash (or short-term investments) that the company might be holding. It's the figure that we subtracted from the operating profit to give us the profit before tax. Interest cover of 10 means that a company can pay the interest on its debt ten times over, which is easily comfortable enough for a company with fairly steady profits. Interest cover begins to concern us when it drops to below 5 or so. Less than this should certainly make you ask a few questions. For companies with very reliable and steady sources of income, it might be OK but, on the whole, it's probably best to stay clear.

Have they been a success up until now?

Success breeds success. While past success doesn't correlate infallibly with future success, it is an important indicator. It may be pretty Foolish of us to assert this in a world where ubiquitous legal disclaimers reinforce the idea that past performance is no guarantor of future performance, but we're going to do just that.

Any company that comes into consideration as an Obviously Great Investment should have been a success for many years, and that success will have carved them dominant industry positions which even further ensure their future success. As we have said before, business success, over the long term, will translate into share price success. If we have found an Obviously Great Investment, then it should, almost always, have a good track record of long-term share price growth. It's worth looking at several different time periods. Start by looking at the share price performance over the last ten years or even longer. Ideally, the share price will have grown steadily over the period but, the stock market being what it is, there will be plenty of ups and downs along the way. Although a ten-year price history is preferable, a five-year (or even shorter) period might be relevant where a company has changed greatly in the recent past or where it has only recently listed its shares on the stock market. However, you should always be wary of placing too much emphasis on short-term stock market movements.

The Internet is a good source of information on this type of thing. If you have a look at Appendix 4, you'll see a list of financial Web sites that provide this sort of information. The best ones will automatically give you a chart showing a share's price history over various periods. The Motley Fool Web site will do this for you and, naturally, we'd love it if you came over to our site and had a look. Try some of the other sites too, though, to see what they offer. Just don't forget to come back!

Basically, you're looking for long-term share price growth of about 10 per cent or more per year, on average. If the future were to continue in the same vein, then with our two or three extra per cent a year from dividends, we'd be doing pretty nicely.

Obviously Great Investments from previous editions

With all this in mind, let's now see if we can apply it to some actual companies. To start with, we can have a look at the companies which, we felt, met our criteria in the previous editions of this book. We started by making ten selections in the 1998 first edition, but we made a couple of changes when the second edition came out in 2000. The eight companies that we've stuck with for the whole four years, from 1998 to 2002, are set out in the following table.

Company	Price on 1/6/98	Price on 1/6/02	Gain/Loss %
AstraZeneca	2545p	3011p	+18.3
Ericsson*	420.9p	151.7p	-64.0
Glaxo	1638p	1404p	-14.3
Microsoft*	2550p	3479p	+36.4
Pizza Express	855p	660p	-22.8
SmithKline Beecham**	1439p	1404p	-2.4
Unilever	670.4p	636.2p	-5.1
Vodafone	137.6p	103.3p	-24.9
Average			-9.9
FTSE All Share			-11.2

* Prices converted to pounds sterling at prevailing exchange rates

** Prices adjusted for merger with Glaxo

We can see that it's been a ropey few years for the stock market overall, with the UK's broad market index, the FTSE All Share, falling by a little over 11 per cent over the four years. Not surprisingly, our obvious greats haven't escaped either, but the ones we've stuck with for the full four years have done marginally better than the index overall, with an average fall of just below 10 per cent. This average performance ranges from strong in the case of Microsoft to frankly dismal in the case of Ericsson and it all serves to underline what we said earlier about spreading your investments over a number of different companies.

We'd like to leave it at that, give ourselves a gentle pat on the back and move onto looking at the companies. Unfortunately, life's not as simple as that and we need to have a look at the changes we made for the second edition to give the complete picture.

The original 1998 selections included Marks & Spencer and Rentokil, the services company. For the second edition, in reviewing these selections, we decided that we'd made a mistake with them and that they should go. As we said about Marks & Spencer:

We'd say that it is an object lesson in what to do when an Obviously Great Investment becomes not so Obviously Great. You can't get it right all the time and if you no longer feel that a company fits the bill, then it's best to get rid of it and find something that does.

Cheap imports from overseas had introduced extreme competition to the High Street and Marks & Spencer began to look as if it was resting on its laurels. On top of that we felt that power had shifted in the overall clothes manufacture and retailing industry towards the clothes designers. Even though we felt that Marks & Spencer would ultimately pull itself out of the mire, it no longer had the strength to match our criteria, so out it went. Since then, the company has indeed made a revival and it may return to greatness, but there's certainly been nothing very obvious about it. Overall, Marks & Spencer was down 53 per cent when we booted it out in 2000 and has since recovered by 44 per cent. If we had held onto it throughout, then it would now be down 32 per cent.

When we reviewed Rentokil in 2000, we came to the conclusion that it didn't fit the third test 'is their position easily defended?'. The company had been a victim of its own success and many smaller competitors were moving in on its patch, undercutting the company on prices and putting pressure on profit margins. As with Marks & Spencer, it was open to debate whether the company would return to former glories but, in any event, there was no longer anything obvious about its merits, so out it went. As sod's law would have it, Rentokil has also made a strong recovery since we kicked it out. In 2000 it was down 64 per cent and, since then, it has bounced back by 83 per cent. If we had left it alone, it would now be down 34 per cent.

For replacements, we chose Diageo and ARM Holdings. We'll say a bit more about these two in a moment. For now, we're just interested in how they've done and, as ever, it's a case of swings and roundabouts. Diageo has risen by an excellent 50 per cent while ARM has fallen by a lamentable 71 per cent. Overall, if we treat the original 1998 selections as a portfolio, putting an equal amount into each company, selling Marks & Spencer and Rentokil in 2000 and replacing them with Diageo and ARM, then the portfolio would now be down by 20.5 per cent compared to the fall in the FTSE All Share index of just 11.2 per cent. If we hadn't made the changes, the portfolio would now be down 14.5 per cent.

Either way, our selections have underperformed the index over the four years since 1998. It's interesting to note, however, that we were comfortably ahead when the second edition came out in 2000 and we were still ahead in January 2002, when we produced an article on our web site following requests to review the performance. It goes to show the changes that can happen over the short-term. As we said in the second edition about the good performance up to 2000:

> *We are still at the stage when what's fashionable will have a greater effect on the share prices than how the underlying business is actually performing. Over the long term, though, business performance will take over as the principal driver of the share prices.*

It's just not Foolish, nor financially fattening in our opinion, to try to second guess what the market views as fashionable and it therefore makes no sense to focus on short-term share price movements. Of course we're up to four years now instead of just two, but we're still a long way from the long-term. Ultimately, it's a question of investing in businesses with strong consistent performances and being patient.

Yet, as you'll have noticed, we didn't show much patience with Marks & Spencer and Rentokil. Were we right to ditch them? It's a tricky question. You have to make a judgement about why you bought the shares in the first place and whether they still fit the bill according to those criteria. According to ours, they were no longer the solid companies that we thought they were and, that being the case, we were no longer confident about their long-term prospects. So we decided to change them in favour of companies we felt better about. We're still happy with the decisions that we made and would make them again. It's true that, as things have turned out, we'd have been better to have hung onto M&S and Rentokil, but a couple of years is a short time in the stock market. In the end, only time, and lots of it, will tell whether we got it right or not, but we're happy to be patient.

What about all the Obvious Greats from 2000, you ask, are they still so great? Is there more tinkering to do? Well there is a little bit. Let's take a look at the companies in turn.

AstraZeneca and GlaxoSmithKline

It's all been happening in the drugs industry. Zeneca has merged with Astra of Sweden to make AstraZeneca while Glaxo Wellcome and SmithKline Beecham have got together to form GlaxoSmithKline. There are several reasons why these companies are merging. First of all, they can make their research and development ('R&D') more effective by sharing resources and cutting out overlapping work. There is also the potential to cut costs in the marketing and distribution of their drugs. Another advantage of being big is that the greater your range of products on sale and in development, the smoother your growth is likely to be.

These companies have some excellent brands, and although most of them aren't really what you'd call 'consumer brands', there's also a sense in which they are. If your life has been saved by Zantac (a GlaxoSmithKline drug), you're unlikely to want to switch (now that Zantac's patent protection has expired) to generic ranitidine, which is the same drug manufactured by someone else and much, much cheaper. That means you're going to kick up a stink when your GP tries to change you from one to the other and she'll eventually give up. Although patents do obviously provide a protected revenue stream for the developing company in the early part of a drug's life, that revenue doesn't simply disappear when the drug comes off patent for the reasons just outlined. And it's not only patients who are emotional and a bit gullible. What about all that trash on your GP's desk? The drug companies spend millions marketing to doctors, who are highly susceptible to their blandishments. In terms of the future, the upcoming science of pharmacogenomics, which deals with the relationship between drugs and genes, holds tremendous promise, both for drug development and also, ultimately, for tailoring drug treatment to individuals.

One problem with drugs companies as investments is that their future prospects depend on them producing new big-selling drugs on a regular basis. Of course the bigger drugs companies, with their higher spending on research and development are more likely to achieve this, but even they have trouble from time to time. So it's difficult to pick the companies which will produce the goods. That was the reason for originally picking all three of Glaxo and SmithKline Beecham and Zeneca. As things have turned out, hedging our bets has paid off, since AstraZeneca is now viewed to have a stronger pipeline of new drugs in the offing than the combination of GlaxoSmithKline. That's the reason for AstraZeneca shares rising 18 per cent, while GlaxoSmith-Kline's have declined.

Taking this approach to extremes, where you fancy the prospects for a whole industry but can't be sure who the winners will be, you could invest in a tracker of that particular sector. For example, there is an exchange traded fund (see Chapter 17) that tracks all the big pharmaceuticals companies across Europe.

Anyway, we're confident about the prospects for the pharmaceutical industry, and we're confident that our representatives, AstraZeneca and GlaxoSmithKline will play a major part in its success.

Ericsson

Ericsson has been up and down like a yo-yo. It was selected in 1998 at 421p, promptly rocketed to about 1450p by 2000 before slumping down to just 152p. You'd be forgiven for thinking that something very funny has been going on and indeed it has. Ericsson was sucked squarely into the technology 'boom and bust' and much of the explanation for its wild share price swings can be found in Chapter 20, Six Lessons From The Technology Boom And Bust.

It's business performance, however, has also suffered a major loss of form. Having coughed up billions for their third generation mobile phone licences, much of it in borrowed money, the network operators have found it hard to find the money to build their funky new networks. Since a large part of Ericsson's range of products go into these networks, it hasn't been a pretty time for the company and for the year that ended on 25 January 2002, the company announced an operating loss of £1.3 billion.

The mobile phones division has suffered too from being unable to compete effectively with Nokia. The upshot has been the merging of Ericsson's mobile handset business with Sony's to form Sony Ericsson. We'll have to wait and see whether this improves the business' fortunes, but it's hardly operating from a position of strength.

Pretty much any way you look at it then, we'll have to put up our hands and say we picked the wrong horse. If there is an obvious great among mobile phone companies, then it's Nokia. Nokia has a stranglehold over the mobile phone handset market, where its brand weighs heavily in its favour, and it's been cutting into Ericsson's market as a supplier of the various gizmos that go into making the networks.

Of course it would have been nice to have worked all this out a couple of years ago when Ericsson's shares were still flying, but we didn't and there's no point crying over spilt milk. It's the way of things that everyone can make money when everything is looking rosy and it often takes a nasty recession to show where the strength really lies. Ericsson may recover, but its strength is far from obvious and it has to be for the chop.

Microsoft

Microsoft's business continues to go from strength to strength. While other software companies have been left wondering where their next profit is coming from, Microsoft saw its operating profits increase by 6 per cent in 2001, following an increase of 10 per cent in 2000. Overall, profits have more than doubled in the five years since 1997. It all stems from the company's world-beating Windows operating system, 'Office' products such as 'Word' and 'Excel' and the 'Internet Explorer' web browser.

Despite all this, it hasn't been an easy time for Microsoft. In a sense it's been a victim of its own success. So complete has its domination of the software market become that the US Justice Department has felt the need to intervene. Microsoft stands accused of abusing its strong market positions to undermine its competitors. Now many people would say, 'So what? Isn't this just what any company with a strong brand and market position would do? It's a free world, or at least it should be.' Others would say that Microsoft has behaved in such an underhand fashion that what it has done amounts to breaking a whole range of laws designed to prevent abuse of a monopoly position, and that's certainly the side on which the US Department of Justice has come down. The debates at the Motley Fool's discussion boards have been somewhat heated, as you can imagine, especially on the US site but also the UK, and there has been a series of articles on the issue.

At one point, it looked like the company might be forced to split in two, with the Windows operating system going into one company and the application and Internet software business going into another. Now it looks as though at least this has been avoided. As things stand at the moment, Microsoft has reached agreement with the US Department of Justice and nine individual States not to carry on with many of the activities that had been the cause of complaint. Proceedings with other States continue, but most commentators agree that Microsoft looks like emerging from the mess relatively unscathed.

Problems might arise for Microsoft in the future as computing evolves away from the desktop PC, but there are millions of PCs and laptops around the world using Microsoft products and it's hard to imagine that they'll disappear just like that. In any event, Microsoft has shown itself to be quick to spot and take advantage of developing industry trends.

All in all, Microsoft is amongst the world's most dominant businesses and it's hard to see an end to that. It stays in.

Pizza Express

After talking about such global giants as GlaxoSmithKline, Ericsson and Microsoft, it seems a bit odd, at first, to move on to Pizza Express. Let's have another look at whether it fits the criteria. First of all, does it have a strong brand? To this, global giant or not, we have to answer yes. Although the brand is, at present, mostly limited to the UK, it is undoubtedly strong here. Few people in the southeast have not heard of Pizza Express and most have tried their products. Penetration throughout the rest of the country is more limited, but the company appears to be succeeding in extending the brand into other regions without affecting its reputation for quality. What about best in business? Well, at the simplest level, that of pizza restaurants in the UK, Pizza Express stands head and shoulders above the competition. In fact, even if we extend this to include UK restaurants generally, Pizza Express comes out favourably as one of the few chains that give the impression of being master of its own destiny.

On the financial tests, Pizza Express also scores highly. In the five years to 2001 profits have more than doubled from £15.6 million to £40.0 million, with a margin consistently around 22 per cent, as the group has expanded its estate of restaurants aggressively.

The slightly awkward question for Pizza Express is revealed by the third test – is their position easily defended? Whether they can defend their position depends, primarily, on whether the consistency of the offering can be maintained as the brand is extended throughout the UK and overseas. In the

UK, the company has an exceptional track record in this respect and we're confident of continued success. However, the requirements of overseas markets are subtly different from the UK and it remains to be seen whether Pizza Express can take account of the differences whilst maintaining its reputation for quality. At the moment the signs are reasonably positive. However, we accept that this is one that needs watching quite closely and, if you're looking for investments that you can safely tuck away and not worry yourself about, then this might not be one of them.

The performance of the shares had been following the business upwards, with a peak of around 950p last year. Since then, however, the company has been affected by the slowdown in sales, particularly in the London market. With dreary statements emanating from other restaurant operators we view this as a short-term phenomenon affecting the whole industry and are more than happy to keep faith with the company's long-term record of success.

Unilever

Unilever owns some of the greatest consumer brands in the world. These include Hellmann's mayonnaise, Bird's Eye fish fingers, Lipton teas, Magnum ice cream, Domestos bleach, Persil and Omo washing powders, Vaseline care products, Signal toothpaste and Calvin Klein fragrances to name a few. This is what we liked about the company two years ago and four years ago and it still is. However, when we originally picked them, we had this to say about their margins:

> 'To be honest, this isn't where Unilever shines. Over the last few years, before tax they've been making around 8 to 9 pence on every pound, but only about 5 pence after taxes. Yikes!'

We're pleased to be able to report good news on the margins front. In February 2000, the group announced its Path to Growth initiative, aimed to speed growth in profits and improve margins by cutting costs and focusing on higher margin products. The costs of the restructuring have been pretty hefty, with £2.0 billion spent in 2000 and £588m spent in 2001, but it does seem to be having the desired effect. Excluding the restructuring costs, margins have ticked up to around 11 per cent for each of the last two years and profits have grown by 16 per cent and then 9 per cent. The ideal business doesn't need to go through restructurings, but 'ideal' doesn't exist. We take comfort in the fact that Unilever is, by focusing on its strongest margins, seeking to improve the things that we see as important. Over the long-term we'd expect it to continue with its record of steady progress and it stays in.

Vodafone

It's been an extraordinary few years for the telecommunications industry and Vodafone has been in the thick of it. First there was the acquisition of Airtouch to give the company a large slice of the US market and then it bought Mannesmann to fill in the gaps in continental Europe. This was followed by the £6 billion purchase of a licence to operate a third-generation mobile phone network in the UK and several billions more to do the same overseas. Unfortunately, all this is mostly by way of jockeying for position for the expected (by Vodafone at least) explosion in wireless data services. A couple of years down the line and it hasn't happened yet and investors are beginning to doubt that it will. This has been reflected in the share price, which after peaking at nearly 400p in 2000, has sunk back to just 103p.

At the root of it all is the wireless Internet, which will give us the means of doing all sorts of wonderful things on the move. We might, for example, want to watch the highlights of last night's football game while we journey to work or we might want to know whether our train is going to be late or we might just want to know where the nearest Chinese restaurant is. The truth is that no one really knows what we're likely to want to do with the wireless Internet, but those in favour are convinced that it offers to add much value to our lives for us not to want to do something with it. Others will say that we can do most things that we want to do with the phones we have at the moment.

We'd place ourselves in the optimistic camp. It's always hard to say where new technology is going to take us, but there's a big shift going on and it's got to take us somewhere. Wherever that place is, Vodafone, as the world's leading mobile network operator, is likely to be sitting there ready to take our money.

ARM Holdings

ARM Holdings designs computer chips. In fact, it designs 'processor cores': the bit of a computing system which executes instructions. You can think of it as being a bit like the brain. It's important to note that ARM doesn't actually make chips, it just designs them and leaves the sometimes awkward task of manufacturing them to others. We like this, because it is in designing things that the real value is added: manufacturing chips is a skilled business, but not half as creative or original as actually designing the things.

Where ARM excels is in the design of small, cheap, efficient processors which only need a little power to drive them and which do not get too warm while they're working. Currently, the most obvious place to find this type of chip is in mobile phones, of which around 80 per cent already carry ARM-designed chips, but there are many other potential markets: cars, 'smartcards', cameras, microwave ovens, anywhere where you need a little bit of basic computing power. For this type of application, ARM-designed chips offer an unrivalled balance of performance, cost and efficiency.

From a business perspective, not much has changed for ARM over the last couple of years, notwithstanding a major downturn in the global semiconductor industry. The company still dominates its markets. If anything, you might say that its position has strengthened. It's also making plenty of money for its efforts, with profit before tax increasing from £18m in 1999 to £50m in 2001 and operating margins standing at an exceptional 31 per cent.

So, in light of all this, how come the share price has dropped by 70 per cent since we wrote about it in June 2000? It all comes down to valuation and investor sentiment. Even though the company has done extremely well over the last couple of years, it was expected to do just that and the valuation that was placed on the company in June 2000, a PE ratio of almost 500, demanded it (remember PE ratios from the previous chapter?). Not only that, but investors were expecting this phenomenal performance to continue long into the future. Nowadays, in the 'post-bubble' stock market, investors aren't prepared to look that far ahead for profits, so the company's PE ratio has dropped down to around 50.

If you remember from earlier in this chapter, we're looking for companies with very promising prospects for growth long into the future, because we believe that the stock market often has difficulty in giving this type of company the valuation it deserves. What we've seen with ARM is that this is not always the case. Back in 2000, investors were more than happy to pay up for profits that were way off in the distant future. On that basis, looking back now, the company's shares were probably overpriced, although we will have to wait many years to be sure about that.

What we can say now is that the stock market is showing some signs of returning to, what we would say, is its more normal myopic state, where a profit isn't a profit unless it was made last year and is sitting in the bank. That's a natural reaction to the excesses that we've seen in the last few years and it's probably a good thing. At least it should make for a better environment for investing in solid growing companies.

We'll say more about the technology bubble and what can be learnt from it in Chapter 20. For the moment, we'll leave ARM by saying that it continues to perform exceptionally well on the business front and there are few reasons to doubt that this will continue. We're more than happy to stick with it.

Diageo

The other new company that we included in the 2000 edition of this book was the drinks company, Diageo. Diageo owns a whole raft of premium drinks brands, including Bell's, Johnnie Walker and J&B whiskies, Gilbey's, Gordon's, and Tanqueray gins, Smirnoff vodka, Captain Morgan rum and Guinness. On top of this, it owns Burger King and has a part-ownership of a range of food brands, including Green Giant and Häagen-Dazs. The company has an overall plan of exiting its food businesses, including Burger King, although it is taking them some time to do it. We're very happy with that strategy, since it's the spirits brands that are strongest and they carry higher margins.

Over the last couple of years, the business has maintained its solid performance, with profit increasing by 12% between the financial years ending in 1999 and 2001. Group operating margins remain at a little over 16 per cent. The one major weak spot is Burger King, where profits have declined since 1999. We can overlook that, since it counts for less than 10 per cent of overall profits and will hopefully be leaving the group soon (although the poor performance is getting in the way of a sale).

This time, we're pleased to say that this performance has been duly reflected in a strong share price performance, with a rise of 50 per cent over the two years. In fact, if anything, Diageo has benefited from the reverse effect to ARM, with investors now apparently prepared to credit the company with better prospects for growth. Anyway, nothing has happened in the last couple of years to change our positive views on the company and we're more than happy to stick with it.

Show Us Some More Companies Fools!

So times have moved on from 2000 and we've ended up ditching Ericsson from our list of companies. We can take a look now at some companies to replace it.

Cadbury Schweppes

How about Cadbury Schweppes? The brands that make up its name have been around for a couple of hundred years and, if it makes sense to stick to what you know, then most of us will be on safe ground here — whether through a sneaky bar of Dairy Milk on the way home or a relaxing gin and tonic when we get there. The group's modern history began with the merger of Cadburys and Schweppes in 1969. This set in motion a period of expansion around the world, culminating in the acquisition of, amongst other things, Dr Pepper/7UP in 1994, Snapple beverages in 2000 and the soft drinks businesses of Pernod Ricard in 2001. Various brands have also been sold, to leave the group focused on Europe, North America and Australia.

After all the comings and goings, the group now comprises, amongst other things, Dr. Pepper (apparently they love it in America), 7UP, Snapple, Schweppes, Orangina and Canada Dry on the beverages side and Cadburys Dairy Milk, Cadburys Creme Egg, Roses, Flake, Crunchie and Wispa on the confectionary side. No wonder the company says its mission is to bring the world 'moments of delight'.

Overall, the company is pretty evenly split between Europe and North America, although the European business is heavily focused on confectionary, while the North American business is concentrated on beverages. So, in terms of sales, you get 39 per cent from North American beverages, 6 per cent American confectionary, 28 per cent Europe confectionary and 10 per cent Europe beverages. Asia Pacific, mostly Australia, chips in with 12 per cent of sales and the loose 5 per cent is 'other'.

1. Have They Built A Strong Brand?
For sure – quite a few of them in fact.

2. Are They Best In Their Business?
Few people would suggest that Cadburys is the best chocolate in the world, but that's hardly the point. We're thinking of investing in it, not eating it, so forget the best chocolate, what we're after is the strongest chocolate business. In this respect as well, Cadburys has some real competition from the likes of Nestle, the owner of Kit Kat, Yorkie and Nestle Crunch, and Hersheys, which is 'big in America'. And then you've got Mars. When you walk into a newsagents and stand before that mound of sweeties, Cadburys might be prominent, especially in this country, but it's a long way from being the only game in town. The most we can say for Cadburys here is that it might be up there in a tie for first place.

At first sight, you'd have to be even more worried about the beverages businesses, with Coca-Cola and Pepsi appearing on the horizon. As well as the eponymous colas they each own a wide range of other soft drink brands, with Coke speaking for Fanta, Sprite and Powerade, while Pepsi can lay claim to Mountain Dew and Lipton's Ice Tea. Every cloud has a silver lining, though, and here it's the fact that Cadbury Schweppes is particularly strong in certain niche areas. The likes of Coke and Pepsi are undoubtedly fearsome competitors, but they don't have a chance against Schweppes in the market for tonic water. You need to ask where the battleground begins and ends. Some drinks compete broadly across the market, while others sit neatly in their niches, giving them a strong position to fight off would-be intruders.

While Schweppes and Canada Dry occupy strong niches, products like Dr Pepper and 7UP compete more obviously with the likes of Coke, Pepsi, Fanta and Sprite in the market to quench our thirst. And they do so from a position of weakness. So, overall, there are some good points and some not so good. Unfortunately, in terms of scale, the good bits are outweighed by the not so good.

3. Is Their Position Easily Defended?

The long history of the main Cadbury Schweppes brands provides some confidence about defending them. The advantage here for the incumbent brands is in the constant repeat purchasing of their products. Every time you buy a bottle of Schweppes tonic or a Cadburys Creme Egg, the company has an opportunity to develop its relationship with you and this makes it incredibly difficult for would-be competitors to break into the market. So we need to look again at the overall balance of the different markets. If you want tonic water, then tonic water is what you want and Coca-Cola, no matter how well it's marketed, won't get a look in. So Schweppes is incredibly well defended. The likes of Dr Pepper and 7UP, however, have more to worry about.

In confectionary, the different product types compete against each other more or less head to head. So, to say that Cadburys dominates the small confectionary egg market, or whatever you might call it, doesn't get us very far since people might easily decide to have a Mars bar instead.

Given the long history of most of the brands, it would be churlish not to give Cadbury Schweppes a tick here. But we've already seen that there are competitors that can probably defend themselves even better. It may well be that they'd make the better investments.

4. Are They Making A Lot Of Money For Their Efforts

Looking at the 2001 year, the group made a healthy operating margin of 16.9 per cent overall. By looking at 'note 1' to the group's accounts, we can break this down into the different areas. In beverages, the group made an excellent operating margin of 23.1 per cent, while on the confectionary side it only managed 13.9 per cent. This would seem to suggest that the beverages businesses have the greater overall quality.

Looking back over the last eight years since the acquisition of Dr Pepper/ 7Up (from the 'Financial Record' section of the group's accounts) we see the 2001 margin of 16.9 per cent was preceded by 16.9 per cent in 2000, 16.2 per cent in 1999, 15.4 per cent in 1998, 14.7 per cent in 1997, 13.8 per cent in 1996, 13.4 per cent in 1995 and 12.0 per cent in 1994. A pattern seems to be emerging. Rising margin must be seen as a good thing — after all, it means you're gradually doing better and better — it does, though, give some cause for concern since it suggests that the business was not firing on all cylinders a few years back. If it's performed badly before, then it will probably do so again. We'd certainly rather see rising margins than falling margins but, on the whole, we'd like to see them consistently high.

It's interesting to investigate why the group margins have been on the up. In this case, the two main divisions, North America Beverages and Europe Confectionary have actually had pretty stable margins over the full eight years. What's made the difference is that the higher-margin North American Beverages business has been growing much more quickly than the lower-margin Europe Confectionary business, so that it now has more impact on the overall results. Since 1994, Europe Confectionary has grown at just 3 per cent per year and has shrunk from 40 per cent of group sales to just 28 per cent. North America Beverages, meanwhile, has been growing at 22 per cent per year, taking its share of group sales from 17 per cent up to 39 per cent in 2001.

Chiefly this change in emphasis derives from the acquisitions and disposals that the group is making. Ideally it would have come mostly from the existing group businesses getting bigger, but you can't have everything. It's encouraging, though, in any case to see the group concentrating on its higher margin businesses.

5. Are They Up To Their Eyebrows In Debt?

Looking at the accounts again, we see that the group had a total of £2.1 billion in debt at the end of 2001 and that during the year it had to pay £106 million in interest compared to its operating profit of £831 million. So the interest bill is 'covered' about 8 times by operating profits. For a company with such stable profits (people still guzzle chocolate and soft drinks in a recession), that's more than comfortable.

6. Have They Been A Success Up To Now?

If we go back ten years to 1st June 1992, Cadburys share price was 219p compared to 500p now. That represents growth of 8.6 per cent per year, compared to the FTSE All Share increasing by 5.5 per cent per year over that period. On top of this, the group has been paying dividends of a few per cent per year, to give total annual returns of perhaps 10 per cent per year. It isn't setting the world on fire, but it's a steady performance.

Overall, Cadbury Schweppes has some excellent brands, some of which dominate attractive niches, but most of which are more general in nature and a little weaker. It's these weaker areas that worry us. Competing with companies like Coca-Cola is only for the very brave and, while we wish the company well, it doesn't quite fit the bill. Let's try again.

Sage

Sage Group is the world's leading supplier of accounting, payroll and business software to small and medium-sized businesses. There are several factors making this an attractive market. First and foremost, by enabling its customers to organise their business effectively and cheaply, it adds plenty of value. Beyond this, though, there is sustainability. Once you've installed Sage's payroll software, for example, it's going to give your business a major headache to switch to something else. When the time comes to buy a more sophisticated accounting product, there's also a fair chance that you'd prefer, other things being equal, to go with the company whose product you already use. As your business grows, Sage will be there to provide you with a new line of software and, unless and until they muck you about, they're likely to be the first port of call.

Naturally, Sage goes to a lot of trouble not to muck its customers about. As part of this, the company offers ongoing service contracts so that customers can keep in touch and learn how to use the software more effectively. This gives Sage the opportunity to consolidate and develop its customer relationships, but it's also a nice earner. In fact, it's now the core part of Sage's business, with 68 per cent of the company's revenue coming from its installed base of 2.8 million customers around the world.

So, whilst Sage is fundamentally a software company, it goes a lot further than that. The company's real strength is in the service it can provide businesses as they develop. There's obvious added value and, for the reasons already explained, it has a very sustainable quality. It's also fair to say that providing the technology to help businesses improve their efficiency is nothing if not a growth market.

1. Have They Built A Strong Brand?

It might not be well-known to consumers, but in the world of back office business administration, particularly in the UK, Sage has built a fantastic brand. In addition to Sage itself, the group owns several other brands that lead in their various markets around the world, such as Peachtree and Ciel, which are leading suppliers of accounting software in the US and France respectively. The stable of brands was improved during the last financial year, with the acquisition of Interact Commerce Corporation, which brought with it the market-leading ACT! customer relationship management soft-ware (as well as around 3 million new customers).

The high proportion of revenues coming from its installed base of customers is a testament to the strength of Sage's brands. It also, of course, introduces a degree of 'repeat purchasing' that should help the company sustain the brands. Through repeat sales, ongoing service contracts, not to mention the daily usage of its branded products, Sage keeps itself firmly in the mind of a loyal customer base and that's just what we like to see.

2. Are They Best In Their Business?

Just as with Cadbury Schweppes, there are difficulties over how we define the market. Is the battleground the market for software generally, or for business administration software or for supplying business administration software to small and medium-sized businesses? In the first case, there are some truly mighty companies, such as Microsoft and Oracle for starters. There are also some very big players in the market for business administra-tion software, such as SAP and Peoplesoft, but these companies are mostly geared to providing solutions for larger companies. Sage's market, focusing on the smaller businesses, is different because it involves a greater degree of hand holding. Its customers need more help in deciding which product would suit them and they need more ongoing service once the software is installed. This greater service element involves different skills and it's where Sage shines. There is competition at this end of the market too, most notable from Intuit's 'Quickbooks', but if you had to choose a market leader in the small and medium sized business section, it would have to be Sage.

In the UK, Sage is undoubtedly top dog. The same can probably be said of France, but in the other important markets of Germany and the United States, it's merely one of a number of significant companies. The biggest problem is the US, where the mighty Microsoft recently marched straight onto Sage's territory with the purchase of Great Plains and Navision. Microsoft said at the time:

> This combination of Great Plains and Microsoft allows us to dramatically accelerate our vision of being the leader in providing interconnected business management solutions to small and mid-sized customers.

Sage might have a large base of installed users, but it's nothing to what Microsoft has through its Windows and Microsoft Office products. This brings us on to the third test...

3. Is Their Position Easily Defended?

The appearance of Microsoft on the scene throws this into some doubt, for the United States market at the very least. It's not by accident that the word 'interconnected' finds its way into the earlier quote from Microsoft. The company has built itself on bundling products together. It can be handy for consumers, but it can also stifle competition. Whatever the rights and wrongs, Microsoft has recently had its knuckles rapped over this. So we know two things. First of all, Microsoft is more than capable of using its established positions in the software market to further its other product areas and secondly, that it will have to tread carefully in future. How this will work out in the case of business administration software for small business is anyone's guess.

As we saw earlier, though, there is more to this market than just selling software. It's more of a service market and it's questionable how good Microsoft is at dealing with that side of things. If you've ever used a Microsoft product, you'll probably be aware of their reputation for doing the unexpected at times and the after-sales service is a long way less than perfect.

So can Microsoft steamroller into this market? We think that it will find the going tough. At the very least it might need a change of emphasis from marketing to service. Sage, meanwhile, has been busy perfecting this end of the market for many years. However the position in North America develops, Sage has some very strong and defensible positions in the UK and Europe and these markets produced 65 per cent of Sage's profits in 2001. We'll need to keep an eye on Microsoft, but we're happy to give Sage a tick here.

4. Are They Making A Lot Of Money For Their Efforts

In the year to 30 September 2001, Sage managed an operating margin of 27 per cent and it's been consistently at around the 25 per cent mark for the last five years. So we can say quite comfortably that they're making a lot of money for their efforts.

Looking at the different parts of the world, the UK business made a 2001 operating margin of an astonishing 38 per cent, while the figures for mainland Europe and the United States were 26 per cent and 20 per cent respectively. That confirms what we've said about the relative strengths of the different areas. Even so, a margin of 20 per cent in the US is not to be sniffed at. It just suffers by comparison to the company's incredibly strong franchise in the UK.

5. Are They Up To Their Eyebrows In Debt?

Looking at the company's accounts, Sage had £191m of net debt at September 2001 and it paid about £7m in net interest during the year. That would amount to an interest rate of just 3.7 per cent and, since that's less than it costs the Government to borrow money, we can deduce that something funny is going on. Looking more closely at the accounts, we can see that most of the debt relates to money borrowed during the year to pay for the acquisition of Interact Commerce Corporation. So all the debt is there at the end of the year, but there isn't a full year of interest costs in the profit and loss account. Assuming an interest rate of 7 per cent (the accounts refer to some of the debt having an interest rate of 6.77 per cent so we shouldn't be far off), we'd expect an annual charge of £13.4 million compared to its operating profit of £128 million. So the interest bill is covered nearly ten times by operating profit. That's plenty.

6. Have They Been A Success Up To Now?

Along with all companies that have anything to do with 'technology', Sage shares have had a nasty time over the last couple of years, falling from a peak of 913p in to 176.5p at the time of writing. With the company's profits grow-ing by 65 per cent since 1999, however, we can reasonably put this down to the market's changing fashions. Looking at the longer term, Sage has seen its shares rise from 9.4p since June 1992 to give an annual growth rate of 34 per cent. 'Nuff said.

With one or two caveats, Sage dominates a very attractive market. In the UK it's making money hand over fist and even where it's weaker it makes healthy profits. All this has contributed to make it a phenomenal investment in the past and we see no reason for this to end. We see it as an Obviously Great Investment. How about another?

HSBC

If we're trying to find companies that will be the engine of future economic growth, we could do a lot worse than look at a company that will probably provide the funding for a lot of it. HSBC, as one of the world's largest banks, is in prime position to do this. The group has evolved from the Hongkong and Shanghai Banking Corporation and is now spread over 81 countries around the world. Profits, however, are still focused on Hong Kong (44 per cent of 2001 group profit) and Europe (48 per cent), which was boosted by the acquisition of Midland Bank in 1992. The remaining Asia-Pacific area contributed 12 per cent of 2001 profits and North America chipped in 7 per cent, while Latin America made a loss, sucking out 11 per cent of profits on account of the economic crisis in Argentina. Anyway, that's enough pre-amble, let's run them through the sieve.

1. Have They Built A Strong Brand?
No one in HSBC's biggest markets, the UK and Hong Kong, can have failed to come across the brand and, although it's less conspicuous around the rest of the world, this is beginning to change. In 1999 an initiative was launched to bring all of the group's operations around the world under the umbrella of the one HSBC brand. The bank aims to be seen as a global force whilst under-standing the local characteristics of different markets and there is, indeed, an advertising campaign in progress to promote just this. It may not be Coca-Cola but, in the financial world, HSBC is about as big a brand as they come.

2. Are They Best In Their Business?
This one's a little more tricky. HSBC is some way from being the biggest bank in the world. In terms of total assets, it stands 6th on the global list behind Mizuho Group, Citigroup, Deutsche Bank, JP Morgan and Bank of Tokyo-Mitsubishi. Total assets, however, only tells part of the story and on the more

important measure of profits, HSBC sneaks into second place with overall annual profit before tax of £5.6 billion, behind Citigroup of the US which made a whopping £15.1 billion in 2001. Now size certainly isn't everything but, in the business of banking, it's undoubtedly important.

The redeeming feature is that Citigroup and HSBC largely focus on different geographical areas. While HSBC is big in Europe and the Asia-Pacific, Citigroup is heavily focused on North America. So with which areas would you most like your investment to be involved? HSBC's presence in Hong Kong and the Far East gives it potential for growth in the emerging economies of that area, but there is undoubtedly more risk.

Of course, even within HSBC's strongest markets, there is competition. The regulatory authorities will see to that. In the UK, competitors include the other big high street banks and, in the Far East, there's Standard Chartered and the big Japanese banks. Overall, we'll give HSBC a hesitant tick on this. There is undoubtedly powerful competition, but HSBC is as strong as any one in its main markets.

3. Is Their Position Easily Defended?

Although there are a number of major players, their identities rarely seem to change, except by way of takeovers and mergers. Looking at the UK banking market, for example, the main players of yesteryear, Barclays, Lloyds, Midland and NatWest are all still there in some shape or form. Midland, the one which HSBC acquired, was originally founded in 1836. The Hongkong and Shanghai Banking Corporation itself was established in 1865. So there's certainly a degree of staying power.

One fly in the ointment for HSBC might be the takeover of Hong Kong by China in 1997. It's hard to know what to make of this. On the one hand, their presence in China presents opportunities for growth while, on the other, there are risks in having such a large portion of group assets and profit located in what is now a communist country – notwithstanding what China have said about Hong Kong continuing to operate as a free market economy.

4. Are They Making A Lot Of Money For Their Efforts

In terms of how they make their money, banks are slightly different from other companies. Instead of making something and selling it, they essentially borrow money and lend it out. This means that the profit margins that you'd normally look at are somewhat confused. The nice thing about banks is that they lend themselves better to looking at the return on assets which, you'll remember from our introduction of the tests, is really the bottom line. Banks come into their own on this measure, because it's much easier to value their assets than it is for other types of business. After all, if a bank lends you £1,000, then it has an asset of £1,000 that it can point to. The only problem is that you might not pay it back, but banks do so much lending that they have a very good feel for how much of their loans will not get paid back. It's called making provision for bad debts and involves a fair bit of chicanery but there's not much in it for the banks to try to flatter themselves because the truth will out in the end.

Anyway, as we've said, a bank borrows money and lends it out. At the same time, it will have a little pot of cash on the side for emergencies. At any point in time, you'd hope that what it has lent out, plus any cash, comes to more than it has borrowed because otherwise it would be, er, bust. The difference between the two is the net assets and it's what represents the shareholders' own money, as it were. Still with us? So the return on net assets is a measure of how much profit the bank is making on it's shareholder's money and you get it by dividing the profit by the bank's net assets.

Looking at HSBC's 2001 results, we can see a profit after tax of £3.8 billion and net assets (also known as shareholders' funds) of £32 billion. So that gives us...3.8 divided by 32...12 per cent, near enough. So, for every pound of the bank's net assets, it generated 12p in 2001, after tax. That sounds all right, but comparing it with the figures for other banks, for example Barclays made 17 per cent and Citigroup 18 per cent, it becomes apparent that something's not right.

Looking at the five year summary of results in HSBC's annual report and accounts, we see that 2001 represents something of a blip since return on shareholders' funds was 17 per cent in 2000, 18 per cent in 1999, 16 per cent in 1998 and an excellent 21 per cent in 1997. So what was the problem in 2001? Looking at the financial review in the accounts, we find this:

HSBC's attributable profit of US$5,406 million in 2001 was 18 per cent lower than 2000 principally as a result of an exceptional charge of US$1,120 million

relating to the situation in Argentina, providing for the Princeton Note settle-
ment, and after absorbing a US$282 million increase in goodwill amortisation
due to the recent acquisitions.

The 'Princeton Note settlement' is explained in a 'legal proceedings' section of the accounts and relates to the activities of Republic New York Corporation before it was taken over by HSBC in 1999. In fact, HSBC was aware of the legal proceedings at the time of the takeover and went ahead anyway. The proceedings have now largely been settled. As to Argentina, you'd have to say that this is the risk of banking in emerging markets and that's something that HSBC does plenty of. So you're going to get these hiccups from time to time. As long as they don't become too regular, or too severe, we're relatively relaxed about it and look forward to getting back to returns in the upper teens.

5. Are They Up To Their Eyebrows In Debt?

Well yes, of course they are up to their eyebrows in debt! They owe money to every current account holder for starters (the ones in credit anyway). In fact, the bank owes £310 billion on customer accounts and about £448 billion in all. Of course the flip side of this is that it has £480 billion in assets, leaving the £32 billion that we saw earlier for shareholders. It's a fairly fine line, but that's the nature of banking and, again, we're going to have to modify our test a little.

What we're worried about, of course, is that the company doesn't go bust and you won't be surprised to hear that the banking authorities around the world are pretty keen on it not going bust as well. For this reason, they specify certain 'capital ratios' which are intended to make sure that banks stay well within themselves. These are now enshrined in the Basel Capital Accord of 2001 and, as is the way of these things, they're horribly complex. You can skip the next paragraph if you like (it's pretty dull), but we'll try to give a small taste of what's involved.

Essentially, a bank's capital is split into two categories: 'tier one capital' and 'total capital'. Tier one capital is, with one or two tweaks, the sharehold-ers' funds that we talked about earlier. Total capital is a looser definition and includes the tier one capital plus, without wanting to get into too much detail, a few other things. You then add up all of the bank's assets (mostly the loans it makes), adjusted to take account of their risk, to give something called 'risk-weighted assets'. The Basel Accord says that your total capital has to come to at least 8 per cent of your 'risk-weighted assets' (the 'total capital ratio') and that your tier one capital has to come to at least 4 per cent of your 'risk-weighted assets' (the tier one capital ratio).

Now it's way beyond anyone but the banks themselves and their regulators to do this sort of calculation, but it does at least give us some benchmarks to measure our bank against. HSBC declares confidently in its 2001 accounts that it has a tier one capital ratio of 9.0 per cent and a total capital ratio of 13.0 per cent. It also goes on to say that it uses 'a benchmark tier one capital ratio of 8.0 per cent in considering its long term capital planning'. So, on the face of it the bank is well within what's required. We can also get some confidence from looking at other banks to see where they stand and we find that Barclays and Citigroup both have slightly lower ratios. In 2001, Barclays had a tier one ratio of 7.8% and a total capital ratio of 12.5 per cent, while for Citigroup the figures are 8.3 per cent and 12.4 per cent.

So banks aren't easy to measure on a debt basis but, keeping things simple, we can see that HSBC is well within industry standards. That's enough for us.

6. Have They Been A Success Up To Now?
After all that banking guff, we're delighted to end up with the simple question 'have the shares been a good investment over the years'. To that we have to answer an unqualified yes. The shares have risen from 111p in 1992 to 850p now, to give annual growth of about 23 per cent per year. On top of that there have been dividends of a few per cent each year, giving a total annual return in the mid to high 20's – very nice indeed.

It's been awkward applying our tests to HSBC, but banks do make up nearly 20 per cent of the UK stock market by market capitalisation and they've tended to make good investments in the past. So, in this the third edition of the book, we thought we'd branch out a little. What we end up with is a bank that has strong and sustainable positions in its main markets and is making plenty of money as a result, notwithstanding the occasional hiccup. It probably carries a little more risk than some other banks because of its exposure to emerging markets, but this also provides opportunities for growth and HSBC does have a decent spread of risk around the world.

If we did need our arms to be twisted, it would come from the 4 per cent dividend yield that the shares currently offer. Providing the dividend isn't reduced (an unusual, though not unknown, event for a bank), we'd be doing better with HSBC than with cash in the bank even without any growth in the share price and that provides a certain level of comfort. As it happens, though, we'd expect the dividend to grow at least in line with average earnings growth. A decent yield with growth at least in line with average earnings is the basis for the excellent performance from the stock market in the past and HSBC looks the part for the future. All in all, we see it as an Obviously Great Investment.

To Sum Up On Obvious Greats

With the notable exception of Ericsson, we're still pretty happy with the companies we picked out as Obvious Greats in the first two editions of this book. On top of these, we'd add a couple more: Sage and HSBC. We're tempted by Cadburys as well, but the group falls down because of the mighty competition it faces. We'll be watching the progress of these and other companies on our website over the coming years. Why not come and join us? It beats the hell out of watching 'Newsnight'.

The Six Obviously Not Great Qualities

As well as looking at a number of Obviously Great Investments in previous editions, we've also looked at six companies that we felt were just as obviously *bad* investments. The reason that we picked them out is that they comprehensively failed one (or more) of our tests for greatness. In fact, they failed the tests so badly that, in our eyes, that made them Obviously Bad. When we reviewed this ragbag, two years ago, we found that every single company had fallen, with an average of minus 40 per cent. Pretty bad investments, then. However, after two years, there was little room for smugness and we said at the time:

We must, as ever, point out that it is still early days: two years isn't nearly enough to decide on how well an investment has performed.

We're pleased to have made this point back then because, as things have turned out, our selection of Obviously Bad Investments have done rather well over the last couple of years, with an average gain of 60 per cent. In some senses, they've been enjoying the opposite fate to the high growth companies. While growth was in fashion back in 2000, the cheap shares, with none of our favoured qualities, had probably been overpunished. And while money has been running away from the growth investments, it's been finding a home among some of the more ropey, though cheaply priced companies.

The best we can say about it, is that every dog has its day. And for the lower quality companies, their day has managed to stretch out for a couple of years now and we're still counting. The trouble is that it's very difficult to predict when these periods are going to occur. Of course it looks obvious now that this was set to happen, but it didn't at the time, which was why everyone was piling their money into the high growth shares. Fashions change in the stock market and rarely before have they changed as rapidly as in the last two years.

So, does this mean that it no longer makes sense to invest in the quality long-term performers that we've been looking at? Is it now time to make a switch and start investing in the lower quality businesses that don't dominate their markets and that don't have control over their destiny? Certainly not! If anything, making such a switch after a period of resurgence in those types of company is just the wrong time to do it. Yet we'd say that they might continue to do well in the near future. As we've said before, we just don't claim to have a clue about the stock market's short-term fashions. The whole basis of Foolish investing is to let the crowds chase each other around while sitting back confident that the strongest businesses, with the best scope for profitable growth, will provide the best returns over the long term. Nothing has changed. In particular, investing in the stock market requires as much patience now as it ever did.

Anyway, after those various excuses, we can look at some of these obviously bad qualities. As we said, they're the opposite of our tests for Obvious Greatness, so we start with not having built a strong brand.

No strong brand – Corus Group

If you don't have a strong brand, then you risk falling into the gloomy world of commodity products. These nasty things exist when there is nothing to differentiate one company's products from another's. The result is that all the sellers in a particular market compete with each other only on price. Not surprisingly, it's pretty tough for anyone to make much of a profit in these circumstances. Things like metals and cocoa beans are commodities and, unless you have some reason for thinking that your cocoa beans are so much better than everyone else's (which is unlikely), then we think you're likely to be on a hiding to nothing.

In the 2000 edition of this book we illustrated this point with Corus Group: the result of the 1999 merger of British Steel and Hoogovens, a steel producer from the Netherlands. As so often is the case in unattractive commodity markets, the merger was essentially a defensive measure. It cut the number of competing companies by one and provided the merged company with 'economies of scale'. This just means that by putting the two companies together, some overlapping costs could be removed. The trouble is that you can't make a silk purse out of a sow's ear. Although the task might seem easier if you have a second sow's ear to play with, ultimately that's an illusion. Remember that we're looking for solid long-term growth and, however you view it, one-off cost savings won't give you this. Despite the merger, Corus remains a company labouring in a competitive market with nothing to say for its products except that they're pretty much like everyone else's. Indeed it has continued to make losses for the last two years and the shares have fallen 10 per cent.

We'd say steer clear of commodity products and we'd continue to steer well clear of Corus Group.

Not best in their business – Somerfield

When we wrote about Somerfield in 2000, it occupied fifth place in the UK grocery market, with a market share of 6.9 per cent, compared to the market leader, Tesco, which had a share of 15.6 per cent. Since then, Somerfield has been on the slide, with its share dropping to 4.7 per cent, while Tesco has extended its position to speak for 16.5 per cent of the market. The company has also continued to make losses, although it's expected to stem that particular tide this year. The stock market has pre-empted the recovery by marking the shares up by a huge 150 per cent since we mentioned them. So there you go. We'd say the battle is far from over and that Somerfield is still at the losing end.

If you were choosing a British supermarket to invest in for the next few decades, would you pick Tesco or Somerfield. To us this sort of question answers itself and, as the great Warren Buffet has famously said 'if you aren't willing to own a stock for ten years, don't even think about owning it for ten minutes'. Scale is important in food retailing, as it can enable a company to get better deals from its suppliers and to get better value from its marketing. With Wal-Mart having entered the UK market through its takeover of Asda, we wouldn't want to be in Somerfield's shoes. Of course, Somerfield may prove us wrong – after all, Tesco has had to climb the ladder to reach the top of the UK market – but we think the odds are heavily stacked against it.

Position not easily defended – Rentokil Initial

Rentokil was initially in our list of Obvious Greats. However, when the second edition came around, we decided that we'd made a mistake with it. Although the company had some excellent and profitable market positions, we felt that we'd overestimated the company's ability to defend them. So much so, in fact, that it prompted us to introduce this new test. We therefore felt it only fair to put forward Rentokil as an example of the test being failed. Well it's come back to haunt us, since Rentokil shares have now recovered by 83 per cent. In our defence, we did say:

> We don't actually think that Rentokil is that bad, certainly not as bad as others on this particular list but, since it was the reason for us inserting this new test, we thought it only fair to use it as the prime example.

But it does serve us right for being a bit cocky! While we'd say that Rentokil probably still fails this particular test, it passes the others with flying colours and that should have been a warning sign to us. So what's a business with very flimsy market positions, that doesn't do so well on the other tests?

We'll go for Airlines this time and, specifically, British Airways. It does have a pretty good brand, but that's about as far as it goes. The market for air travel has been fiercely competitive pretty much ever since the Wright Flyer made its first wobbly flight and profits have been elusive. For years, British Airways kept itself going under the protection of Government ownership, but since its privatisation in 1987, it has had to fend for itself in the big wide world of private ownership. The shares have managed to crawl up from 125p to 203p, but it's been a turbulent ride. The picture now is as rough as ever, with the profitable North American route suffering since the 11th September tragedy and with European short-haul routes getting massacred by competition from the more efficient low-cost operators such as easyJet and Ryanair.

We're delighted to fly with British Airways and even more delighted that the competition keeps the flights so cheap. We'll steer a long way clear of the shares, though.

Not making a lot of money for their efforts – Pura

In the first and second editions we used Pura, the supplier of oils and fats formerly known as Acatos & Hutchison, as an example of a company not making a lot of money. Indeed 1998 and 1999 produced losses. The last couple of years have at least seen a return to profits, although it's hardly convincing, with operating margins hovering around the 1 per cent mark. Nevertheless, it's been enough to push the shares up from 55p to 80.5p since 2000. So it's another 'obviously bad investment' that's done rather well over the last couple of years. Mind you, it's still well below the 237p that we picked them out at in 1998 and it's also a long way below the 120p mark that the shares stood at ten years ago.

We wouldn't classify ourselves as experts in the oils and fats market, but we'd conclude from looking at Pura that there's something not right with it. Pura remains a business that we'd leave well alone.

Up to their eyebrows in debt – Eurotunnel

It took 150 years for them to get around to building the Channel Tunnel. It often seems like it'll take them another 150 for it to get out of debt. The company keeps rescheduling its debt and, eventually, it will probably be making enough money to pay the annual interest bill. When this will happen, though, is still anybody's guess. In fact, some people argue that the time has already come. The thing is, Fools, that if there is serious debate about whether a company's debt is actually covered or not by its profits or whether its debt pile is just getting bigger and bigger, then it is going to be a long way from being an 'obviously great investment'. In fact, if there is this much doubt about normally such a simple matter as a company's ongoing viability, then it would take much, much, braver Fools than us to go anywhere near it. If you want a flutter and you're bored of the horses, then have a go with Eurotunnel but we think that the time for it to be considered as a long-term investment is still some way away.

Not a success up to now – Rank Group PLC

Good companies are generally good for a reason and, over the long term, this will (and will have) come out in the share price. If you find a company whose share price hasn't performed for years, then there's a good chance that there's something wrong with it. That doesn't mean that some investors won't make money from it: the share price goes up and down and some will be lucky. But we're looking for steady long-term growth and companies whose share prices have been yo-yoing steadily sideways, or worse still downwards, are not the best place to find it.

We selected Rank Group for this slot back in 2000. It has a range of interesting brands, including Mecca Bingo and Hard Rock Café (would you believe that there are now over a hundred of these in forty-five countries around the world?), but it looked like something had been going wrong, somewhere along the line. Having peaked at 545p in 1996, the shares had slumped to 141p. Since then, however, there's been a partial recovery and we're back up to 280p. So what do we make of that? Normally we'd dismiss it as an unpredictable and relatively uninteresting short-term price movement. But then this test is all about price movements and, while we'd rather be looking over ten years or so, over which time Rank has still been pretty lousy, the fact that the company has done well may, possibly, be an indication of it doing something right again.

So it's time for a fresh face. There are plenty of examples of poor share price performances over the last couple of years, mostly in the technology sector, but remember that we're thinking long-term. Over ten years, one of the worst performers we can find is Coats plc (formerly Coats Viyella). Back in June 1992, the shares stood at 209p and they're now at just 53p. Something somewhere has not been going right for the company. Naturally, shareholders will see to it that any company with this sort of performance will make some big changes. For Coats, that's involved selling much of its business to leave it focused on sewing threads and zips and the retail businesses of Jaeger and Viyella. It may be that these are now profitable niche businesses, with a decent future, but given the history, it's not possible to be very confident about that. Until there's evidence of a major turnaround in performance, we'd stay clear of it and we suggest you do too.

Buy What You Are

So, where do you look for your investments? We've already talked about buying what you know and it's hard to imagine getting much more Foolish than that. Buying shares in companies whose products and services you know to be worthwhile is an excellent start. As you become more engaged in the growth of your future wealth, however, you're going to find yourself looking more and more deeply at the way in which your own individual life is supported by the products around you. Look at what you use in your job, what your company produces, what your competitors produce, what you use in your leisure hours (you do have some, we hope), and what your family uses. If you're anything like us, you'll soon be saying to yourself: 'Hmm, this is a good product, but how would I market/manufacture/ advertise it better?' Say that to yourself about most of the products you use and you'll often come up with a great idea for how to do it better because you – the end user – are just the person to see the openings and opportunities that the company's management has overlooked. All you then have to do is send your idea off to the company, offering to enter negotiations for a licensing fee for your brainwave, sit back and let the royalties flood in. (Dream on.)

Occasionally, you'll find a product or service that you don't think can be bettered, one that is so expertly marketed and correctly targeted that you are speechless, dumbstruck with admiration. Congratulations! You have possibly just found a great investment. What you must now do is find out all you can about the company and crucially, whether it's publicly or privately owned. If it's privately owned, then tough luck: this company is going to have to go on your wish list, just in case it does one day decide to go public.

If it's a quoted company, then that's marvellous, but hold your horses, put the padlock back on your wallet, you have some *work* to do. First, you need their annual report and from there you want to know its history, what other products it produces, what future plans it has, its numbers (Is it growing? Is it profitable? What's its market cap?) and what other people think of it. Look up recent articles about it in the press and ask the company themselves to send you copies of any recent analysts' reports: these can be illuminating. In doing all this, you'll find that the Internet, if you have access to it, can be very useful. We've mentioned before that most companies have their accounts and a host of other useful information on their Web site. There are also a number of sites that provide financial commentaries on different markets and industry sectors and some that provide areas where you can discuss your ideas with others. There's a list of some of these sites in Appendix 4, but you do know which Web site's the best, don't you?

Anyway, after that brief commercial, let's get back to business. If you're convinced that the company you've found is the best thing since Mother's Pride, you believe its product fills a unique niche, it is expertly managed and it satisfies all the financial criteria you will have by now developed for a company you're prepared to invest in, then go ahead – put your money where your mouth is!

A(nother) word of warning, however. If you're looking at a small capitalization company, you're going to have to be much more canny and you'll have to keep a much closer eye on your investment than if you're simply choosing consumer giants of the type we've mostly been talking about here. Pizza Express is the closest to a smaller company share that we've mentioned (positively anyway) in this chapter, and you'll remember that we said we'd need to be keeping half an eye on it. As companies get smaller, then you'll probably need to spend more and more precious time keeping track of it. That said, there are real profits to be made in using the specialist knowledge you use in your daily life to invest in companies that reflect what **you are**, whether those are small growth companies or multinational conglomerates.

For now, though, congratulate yourself that you have successfully ploughed through the largest chapter in this book, take a break, stretch the legs and come back refreshed, bright-eyed and eager for the next chapter: The Ten Most Common Investing Mistakes.

13

The Ten Most Common Investing Mistakes

The man who makes no mistakes does not usually make anything.
Edward John Phelps, Mansion House speech, 1889.

If you're the type who likes helpful restatements and summaries of the major portions of a book, read on. We are going to wind our way gently towards the close of this part with the ten most common investing mistakes we see people making as we wander through the online and offline worlds. There are other common ones besides these ten, but if we could all just prevent ourselves from making these, the world would be a much safer place to invest.

No. 1: Buying What You Don't Understand

Baptisms of fire are common in the stock market. Poll the investing public and you're likely to find that most of them didn't have a clue what they were buying when they made their first investments, and many of them still don't. Cousin Dennis, the chap who can't programme his video, he's starting a Web publishing business. 'Five thousand, that's all I need from start-up investors. It's a dead cert. No one's done this before. I'll double your money in six months.' And you what? You gave it to him?!

Or maybe a colleague at work has a hot tip on a biotechnology company, which he whispers to you over the coffee dispenser. 'Psst! Thunder-Box Biomedical. Hot new products. A new oscillo-proteinase inhibitor, goes like the clappers,' he says, talking in biotech-speak. 'Ripe to be bought out by one of the big pharmaceuticals, too. Get in now before the price hits the roof!' Uh-oh – you don't really understand a word of it, do you?

The pathway to superior investing is unfortunately littered with speculations in low-grade, cash-burning outfits, hyped to the heavens and with operations that are largely unfamiliar to their shareholders. But any investment that you don't understand is a mistake, even if it does beat the market for you. Allow us to make our point by going to an extreme. Would you buy Vodafone or ARM Holdings solely on the basis of what you have read here? Oh, you know the basis for our thoughts on these businesses and their great prospects for the next few decades. But hang on. We're just a bunch of Fools. Would it be particularly intelligent to rely solely on our ramblings when:

- you can come and discuss them with thousands of other investors (including ourselves for that matter) at the Motley Fool Online *right* now;
- you can phone them directly, ask for their latest company reports and any analysts' reports they happen to be giving out (for free), and run them past your investment club, mother or work colleagues for further insights;
- you can tap instantly and for free into the growing amount of information available about them over the Internet including, most likely, their own corporate Web site?

The salient point here is that the story of your epic journey into the world of savings and investing has as its antagonist anyone who tries to rush you. If you've found any useful investment principles in this book, read them again. Soak them up slow-w-w-ly. Get hold of one or two other books. Read them. Slow-w-w-ly. Becoming accustomed to this sort of approach and deliberation will benefit you as an investor; it's the direct opposite of what most people do, which is to rush to act quickly on the recommendations of others. And by 'others' we mean anybody or anything: an advisory stockbroker, an online investor, your lucky rabbit's foot, great-aunt Cicely in the middle of one of her winning streaks, or even the Chief Executive of the company in which you are about to invest.

You 're responsible for your investments and so you had better verify any information or analysis you are presented with. Be canny, not gullible.

No. 2: Focusing on Your Short-term Performance

It's unfortunate that no matter how frequently the Miracle of Compound Interest is evoked, with the mightiest profits appearing at the far end of an investment life, some investors continue to believe that profits up front, profits today, are meaningful. Which is a shame. Because, in many cases, that impatience results in flawed logic, poor investments, frightful indigestion and pacing the floor after midnight.

It isn't worth it.

In Chapter 7, we quoted a section from Warren Buffett's 1997 Letter to Shareholders. We like it so much that we're going to repeat it:

> *A short quiz: If you plan to eat hamburgers throughout your life and are not a cattle producer, should you wish for higher or lower prices for beef? Likewise, if you are going to buy a car from time to time but are not an auto manufacturer, should you prefer higher or lower car prices? These questions, of course, answer themselves.*
>
> *But now for the final exam: if you expect to be a net saver during the next five years, should you hope for a higher or lower stock market during that period? Many investors get this one wrong. Even though they are going to be net buyers of stocks for many years to come, they are elated when stock prices rise and depressed when they fall. In effect, they rejoice because prices have risen for the 'hamburgers' they will soon be buying. This reaction makes no sense. Only those who will be sellers of equities in the near future should be happy at seeing stocks rise. Prospective purchasers should much prefer sinking prices.*

Most of us, for at least the five years to come, are going to be net purchasers of hamburgers, er, sorry, shares. So, if our investments fall in value, then that is a good thing, because it will allow us to purchase more shares that we value as long-term buys for lower prices. Our existing long-term holds may have fallen slightly in value, but it doesn't matter.

Remember that 20 per cent of £1000 is £200. And 20 per cent of £100,000 is £20,000. As time expands your base of capital, each later year of growth will provide substantially more profits. Let's hark back to Anne Scheiber, the

American who started with $5000 in 1944. Back then she earned less than $1000 per year. By the time she died in the mid-90s, she was earning more than $500,000 in dividends alone and an average market year brought in more than $2 million in paper gains.

It's the tomorrows that build wealth, not the frenetic activity of the todays. What your portfolio does in the coming week is several orders of magnitude less important than what it does between the years 2005 and 2010, or better yet, 2015 and 2020. To buy and sell your shares on the back of short-term market fluctuations will mortally wound your wallet as you try to predict which way the dice is going to roll next. The trading commissions will eat into your profits and you'll become one of those sad, skeletal souls who dances to the tune of a share pager which bleeps whenever your chosen shares move more than a specified amount. Can you afford to let yourself exist on this level, a level which can only be sustained by frequent injections of caffeine, adrenalin and whisky? We say: '*Nyet!*'

Truly, Fools: 'Lift thine eyes from the dust of the short term, up, up unto the Heavens and regard the glory that is the long-term panorama!'

No. 3: Finding Yourself Becoming Enduringly Bearish

Bears, bulls – do you know them? Bears think the glass is half-empty, bulls think it's half-full. Bears think the sky is perpetually poised to fall on their investing heads, bulls fall headlong over their own two feet in their rush to invest *NOW* in this amazing market that is going to be climbing to the skies for ever. Don't miss it!

Moderation, the Middle Way. Whatever you want to call it, a long-term investor can't live without it. Excessive bearishness, though, as much as excessive bullishness, will injure your investment returns. Possibly, it will injure them mortally. There is, you see, no 'right' time to invest, no point at which the economic signs, the market sentiment and the pattern of goose entrails all come together to give you the green light. In a rising market, well, things are looking overvalued and the market may just be on the point of crashing. You'd look pretty stupid, wouldn't you, if you invested now? Best just to wait a bit. In a falling market, you're never quite sure how far it's going to fall. I mean, it might just keep going down and there's no sense in buying something that is *decreasing* in value. That would just be stupid! Then the trough comes and you're a whisker too late and the market's climbing again. You missed it, but maybe this is only a temporary rally. A friend of yours who likes to look at charts of share prices has said that this is a classical 'Double nelly, triple salco' appearance in the star – oops, FTSE 100 – chart and signifies another impending downturn. And then you decide he's wrong and that the market is on the way back up, but now you're aching at having missed your chance earlier on and …

And so it goes on. It's a disease. You can never be a perfect parent, only a 'good enough' parent, and so it is with investing. No one, not even Warren Buffett, can invest without regrets. They are part of the game, and trying to invest without incurring any will not move you forward. Repeat to yourself your Foolish mantra: since 1869 the London stock market has provided an annual return of 9.5 per cent on average. It has, on average, doubled investors' money every seven and a half years. Why now should this precedent suddenly be shattered? There's no real reason why it should be. In any event, even if the returns from shares are lower over the next few decades, the evidence is overwhelming that the returns from other forms of investment are likely to lower still. Just recognize that you don't need to get it perfectly right or perfectly timed to come out the other end clutching a profit.

Remember that you are now a card-carrying contrarian. In fact, you won't be disappointed if you buy and six months later things start tumbling down, because you're a regular saver and you *like* bear markets. They give you the opportunity to pick up even more great businesses at bargain prices, or even to buy the whole market at a bargain price by sinking more of your funds into an index tracker. What a terrific business this all is!

Don't be a bear. Instead, be a 'good enough' investor, a long-term, patient bull, for this, history tells us, is the true nature of the market.

No. 4: Believing the Financial Press Is Expert

Do financial advisers have your best interests at heart? Is every fibre of their being dedicated to your long-term enrichment? Do financial journalists go to bed at night wondering if they have done the best they can by investors that day? The answer, by now, is obvious. So, what sells newspapers and gains television viewers? If you said 'Alarm, despondency, froth, short-termism', you wouldn't be far off the mark. It isn't often that you see the true power of Brother Time and Sister Logic played up in the financial press. To date, the media has shown little interest in speaking to the patient private investors who tuck money away into shares and hold them for decades. Not that there is much to say to them and that is partly the point. In the media's race to present (or design) the latest controversy and in its obsession with *today*, the business press largely ignores the variable of time. The great self-sufficient investors haven't created their wealth over the last forty years by buying on the rumour and selling on the news. They buy on the research, their own research, and often don't sell. At an investors' conference in 1997, an elderly gentleman talked with us about his decades of investing, chuckling that it seemed like everyone from investment firm to financial newspaper had tried to rock him out of his position in Schering-Plough, one of the leading US drug companies over the past forty years. 'And, thank God, I ignored them all and held straight through.'

Thank God, indeed. He made $7 million out of that investment.

It's controversy and disaster that sell in the media business. Train crashes and terrorist bombs, estranged celebrity couples and ethnic cleansing, and ... the collapse of the stock market. The editing process at most newspapers is heavily biased in favour of matters catastrophic.

When we return once more to Warren Buffett, who claims not to read financial papers, we're reminded of what matters. Private investors have quietly and methodically grown their savings for decades. No, they aren't half as exciting as the collapse of Barings Bank or (*sigh*) the next market collapse, so they don't often gain coverage from the press. But they do seem to be making a good deal of money this century.

Now, none of this is to imply that the market won't lean this way and that, that it won't crumble again, perhaps even soon. At some point, it will. But the average investor (median age of 34) has four decades ahead in which to invest. Whether the market drops by 30 per cent tomorrow is of supreme *inconsequence* to most individuals. Regrettably, that decline is of supreme *consequence* to the financial media, on the look-out for casualties and collision. And therein lies the inversion of interests, pitting patient reader against desperate writer. In a world where learning was prized over controversy, those financial papers whose currency is hype might become worth reading. We're not quite there yet.

No. 5: Concentrating Your Attention On Share Price

One of the frequent mistakes of the novice investor is to be overly preoccupied with share prices. Our first inclination as investors is to believe that a share trading for 150p is less expensive and holds greater potential for reward than one trading at 1500p. Seems reasonable, doesn't it? After all, we've been buying products all our lives and things that have a lower price are cheaper. Simple.

Unfortunately, this principle doesn't hold when it comes to the stock market. A share price in and of itself is meaningless. Oscar Wilde is, as he is so often, on the side of the Fools: 'Nowadays people know the price of everything and the value of nothing.'

What is the total value of a business? Let us hark back to Chapter 11, 'A Share Primer', and reiterate that the total value of a company equals the number of shares times the price of those shares. Thus, if Alan's Aardvark Adventures PLC has 100 million shares, each priced at 150p, the company is valued at £150 million (150p x 100 million = £150 million). And Ethelred's Elephant Enterprises PLC, with 5 million shares trading at 1500p a share, is priced at £75 million. In this case, the 1500p share represents a lower-priced company than the 150p share. The cheapness of a share depends on the total value of a company, not whether it is trading at 150p or 1500p.

To combat the tendency to focus on share price, imagine that all of the shares in your portfolio were trading at 1000p a share. Further, imagine that every share on the market were trading at that price. Now, which companies would you invest in? Would you buy that tin-cup-waving, self-promotional Caspian Sea oil driller, or would you buy Diageo? Would you become an owner of debt-crippled Eurotunnel or would you buy an ownership position in debt-light GlaxoSmithKline?

Shield from view the daily to-ing and fro-ing of share pricing and you will naturally bear down more rigorously on the businesses you are buying. In doing so, you will have avoided our fifth giant investing miscue. Now, on to number six.

No. 6: Buying Penny Shares

'The exception proves the rule.'

It would be so appropriate to quote this pithy saying now, as we move swiftly from telling you that share price doesn't matter to telling you that in some ways it matters a great deal. We'd love to quote it, but the fact is it's a nonsense. 'Proves' in this context has the same meaning as 'tests', as in 'proving ground'. The exception 'tests' the rule. Doesn't make sense, does it? How did this happen? How did the meaning of this ubiquitous phrase become so distorted over the years? All will be revealed in the forthcoming *Motley Fool Guide to Life, Loving and Comparative Etymology*. Until then, tingle at the mystery that is the English language and reflect that the following statement is indeed true:

Penny shares *will* seriously damage your wealth.

Penny shares refers to shares whose price can be measured in multiples of just a few pence and whose market capitalization can usually be measured in just a few million pounds. When companies go public, they often don't do so with an initial share price measured in multiples of just a few pence. Companies whose shares trade in pennies have often *earned* their way to the bottom of the heap.

If a share trades at 8p, then an increase in price to just 10p is a 25 per cent gain, a far easier move, you might think, for a share to make than, say, from 1000p to 1250p. 'Penny shares offer quick and easy profits.' Newsletters exist and prosper on this principle and purport to guide the naïve investor into stunning profits by offering tips on which penny shares to buy. Fellow Fools, if it were so simple, we wouldn't be writing this book and if you wanted to contact us, you'd be dialling the country code for the Seychelles first. Briefly, the rub is:

● Since the number of shares in the marketplace is so small and the amount of solid news so scanty, hype and rumour are likely to be the biggest motivators of penny share price movements.

- The small number of available shares can make them exceedingly difficult to buy or sell – remember every purchase or sale requires another party to complete the transaction. The technical term is that these shares are *illiquid*.
- The spread between buying and selling prices (the 'bid-offer spread') can be so large as to rub out any potential profits.
- Whereas the share price of GlaxoSmithKline or Unilever will (almost certainly) never fall to zero and is highly unlikely ever to be cut in four, this kind of thing is not just possible, it is *likely* with penny shares.

There are no consistent, long-term profits to be made in penny shares. If you like to throw away money on the roulette wheel, then penny shares are for you. Our bet, though, is that if you've invested weeks of unrelenting misery to get thus far through the book, you're not the Johnny-Go-Lightly, betting type.

So, what exactly *is* a penny share? Where is the cut-off? How do you decide by price alone what is a volatile, unpredictable investment, more likely to end in tears than not and, importantly, how do you make sure you don't also end up excluding some great, up-and-coming companies with a novel product or an original idea? It's a tricky question to which there is no right answer and in the early days of the Fool UK we had quite a long discussion on this topic on our online message boards. We use the following criteria when deciding whether we are prepared to consider a company as an investment prospect:

> *Share price greater than 50p*
> *Market capitalization greater than £30 million*

Some will think this too high, perhaps others will think it too low, but it's a level at which we feel comfortable. Don't worry if you don't agree with us precisely. As long as you're discussing just where the cut-off point should be set and not the whiz-bang investment opportunities that penny shares offer, you've got the right attitude.

Having avoided six potentially fatal errors, you're in pretty good shape, but look what else is waiting to drag you down into investment hell …

No. 7: Not Tracking Your Investment Returns

With the Internet and with a variety of software packages available, tracking the performance of your investments is easier than ever before. If you type in your investments, then the Internet will do the rest for you, updating continuously to show you how things are going. As we've said before, you shouldn't spend all day following their movements (again, unless you're Uri Geller), but you should make a point of checking from time to time to see how you're doing both overall and against the market average. How have your 'Obviously Greats' performed over the past two years? Has your strategy to buy ownership positions in predominantly small technology companies proven fruitful? Is your financial adviser beating the market, after the deduction of all management fees?

Not knowing whether your investments are thriving or barely surviving from year to year is somewhat akin to not knowing how your favourite football team is doing, or worse: how your children are doing at school, or how old you are. The process of checking your portfolio's performance against the stock market should be painless ... nay, joyous.

Too many investors don't know how their savings did in 2000 or in 2001 or over the past decade. There are entire investment clubs that perform wonderful research, do a top-notch job with analysis and yet, at year end, don't know how their investments have performed relative to the Footsie. Much as we enjoy the process of researching businesses and investing, measuring performance is critical. And in too many instances, our lack of attentiveness to the numbers brings good humour to the financial services industry. Not just a few unit trusts have run advertisements that read, '1995 was a great year. Our fund rose 26 per cent!' This in a year when the market climbed 35 per cent. The investor tracking returns knew to sell off that unit trust for promoting its own mediocrity.

No. 8: Not Diversifying Your Portfolio

There is a lot of discussion about how much diversification a portfolio needs. Without going into the ins and outs, the general view is that investing in somewhere between ten and fifteen different companies should be enough.

Fewer than ten holdings leaves you a bit too exposed to one or two (or perhaps more) of them going wrong, whereas more than fifteen doesn't really do much to reduce your risks, but it might well increase your costs and make it harder for you to keep track of what's going on. Of course, if you got up as high as, say, thirty shares or more, it would be very hard to beat the market average (because your portfolio would now be close to mimicking it) and you'd have to ask whether you might be better off (because of things like costs) just going for an index tracker.

Don't forget, though, that buying shares in, say, twelve different companies won't spread your risk much if they're all in the same industry sector and subject to the same economic forces. You need a range of different business types. A football team is unlikely to win many matches if it is made up entirely of strikers, unless, by some freak of chance, the entire game happens to be played out in the opposition's penalty box. Instead, you need to pick a team that will cope, as well as possible, with the whole range of circumstances which might come your way, both in attack and defence. The same goes for shares – you need to build a portfolio that isn't dependent on things turning out a certain way.

Similarly, there's not much point in having twelve different shareholdings if you put £1000 in eleven of them and £11,000 in the twelfth. This twelfth company would make up 50 per cent of your portfolio and it would be more like having only two shares. Over time, some of your shares will do better than others and, gradually, one might grow to make up an uncomfortably large portion of your portfolio. You'll therefore need to sell a bit to reduce it, perhaps investing more in one of the others, or in a totally new company that you like the look of. When to do this is largely a personal matter. It has to do with how you feel about risk and taking into account the costs of making the changes. If you consistently tinkered with the holdings in your portfolio so that they remained in constant alignment, you'd end up, through dealing commission, giving the bulk of your portfolio to your stockbroker. Our recommendation is that portfolios of greater than £10,000 never have more than 15 per cent of their capital initially invested in any one share. From there, we recommend that you start to think about lightening any holdings that grow to become more than about 25 per cent of your total portfolio. Let's walk through a brief example, with a £20,000 portfolio. First, you would never invest more than £3000, or 15 per cent, in any one company. Then imagine that your portfolio took this shape two years hence:

Purchased	No. of shares	Security	In at	Now	Value
May 2000	3370	Alfie's Chip Shops	89.00	402.00	£13,547.40
Nov. 1999	450	Soup and Snails	578.00	848.00	£3816.00
May 1999	850	Happy Holidays	220.00	401.00	£3408.50
Jan. 1999	900	Eileen's Cakeshop	278.00	343.00	£3087.00
May 1997	450	New World Mining	330.00	555.00	£2497.50
Aug. 2000	550	Shaving Kits	490.00	318.00	£1749.00
Aug. 1999	2900	Pronto Pilchards	100.00	49.00	£1421.00
April 2000	1200	Motley Fool UK	250.00	68.00	£816.00
TOTAL:					£30,342.40

In this scenario, you'll see that although no initial investment exceeded 15 per cent, one of our holdings has exploded. Alfie's Chip Shops has more than quadrupled; our holding in Alfie's has swollen to over 40 per cent of the total value of our account. Red lights should flash here. The portfolio has become overweighted in one direction. It's time to slack off on Alfie's, even though it's been our top performer. Before leaving this section, did you notice the shaggiest, smelliest, wettest dog in our portfolio? Yikes!

No. 9: Not Being Online

Even if the share prices of the companies involved have been flying all over the place, the growth in activity on the internet has been one of the big stories of the last few years. Investors from across the planet are tapping into a network of resources that dramatically outdoes the amount of information available via any other medium.

The Motley Fool UK (www.fool.co.uk) services conversations between stockbrokers, analysts, consumers and private investors far removed from the City. In a few short years, we have gone from a world where only the wealthiest individuals and the largest institutional investors could gain access to valuable information and research. Today, the beginner investor with a personal computer and a modem can click into ongoing conversations about personal finance, business and investing that are educational and inclusive.

It is a profound mistake for anyone with access to the Internet – either at home, school, or via a local library – not to take advantage of the resources and the opportunities to have your individual questions answered online. A mass conversation about savings and investing is occurring even as you flip through these pages. And it's a discussion that is changing the way the money world works, an ongoing transformation that greatly works in favour of the individual.

As consumers band together and negotiate with the big boys on a far more level playing field, the balance of financial power is shifting. If you can access the Internet, you should give Fooldom a whirl, as well as a number of other sites which we have detailed in Appendix 4, 'Useful Web sites'. Rather than learning by passively reading, you can, with your networked computer, learn through co-operative endeavour.

No. 10: Spending Far Too Much Time on Investing

It seems only right that we close down our investing don'ts with a recognition that many of us fall into the trap of dedicating too much time to money management. If this notion seems ludicrous to you today, don't be surprised if in three years you systematically check your shares each morning and find yourself in regular conversations about the prospects of JJB Sports and the future market for Manchester United football shirts with your athletically challenged third cousin Rupert.

Studying businesses, becoming a part-owner of enterprises, and talking about your smartest and dumbest investments is actually a great deal of fun. The very brightest among us find ways to involve ourselves just enough to wallop the market's average returns, to learn much from the ongoing investigation, but never (or rarely) to compromise the other joys of life – grandchildren, a picnic lunch, handling the wheel of a sixty-year-old MG, sleeping until lunchtime one Tuesday in April.

Very few investors completely avoid at least one period in their life when they spend too much time thinking about their money, when they become consumed by their savings growth. In the very dreariest of scenarios, some even take to trading shares each day, while passing the daylight hours in torn pyjamas, bathed in the unearthly glow of a computer monitor, blindly reaching to their left and unknowingly eating a two-week-old tuna sandwich off the wrong plate. Although we find it hard to imagine a scenario where this sort of trader makes money and beats the market, even so, can you imagine this sort of living? Can you imagine eating that sandwich? Can you imagine that taste going unnoticed?

As captivating as the market can be, as much fun as the whole process of saving and investing is, verily it does not take the place of living. The blend of online services, the study of business and market-beating investing has proved nearly irresistible for some. Take heed, though, at the words of W. H. Davies in his poem 'Leisure' of 1911:

What is this life if, full of care,
We have no time to stand and stare.

What You've (Maybe) Already Got

What You've (Maybe) Already Got

It is the folly of the world, constantly, which confounds its wisdom.
Oliver Wendell Holmes, *The Professor at the Breakfast Table*

The first step into the world of investing, for most people, is some form of product created and managed by a financial services company. This section of the book is dedicated to the most common of these, sometimes very peculiar, animals. We'll start by taking a lively stroll (we wish) through the confusing and sometimes dangerous world of pensions, then we'll leap across the disturbing abyss of endowments before arriving, safely we hope, in the tranquil paradise of the individual savings account. Finally, we'll look at the differences between unit trusts, investment trusts and other weird savings vehicles, such as Open-Ended Investment Companies (OEICs) and Exchange Traded Funds (ETFs).

Throughout the section, it's important to keep in mind that all of these things are just a form of investment wrapper. Think of them as clingfilm. Clingfilm does not change what's inside, merely the effect of the outside world on it. If the contents are good, like a slice of mature farmhouse cheddar, they stay good. If the contents are bad, like four-day-old fish pie, then they stay that way. When you hand over your hard-earned cash to some financial services company, they must invest it in order to provide the returns that you expect. Generally, they will invest your money in a range of different investments including cash, gilts, property and, of course, shares. Sometimes, they might use complicated financial instruments to guarantee a particular level of return, but these have to be paid for. Fundamentally, the underlying risks and returns that you find in the product you are buying will be the same as if you had bought those underlying investments yourself. If your product provider does the financial equivalent of serving up a slice of four-day-old fish pie, any amount of financial clingfilm isn't going to make it taste any better.

So what, you might well ask, are these wrappers all about? Well, in the case of pensions, endowments and ISAs, they're there to keep the taxman's greedy little fingers off them. The Government knows that it can't possibly pay to look after us all in old age, so it lines up a few tax breaks to help persuade us to look after ourselves. An added advantage of 'Collective

Investments' is that, by grouping together with lots of others, we can often achieve a better spead of investments than we could on our own. So, you get a good spread of investments and you might save some tax. Sounds good, doesn't it? The trouble is that none of this is achieved for free. When you give someone else your money to look after, they charge for it. So, when you are trying to find a suitable product for yourself, you need to compare the product's charges with the benefits that the particular product is designed to provide. Remember also that, as we found with actively managed unit trusts, the charges will often be the very reason that a product fails to achieve what it sets out to do.

OK, have you packed your toothbrush? Off we go.

14

The Dangerous
World of Pensions

*Was it a friend or foe that spread these lies? Nay, who but infants question in
such wise? T'was one of my most intimate enemies.*

Dante Gabriel Rossetti, *'Fragments'*

How many times have you heard people say: 'I really must do something
about my pension, but I don't understand a word my financial adviser says.'
Maybe you've said it yourself. Generally, the conversation stops there,
accompanied by uncomfortable downward glances, shoe shuffling, a general
feeling of unease and mutterings along the lines of 'Gosh, it's so hard to
know, isn't it? I mean, I just don't understand all that stuff ...'

It's a shame alright, but it's not surprising that people don't discuss their
pensions, as they have never received any education about them. They find
the whole subject intimidating in the extreme and the last thing the professionals would like is for people to be considering these investments from a
knowledgeable standpoint. Just why this is, we are about to see.

You've Got to Have a Pension, Haven't You?

Well, yes, and then again, no. Before we answer this in a slightly more helpful manner, let's take a quick look at what pensions actually are and take a
Foolish jaunt through the thorny issue of annuities. If you already have a
pension yourself, our guess is that you'll be quite interested to hear what we
have to say in this chapter. If you don't yet have one, then we hope it will also
provide some food for thought, because sure as goldfish swim, the Pope is
Catholic and the Shipping Forecast must mean something to someone some-

where, there is a financial adviser out there who is going to try and sell you one of these. Soon.

What is a pension?

A pension is an income that you receive after you've stopped work. To build up a big enough pot of money to provide that income, someone has to do some saving. What makes one pension scheme different from another is down to how this money is saved, who it is saved by and how the income is eventually generated.

As we said in the preamble to this section, to encourage us to save enough for our retirement, the Government provides a tax break. So long as a pension scheme fulfills the criteria they have set down, then the money that goes into it comes out of your pre-tax earnings. Think of it this way: you put some money in, then the Government chips in the tax that you have paid (or would pay) on that money. These contributions form a pension fund, which is invested over the years until your retirement. In theory all this seems dandy. In practice, life is once again about to take a shot across your bows. There are (more than) a few complications along the way.

We're going to take a look at the state pension, occupational pensions and private pensions (commonly known as Personal Pension Plans).

The State Pension

The state pension scheme basically comes in two bits – the 'basic pension' and the 'State Earnings-Related Pension Scheme' (SERPS).

Basic pension

It is slowly being abolished, as we saw in Chapter 1. Slipping in a 2 per cent drop in growth was a shrewd manoeuvre by the Thatcher Government in 1981. The Tories, in the aftermath of their 1979 landslide, realized that, since there was no investment fund out of which pensions were being paid (they are paid by the National Insurance contributions of those currently working), the rapidly ageing population was going to mean that pensions at the current levels were going to become too expensive. So they cut the rate at which pensions appreciated from average earnings growth down to the rate of inflation. The Labour Government has restored the link with earnings for a few years but, ultimately, it's a case of pushing water uphill. There just won't be enough people in work to pay for the pensioners and, by the time many people reading this book retire, they'll be lucky if the weekly state pension buys them a bottle of blue hair rinse and a packet of Mr Kipling's jam tarts. It's also worth bearing in mind that not everybody qualifies for it – you have to have made a minimum level of National Insurance contributions. (Roughly speaking, you'll be OK if you've earned at least the same amount as the basic pension for most of your working life). Do not factor the state pension into any of your retirement calculations.

The State Second Pension and 'Contracting Out'

The basic pension replaces your lowest slice of income (that is, up to £75 per week currently). The State Second Pension (which until this year was called SERPS, short for the State Earnings-Related Pension Scheme) is designed to replace your income from £75 per week to £585 per week. It is 'earnings-related' because the more you earn (up to £585), the more you get. However, as you move from £75 to £585, your income is replaced at different rates. The idea is to give more of a benefit to those on lower incomes. So, anyone earning between £75 and £208 per week (all these figures are for the 2002/3 tax year), will accrue their State Second pension as though they were earning the full £208, as will carers and those suffering long-term incapacity. The rate of accrual for those earnings up to £208 is 40 per cent. Earnings between £208 and £473 accrue the State Second Pension at a rate of 10 per cent and, for earnings between £473 and £585, the rate is 20%.

Right, got all that? Good, but it's all set to change in a few years' time, with phase two of the introduction of the State Second Pension. The thinking is that it will become a flat-rate pension equivalent to 40 per cent or so of your earnings up to £208 per week, although this figure will rise over the years. Come to think of it, there's every chance they'll change their mind about it again before we get there, so no one really knows what will happen.

This sort of tinkering, whether it's good or bad, certainly makes the State Second Pension rather unpredictable and, if you really don't want to place your faith in the Government, then there is the option of 'contracting out'. If you do this, then instead of accruing the State Second Pension, you get national insurance 'rebates' to put into your private or occupational pension and the idea is that these are enough to make up for the State Second Pension benefits that you're giving up. Whether they do or not is another matter entirely. People will argue about whether or not you should contract out until the cows come home, without ever reaching much of a conclusion. The good thing about this is that it probably means there isn't much in it for most people. One thing people do seem to agree about is that contracting out doesn't make sense once you get much beyond the age of forty.

So the State Second Pension is an add-on to the basic state pension and it's handy for that, whether or not you choose to contract out. But again, it's unlikely to form the basis of a comfortable retirement and we suggest that you don't count on it amounting to much. Instead, it might act as a safety valve if you reach retirement and haven't saved enough.

Occupational Pension Schemes

Forty years on the shop floor at Harding & Sedgewick ends with a handshake, a carriage clock and a generous pension to reflect the hard work and faithful service of a lifetime:

> *'Thank you, Higgins. Any plans for the future, my man?'*
>
> *'Well, sir, there's an allotment to dig and the cricket to watch. And may I say what a fine company this has been to work for over the years and what gentlemen you and your father before you have been. It has been an honour to work my fingers to the bone fourteen hours a day for a pittance of a weekly wage and a five shilling bonus every other Christmas. The outstanding growth in your personal wealth over that time and the way in which I was allowed to shine your shoes on my birthday have been a source of great pride to me. Truly a privilege, sir. Thank 'ee.'*

Yes, those were the days, the days of Mrs Miniver and Morris Eights, of the Movietone News and good old British honesty and pluck and people jolly well knowing their place. Those days, though, are largely gone. While occupational pensions can provide a sound retirement income and should generally be opted for rather than against, the picture is not quite so clear as it was back then, when the sun always shone in June and we knew with such certainty who the baddies were.

The best occupational pensions are to be found in the public sector. If you are in the police force, your pension will be generous indeed and will be paid for out of the organization's budget, not an investment fund. Elsewhere, though, and especially in the private sector, pensions are paid out of an investment fund into which both employee and employer contribute. This fund will be invested in a variety of things, although generally it is heavily weighted into equities. That said, the equity investments are more likely to take the form of the underperforming unit trusts we've already talked about. There are two basic types of occupational pension scheme: defined benefit and defined contribution.

We're already getting into jargon here with 'defined benefit' and 'defined contribution', but all this boils down to is who takes the risk of the investments not performing well enough. Having an idea of who takes the risk is something well worth knowing. With a *defined benefit* pension scheme, the final benefit is what 'defines' how much the policy is worth. In effect, the final benefit – aka 'how much you get' – is guaranteed. Typically, your eventual benefits from this type of scheme are defined as a proportion of your final salary and they are often referred to as 'final salary' schemes for this reason. With these pensions, your retirement income (and any lump sum that you stand to get) simply comes out of the total pension pot that your employer has been building up over the years for all employees. If the investments have performed badly and there isn't enough in the pot, then your employer has to stump up the difference. Of course, if the investments perform well and there is extra in the pot, then the employer gets to keep the extra. (There's always a pay-off for taking risk, right?)

In a *defined contribution* pension, the value of the policy is defined by what is put into it. For this reason, they are sometimes known as 'money purchase schemes'. The level of your final benefit depends on how well the investments in your scheme perform, and are therefore not guaranteed. If the investments perform well, then you will get the extra benefit. However, if performance is poor, then you'll end up with a lower retirement income than you were hoping for. In this case, it's you that takes the risk, not your employer.

Defined benefit occupational schemes

As we've just seen, defined benefit occupational schemes pay you benefits based on your final salary (or an average of your salary for the last few years of your employment). Typically, the benefits will involve a lump sum and an income for life. There may well be a number of useful frills, such as life insurance and a pension for your spouse if they survive you.

The lump sum and income are generally expressed as a fraction of your final salary per year of service. Imagine that you are getting retirement income of $\frac{1}{60}$ of your final salary and a lump sum of $\frac{3}{80}$ of your final salary per year of service, and you have 20 years of service. You will stand to receive $\frac{1}{3}$ (that is, $\frac{20}{60}$) of your final salary as income and $\frac{3}{4}$ (that is, $\frac{60}{80}$) of your final salary as a lump sum.

Defined benefit schemes are generally pretty attractive because your employer takes the risk of things not working out on the investment front. Unfortunately, this fact is not lost on most employers and they are stampeding to change to the next option.

Defined contribution occupational schemes

The effect of a defined contribution occupational scheme is similar to having a personal pension (which we're coming to next) into which your employer makes contributions. Your benefits depend on what is put into it (and how the investments perform). At retirement you get a tax-free lump sum and the remainder of your fund must be used to purchase something called an annuity. How much of the fund you can take out as a tax-free lump sum depends on final salary and length of service.

Some schemes offer you a choice of how much to put in. For example, your employer may offer to match the amount you put into the pension by contributing the same amount again. This can make for tough choices. Your employer will work out how much to pay everyone as a salary, taking into account the average amount that it has to contribute to everyone's pension. The effect of this is that if you are putting in less than average, then you are missing out on an employment benefit. However, just because your employer has offered to put money into a pension scheme if you do, it doesn't necessarily mean that you should. It really depends on the level of the contributions. If your employer offers to match your contributions (or better), then it would almost certainly make sense to take it. However, if your employer only puts in, say, £1 for every £9 that you put in, then the decision is more difficult: other factors about whether or not to opt for the pension will probably be more relevant.

Preserved benefits and transfers

Under an occupational scheme, if you have worked for an employer for two years you get to keep the value of any pension benefits that have built up if you change jobs. Either you can keep the 'preserved benefits' in the old scheme, or you can get the old scheme to transfer enough money (called the 'transfer value') to the new scheme to give you the same benefits that you had already built up in the old scheme. The trouble with transferring is that it often costs you money to do it. If you have worked for less than two years with an employer, you basically just get back any contributions that you've put in.

AVCs and FSAVCs

This is an option for people who are members of an occupational scheme, but who don't think their benefits are going to be enough. An AVC scheme is run by the employer to enable people to top their pension contributions up to the maximum allowed. AVC stands for Additional Voluntary Contribution. Where your employer does not offer an AVC scheme (or even if they do, but we'll come to that), you can contribute to an FSAVC scheme (which stands for Free-Standing AVC).

As you might imagine, an AVC (or FSAVC) for a defined contribution pension just increases your contributions, although they might be in a slightly different place from your main scheme. Where an AVC scheme is available for a defined benefit pension scheme (generally only in the public sector), your contributions can purchase 'added years'. In other words, you are buying extra years to be taken into account in calculating your final salary benefits.

An AVC, sponsored by your employer, has an advantage over an FSAVC because of 'economies of scale'. In other words, by grouping together with your fellow employees, the overall charges tend to be lower. FSAVCs are very similar to personal pensions we're shortly going to hear about. They generally have similar, punitive charging structures, your fund will be channelled into the same kinds of underperforming investments and they are sold by the same people. Take a look at this quote from an article in the *Financial Times* of 25 April 1998:

> *Bacon & Woodrow, one of the biggest pension analysts, warned recently that the stand-alone alternative to company-sponsored AVCs – free-standing AVCs (FSAVCs) – is being sold inappropriately.*
>
> *Indeed, B&W said this week that about a quarter of pension schemes contained members who had paid commission to a salesperson, only to end up with an FSAVC identical to the in-house AVC – except for higher charges to cover the commission.*

So it came as no great surprise when the Financial Services Authority (FSA) launched a review into the selling of FSAVCs. The review has focused on about 10 per cent of FSAVC sales where it meant that the investor may have missed out on employer contributions to an available AVC scheme. Anyway, the bottom line on this is that, if you have an occupational pension scheme and want to top up your contributions, an in-house AVC scheme is likely to be a far more attractive option than an FSAVC scheme.

Who puts the money in

One final thing to think about with an occupational pension is who puts the money in. In a pension scheme offered by your employer, you might put a bit in each month and so might your employer. Sometimes, in fact, your employer might offer to match your contributions. Sounds good, but let's think of it in another way. You, as an employee, are worth a certain amount to your employer and (so long as you, and/or your union, make the right noises when your pay is reviewed) hopefully this is the amount that you are paid. It makes little difference to your employer whether all your benefits come in the form of your salary or whether your salary is five per cent less and he pays five per cent into a pension scheme for you. What matters is your overall package. If your employer offers what is generally considered to be an attractive pension scheme, then ask yourself how much more salary you could be paid if you didn't take the pension.

Of course, much of this is fairly academic since few of us actually have that much control over our benefits package. Still, it's as well to think about things in this way.

Good and bad

Taking into account the previous section and reckoning that we don't have the option to take our employer's contribution to our occupational scheme in the form of extra salary or a tube of Smarties on our desk every morning, what makes occupational pension schemes attractive is that contribution from the employer. What makes them less attractive is the fact that they're not very portable. Since you are unlikely, these days, to be spending the whole forty years of your career at Harding & Sedgewick – the average person changes job five times in their working lives and less than 5 per cent of men and 1 per cent of women stay in the same job for thirty years – this could leave you with a number of small pensions, each paying out not very much. If it is portable, you're still likely to lose out to some extent.

There are good things, then, and bad things about company pension schemes. As throughout this book, we don't seek to tell you what you should do and what you shouldn't do – that would be pointless; what we seek to do is give you the information to make informed decisions on your own behalf. What we hope you will take away from this short section is that, for most people, an occupational pension is probably not going to provide the single, all-encompassing answer to a prosperous dotage.

Avanti!

Personal Pensions

The late 1980s. Thatcher's generation of self-employed entrepreneurs is busily engaged by turns in quaffing lager, racing around in Ford Escort XR3i's and revolutionizing the British economy, but none of them, of course, has access to an occupational pension scheme. We have to presume this didn't please the boss and following a gentle word in the ear of Nigel Lawson, the Chancellor of the time, an acronym was born:

'Unfair, Nigel! These are my children. Go and DO something about it!' Roars

the 'T', eyes ablaze with fury and index finger pointing to the door of the Cabinet Room.

'Immediately, Ma'am,' ripostes Mr Lawson and scurries off to do the Leaderene's bidding.

PPPs, or Personal Pension Plans, were introduced to give self-employed people, or those working for small businesses without occupational schemes, a crack – as they like to say in the Sunday newspapers – of the pensions whip. Essentially they are *defined contribution* schemes into which you contribute out of your pre-tax earnings. In other words, whatever you contribute, up to certain limits, the Government will also chip in the tax that you would have had to pay on that income. The fund then grows over the years then, on retirement, you can take up to 25% of your fund as a tax-free lump sum, while the remainder must be used to buy something called an annuity to provide an income.

The contribution limits depend on your age and salary, moving from 17.5% of salary for those under thirty-five, up to 40% for people that are above sixty. Recent rule changes mean that you can contribute up to £2,808 (for the 2002/3 tax year) to a personal pension even if you don't actually work and don't therefore have any earnings (and the Government will still chip in the tax even though you haven't paid any, taking the total possible contribution for a non-earner up to £3,600). If you've earned less than £30,000 in one of the last five tax years, in most cases you'll also be able to contribute to a personal pension even though you're already involved in an occupational scheme. (There are more details on all of this in the Inland Revenue Leaflet PSO2.)

Simple? No, definitely not.

First, it was with PPPs that the financial professionals got their knickers in a very painful twist in the late 1980s and early 90s. By encouraging people to purchase their (expensive) plans and to abandon the perfectly good occupational schemes many of them were already in, they were giving disastrous financial advice, which would leave most of these people at a financial disadvantage in years to come. This has become known as the 'Pensions mis-selling scandal' and the precise reasons it arose (the companies involved were making a killing from selling these policies) will become painfully obvious as we consider the issue of investment charges in just one short paragraph from here. Suffice to say that some of the biggest names in financial services were implicated to the tune of billions of pounds of compensation, which they are now having to pay to those they disadvantaged by their phoney advice. The issue was supposed to be in the process of being resolved in early 1998 (with some judicious prodding from Parliament and fines for those who were reluctant to pay compensation), when it all hit centre stage again. The Government decreed in February of that year that the companies would have to investigate another 1.5 *million* cases, pushing the likely compensation bill from £5,000 million to beyond £11,000 million at a single stroke. The minister responsible referred to this as 'an awful lot of money' and we're with him on that one.

Next comes the thorny issue of charges. Let's cast our minds back for a moment to Chapter 2, 'The Miracle of Compound Interest'. There we saw how important it was, nay vital, to start on the investing trail as soon as humanly possible. Time and patience are the friends of the Foolish investor. What think you, then, Fool, of giving up 80 per cent or more of your first two years' contributions to a PPP in charges? This is money that will go not into your future, but into someone else's, either the financial adviser who sold you the plan, who takes it as his commission, or else the investment company itself. That's 80 per cent or more of the first two *paramount* years: also an awful lot of very important money. The process by which this money is taken from investors is called front-end loading and it's as bad for investors as it is good for the people selling the pension policies. And (are you still with us here?) it gets worse, breathtakingly so. Often, if you change the amount of your contributions, the company will restart the punitive charges schedule. Look at this e-mail from David Carter in 1998:

I increased my contribution to £300 [from £100] per month with effect from May 1st 1998. Then came the shock disclosure and here I do quote, because I was flabbergasted when I saw:
'HOW MUCH WILL THE ADVICE COST?'
'Company X will provide services and remuneration for arranging and servicing this increase [sic] to your plan amounting to £77.11 per month on average in the first year and a variable amount per month thereafter, being for

example £64.50 on average in the second year, £15.28 in the third year and £24.28 in the final year. These amounts have been included in the deductions shown above and are determined by the size of the contribution increase and payment term.'

Now, I've never been much of a jargon man myself. But to my simple thinking, this all adds up to a total of £2200 over four years just to service an increase to my premium – I even had to write the letter authorizing the increase to the company direct debit!

I rang my Company X salesman (I've never accepted their term of 'advisor') who I've known for thirteen years. He was upset that I should question this 25 per cent (averaged over 4 years) charge. He compared it to my fees for recruiting staff for my clients (average: 20 per cent of first year's remuneration). I respectfully pointed out to him that I don't make any charges when a client increases someone's salary! (Anyway, isn't the first year's fee 40 per cent?)

He's coming to see me tomorrow to try and sort it out. He asked me to find out whether other pension providers charge less – probably so that he can show me how well the Company X investment out-performs any other that I might choose. I don't want to play that game and told him that I shall not be doing any business with Company X again.

Sadly, what happened to David happens to many people with personal pensions who think they're saving more and more for the future. Each time they increase their contributions, they don't realize they are paying directly into the pockets of the people who are running their policy.

Now, interesting things also happen when you stop paying into your Personal Pension Plan earlier than you'd planned. There could be a variety of reasons for this, which were nicely detailed in an article in the *Independent* on 15 November 1997: Lincoln, a PPP provider, found that 45 per cent (!) of its pension premiums lapse within three years and, to their credit, commissioned research into why this was so. This research revealed that 34 per cent lapsed due to unemployment, 23 per cent due to career breaks to raise a child and 20 per cent because people were offered a good occupational scheme – in other words 77 per cent of lapses were due to perfectly acceptable reasons, not just people jibbing out for no reason.

Let's turn again to the pages of *Money Management*, the magazine of choice for the financial services industry. Brace yourselves for the riveting story behind the paid-up value and the transfer value. If you decide to stop paying into your PPP, you can do one of two things: leave the money where it is or transfer it out. If you transfer it elsewhere you get (no great surprises here) the transfer value. If you leave it where it is, the company will credit you with a paid-up value that will then grow until the end of the term and you can take whatever benefits might be coming your way. So far, so good, but you won't be surprised to hear that some of the transfer values were truly appalling. Consider the case of a thirty-year PPP with J. Rothschild Assurance, in which contributions of £200 per month were stopped after two years. Now, um, 24 x 200 equals, um, 4800, right? No, that can't be right, let's check it again, 24 x 200 equals …

(Sounds of head-scratching, whistling, pencil scribbling through long multi-plication sums)

… um, yes, 4800.

Now, in this case, the transfer value of the fund after two years is actually only £1473 – in other words 69 per cent *lower* than the contributions paid in. Just 69 per cent depreciation in two years: now, that's investment!

Fair enough, you might say (we wouldn't), they have to penalize people who decide to leave early, but take a look at their paid-up value: that's a whopping £4788. This is just about what you've paid in contributions and a definite incentive to leave the money where it is, rather than transfer it else-where. Not bad, you might think (we wouldn't): zero growth after two years. Leave it there and it'll grow nicely, you might think. Wrong! If we then move on to the maturity value of this £4788 at thirty years, we see that it is only £13,826, or equivalent to a paltry return of around 4 per cent per year.

Now, picture for a moment having had the misfortune of being sweet-talked into a Rothschild plan that you found you had to leave for one reason or another. The consequences are nothing short of catastrophic. For you, anyway. However, someone, somewhere is getting the benefit of all that compound interest on 4800 – 1473, or £3317 over thirty years. Nice work if you can get it, we say.

Stakeholder Pensions

The introduction of so-called 'Stakeholder' pensions has improved the situation greatly because, to describe itself as such, a pension plan must meet some very strict, and we must say pretty Foolish, conditions. Essentially these come under the headings of charges, access and terms, rather like the 'CAT' standards that we'll talk about when we get onto ISAs. The key points are that:

- Schemes may only charge a maximum of 1% per year of funds accrued.
- There must be no up-front charges.
- Payments into the scheme must be flexible — so you can stop, start, increase or cut your monthly payments without penalty. The minimum payment is £20, but schemes can choose to require even less.
- Transfers in from other pension schemes must not be charged for — although if you're thinking of transferring your current pension into a stakeholder, your old pension manager can charge you for leaving their scheme. But you can't be charged for leaving a stakeholder scheme.

So, while a stakeholder pension might not be the best pension product on the market at any one time, it should be pretty close to it. In a sense, they're the pension equivalent of the index trackers that we've talked about so much already. In fact the Wise pension fund managers have found that they can only manage to make Stakeholder pensions work for them by actually making them index trackers. There has also been a certain reluctance in the industry to provide them, but this has only matched by an apparent reluctance on the part of the investing public to make use of them. You see the 1 per cent limit on charges doesn't leave much room for an advertising budget. Anyway, given that they're based on an index-tracking approach, have low charges and are relatively transparent, they certainly constitute a Foolish pension option.

Self-Invested Personal Pensions (SIPPs)

Another Foolish pension option is the Self-Invested Personal Pension or SIPP. Like the stakeholders, these are just a form of personal pension with a slight nuance of their own. In this case the nuance is that you, as the name suggests, make the investment decisions. By putting a SIPP wrapper around your investments, you get the same tax benefits as for personal pensions generally, but you also have to live with the same restrictions: principally that you can't get at the money until you retire and then you have to use 75 per cent of it to buy an annuity (we are coming to these!).

SIPPs used to be prohibitively expensive unless you had a very large pension fund, but low-cost versions are beginning to crop up over the Internet, potentially widening their audience. Having said that, SIPPs clearly won't suit everyone because not everyone trusts themselves to make their own decisions with their pension fund, but some Fools certainly prefer it that way (remember how badly the professionals manage at it). You could, of course, have a SIPP and just buy index trackers to put in it, but then you might as well use a Stakeholder in the first place. It's worth pointing out at this stage that you can transfer a stakeholder into a SIPP for no cost, so a reasonable plan is to start with the former and move to the latter if you get advanced in your Foolish education and fancy doing it yourself.

Annuities

This word annuity has been cropping up a lot, but we didn't get into any detail about what it actually means. We're sorry about that, but now's the moment to make up for it.

The Government – and you won't be surprised to hear this – doesn't trust you a great deal. It doesn't trust you not to blow the entire amount of your retirement fund on General Montgomery at 50–1 in the 3.30 at Kempton Park. It doesn't trust you not to blow the whole caboodle on a two-week orgy of high living in a pink Rolls-Royce with personalized number plate 'FOOL 1'. It doesn't trust you not to blow the lot on a dead-cert investment in an emerald mine in the Venezuelan interior or on Russian Ministry of Finance junk bonds. You see, if they did trust you not to do any of these things and you let them down, then they would end up having to feed and house you and that's why they make you buy an annuity with the money you have accrued in your personal pension or AVC fund. It's a very sensible decision on their part, they see it as just return for their generosity in giving you tax relief on your pension contributions for all those years, and it lets them avoid what could potentially be a whole lot of bother. For you, though, it may not be so good. Let's see why.

An annuity is the way in which you convert the money you have built up in your PPP or AVC fund into a regular income to see you through your retirement. It works broadly like this:

- You retire.
- You take the dosh in your PPP or AVC fund and use it to purchase an annuity, either from the company with which you already have your policy, or another company (for the privilege of which you may be charged a penalty by your original company).
- The annuity pays you an income until you die.
- You pay tax on that income.
- The precise amount of the income depends on how long the annuity provider expects you to live. Women, who live longer than men, receive less than men of the same age. Older people receive more than younger people. (And students of the macabre will note that with some companies, fat smokers can negotiate larger payments than slim non-smokers. We should have put vouchers for a large doner kebab and a packet of twenty Benson & Hedges at the back of the book. Enjoy them while you can!)
- Unless you have agreed to accept a substantially reduced initial annuity income, the amount you will receive will not increase with inflation.
- Unless you have agreed to accept a substantially reduced initial annuity income, your spouse may get nothing when you die.

Now, you and your spouse both die. BIFF!

- When you and your spouse are both dead, the annuity ends and your relatives or favourite charity get nothing.

One of the problems with annuities is that these days we are living too long for them, and the rate of inflation is just that little bit too high to make them last. With the basic annuity, an insurance company effectively takes your money and uses it to buy some gilts. It buys gilts because it needs something that is considered to be low risk and that provides an income. But people reading this book may be looking at twenty, thirty or even more years of retirement. You'll remember from Chapter 4, 'The Bible of the Long Distance Investor', that gilts tend to make a pretty poor investment over that sort of period. Let's do a thought experiment to look at why annuities are not powerful investments:

Hermione is fifty years old and wins the lottery: £1,000,000 in cool, gleaming pound coins. She can't be bothered with thinking about all this tiresome business of investment, she has no relatives and all she wants is a steady income with which to enjoy herself, so she uses it all to purchase an annuity. At the rates prevailing in summer 2002, this will buy her an annuity income of about £60,000 per year. Whoopee! But remember, this will not increase with inflation. Assuming that successive governments manage to achieve their inflation target of 2.5 per cent, Hermione will enter her seventieth year with an inflation-adjusted income of £36,161 (that's the real value of her intial £65,000 after it has depreciated at 2.5 per cent per year). Not bad still, but she's beginning to think hard about whether she can really afford two cruises a year. She tightens her belt and, a true warhorse, makes it to her ninetieth year. Now, her income has fallen to the equivalent of only £21,794. She can just about keep herself fed and warm in the winter, but a cruise? Forget it!

In fact, things are a little worse than this when we compare the income to average earnings since, as we've seen before, this tends to increase at a rate of about 2 per cent more per year than inflation. Adjusting for this, and it seems only fair to do so, Hermione's income at ninety would be the equivalent of just £9,512. And, of course, when Hermione's time eventually comes to depart for the longest cruise of all, there'll be nothing left to leave to her great nephew Timmy. She will have forfeited Most Favoured Ancestor status. To think she was once a millionairess.

As an alternative, Hermione could have used her lottery win to invest in a range of income producing shares. We'll say more about this in Chapter 19, Investing for Income, but there's a wide selection of strong companies around that provide income, through their dividends, of about 4% per year, with fair prospects for this to grow over the long term at least alongside growth in average earnings. Taking this approach, our lady of leisure will have had to make do with just £40,000 per year from the start, but that income could be expected to maintain its spending power whether she survived to 75 or 105. And, of course, when she does finally snuff it, the million pounds will still be left intact for Timmy. In fact, you'd expect it to have grown in line with average earnings.

Of course, by going down the shares route, Hermione will have had to take on some risk. Over the short term, shares prices can be highly volatile but, as we saw in Chapter 4, The Bible of the Long-Distance Investor, they haven't done worse than gilts in any 30-year period since 1869. It's also important to note that, if the share prices are volatile, it's because investors are changing their mind about how much its worth paying for a particular company's stream of dividends. The stream of dividends, itself, tends to change much more gradually. All companies can go through bad patches and sometimes, they even stop paying a dividend entirely for a few years but, across a broad portfolio of shares, or some high-income investment trusts (as we'll see in Chapter 19), the overall income is highly unlikely to reduce substantially. In any case, the nightmare economic scenarios that can have this sort of disastrous effect often involve large doses of inflation and that would have done Hermione's annuity income no favours as well.

Annuities do have one advantage in that they're calculated to use up your pot of pension savings over your anticipated lifetime. This means that you can buy yourself some certainty and make use of your full pot of money, having nothing left when you die. However, the longer your expected lifetime, the bigger the price of that security. Over periods of 30 years or more, the chances are that you can do at least as well with a portfolio of 'high yield shares' and still have the money left over at the end.

Reprise: 'You've got to have a pension haven't you?'

We feel a little more able to answer this now and the answer is 'Nope'. While it's probably a good idea to contribute to your occupational scheme – as long as you don't switch jobs too often – the case for personal pensions and FSAVCs is much more difficult. Their inflexibility and the compulsion they bring to purchase an annuity counterbalance the undoubted advantage of the tax relief they attract. Then there are the charges to think about. We can't see any sense in going for the traditional Personal Pension Plans, with their typically exorbitant charges, in preference to cheaper, non-pension, options. However, the picture here has been improved greatly by the advent of Stakeholder pensions and cheap SIPPs. These have charges to match the low-cost non-pension approaches, but you still have to balance up the tax advantages of pensions against their inflexibility and the compulsion to buy an annuity.

Bear in mind, also, that other investment wrappers provide tax relief, too: most importantly, the ISA. With a pension, you get tax relief on the money you put in, but you get taxed fully on your eventual income when you retire. With an ISA, on the other hand, you don't get any tax relief on your contributions, but the eventual income comes to you free of tax. We'll say more about this comparison towards the end of the chapter on ISAs but, for the time being, just bear in mind that pensions are tax-deferred investments, they are not tax-free investments, whatever pension salespeople would like to have you believe. It's almost as though you say, 'Don't pay me that bit of salary now, pay it to me when I've retired instead.' When it is paid to you in retirement, it will still most definitely be taxed.

There is, though, one overriding reason why you might want to contribute to a pension plan and that is if you wouldn't be able to keep your grubby paws off the money otherwise. Most other types of investment will allow you to raid your funds before you really should. With a pension plan, you can't get any benefit from the money until retirement, no ifs ands or buts, and even then, apart perhaps from a lump sum, you can only use the money to provide yourself with an income. A pension will also, incidentally, protect your savings against being raided by your creditors if you were to be made bankrupt.

Be honest with yourself and if you haven't got the discipline to leave your savings untouched, then start looking around for a Stakeholder, or perhaps a SIPP if you're the adventurous sort.

15

The Disturbing Abyss of Endowments

O wombe! O bely! O stynkyng cod Fulfilled of dong and of corrupcioun!
Geoffrey Chaucer, *The Canterbury Tales*: 'The Pardoner's Tale'

For years and years, if you didn't have an endowment policy, you didn't have an investment. Endowment policies were the mainstay of the investment market and were commonly sold in conjunction with mortgages. You paid the interest on the mortgage and a small amount also went into an endowment policy. When the mortgage term was up, the endowment policy matured and paid off the loan on the house. Neat. Easy. So neat and easy, in fact, that by the end of the 1980s, 80 per cent of UK mortgages were backed by an endowment policy.

Before we go any further, let's hear a few comments about the life assurance industry in general (the people who sell endowments) from a former Deputy Chairman of one of the companies implicated in the pensions misselling scandal we've already heard about:

> ... for the last twenty years the big life assurance companies in this country have systematically been ripping people off ...

Steady on! He continues:

> ... the high turnover in salespeople, the commission system and the practice of front-end loading all lend weight to the accusation that there has been a

massive distortion ... by the life assurance companies ... of the British retail savings market ...

Phew! Whose side is this fellow on? These comments were quoted in a book entitled *The Last Days of the Credit Culture* by Jonathan Mantle.

So, What Is an Endowment?

Endowments are a form of life assurance policy with a savings and investment mechanism built in. What happens is that the policy holder pays premiums and then, after a predetermined period of time (normally twenty-five years when linked to a mortgage) or on death, the insurance company pays out a sum to that policy holder. Sounds innocent enough, but like so many things in this deceptive ol' Wise world, it isn't. The added complexity of the products give financial services companies all the opportunity that they need to cover up what are, in most cases, indecent commissions and charges. By now, you won't be surprised to hear that our Wise friends generally don't need asking twice to take advantage of this. You also won't be surprised to hear that these commissions and charges, which come straight out of the money you pay in, are the very reason why they prove to be such lousy investments. Did you notice the words 'front-end loading' in the second of the two quotes above? We've come across that before in the chapter on pensions. Yes, the same thing happens with endowments. The salesperson largely creams off the first couple of years' contributions, pockets them and leaves you fighting to keep your head above water. Fighting so hard, in fact, that it may be as much as seven years before you break the surface again. The surrender value (i.e. what you'd get if you cashed the policy in) can take this long to even approach the value of the contributions paid in. In fact, let's not do our own dirty work, let's quote the industry's own magazine, *Money Management*, again. In a review of endowment mortgages in July 1997 it said:

In most cases, even after seven years, ... endowment surrender values do not even return premiums paid. The average yield on seven year surrender values is –0.9 per cent.

Pardon us, but haven't we been here before? It can and often does take this long for the transfer or paid-up values of PPPs and AVCs to break even. We're starting to see some common threads emerging. Low returns, massive charges, inflexibility: all these things characterize the investments that people out there want to sell you. You know, sometimes we get financial professionals coming to our site and telling us we're misleading the public, that we're giving those fellows a bad name. Well, it seems to us like they're more than capable of doing it themselves. Anyway, to understand endowments better, we need to take a little step back in history and see how they developed.

The original pure endowment

The original incarnation of endowments was the 'pure' endowment. In the finest traditions of insurance, these policies guaranteed to pay a definite sum on death or maturity. When sold alongside an interest-only mortgage, this made a good deal of sense, since it was a definite sum that would be required to pay off the mortgage at the end of the term. Essentially the effect of this would be identical to having a repayment mortgage together with pure life assurance (that is, which only pays out on death, not at the end of the term). Both approaches would guarantee that your mortgage would be repaid on death or at the end of the period of the loan. The question you then have to ask with this type of endowment is 'What's the point of it?' Why not just get a repayment mortgage together with some pure life assurance? Why bother the insurance company with the repayment part of the mortgage, since this will surely just add to costs? In the dim and distant past, there used to be some tax relief on the premiums paid into life assurance products, but after this was scrapped, it became very hard for the insurance companies to sell these products. They therefore needed to think of something to sweeten them up a little.

With-profits and unitized with-profits endowments

What insurance companies (and their salespeople) found was that it was a lot easier to sell endowments if they could suggest to prospective policy holders that there might be a 'windfall', over and above the mortgage repayment, at the end of the policy term. They therefore devised the 'with-profits' endowment. With these, they took the premiums that you paid them, took out the life assurance bit and invested the rest on your behalf, the plan being that you would get the proceeds from these investments and this would pay off your mortgage with, hopefully, a bit to spare.

What had in fact happened was that the householder, rather than the insurance company, had suddenly started to carry the risk of the investments not doing well enough to pay off the mortgage (remember how important it is to know who is taking the risk in any given situation), which effectively meant that the apparent benefit of the 'windfall' was no more than cosmetic. Householders could create the same result by channelling the money into (lower-charging) investments themselves. Of course, the sellers of endowment policies didn't really want people to realize this and, as we'll see in a moment, it is more than fair to say that, on many occasions, they were economical with the truth when selling these policies.

The investment element of with-profits endowments is added to policies in a fairly unusual manner. At the end of each year an annual or 'reversionary' bonus is added to the policy. Once added, this cannot be taken away. The effect of this is that the value of your policy won't fall (although it can still go up only very slowly). In addition to annual bonuses, a terminal bonus is added at the end of the term. Initially this seemed like a good idea. Unfortunately, the insurance companies realized that it didn't give them very much flexibility. Gradually, therefore, the terminal bonus has come to represent more and more of the investment return (at the expense of the non-removable annual bonuses) so that now terminal bonuses can account for as much as 60 per cent (or more) of the final value of a policy. So their final value is barely more reliable than if an investor had invested the money themselves without troubling the insurance company (and therefore making substantial cost savings).

In the world of PEPs and ISAs (which we look at in the next chapter), it seems odd that many people are still persuaded to pay their money into a with-profits endowment that will frequently have no value for several years, thus locking them in whether they like it or not. By contrast, should you wish to, you can get at your ISA funds at any stage. In addition, the underlying investment mix of a with-profits policy is, at best, the same as can be had from an ISA, but with higher charges. It is therefore difficult to see any reason why the investment performance of a with-profits endowment should be as good as a cheap ISA. True, the Government has only said that ISAs will be around for ten years, but it seems almost inconceivable that there would be no form of tax-free savings vehicle after that.

Unit-linked endowment policies

In order to boost the attractions of endowments further, the insurance companies decided to produce a version linked to their managed unit trusts. Instead of the complicated business of bonuses that you get on a with-profits endowment, with a unit-linked endowment the value of your investments just go up and down with the value of the unit trust that your endowment is linked to. This has the benefit of being a more transparent structure, in terms of returns as well as charges, but it makes the comparison with ISAs even more stark. Let's assume we're looking at the same unit trust. What's the point of buying it via an endowment, and possibly paying in money for years before it has any value at all, when you could pay into an ISA, a fund that will be available to you whenever you should want it? On top of this, of course, there is the fact that the vast majority of the unit trusts that these endowments are linked to will underperform a good cheap index tracker.

Endowment Mis-selling

It's pretty clear that endowments have come a long way from the original no-risk product. These days, their risk profile is not significantly different from the underlying investments that homeowners can buy themselves to back their mortgage. In both these cases – buying the investment yourself in the form of an ISA or buying an endowment – you are taking the risk that you will not, in fact, be able to repay your mortgage at the end of its term, in favour of what you hope will be greater return. If this is so, why would you choose to take this risk in an endowment policy which is extraordinarily costly and inflexible? As we'll see in Chapter 18, 'Be Your Own Landlord', the only way that repaying the sum at the end of the mortgage can be guaranteed is by taking a repayment mortgage, where you actually repay a bit of the capital each month until it's all gone (typically after twenty-five years). Unfortunately, in their endeavour not to miss out on the several thousand pounds of commission that selling an endowment can earn, it seems that a great number of financial advisers and salespeople have been rather slow to point this out.

This has prompted the Financial Services Authority (FSA) to undertake a review into the 'mis-selling' of endowments. The FSA's view is that, where the extra risks of an endowment mortgage over the repayment type have not been made clear, there 'may have been a mis-sale'. Compensation that is then payable is the difference between the endowment-holder's position and the position they would have been in with a repayment mortgage. This is reasonable, as far as it goes. The trouble is that it doesn't consider whether endowments are a suitable means of saving to repay the capital on a mortgage where the homeowner *is* prepared to take the risk of an 'interest-only' mortgage. Whether or not a repayment mortgage should have been recommended, the extra charges on an endowment and their consequent sub-par performance means that there are very few circumstances in which an endowment can be considered a more effective means of repayment than a cheap ISA alternative.

In addition to the issue of mis-selling, the FSA has recently lowered the percentage growth figures that endowment salespeople are allowed to use to sell endowments and review existing ones. The effect is that, on the new projections, many endowments sold in recent years are now 'not on track' to pay off their mortgages. This has meant that the endowment providers have had to write to policyholders explaining this. First of all, it's important to point out that there is no great reason for panic. If the projections are lowered, then policies with insufficient leeway are bound to fall short on the new projections. The question to ask is why the projections have been lowered. The answer to this is that we are now in a lower interest rate environment than we were. Interest rates are expected to remain low and this means that the returns from all investments are now expected to be lower than they have been in the recent past. The flip side to this is that the interest rates on mortgages are also expected to be lower. The solution, then, for anyone who has an interest-only mortgage (whether it is backed by an endowment or an ISA), is to take the money that you're now saving on lower interest rates and add it to the money that you are investing (we would suggest, though, that you do this through a cheap index-tracking ISA rather than topping up the endowment). Alternatively, you could take the safe option and use the extra money to pay off a bit of the capital on the mortgage each month (in other words, convert to a 'part-repayment' mortgage).

We'll talk more about the pros and cons of different types of mortgages in Chapter 18. For the moment, suffice to say that the financial services industry has yet again failed to cover itself in glory.

So, Where Does This Leave Us?

Even though the proportion of mortgages being sold with endowments is now apparently down to around 10 per cent, we Fools would say that this is still 10 per cent too many. So, the first thing to say is – **don't get one.** The only possible situation that we can think of where they *might* be a good thing is as a savings vehicle for a higher rate taxpayer who is already making full ISA contributions. However, even in this case, we'd say that you'd be better off investing directly in the stock market and holding for a long period. Careful tax planning should remove any benefit that the endowment might have had.

What if you're one of the unlucky people who have already got an endowment? The first general suggestion that we can give for anybody worried about their endowment is to get hold of the FSA factsheet on endowment mortgages. You can get this by phoning 0845 606 1234, or you can find it on the FSA Web site, which is listed in Appendix 4. The second general pointer is to say that there is no reason to rush into anything. You should think long and hard about your situation and discuss it with others. You might even want to pop by our Web site and see what others have chosen and are choosing to do with their endowments. As you can probably imagine, it's something of a hot topic. If necessary, take professional advice. However, if you do want to do this, we'd suggest that you make sure that the adviser has no conflict of interest with your position. This will generally involve finding a financial adviser who doesn't earn commission from selling endowments.

There are a number of possible options for your endowment and you should contact your provider to find out which of these are available to you. When you have this information, think about it from first principles. Forget what has gone and think about the future. What are the costs associated with your endowment from now on? What is the likely performance of the endowment from now on? What would be the effect of selling the endowment and reinvesting the proceeds in something better? What would be the effect of stopping contributions at this stage?

If you have a with-profits endowment that is more than about seven years old then it might have a sale value. Bear in mind, though, that, if you sell, someone is buying it because they think it's cheap. They will have taken into account the effect of ongoing charges and the likely terminal bonus and they will have decided that it is a good deal. You therefore need to have some reason for thinking that it is a good deal for you too. For instance, the buyer might think that endowments are lower risk than, say, index trackers. They might therefore be prepared to accept a slightly lower future return from the endowment than you might expect to get from the tracker. You, on the other hand, might think that endowments don't significantly reduce your risk and that you'd therefore rather have the money in a tracker or you might simply want to revert to a repayment mortgage.

If you do decide to sell your endowment, you're really not giving yourself a chance of doing better unless you make absolutely sure that you get the best possible price for it. First of all, you can get a free brochure on buying and selling endowments from the Association of Policy Market Makers on 020 7739 3949. With this and the details of your policy in hand, you can go about collecting a number of quotes for your policy. Don't be afraid to tell them that you have higher quotes from elsewhere: they're bound to start low and move up. This point is amply illustrated by a post from Jonathan Teague on the Motley Fool's Endowments discussion board on 29 January 2000:

Hi all,

I'd just like to relate the happy tale of my recent endowment sale.

I had been paying into an endowment with the Pearl since Feb 89 and for the past year had been reading the Money section of the Sunday Times, listening to the various personal finance programmes on the radio and wondering if continuing with it was entirely sensible. Then, WHAM, in November I discovered the Fool. Well to cut a long story short I spent considerable time getting past performance information out of the Pearl and came to the conclusion that the future did not look rosy for the endowment and it was time to consider selling and reinvesting.

The surrender value was 9284. Amazing, a whole 3.78 per cent annualized return on the monthly investments (deducting an allowance for the life cover). Gee, was I impressed?!

Well I contacted most of the TEP [Traded Endowment Policy] traders (all online with the exception of Neville James) and the offers started to come in:

Policy Trading Company: Sorry – can't beat Life Co
Absolute Assigned Policies: 10,744
Policy Plus: 10,740
Surrenda-Link: 10,923
Beale Dobie: 11,809
Policy Portfolio: 12,200
Neville James: 12,750

An astounding range. How can one company not beat the surrender value and another give over 30 per cent more?

This is where things got interesting, basically I didn't do anything for a fortnight (the Fool does not act hastily) and the phone rang – Beale Dobie wanted to know if I liked their offer, I told them about the higher offer and they said they would 'see'.

Promptly in the post.
Beale Dobie: 13,007

Blimey, mate! Now 40 per cent more than surrender value and almost 1200 more than their original offer. But then ... the phone rang again, Policy Portfolio this time – they too would 'see'.

Next day.
Policy Portfolio: 13,800

Sorry! Is this real, that's 48.5 per cent more than surrender and 13 per cent more than PP's original offer. Anyway, after giving some of the other offers yet another 'go' I concluded that this really was the best offer and went for it. The paperwork was dealt with very efficiently and in less than two weeks the cheque arrived.

So if you decide to sell the morals are –

1.Don't immediately accept the highest offer from the first batch – let them fight – they will!

*2.Get quotes from as many of the traders as possible (you can ask for quotes from almost all of them online). You never know which one will give the best offer for your policy. Imagine if I had only picked Policy Trading Company, Absolute Assigned Policies and Policy Plus to get quotes from – **that would have cost me £3000!***

Well I'm now well on the way to being a fully paid-up Fool. It's all going into trackers from now on.

Incidentally the 13,800 represents an annualized tax-free return of 10.73 per cent on the monthly investment, not bad so I'm not too upset. Yes, if I had invested in a tracker from day 1 I would have over 20K now but you can't regret the past – you just have to make damned sure you learn from it!

Fool on,

Jon.

We'd add just a couple of things to Jon's comments. Having got your highest offer, it could be worth putting the policy up for auction, with the offer that you've received as the 'reserve price'. If the auction beats this, then well and good; but if not, you have the other offer to fall back on. A company called H. E. Foster & Cranfield carries out weekly second-hand endowment policy auctions and, strangely enough, has done so since 1843. You can contact them on 020 7608 1941.

If your endowment policy is a unit-linked policy or is only a few years old, then you might not be able to sell it. In this case, you could think about surrendering the policy. You can get the surrender value from the endowment company and then try to work out, along the lines mentioned above, whether you think that the surrender proceeds (if any) could do better for you outside the endowment than inside it. The sums can be quite tricky, but it is well worth making the effort to look into it, rather than risk being tied into an underperforming investment for twenty years or more.

If you feel uncomfortable about selling or surrendering your endowment, you may have the opportunity to make your policy 'paid up'. The effect of this is that your accumulated pot of money stays in the endowment, but you stop making further contributions. The money that would have gone into contributions can then be used to pay into an alternative, and hopefully better, investment or, alternatively, into repaying your mortgage directly. One final point to make if you are considering disposing of, or stopping contributions to, an endowment is that you will be losing your life assurance cover. If you have dependents, then the chances are that you should replace this.

In Conclusion

In the unlikely event that anyone hasn't realized that we absolutely hate and detest endowments, let's summarize by saying that endowments are inflexible, high-expense, underperforming investments that line the pockets of the Wise at the expense of the public. If you want life insurance, which, by the way, is basically just the same as life assurance, buy just that – 'term' life assurance, no more no less, and put your money for investment into real investments, Foolish investments. If you do want out, it will almost certainly pay you to sell, if you are able to, rather than surrender. Here, to end our consideration of endowments, is an editorial quote from the *Daily Telegraph* of 31 August 1991, at the height of the endowments boom:

> *It cannot be said too often that the advantages to the householder of an endowment mortgage are as nothing compared to the gain to the policy salesperson, that life assurance has nothing to do with house purchase, and that savings-related life assurance is a waste of money.*

16

The Tranquil Paradise of ISAs

For my wish … I desire most marvellous things; just a fine bauble and a hood
garnished with long ears and bells that make a marvellous noise …

Recueil de Poésies Françaises

The Government is very keen for us to save for our future and it provides tax incentives for us to do so. Unfortunately, as we saw with pensions and endowments, these tax incentives are sometimes overwhelmed by a variety of catches. Fortunately, though, every now and again, the Government hits the nail on the head and gives us exactly what we want (or very nearly anyway). This is what happened when the Personal Equity Plan (or PEP) was introduced in the late 1980s. PEPs were a means whereby any old Fool could invest money in shares while sheltering the returns from the taxman. Not surprisingly, they've proved to be extremely popular and they are still around today, although no new money can be added to them. These days, we have Individual Savings Accounts (ISAs) to put money into and, although they are a bit complicated, they remain every bit as lovely as PEPs used to be.

What? The Fools are actually endorsing a financial product?! Have they gone mad? Well, we must admit that after writing the previous couple of chapters it does feel a little strange. Perhaps this outflowing of joy is a result of the pain and sorrow of what has gone before, but we really do like ISAs a lot. The main reason for this is that, with a few reasonable limitations, you can put pretty much whatever investments you like into them. This means that we're in control. We can sit there with our ISA and say, 'Mmm…I'll have a bit of that and a bit of this and, oh yes, a bit of that.' It also means that they have a very transparent charging structure. You can see exactly how much it is costing you and, as a result, ISA providers are in intense competition with each other to provide them more and more cheaply. All very Foolish.

When you buy an index tracker (or an underperforming managed fund), you can generally buy it pre-wrapped in an ISA. The nice thing about doing this is that the manager of the index tracker will typically throw the ISA wrapper in for free, keeping your costs down. Alternatively, you can buy your own ISA wrapper (called a 'self-select ISA') and put what you like into it yourself. The trouble with this is that you'll have to pay for the ISA and then pay for what you put into it on top. For this reason, self-select ISAs tend to be used only where you are putting shares directly into the ISA, since, with the big exception of dealing charges when you buy and sell, shares have no additional ongoing costs.

Once you've got your money in an ISA, you won't get charged any income tax on interest received on it and you won't get charged any extra tax (in addition to what the company has already paid) on any dividends from companies (we talked about dividends in Chapter 11, 'A Share Primer'). In fact, until 2004, you get back a tiny bit of the tax that the company has paid. On top of all this, you don't get charged any capital gains tax when you sell investments within the wrapper, and you don't incur any tax when you take money out of the ISA. We'd really like to say that it's as simple as that and move on to the next section of the book. Unfortunately, as ever, the devil is in the detail. Thankfully, for once, the detail does nothing to reduce (or, for that matter, improve) the usefulness of the product. It serves only to make the head a bit sore.

The Detail

There are two basic types of ISA: the Maxi-ISA and the Mini-ISA. It's pretty important to be clear about the differences because, in each tax year, you are allowed (assuming that you're a UK resident aged eighteen or over) to invest in just one of the two types. Each type has three separate components: cash, stocks and shares, and insurance. The difference between the two is that in the Maxi, they're all mushed together into the same account, whereas with the Mini, each of the bits are in different accounts. It's perhaps easiest to think of the Maxi as being like one big teapot into which you can put up to three different types of teabag (that is, one teabag for cash, one teabag for stocks and shares and one teabag for insurance). Since it's all in one teapot, only one person can be mother. In other words, you have to pick one financial organization to run the whole Maxi-ISA for you.

Similarly, you can think of the Mini-ISA as being like three small teapots, each of which can contain a different teabag (except you can't have the same type of teabag in two different pots). So, if you like the interest rates on someone's cash Mini-ISA, but you don't like the charges on their stocks and shares Mini-ISA, then you can open the cash Mini with them, but go to someone else for the stocks and shares Mini. Before we leave our teabags analogy, we should just say that we don't much like the taste of insurance teabags. We don't like the confusion between insurance and investment at the best of times and we really can't work out who would want to put insurance policies into an ISA. It looks like we're not the only ones. Very few financial organizations offer them and in the first nine months of the ISA, only £44 million had been put into the insurance component compared to more than £17 billion into cash and stocks and shares. Really, then, we'd say that you can simplify matters greatly by just ignoring the insurance component and concentrating on the other bits.

Now we've got the difference between these Maxis and Minis sorted out, let's have a look at the annual limits. For the 2002/3 tax year, you can invest up to £7000 in a Maxi-ISA. You can put as much of this into the stocks and shares component as you like, but you can only put up to £3000 into the cash component. For Mini-ISAs, the limits are £3000 for a stocks and shares Mini and £3000 for a cash Mini.

Each new tax year brings the opportunity to make fresh subscriptions to an existing ISA, or to open a whole new ISA. Of course, if you keep opening a new ISA each year, things are going to get pretty complicated. To simplify matters, transfers from one ISA into another are allowed. However, the components must remain the same. So, once you've gone for the stocks and shares component of a Maxi-ISA or a stocks and shares Mini, you can move it around all over the place, but it must always remain in stocks and shares. Similarly, when you've gone for a cash component, it must always stay in cash. Any transfers like this do not count for the purposes of each year's allowances.

As you can probably imagine, you can only really put cash (and one or two things that are very like cash) into a cash ISA. The fun starts when you get to the stocks and shares bit. Here you can put in most of the things that you might want to. You can put shares in it, so long as they're quoted on a major stock exchange (there's more about what that means in Chapter 11, 'A Share Primer'), you can put most unit trusts and investment trusts into it and you can put gilts and corporate bonds into it. You can even hold a bit of cash in it, but this must be for the purpose of buying the other investments that we've just mentioned. You can't hold cash in a stocks and shares component 'for the sole purpose of sheltering interest on cash deposits from tax'.

The Government has designed a scheme to help people tell which ISAs meet certain minimum standards. It's designed to reassure us a bit and it does just that. It's a voluntary code and it in no way guarantees returns, but if an ISA is CAT-marked, it does tell you that certain conditions are met. CAT stands for Charges, Access and Terms, the three areas that the standards cover. For Charges, the provisions are that cash ISAs can make no charge at all, and stocks and shares ISAs can only charge up to 1 per cent of the value of the ISA per year. For Access, you've got to be able to get at your money within seven working days. The most important part of the Terms bit is that the interest rate on cash ISAs can't be more than 2 per cent below the base rate, at least 50 per cent of stocks and shares ISAs must be invested in Europe and unit trusts must have the same buying and selling price.

Wrapping Up

Stocks and shares ISAs are very well suited to saving for retirement. You can start off with most (or all) of the investments going into shares to grow nicely over the long term, then when you get to retirement, you can switch part of the accumulated fund into gilts or corporate bonds to provide a higher immediate income and less short-term risk (although, as we'll see in Chapter 19, Investing for Income, you shouldn't be too hasty to move into this type of investment). The beauty of this is that this income is received free of income tax, whereas the eventual income from a pension gets taxed. All things being equal, this amounts to the same thing. This is because of a fancy mathematical concept called 'Multiplicative Commutativity'. Simply put, it just means that with multiplication, it makes no difference what order you do it in. For example, look at the position for a higher rate taxpayer (i.e. 40 per cent) who has £1000 to invest pre-tax and gets 9 per cent growth for three years before drawing income at a rate of 5 per cent. Tax of 40 per cent before the money goes into the ISA leaves him with £600 ('1000 x 0.6'). This grows at 9 per cent a year for three years (that's the '1.09' in the equation) and is then drawn at a rate of 5 per cent (that's the '0.05'):

ISA: £1000 x 0.6 x 1.09 x 1.09 x 1.09 x 0.05 = £38.85

Meanwhile, in the pension, all the money goes in up front (i.e. there's total tax relief on it), but the income gets taxed at the end:

Pension: £1000 x 1.09 x 1.09 x 1.09 x 0.05 x 0.6 = £38.85

Each year's income is the same for the ISA and the pension: £38.85. Not a lot of people realize this. But now you do.

Unfortunately, this position is confused by a couple of factors. First of all, the tax benefits of an ISA are not quite this simple. Although the interest on bonds and cash attracts full tax relief, there is only partial relief on the income from shares, which you get in the form of dividends. In effect, because the company that you invest in pays tax on its earnings, the income from shares is automatically taxed at the basic rate (give or take a little) – even in an ISA. You therefore only really get a tax benefit on the income from shares in an ISA if you are a higher rate taxpayer in retirement (because you avoid having to pay an extra bit). Since part of the point of going along the ISA route is to keep some money in shares after retirement, this reduces their appeal some-what, but at least you're not compelled to buy an underperforming annuity as you are with a pension. Secondly, the above example assumes that you will pay the same rate of tax in retirement as you do during your working life. In practice, your income (and therefore tax rate) in retirement is likely to be lower. Again, this makes the pension route a little more attractive.

Other benefits of saving via the pensions route are that, if you lost your job, you'd have to use up most of your non-pension savings before you qualified for any welfare benefits. Similarly, any pension that you have is protected if you are made bankrupt. The last main benefit of pensions is that the contribution limits are much higher than for ISAs. If you are already making full ISA contributions, the tax benefits of pensions become much more obvious.

The big problem with pensions is the requirement that we keep harping on about to buy an annuity with the bulk of the fund that you build up. As we saw in the chapter on pensions, annuities leave a lot to be desired, and that's putting it politely. If you're lucky enough to have a long retirement, their real value can be considerably eroded and you don't retain the money to leave to someone in your will.

Pensions are also very inflexible. Once money has gone in, it can only come out in the form of the lump sum on retirement and your retirement income. The flip side is that this does at least impose some discipline on you. If you think you're liable to blow all your savings at the drop of a starter's flag, then a pension could well be the way to go.

All in all, there are as many different arguments about the pros and cons of pensions over ISAs as there are different types of pensions and ISAs. The important thing to take on board is that the decision, either way, is generally not clear-cut. If someone tries to tell you that a pension is unambiguously a good idea, then there is a fair chance that they have an expensive pension to sell you.

A stocks and shares ISA is also a suitable means of repaying a mortgage. You can keep paying into the fund over the term of your mortgage and then, when the time comes, cash it in free of tax and use the money to repay the loan. At any stage during the term of the mortgage, you can decide that you'd rather just use the fund that you've built up to repay part of the mortgage (or even all of it if the fund has grown big enough). We'll talk more about the pros and cons of investment-backed, or 'interest-only', mortgages in Chapter 18, 'Be Your Own Landlord'. For now, although hopefully we don't need to, we just want to reinforce the point that if you want to go down this route, a good cheap ISA investing in shares is far more likely to make sense than the dreaded endowment.

Cash ISAs are a very good way of keeping a reserve fund for emergencies. You can get at the money whenever you need it (with a CAT-marked ISA anyway) and, in the meantime, it's earning tax-free interest. The one snag with a cash ISA is that by having one, you might hit the annual contribution limits and reduce the amount that you could be paying into a stocks and shares Maxi-ISA. In this case, we'd say that the stocks and shares should take precedence (no surprises there). Still, most people aren't in a position to save this much, in which case a cash Mini-ISA to go with a stocks and shares Mini (or a cash component in a Maxi-ISA) could make a lot of sense.

All in all, ISAs are a flexible, transparent and generally pretty cheap way of saving for most things and they offer very useful tax advantages. They're a bit complicated, but we love 'em. And so should you.

17

Unit Trusts, Investment Trusts and All Sorts

There are few sorrows, however poignant, in which a good income is of no avail
Logan Pearsall Smith, *Afterthoughts*

Pensions, endowments and ISAs are the investment wrappers that bring with them tax advantages, but there is a range of other 'collective investments' that enable investors to group together to have their money managed by someone else. The most common examples are unit trusts, open-ended investment companies ('OEICs'), investment trusts and exchange-traded funds ('ETFs'). In fact, almost all ISAs and quite a few pensions are themselves just wrappers around these more basic collective investments. So where you might have the 'Permanently Improvident UK Performance Unit Trust', Permanently Improvident will almost certainly give you the option to buy that unit trust pre-packaged within an ISA and there might well be a pension as well. In other words, you can wrap your tax-protective clingfilm around all sorts of things and, in many cases, it will be some other collective investment in the first place. One thing to make sure about is that you don't get charged twice for the two different wrappers.

There is a huge range of pooled investments available, but they break down into two main types, "open-ended" funds and "closed-ended" funds. Open-ended funds include unit trusts and OEICs, while closed-ended funds are generally referred to as investment trusts.

Unit Trusts and OEICs

Unit trusts and OEICs are known as open-ended, because their size is not limited. Imagine that you have £10,000 invested in a unit trust that has a total of £10 million of assets. If you decided to withdraw your investment, then the fund's total assets would go down to £9,990,000. However, if you decided instead to add another £10,000 to your investment, then the total assets would go up to £10,010,000. The effect of this is that if a fund suffers a large number of "redemptions" (that is, withdrawals), then it will have to sell some of its investments in order to provide the money for the investors that are pulling out. Similarly, when lots of people are adding money to a unit trust, that trust has to buy more investments in order to maintain its investment profile.

The main implication of this is for costs, because if you're going with the crowd, you'll have to pay for some of the costs of the underlying fund buying the new (or selling the old) investments. If you cash in your units, for example, when everyone else is buying, then the fund won't have to sell investments on your behalf and this might save you some money. Overall, though, as you'll hopefully have noticed from the rest of this book, we're not great believers in the frequent buying and selling of investments. Far better to invest steadily over the long term and, on that basis, you shouldn't be paying much attention to what the crowds are doing.

You can purchase units in a unit trust or OEIC either by contacting the provider directly or through a broker or financial adviser (salesperson). OEICs, by the way, are essentially just a European form of unit trust. In recent years, unit trusts in the UK have been turning themselves into OEICs so that they can also be marketed in Europe. Anyway, the best way to invest in them is, as ever, generally going to be the cheapest way. If you go through a broker or financial adviser (salesperson), it is worth checking that their fee or commission is absorbed within the charges made by the provider. You don't want to be charged twice.

Unit trust and OEIC providers generally calculate their prices once a day at around noon, in accordance with FSA regulations. This is where the main difference between unit trusts and OEICs arises. With a unit trust there are generally two prices, a "bid" price and an "offer" price. Purchases are made at the offer price and sales are made at the bid price. The difference between the two prices may or may not also incorporate an initial charge. OEICs have only one price, with the initial charge being taken as a separate commission.

How your order is turned into units is also the subject of detailed FSA regulations but, generally, they will be bought for you when the price is next set. If you make your order in the afternoon, this could therefore be the next business day. After the transaction is completed, you will be sent a contract note. You should hang on to this.

Once your money is in the trust, it is held by the fund's trustee for your benefit. Technically speaking, the trustee employs the management company to manage the fund according to its objectives. It is the responsibility of the trustee to ensure that this is done correctly. In the case of an OEIC, the trustee is called a "depositary", but the effect is basically the same. However, the funds are marketed under the name of the management company and you probably won't get to hear about who the trustee is. This doesn't really matter, since the trustee, whoever it is, has to operate in a clearly defined way according to the law.

There is a huge range of charges between different funds. Some will charge as much as 6% as an initial charge with ongoing management fees of 1.5% per annum, or sometimes even more. By contrast, some have no initial charge and ongoing fees of only 0.5% (or less). Some unit trusts and OEICs have "exit charges" whereby they take a percentage of your money when you remove it. Needless to say, you need to be fully aware of all the charges before you invest.

You might have gathered already that our favourite type of unit trust is the index tracker. With these, your money is managed in a way that's intended to provide the market average return, while keeping costs to a minimum. Because they cost less, they tend to do better than the vast majority of actively-managed unit trusts. We've already been into a fair bit of detail about why this is in Chapter 7. There's also a lot of detail in Appendix 2, 'What Makes A Good Index Tracker'.

Investment Trusts

The easiest way to understand closed-ended funds, or investment trusts, is to think of them like a company. This is because that is exactly what they are. Just like any other company, they issue shares to raise money from shareholders and then invest that money. The difference between investment trusts and normal "trading" companies, is that they invest their money in the shares of other companies rather than in physical assets such as factories or grocery stores or mobile phone networks. Since they are like a company, they are also able to borrow money to invest (which is not allowed for unit trusts).

You buy shares in an investment trust in much the same way as you would a normal company, that is, by contacting a stockbroker. Some of the larger investment trusts also run schemes whereby you can invest small amounts on a regular monthly basis. Since you buy investment trust shares just as you would shares in a normal company, the charges are the same also. So, you suffer stockbroker's commission on buying and selling. In a way, this is comparable to an initial charge and an exit charge on a unit trust. However, if you use a cheap broker, they should be relatively small. On top of commission, you lose a small amount as the difference between the bid and offer prices of the shares of the trust. However, again, this tends to be a relatively small amount.

In addition to these charges for buying and selling investment trust shares, you pay an annual management fee and other ongoing administration costs. Again, think of it as though the investment trust is a company (because it is). The annual management costs are the equivalent of a company's head office costs. Sometimes, the investment trust manages itself, through its own employees, and sometimes it 'outsources' the management to an external fund management company. Whichever way it does it, though, the investment trust, just like any other company, is obliged to do the best it can for its shareholders — and that's you. To put it another way, investment trusts have to act in their investors' interests.

This has some important knock on effects. For starters, investment trusts are not able to advertise themselves, because they couldn't justify the expense as being in the interests of shareholders (although the Association of Investment Trust Companies does do some marketing, funded by a small annual levy from the different companies). Unit trusts, meanwhile, spend a huge amount on marketing and this has to be paid for by someone. Needless to say that as a unitholder in a unit trust, that someone is you. So, unit trusts tend to have higher charges than investment trusts and, as a result, they've tended to perform worse over the years (at least the actively-managed ones with the big charges have).

Another important point about investment trust charges is that as the company gets bigger, then it costs less and less to manage, as a percentage of its overall assets. After all, it doesn't cost much more to manage £1 billion as it does to manage £10 million. The benefits of these economies of scale have to be passed on to the shareholders and the upshot is that the very big (generally very old and established) investment trusts have very low charges indeed — sometimes as low or lower than index trackers. This point was borne out by research undertaken by Fitzrovia Research a couple of years ago.

Net Assets Of Trust (£m)	Average Investment Trust Charges	Average Unit Trust Charges
All Sizes	1.46%	1.53%
More than £10m	1.40%	1.48%
More than £20m	1.35%	1.45%
More than £50m	1.11%	1.42%
More than £100m	0.99%	1.39%
More than £250m	0.75%	1.34%
More than £500m	0.57%	1.36%
More than £1,000m	0.36%	1.32%

Another effect of investment trusts being companies is that their share price, at any point in time, is dictated simply by what investors are prepared to pay for them, and may be some way away from the true net asset value of the company. In fact, the share price is generally some way below the net asset value. Imagine an investment trust with £100 million of investments and 100 million shares. The 'net asset value per share' would be 100p. Yet the shares might change hands for just 90p.

One reason is that you could buy the same portfolio of shares yourself directly in the market, without suffering the ongoing management charge. So, the price of the investment trust needs to be discounted by an amount to take account of its charges (it's head office costs, as it were). You should probably assume that this 'discount' makes no significant difference to the capital value of your investment. After all, if there's a ten per cent discount on the investment trust when you buy it, it will probably also be there when you sell so, overall, it will make no difference. In any case, investing should be a long term undertaking and, over decades, the growth in the investment trust's assets will make far more difference to the investment than the odd few per cent change in its discount.

The discount does, however, have an interesting effect from an income point of view, because the dividends that an investment trust pays out leave the company *without* a discount. Let's say we had £1,000 to invest and we wanted it to go into shares generating dividends of 3 per cent per year, making a total of £30. We could either just go ahead and buy the shares ourselves, or we could do it by buying shares in an investment trust. The investment trust might be priced at a discount of, say, 10 per cent, which would enable us to buy £1,111 of underlying assets for the same £1,000 (£1,000 is 90 per cent of £1,111). These would generate dividends of £33.33 per year (3 per cent of £1,111). Whether we'd be better off with the investment trust, would depend on whether or not the extra £3.33 was wiped out by the costs of running the fund. In this case, so long as the charges are below 0.33 per cent per year, then we'd be better off with the investment trust than by buying the shares ourselves. As we can see from the research from Fitzrovia, the largest investment trusts have charges in this sort of range. It's fair to say, therefore that the largest Investment Trusts can make very Foolish investments.

Exchange Traded Funds

Exchange Traded Funds are a new form of collective investment that deserve a brief mention. An ETF is a sort of cross between a closed-ended fund (that is, an investment trust) and an open-ended fund (that is, a unit trust). As far as you or I are concerned, they appear "closed-ended" like an investment trust. You buy and sell them through a stockbroker just as you would any company or investment trust. However, for financial institutions with loads of money, exchange traded funds suddenly become open-ended, like unit trusts. This means that the ETF managers are prepared to issue new 'shares' and redeem (that is, take back and cancel) existing ones as long as you're prepared to do it in very large chunks. In other words, the offer is open to institutions, but closed to us.

At first sight this preferential treatment for institutions would appear to be a little unfair. "Another stitch-up by those Wise fund managers," We hear you say. Well, not quite. Open-ended funds have the advantage of not having "discounts": the trouble with them is that all this issuing and cancelling of units costs rather a lot in admin fees. This tends to give closed-ended funds an advantage on costs.

The idea of ETFs, then, is to get the best of both worlds. If the shares start slipping towards a discount, then some Wise "institution" will swoop in, buy as many as they can and go along to the managers, demanding that they cash them in. The result is an insignificant discount. The advantage of not having to worry about issuing or cancelling the odd £100's worth of units for us lot is that major cost savings are made. The result of this is that charges can be kept very low.

The ETFs that are currently available in the UK are sold under the 'iShares' banner and managed by Barclays Global Investors. The principal product is the iFTSE100 which, as the name suggests, is designed to track the FTSE 100, but there are others covering different markets and sectors, like the iFTSE Euro 100, the iBloomberg European Pharmaceuticals, the iBloomberg European Telecoms and iBloomberg European Financials.

Horses for courses

Which fund is best for you will depend on what's most efficient for your own individual circumstances. If, for example, you have a lump sum to invest, then you might decide to invest it in a large general investment trust, to bene-fit from its large discount. The trouble with this is that, since it isn't an index tracker, it wouldn't necessarily get the average return on the market, so there's more risk. But perhaps you don't want the average return of the UK market. Some of the largest investment trusts include some foreign invest-ments and it may be that you want some exposure to those markets. If you're worried that your particular choice of investment trust might do particularly badly, then you could buy several of them, assuming your lump sum is big enough for that to be efficient. If you bought the biggest five 'global growth investment trusts', for example, you'd end up with a very widely diversified pool of investments, with low charges and possibly a nice discount.

Open-ended funds, such as Unit Trusts and OEICs, on the other hand, are set up to deal with regular inflows of cash, so they might be more suitable for saving smaller amounts on a monthly basis. If, for example, you wanted to save £200 per month, you'd only have enough money to make a lump sum investment once or twice a year. With a unit trust, however, you can just drip the money in monthly with no extra charge. It will also normally not cost extra to wrap the unit trust up inside an ISA. Investment trusts sometimes provide an option for monthly savings and ISAs, but it has to be fair to the existing shareholders, and will therefore probably cost extra. As we've said about a million times already, if you're going to go for regular savings into a unit trust, then an index tracker will almost certainly give you the best balance of risk and expected investment performance.

Exchange traded funds probably shine most for lump sums and where you want to gain specific exposure to a particular sector or market. There are brokers that provide the facility to save regularly into specific ETFs, generally the iFTSE100, and into an ISA, but it will cost them extra to provide this, so you should expect to find those costs being passed back to you.

One way or another, there are good and bad points about all the different types of investment vehicle. The trick behind finding what's right for you is to decide what you're trying to achieve and then find the most efficient way of achieving it. If you make things efficient for the product provider, then they ought to be able to make things cheap for you. Having said that, always check precisely the charges on any product you buy and research precisely the type of thing that their money gets invested in.

What You've (Maybe) Already Got: A Pause for Thought

If all the foregoing seems complicated and you've only half grasped it, go back and read it again. Maybe not right now – you probably need a break and a stiff drink – but sometime soon, perhaps after you've read more of the book. It's important that you do it, though. The contents of this section will help you make informed choices about how you're going to save for your future and which Wise products you may – or may not – like to buy. If you understand the contents of the last three chapters and Chapter 6, 'Be Your Own Financial Adviser', no one will ever be able to pull the wool over your eyes again and you'll be in a fine position to make your own decisions about your financial future. That's pretty Foolish.

If you're happy you've ingested it all, then 'Bravo!' And onward.

Bits 'n' Bobs

18

Be Your Own Landlord

The best thing we can do is to make wherever we're lost in look as much like home as we can.

Christopher Fry, *The Lady's not for Burning*

They do things differently in Belgium. Take Monsieur et Madame Albert Chips-Cooked-In-Lard-Why-*Do*-They-Do-That-It-Really-Spoils-Them as an example. Monsieur Albert is a branch manager at a small bank in Brussels. Madame is a clerical officer at the country's (and therefore the world's) leading Cream Cake Development Institute. With sensitive documents such as *'L'éclair: crème ou chocolat?'* and *'La pâtisserie: l'avenir'* passing across her desk on a daily basis, we can see that both Monsieur et Madame occupy jobs of the greatest responsibility. Their teenage twin boys, Philippe and René, have broad interests ranging from *'le football'* to *'le football'* and back again, and there is nothing to mark this family out from the vast majority of the Belgian bourgeoisie, including the fact that they do not own their dwelling place.

The four-bedroomed apartment in a respectable part of town that they've inhabited for years is rented. Like many respectable people on the Continent, they have never felt the need or inclination to buy their own place to live. Why is this? We have no idea, but doubtless PhD theses have been written on the subject and universities are even now offering courses on 'Comparative Home Ownership: Europe and Britain in the 20th Century'. You'll tell us we should enrol for one of these and, yeah, maybe we will (read: 'When Hell freezes over'). In the meantime, though, let's do some brainstorming about property as an investment. Is it a good one? In Britain, we seem pretty convinced that it is. On the other hand, in Belgium – and in much of Europe – many people seem convinced that it is not. Someone somewhere in Europe thinks that it is, though, because that someone is Monsieur et Madame Albert Chips-Cooked-In-Lard-Why-Do-They-*Do*-That-It-Really-Spoils-Them's landlord and they clearly think it's worthwhile. We'll say more about this in a moment but, first of all, let's take a quick look at property as an investment.

Property as an Investment

The first thing to spot about property is that it is a *real* asset. 'Real' as in it is actually there. Bricks and mortar and all that. As a real asset, it is worth what people are prepared to pay for it. This is very similar to shares, but it is very unlike other types of investments, such as gilts and cash, which are worth a fixed amount of pounds. The value of gilts and cash (which you might call nominal assets) is defined by the value of the pounds that they represent. As we have seen, the value of pounds fluctuates and, over the long term, inflation has meant that the tendency has been for them to fall in value. In fact, since the economy (including the Government) operates by investing a large number of borrowed pounds, there are good reasons for thinking that, over the long term, if the value of the pound consistently rose, we'd all go bust. For this reason economic policy is generally organized to encourage a steady decline in the pound's value. You can see this from the Bank of England's inflation target of 2.5 per cent. The aim is not to maintain the value of the pound, but to allow it to fall. Over the long term, the interest earned on cash and gilts has been scant consolation for this. The effect of all this is that investing in real assets such as shares and property, although it introduces a certain amount of short-term risk, is the best way of maintaining or increasing the value of your money over the long term.

So property is similar to shares and Fools tend to like it as an investment. But there are some big 'buts'. The first of these is that property is a difficult thing to invest in. You can't just set up a standing order for £100 per month to buy a share in the 'property market average', as you can the 'stock market average' when you purchase an index tracker, since there is no such thing as a 'property exchange'. When you buy a property, it's like buying an entire private company (that is, one that isn't listed on any stock exchange). This means that the process of buying and selling property is fairly expensive, involving, amongst other things, surveys, legal fees and extra stamp duty. It also means that most people are really only in a position to buy one (or maybe two) of them at any one time. This doesn't do very much for spreading your risk. So in some ways, investing in property is much more inefficient than the stock market and, except for the mega-rich, it is much harder to achieve a spread of risk.

The other thing about property is that because you generally have to buy it in very big chunks and most of us can't afford to buy these big chunks outright, we tend to have to borrow big sums of money from someone else to do it. When we borrow money to buy a house, we are borrowing a fixed (that is, nominal) sum to invest in a real asset. This is called gearing. If we buy a house for £100,000 with a £90,000 mortgage, then we have invested £10,000 ourselves. If the house then increases in value by 10 per cent to £110,000, the value of the £10,000 that we put in has actually increased by 100 per cent to £20,000. However, the flip side to this is that, if the value of the house falls by 10 per cent to £90,000, then the value of the £10,000 that we put in has fallen by 100 per cent, to zero. Our short-term risk is dramatically increased but, since we expect the value of our house to increase over the long term (if only because of inflation and increases in average earnings), our long-term returns should also be increased. This gearing effect is, for many, one of the attractive aspects to property as an investment.

Being Your Own Landlord

As we said above about our Belgian friends, just because they don't own their home does not, of course, mean that nobody does. Someone has to own every house and, if you don't own it yourself, you'll have a landlord that you rent it from (if it's council property, then the council will be the landlord). This landlord clearly thinks that it's worthwhile to own the property, otherwise they wouldn't do it. The landlord either ties up their own money, or they borrow money on a mortgage, just as you could have done. The landlord then goes and charges you just enough rent to pay for the upkeep of the property and still provide a good enough return to justify them tying up their money, or a good enough return to pay the mortgage and leave them with a profit. So, if it's profitable for your landlord to own your house (and if they've any sense then they'll fix the rent so that it is), then you have to ask yourself why you shouldn't just *be your own landlord*. That way, you can make the profit that your landlord would have been making from you. In fact, it makes even better sense, since you, yourself, are the most efficient person to be owning your home. You don't need to charge yourself a deposit, you don't need to worry that you might run off without paying rent and you don't need to worry that you might start squatting in your own home (or let anybody else do so). A landlord needs to charge a tenant just a little more than otherwise to take account of the chances of these things happening but, if you do the job yourself, you know that they're not going to happen. You therefore save yourself money.

Buy Your Home, but Do It Foolishly

All this tells Fools a few key things about buying their home. First of all, it's generally a good thing to do, if you can afford to. Secondly, though, it is a risky thing to do in the short term and, if you do take the plunge, you have to make sure that you can do it for the very long term. We've said several times in this book that you need to think of shares as investments for at least five years, and preferably more. Well, you need to think of property as an investment for at least ten years and preferably much more. As with shares, you can change properties in the meantime (although, as we've said, the costs of doing so are a lot higher than for shares), but you need to invest in property, as a class of asset, for the very long term.

Mortgages, as we'll see, tend to last for twenty-five years and you should make sure that you can stay the course. If interest rates rocket skywards in ten years' time, you should feel confident that you will be able to keep paying the interest on your mortgage. This generally happens when there is high inflation, and you'll feel the pain of that in your wallet each month. High inflation, though, also means that the amount of money you had to borrow for the mortgage in the first place will start to look more and more insignificant, which means that high interest rates are not necessarily a bad thing for the long term value of your property. In fact, much of the increase in house prices over the last thirty years can be put down to high inflation, despite the high interest rates that have often accompanied it.

In the *short term*, though, high interest rates can be a very bad thing for the current value of your property and, if increases in interest rates mean that you can't keep paying the interest on your mortgage, then you'll generally find that it is absolutely the worst possible time for your bank to repossess and sell your home. Apart from the possibility of some nasty 'negative equity' (where the value of your house is less than the value of your mortgage), economic conditions are likely to be bad and it may be hard to find employment.

This is beginning to sound very scary, but it isn't really meant to. We're just re-examining the old long-term/short-term perspective that we've already talked about so many times in this book. Buying your home is generally a good thing to do, but do it as a long-term investment and make sure that you don't get caught short. In other words, buy your own home, but do it Foolishly.

Which Property, When and for How Much?

The questions of which property to buy, when to buy it and how much to pay are often the questions that cause people most headaches, but if you think about things Foolishly, this needn't be the case. The answer to the first question is simple. You are buying your own house, as we've said, to be your own landlord. So, the house that you buy is the one that you want (and can afford) to live in. It really is as simple as that. Find the house with that wonderful view, that rambling garden, that short journey to work or that gentle stroll along the lane to your local pub and buy it. To buy a house and live in it just because you think it will make a good investment is putting the cart before the horse. You only have one life and to spend it living in a house that doesn't work for you is a big waste of time. Besides, why are you so much surer that it will be a good investment than the person you're buying it from? The better the prospects for an area, the more the property should be costing you in the first place. In any event, you should have sufficient confidence in your own taste: if you buy something that you like and you look after it, the chances are that there'll be someone who wants to buy it from you when the time comes for you to move on.

So you buy the house that you want to live in, but when do you buy it? Well, you'll be pleased to hear that the answer to this is just as Foolish. You buy it when you want to and when you're able to. Just as Fools don't try to time the short-term fluctuations of the stock market, they don't try to time the short-term fluctuations of the property market. The state of the property market should take account of people's expectations about interest rates and prices in the future and there's no point in holding off because Leo, your estate agent friend, thinks in all his Wisdom that 'the property market looks a bit high at the moment'. In our experience, people who hold off from the property market because they are expecting a big crash suffer a similar fate to those who hold off from the stock market for the same reason. There are always reasons for thinking that the market might fall in the short term, just as there are always reasons for thinking that it might rise. All that we can say with any degree of confidence is that, over the long term, investing in property is a good thing to do. So, when you can afford to buy a home, find the one that you want (and can afford) to live in and go for it.

How much should you pay for your dream home? Well, given the answers to the previous questions, you can probably work out what's coming. You pay what it costs. Here, though, there are some very important riders. First of all, you should only be buying a house that is genuinely up for sale. It's not going to make sense for you to pay twice as much as a house is worth because the current owners love it so much that they really don't want to sell. The only way that you can get a proper guide to the value of a house is if it is on the market.

Next, you look around your dream home and you're told that the asking price is £100,000. What do you do then? Well, you 'um' and you 'ah' and, making sure you don't sound too keen, you say that you want to go away and think about it. You are now in a negotiating situation and there is a large amount of money at stake. Have a look around some similar properties in the area and find out their asking price. Preferably, you should find out how much similar properties have actually sold for. Is your dream home in the same ball park? Be very careful about anything that the seller's estate agents tell you – remember whose side they're on. Another thing to do is to think about how much it would cost to rent the home. The rent that you'd have to pay should always be a good bit more than the cost of a 100 per cent mortgage (to pay for upkeep and to give the landlord his profit). When you've thought carefully about all this, you put in a tentative offer to the seller's estate agent. Don't be afraid of pitching it quite a bit below the asking price: if nothing else, you can learn a lot about the property's value from the response you get. The last thing you want is an immediate acceptance of your first offer. If you get this, you'll know you've pitched it too high. The seller will always tend to pitch the asking price higher than the price they expect to get, so you should always be very reluctant to go above this price. If someone else is interested and the bidding, as it were, gets above this level, then it's probably a good idea to walk away and start looking for another dream home. Remember that you're happy to pay what the property is worth in current market conditions, but you need to be very careful not to pay more than it's worth.

The final point to make about how much you pay is a repetition of a point that we've already made several times. Too many people fall into the trap of buying as expensive a house as they can afford. **Don't do this**. It can be very tempting – we all want somewhere nice to live and it's a very good way of impressing our friends, but it's just not very Foolish. If you can't keep up the mortgage payments, for the long term, then you can end up without anywhere to live and your friends won't be very impressed at all. Work out how much the mortgage interest is going to cost you and double it. If things got this bad, could you keep up the repayments? It's bound to be painful, but if you think they'd be too high then you perhaps need to be looking at something a bit cheaper. The bottom line is that to play the mortgage game profitably, you need to be able to play it for a long time, through good times and bad.

Mortgages

Referred to in everyday language as the 'bloody mortgage' and most commonly incorporated into the phrase 'Well, it pays the bloody mortgage, I suppose' when referring to one's job of work, the mortgage is the cheapest form of long-term loan there is. It's cheap because the lender takes your home as security for the loan and houses are unable to change their name and leave the country. If you don't keep up your repayments, then the lender steps in, sells the house for what it can get and keeps enough to repay the loan. Simple as that. When the lender sells the house, they'll only get what the house can fetch at that time, there's no obligation for them to wait 'until the market recovers'; they just go in and do it. If that means that the money you had put into the house goes up in a puff of smoke, then that's hard cheese. In fact, if the lender can't get enough for the house to cover the loan, you'll still owe them the difference and they can come after you to get it. No wonder we keep saying that you need to stay within your limits. Anyway, that's all the down side to mortgages.

The up side is that the rate of interest is very low. Only a percentage point or so above what the Government pays to borrow money and, since the Government prints the stuff and effectively carries no risk at all, that's a pretty good deal. It is this fact that makes mortgage debt Foolish, whereas just about all other forms of debt are distinctly unFoolish. It is, however, only Foolish if you keep well within yourself. Sorry, did we make that point before? It must be beginning to grate now. It's just that we think it is the single most important thing in this whole chapter. Anyway, we've made our point now and we promise to drop the matter, except maybe for a quick mention at the end for those readers who lost patience with all this rambling and skipped ahead. Now, where were we? Oh yes, mortgages are a good cheap way of borrowing money (can you hear the sound of tongues being bitten?).

As with any loan, there are essentially two different things that you have to do with it. You have to repay the capital on the loan and you have to pay the interest on it. It is how you do these things that makes one mortgage different from another.

Repaying the Capital on Your Mortgage

There are basically two ways of doing this. Either you pay it back bit by bit over the course of the mortgage (which we'll assume to be twenty-five years, but this can vary) or you can pay none of it back at all over the twenty-five years, and pay it all off in one go at the end. The first of these approaches is called a repayment mortgage and the second is called an interest-only mortgage. On top of these approaches, there is another, called a current account mortgage, which is essentially a hybrid of the two.

Repayment mortgages

With a repayment mortgage, you start with a large pile of debt on which you have to pay a large amount of interest. On top of this interest, you pay back a tiny bit of the capital each month. As each month goes by, the amount that you owe is reduced and the amount of interest therefore falls as well, allowing you to pay back a bit more capital. The mortgage is structured so that the payments remain broadly level (subject to fluctuating interest rates), but an increasing amount goes on repaying capital and a correspondingly decreasing amount goes on paying the interest. By the time you get to the last few years of the mortgage, most of the monthly payments are going into paying off the capital and the amount you owe starts falling more and more quickly until, at the end of the mortgage, it is all paid back. The beauty of this is that if you keep making the payments, you know that, come what may, at the end of the mortgage you'll have paid everything back. For this reason, repayment mortgages are the least risky way of repaying a mortgage. A lot of people prefer to do it like this. We can see why, since they've already taken on a fair bit of risk with the mortgage in the first place.

Interest-only mortgages

The riskier option, but the one that is potentially more profitable, is to take an interest-only mortgage. With this approach, you owe the same amount of capital and therefore have to pay the same amount of interest (subject to fluctuating interest rates) throughout the term of the mortgage. All you do each month is repay the interest. How, then, do you repay the capital? Well, in addition to repaying the interest, you put a bit aside each month into a savings plan and then, at the end of the mortgage term, you use the accumulated pot of savings to repay the mortgage. In this case, you are taking a risk as to whether you can repay the capital. If your savings plan doesn't do its job, then you might have a shortfall when the time comes. The up side is that, if your savings plan more than does its job, then you might have a fair bit left over.

A good way to think of interest-only mortgages is to think that the money you are saving is money that you are not using to repay the mortgage. If you're saving at the rate of £100 per month then, after ten years, you will have paid a total of £12,000 into your savings plan. This is £12,000 that you could have used to repay the capital on your mortgage. For it to make sense to save the money rather than use it to repay capital, the savings need to be making a greater return than the rate of interest you're being charged on your mortgage (that is, on the capital that you haven't repaid). For you to have a chance of doing this, you really need to be saving the money in the stock market and, if you do so, then there is a good chance that an interest-only mortgage will work in your favour. After all, the rate of interest that you pay on your mortgage is linked to the rate of interest on cash deposits and, as we've seen, over the long term (like twenty-five years), the returns from shares tend to leave cash deposits miles behind. With an interest-only mortgage, you are therefore effectively borrowing money at mortgage rates in order to invest in the stock market. In the past this has proved to be a very profitable thing to do and there are good reasons to think that this will remain the case, BUT there is no doubt that there is risk involved. In fact, having borrowed money to buy your house, you are now borrowing money to invest in the stock market. For many people this is too much borrowing and too much risk and they prefer to go the repayment route. One thing is for sure: if you do decide to go for an interest-only mortgage, make sure that you think long and hard about the risks involved and your tolerance for them before you do it.

If you take an interest-only mortgage, then, how do you work out how much to save? Generally, your lender will have pretty firm idea about this and they're likely to point you in the right direction. It pays to be conservative. If you end up saving a bit too much, then that's well and good. If you end up saving not enough, then you're not going to be able to repay your mortgage on time. To do the calculations yourself, we'd suggest that a good starting point would be the rates that the Financial Services Authority uses for its growth projections. Currently these are 4 per cent, 6 per cent and 8 per cent. Naturally these are conservative projections. We'd say that 4 per cent really is ridiculously conservative, but why not split the top two and use 7 per cent? Even so, this is a long way behind the stock market's long-term historical growth rate. Still, there's nothing wrong with saving too much. Once you've picked a growth rate to use, have a read of Appendix 1, 'Coping with Compound Interest', which explains how to use this to work out how much you need to save on a monthly basis to reach a particular amount. If you fancy saving on a bit of brainpower, then you could try the compound interest calculations on the Motley Fool website. You should also bear in mind that long-term investment returns are linked to long-term interest rates (although they should amount to a bit more). Therefore, if interest rates start to fall and your monthly mortgage payments fall, you should increase the amount of your monthly savings by the difference. The flip side to this is that if interest rates rise, then you probably don't need to save quite as much, BUT remember what we said about being conservative!

The final decision to make about interest-only mortgages is which vehicle you should use to do the saving. Traditionally, this type of mortgage has been backed up by an endowment policy. We examined these in some detail in Chapter 15 – or rather we tore them limb from limb before feeding the remains to a flock of hungry vultures and exorcizing their dark spirit with a series of ancient Druidic incantations. Suffice to say here that these are an expensive, inefficient means of paying off your mortgage, whose major pay-off is to the person who sells you the policy. Back in the Dark Days of the late 1980s, well over two-thirds of British mortgages were backed by endowment policies. Following the justifiably horrendous press that they've received recently, we're pleased to say that this figure is now down to around 10 per cent. Still, in our opinion, it's about 10 per cent too many. With interest-only mortgages backed by endowments not even making it past the regional heats for Miss Mortgage Fool 2000, who is going to win the cruise to Barbados, the modelling contract and the free year's liposuction? (You're going to think it's fixed, we know you are, but it honestly isn't.) And the winner is ...

'Oh, Ladies and Gentlemen, the tension here at Fool Central is unbearable and I just can't seem to get this envelope open ... Ah, here we are! ... I can't believe it! It's so wonderful! It's so marvellous! She's so beautiful! Step up onto the podium, Miss Mortgage Fool of 2000, Miss Agnes Index-Tra-a-a-acker!'

'Well, Agnes (sotto voce: 'That's right, stand here, luv, and flash yer gnashers into the camera with the light on'). It's a great honour. You've done so well and against such strong competition. What does winning here tonight mean to you?'

'I weell use my poseeshun as Meess Mortgage Fool to work for world *peace, spread ze Folliculitis and I love all children and ze animals. I love you all so much! Mwwoooh, my darleengs!'*

'Thank you, Agnes! I think you meant "Folly" there. "Folliculitis" is a nasty skin infection, as we all know! Har! Har! Isn't she wonderful, Ladies 'n Gennulmen?'

Having read this book this far, this should come as no great surprise. Shares are the best way of saving for the long term and index trackers are the best way to get a good spread of shares with regular savings. Very experienced Fools might say that they prefer to choose their own shares and that's OK, so long as they bear in mind that they are betting their ability to repay their mortgage on their ability to choose good enough shares. We're confident that buying great shares for the long term, as we suggested in Chapter 12, 'Obviously Great Investments', can do a good job but the task of repaying your mortgage is probably best left to the simplest, safest, yes we'll say most boring option. A good cheap index tracker it is then. If you were paying attention when we talked about ISAs in Chapter 17, then you'll know it goes without saying that this index tracker should be wrapped up in an Individual Savings Account (ISA).

And now for some numbers

Having looked at the difference between repayment and interest-only mortgages, let's have a look at how this might all pan out in practice. To take one mortgage as an example, we'll look at the Standard Life 'Future Perfect' mortgage and imagine we wish to borrow £100,000 to repay over twenty-five years. The Future Perfect mortgage is, in fact, no longer available, but it seemed like a good product to use as an illustration since it has a 'capped' rate of 6.25 per cent for the full twenty-five years of the mortgage. For sake of argument, let's assume that interest rates don't drop during the whole term, so the 6.25 per cent remains constant too.

For a repayment mortgage, our monthly payments on the £100,000 loan would be £659.67. If you keep paying this for twenty-five years, then the debt will be gone by then. At the beginning of the mortgage, £520.83 of the £659.67 monthly repayment relates to interest (the remaining £138.84 going in repayments of capital). If we didn't pay down any of the capital, our monthly interest charge would stick at £520.83 for the life of the mortgage. BUT, we can use the remaining £138.84 that we save on the monthly payments to put into an index tracker. Over twenty-five years, this would need to grow at 6.4 per cent for us to end up with the £100,000 to repay the mortgage. If it did this, then you'd have made the same overall monthly payments as with the repayment mortgage, and you'd have the same end result. However, if your tracker grew at more than this 6.4 per cent, then you'd end up doing better with the interest-only approach. For instance, if we assume a rate of growth of 10 per cent, then you'd end up with £172,600 after twenty-five years. With this you could pay off the mortgage and still have £72,600 in your pocket.

Of course you can't necessarily rely on getting a return of greater than 6.4 per cent, even if that's what has happened in the past. This is where the risk comes in. For instance, if over twenty-five years your tracker grew at only 5 per cent, you'd end up with just £81,655; that is, £18,345 shy of repaying your mortgage. Again, there's more about doing this type of calculation in Appendix 1, 'Coping with Compound Interest'.

Current account mortgages

These are new. They effectively allow you to carry the mortgage debt in a bank account. Your lender sets a limit on how much you can borrow and then, so long as you keep below this, you can let the total amount of your mortgage debt fluctuate, upwards or downwards. This means you can treat it like an interest-only mortgage if you want, where you just pay the interest each month, or like a repayment mortgage where you pay back a bit of the actual loan each month. You can repay the loan more quickly than in the traditional twenty-five years or, if you like, you can pay it back more slowly.

If all this is sounding as though current account mortgages are supremely flexible, then that's because they are. Be careful, though, because with flexibility comes responsibility. If you don't make the effort to reduce the mortgage, then it won't reduce. In fact, if you're allowed to skip a few interest payments and do, then the mortgage will actually increase. If you're the interest-only mortgage sort of person and you're using the money saved to invest, then you might not see this as a problem. But you need to make sure that what you are doing is a conscious and well-considered decision and not just a bit of financial slackness.

Another benefit of current account mortgages is that you can effectively use them to save cash tax free. However much your current account is in credit, then that sum is effectively knocked off the outstanding amount to repay on your mortgage. Imagine that you have £10,000 that you want to save in cash. With a normal mortgage, the interest payments that you make will not be affected, as your mortgage and your bank accounts are completely separate. This means that, ISAs aside, you'll pay tax on the interest that you're getting on the £10,000 in a deposit account. With the current account mortgage, on the other hand, the cash that you save goes directly into paying off your mortgage. You can get the cash back out at any stage but, in the meantime, you're not paying tax on any interest that you've earned, because you haven't earned any. Sounds bad, hey? £10,000 saved and not earning any interest. What's the point of that? Well, by reducing the amount of your mortgage by £10,000, you've reduced the amount of interest that you have to pay on it, which more than corresponds to the interest you would have earned on the money in a deposit account.

The current account mortgage lets you have your cake and eat it. Because your overall borrowing can go up and down, you can effectively have a cash reserve without actually having any cash. Neat, hey?! Not only that the sums don't have to be as high as £10,000 to work in your favour. With the interest on the loan calculated on a daily basis, the few days (as long as that?) that your bank account is in credit at the beginning of the month after your salary has been paid will also count and save you money on your mortgage. Over time, this could add up to a very significant saving.

Before we get carried away, we should say that, at the moment, the market for this type of mortgage is relatively young and there are only a few of them around. This means that the competition among the providers is fairly limited and you might have to pay a slightly higher rate of interest than you would for a more conventional mortgage. Still, you might well feel that it's worth it for the advantages and, as these things prove more popular, so the interest rates should become more competitive.

Paying the Interest on Your Mortgage

The first question to ask here is where do interest rates actually come from? Knowing the answer certainly won't make you sparkle at parties, but it is one of those things worth knowing anyway. The answer is that they are set by the Monetary Policy Committee (MPC) of the Bank of England. If the MPC thinks that the economy is doing rather too well, potentially setting off a nasty bout of inflation, then it will put up interest rates to slow things down. On the other hand, if the MPC thinks that the economy is going too slowly, and that inflation is not a real threat, then it will bring interest rates down to try to get things going again. The MPC tries to make small adjustments well ahead of events (about eighteen months ahead), so as to avoid the need to make big adjustments later. If it fails to put up interest rates when it should, then the chances are that inflation will increase and, ultimately, rates will have to go much higher than they otherwise would in order to bring it back under control. It's a case of a stitch in time saving nine.

The base rate is effectively the rate of interest at which the Government borrows money in the very short term. The Government has the best credit rating there is, so if it is prepared to pay, say, 5 per cent to borrow money, then everyone else will have to pay a bit more. After all, why would a bank take only 4 per cent from you and me if it can get 5 per cent from the Government? How much more everyone else has to pay depends on how good a risk they are. If you put your house up as security, then you're a pretty good risk and you should only have to pay slightly more than base rates, perhaps 0.5 per cent to 1 per cent more.

Tracking and variable rate mortgages

When you get a tracking mortgage, your interest rate 'tracks' the base rate. Say you get a tracking mortgage on which you pay the base rate plus 0.75 per cent. This means that if base rates are 5.0 per cent, then you will be paying 5.75 per cent. If base rates go up by 0.5 per cent then you'd be paying 6.25 per cent. Fair enough.

Variable rate mortgages are similar to this, but perhaps not quite so good since they are slightly less predictable. In this case, your mortgage provider sets rates pretty much how it likes. It has savers to whom it must pay interest and it wants to make a profit, so it would like to charge you as much as possible. However, it can't charge too much or all its borrowers will simply move to someone else who's charging less and then where will it be? Taking all this into account, each lender's variable rate is likely to float around a bit above the base rate. In fact, it is likely to float around at about the same sort of premium to base rates as a tracking mortgage. The difference, and the reason for preferring the tracker, is that with the tracker you know exactly what the deal is and it's not subject to the fickleness of your mortgage provider. (By the way, don't get confused with index trackers here – we're talking about something different. A tracking mortgage simply refers to the way the interest rate is calculated. An index tracker is a type of investment you may or may not be using to pay off the mortgage in the end.)

Fixed rate mortgages

With a fixed rate mortgage, as the name suggests, your interest payments are fixed for a certain period. This period is typically anything from a year to ten years. So, if you have a mortgage with the interest rate fixed at 7 per cent for five years, your monthly interest payments on the outstanding capital will be set at that rate for five years.

To understand properly how fixed rate mortgages work, you need to think about the gilt market. In just the same way that the base rate determines what interest rate the Government pays on its short-term debt, the 'redemption yield' on gilts determines the interest rate that the Government pays on its medium- and long-term borrowings. The redemption yield on gilts therefore also dictates the interest rate of fixed rate mortgages. Most broadsheet newspapers will have a list of gilts, together with their yields, somewhere in the business section. If you are looking at a five-year fixed rate mortgage, then you want to compare it to the redemption yield on gilts with a maturity date five years from now. In other words, if it's now 2002, then you want to look at a gilt called something like Treas 5% 2007. Make sure you're looking at the column for redemption yields, rather than the column for the interest yield or flat yield (which are different).

As with variable rates and trackers, you will generally pay a small premium (of perhaps 0.5 to 1 per cent) on the rate that the Government pays (that is, the redemption yield on the relevant gilt). So, if you are offered a five-year fixed rate mortgage at 5.5 per cent and you see that the redemption yield on a five-year dated gilt is 5.0 per cent, then you know that it's a pretty good deal. Sometimes you might see a deal where the interest rate is less than the gilt yield. If this is the case, then there is often a catch in the form of a lengthy tie-in period or something similar. If not, then the provider is probably relying on enough borrowers being too lazy to move when the rate eventually goes up. If you go for something like this, then make sure you're not the lazy type because it could end up costing a lot more in the long run.

The effect of a fixed rate deal is, of course, that your repayments will stay the same for the period of the fix. This provides a bit of certainty for your budgeting. However, once you have fixed the deal you are, to a greater or a lesser extent, committed to it for that period. If interest rates go up, then you'll sit back smugly, thanking your lucky stars that you decided to fix your interest rate or congratulating yourself on your vision and perspicacity. On the other hand, if interest rates fall, then you will have to watch enviously as variable rate mortgages get cheaper and cheaper, while blaming your spouse for talking you into a fixed rate mortgage in the first place. In this situation, it will, most likely, cost you to get out of the deal. This is entirely reasonable, since you wouldn't let the bank back out of the fixed rate deal if the rates went up, and you can't have it both ways. Different mortgage deals have different penalties for copping out early. There is no such thing as a free lunch and, where the penalties for early redemption are slack, the borrower will have to pay for this with a higher interest rate. So, if you hunt around for the cheapest five-year fixed rate deal on the market, don't be surprised if it also contains the toughest redemption penalties. If you want the cheapest interest rate, then you'll have to accept the least flexibility. If you don't like the idea of being tied in, then rather than looking around for slack redemption penalties, you should probably be looking at a tracking or variable rate deal instead.

Bells and whistles

What we've done here is try to simplify the important elements of a mortgage. However, there are literally thousands of different types of mortgage on the market. They are littered with extra frills like 'cash-back' deals and 'discounted rates'. It is safe to say that we don't much like this sort of thing. They are generally just a way of muddying the waters so that the providers can end up charging us more. They know we love a discount and they know that dangling some cash before our eyes (to buy that washing machine) is going to get us right where they want us. Remember that there is no such thing as a free lunch and the more unnecessary bells and whistles that attach to a mortgage, the less likely it is to be the best value. Remember to keep things simple.

A word on the different types of mortgage

The way the interest is calculated on your mortgage is an entirely separate issue from whether the mortgage is a repayment type or an interest-only type. This means you can have a repayment fixed rate, variable or tracking mortgage or an interest-only fixed rate, variable or tracking mortgage. Sorry if by now this seems ridiculously obvious to you, but it is a point of confusion for quite a few people so we just wanted to make sure it was all completely clear.

Summing Up on Mortgages

First of all, decide how you want to repay the capital. If you want the least risky option, then this will mean a repayment mortgage. If you can stomach a bit of risk, then there's a very good chance that an interest-only mortgage will work out better in the end. If you want the maximum flexibility over your repayments, then one of the new current account type mortgages might suit.

As far as paying the interest is concerned, bear in mind that no one, despite what they might want you to believe, knows where interest rates are headed. If anyone really knew what was going to happen, they'd be busy making a fortune on the gilt market. They certainly wouldn't be trying to sell you a mortgage. The gilt market takes into account the market's best guesses, and is therefore the best guide as to where interest rates are heading. Fixed rate mortgages are dictated by yields in the gilt market. The yields in the gilt market, in turn, are dictated by the market's best guess as to where the base rate is headed and the base rate dictates the interest rates on variable rates and tracker mortgages. Phew! Anyway, the effect of all this is that, all things being equal, a fixed rate mortgage should reflect what the market expects a variable rate or tracking mortgage to cost you over the same period. In other words, it should make no real difference which type of mortgage you go for (so long as you get the cheapest available of the type you're looking at) and you shouldn't get too het up about it. However, for peace of mind, there's a lot to be said for a straightforward five-year fixed rate deal. At least that way you know where you are for five years and can budget accordingly. The choice is yours, and now that you have all the facts you're in the best position to make it.

Finally, we just want to return to that point that we made several times at the beginning of this chapter. The best mortgage is one that you can easily afford – even if interest rates rocket. For the whole homeowning thing to work well, you must make sure that you can stick it out for the long term, through good times and bad. That really is the last time we'll mention it. Now let's move on and see how we might get our hands on one of these, how you say, mortgages?

The Five Steps to a Successful Mortgage

It's always been our personal experience, and people have been telling us over the last few years, that there is a yawning chasm between knowing the theory and feeling able and confident enough to put that theory into practice. That's why here we'd like to include some practical steps on how to get the mortgage you want. Your mortgage is going to be with you for a long time and it's worth putting just a little effort into getting it right.

Step One: Do not buy a mortgage from anyone who spontaneously offers to sell you a mortgage

These people should be approached with the greatest caution, as they can be very convincing. They are, however, looking at you as a potential gold mine and will almost certainly try to sell you an endowment as well. On no account let them get between you and the exit: instead speak soothing, polite words, avoid eye contact (this can be dangerous) and back slowly out of the door. If you do this skilfully enough, they will still be talking to an empty room as you turn the key in the door of No. 1 Fleapit Mansions, your current, luxury residence.

Step Two: Also do not buy a mortgage during a face-to-face encounter

You know what you want. You do not have to be 'sold' to. Agreeing to a face-to-face encounter with a mortgage salesperson is agreeing to the possibility that the salesperson may be able to change your mind and sell you what he/she wants. If this is the case, then you are not ready to buy a mortgage.

Step Three: You're the customer, so act like one. Go out and shop!

It's easy to think that the people who lend you the money to buy your house are being kind to you, that they are doing you a favour. This is wrong. You are doing them a favour by gracing them with your custom. Try not to forget this, as it helps in the game of psychological one-upmanship on which you are about to embark. *They* have to earn *your* business; you do not have to prove yourself worthy to them. Be upfront, pushy even. If the person on the other end of the line is starting to sound exasperated or is even putting on mock offence, then go elsewhere. The likelihood of your causing real offence with your polite questions is small and remember this Foolish law of personal finance:

It's your life and it's only their job.

Step Four: Log on and/or pop down the newsagent's

In the first edition of this book we said:

> 'We'd love to be able to say to you that you can do all the shopping you need for a mortgage on the Internet, but it just isn't true. There is certainly a lot of information there but, to make sure you've seen everything that's available, you'll end up falling back on the telephone and that's where the magazines come in. They have listings of all the mortgages and mortgage companies and also large glossy advertisements with telephone numbers and, occasionally, Web site addresses.'

Well, times have moved on a lot. These days there are a number of sites online that offer comparative lists of mortgages and which allow you to search according to location, how large a mortgage you need, what type you're after, etc. You may still want to buy a copy of What Mortgage or Your Mortgage or anything with 'mortgage' in the title from the newsagent's to give you an overall perspective, but it's by no means a necessity.

Step Five: The chase

Park yourself by the computer and/or the telephone with the Foolish mortgage-hunter's survival kit: pen, reams of paper, cup of tea and one box of Jaffa Cakes, comfort-eating for the use of. By now you've decided what you want. Let's assume you've decided on the Foolish combination of a five-year fixed rate interest-only mortgage, backed by an index tracker. You either log on and start searching various Web sites to find a mortgage (useful Web site addresses are listed in Appendix 4) or start phoning likely-looking organizations on your list. To help you through the potential trauma of such a phone call (and you may still have to resort to the phone even if you find what you want on the Internet), here's an example of how it might go:

DIRECT MORTGAGES FOR FOOLS. Hello, Direct Mortgages for Fools, how can I be of Foolish assistance today?

YOU. Hello. I'm interested in a five-year fixed rate interest-only mortgage, which I will back with an index tracker. I'm wondering what you've got to offer me.

(This is a good start. You're confident and you've shown you know a little bit about the subject. The person on the other end is already saying to themselves: 'For this is a Fool!')

DIRECT MORTGAGES FOR FOOLS. Certainly, we have the blah, blah …

(If you're lucky at this point, they will indeed give you the information you ask for. If you're not, you may find yourself giving away a load of demographic information designed to ensure that you and your family unto the seventh generation shall receive direct mail from these people. If that is the case, then you may want to ask them to cut through the malarkey and get to the point.)

DIRECT MORTGAGES FOR FOOLS… . and then we have the ValuePlan Five-Year Fixed Rate Mortgage.

(You're going to be faced with a bewildering array of superficially enticing

schemes designed to make you buy one of DMF's mortgages. We go into some of the permutations below – you'll figure them out pretty quickly and it doesn't make for the most exciting of reading – but just remember that if it looks too good to be true, it definitely is.)

YOU. Sounds interesting. I wonder if you'd send me some details? *(You're for it now. They really are going to ask you a whole lot of questions about your income, spouse's income, other debts, etc. They need this to make up a proposal for you which they will then send out. Despite the rigour of this interrogation and the professional, personalized nature of the proposal when it arrives, be reassured that this commits you to nothing.)*

DIRECT MORTGAGES FOR FOOLS. No problem. May I just ask how you are planning to pay off the amount of the loan at the end of the mortgage term?

(At this point, you say either that you're going to link it to an index tracker as you pointed out at the beginning and you already have one in mind, thank you very much, or else that you will be making regular contributions into a self-select ISA and building up an equity portfolio. If you plump for the latter, sound very confident and knowledgeable. In fact, if you plump for the former, be very confident and knowledgeable.)

DIRECT MORTGAGES FOR FOOLS. That sounds interesting, sir/madam. I wonder if you've considered one of our endowment policies? They have quite impressive bonuses at the end of the policy, they provide life assurance as well and they are portable.

(You didn't sound confident enough, did you? DMF thought there was just the minutest chance that they could flog you an endowment policy. Remember, it means a lot to them and they're going to try very hard. They always use the life assurance thing, because you generally need to have life assurance to cover your mortgage and they always plug the fact that you can keep the same endowment policy if you move house – i.e. they're 'portable'. Luckily, you were ahead of them and you reply:)

YOU. Thanks very much, but I'm not all that impressed with endowments in general. I'll be shopping around for the best deal I can find in level term life assurance and the index tracker's portable in any case.

(Great stuff, Fool! Yes, you've done really well. Level term life assurance

is what you will need and unless DMF is willing to offer you the best deal, don't buy it from them. Level term simply means that you will be insured for the whole sum of the loan for the whole period. If the credits start to roll before your time – or what you thought ought to be your time – then the insurance company pays out on the policy. If you survive until the end of the policy and pay off the mortgage as planned, the insurance cover finishes and you get nothing. Except the satisfaction of having survived, that is. If DMF can't sell you an endowment policy, they may push their life assurance pretty hard and if they do, it may well be a 'with-profits' policy in which there is an investment component (and an even larger charges component) to it. Decline it. You have the information you want, it is now time to make your excuses and leave.)

DIRECT MORTGAGES FOR FOOLS. Thank you very much, I'll get that proposal out in the post to you today.

YOU. Thanks a lot, I appreciate it. Byeee.

There, it wasn't too bad, was it? And the reason is that you knew what you wanted beforehand and were in control throughout. Granted you've had to expend five weeks of unremitting misery to get to this point in the book, but it's starting to pay off. You now move on to the next likely-looking candidate in the magazine:

GERBILS PROVIDENT. Hello, Gerbils Provident – two hundred years of faithful service to rodents and other small mammals – how can I help?

We'll be honest here. This is going to take you a couple of hours one Saturday morning to sort out. Perhaps even a bit more by the time you've sorted through all the paperwork you're going to get sent and made your decision. But it'll be worth it.

The MIG and Life Assurance

One more sting in the tail for house purchasers that it's worth knowing about is the Mortgage Indemnity Guarantee premium, or MIG. It can have other names, too, but whatever it's called, it's a one-off premium that can amount to £1500 or more, which you generally have to pay if you are taking out a loan of more than 75 per cent of the property value. You see, the statistics tell the mortgage companies that loans of this kind of size are more likely to be defaulted on. Hmm, so that means the MIG insures you against not being able to repay the loan and you won't lose your house ...? Sorry, it insures *them* against your not being able to repay the loan. They'll still repossess it, you'll still lose it and they'll still sell it on for whatever they can get for it. What's the point of it for the buyer, then? Good question. At the time of writing some companies are starting to abolish the MIG and it's a trend that we hope will continue. Good riddance!

Generally, people assume that they will need some life assurance to go with their mortgage. In fact, this isn't necessarily the case at all. If you can keep your mortgage down to 75 per cent or so of the value of your property, then there's a good chance the mortgage company won't require you to have any. Sure, people will try to sell it to you, but think about whether you really need it. If you don't have any dependents, you almost certainly don't need it. If your mortgage outlasts you, then the lender can get its money back when the house is sold. That is, after all, one reason why it took security in the first place. By avoiding superfluous life assurance, you can save yourself sizeable sums which you can add to your savings – a far better use for the money. If you do have dependents, then you still might not need *more* life assurance. While providing for your family in the unlikely event of your demise is something that everyone should think about and this will generally mean taking on some life assurance, if you've already got this sorted out then there is no definite reason why you should increase it just because you've got a mortgage. Maybe you should, maybe you shouldn't. It depends on the particular situation – the point to bear in mind is that it is a separate issue.

Be Your Own Landlord – The End

Sounding a bit complicated? Starting to wonder if it's all worth it? Don't! It's actually not all that complicated when you get into it and it's too late, anyway. You see, you may want to give all this over to someone else to manage, but you've ruined it. You now know too much. You've passed the point of no return and should have put this book back on the shelf in the shop immediately after you picked it up, silly Fool! For you now know that many of the people who are trying to sell you a mortgage are trying to make a fast buck, that some mortgages are far worse for your health than others and that these are the ones that will be pushed hardest at you. You can't unlearn any of this stuff and while some say that ignorance is bliss, we say that when it comes to investment it carries a pretty hefty price tag and actually isn't all that blissful anyway.

Being ignorant and having to rely on others to make *your* financial decisions on *their* behalf is a little like one of those falling dreams when you tumble off a cliff and can see the ground coming towards you, but can't do anything about it. Sometimes you actually go on and hit the ground, but at other times you manage to wake yourself up with a start before you do, and that's what happened to you when you picked up this book on that fateful Tuesday afternoon in Bromsgrove. There's no going back and while that may feel a little burdensome at times, on the other hand the financial benefits are potentially enormous and the 'feelgood' factor is pretty strong too. You are now a fully-fledged, card-carrying Fool, managing his or her own investments, captain of your fate and mistress of your soul. It's exhilarating, so savour it. After all, anyone who has got this far through a book on investment has earned it.

19

Investing
For Income

Behold, how good and joyful a thing it is, brethren, to dwell together in unity!
Psalms cxxxiii

If you've reached this far in the book, we hope we've managed to persuade you of the need to build up a large pot of investments to pay for your woolly socks in retirement. You'll also, hopefully, have picked up on the point that this sort of long-term saving is a job for shares, whether held directly or in an index tracker, all wrapped cosily inside an ISA or maybe a pension, or more likely both. You might also have noticed that we've left a gaping hole in all of this, because at some point, we hope, you're going to reach pay-back time and all those lovely investments will need to be put to work to generate an income.

If you've been saving via a pension then you haven't much choice about how to produce your income. As the law stands at the moment, you have to use the bulk of the money to buy an annuity. Remember these from Chapter 14? The way they work is that you buy an income for life from a Wise financial services company. They work out how long you're likely to live and base the income that they'll pay you on that. Some people will live a little longer than expected, but they'll be subsidised by those that shuffle off sooner than expected. Naturally the provider of the annuity works it so that, on average, they make a little bit of profit.

While annuities do provide you with certainty and a reasonable level of income at the beginning, they suffer precisely because of this. It means that the provider has to back up your annuity by investing its money in very low-risk investments, largely Government bonds (aka gilts) and, as we saw back in Chapter 4, these don't hold their value very well over a long period of time. So your annuity income can start to look quite meagre if your retirement blooms into your eighties and beyond. Certainly, you can be sure that the late Queen Mother, bless her soul, didn't keep going on an annuity purchased in 1960. A generous, Queen Mum-type, income purchased back then, when the average wage was a little below £15 per week, would hardly keep you or me going now.

An irony with annuities is that if you don't live very long, then you lose out and, if you do live for a long time, then you don't do very well either. The fundamental problem from which everything else flows is that the income they produce, for all its certainty, is backed up by not very good long-term investments. There are various little add-ons you can buy that partly deal with some of these problems, but they all have to be paid for and that means a reduced level of income in the first place.

For example, at the time of writing, £100,000 will buy a basic annuity, for a typical 60-year old non-smoker, of £7,469 for a man and £6,992 for a woman (women get less because they're expected to live for longer). As an alternative to this, you can get an inflation-proofed, or index-linked, annuity. With these, your income increases along with inflation and, while that's no bad thing, it only gets you so much of the way there. If you want your spending power to remain fully intact, relative to everyone else, then you need your income to be tied to growth in average earnings, which tends to run at about 2% ahead of inflation. In any case, inflation-proofing will reduce your annuity income, at the start, to £5,350 for a man and £4,874 for a woman.

Another useful option, for couples, is to buy a 'joint-life' annuity. Typically, these will pay an income while both you and your partner are alive and then half that income to the survivor for the rest of their days. This will reduce the income for a 60-year old couple to £6,890. If you wanted it to be inflation proofed as well, then the starting income falls to £4,782.

There are various other little wrangles you can go for. For instance, you can add a proviso that if you die within 5 years, then you (or rather those you leave behind) get your money back. But again that will reduce your income and besides, knowing your luck, you'll die after 6 years. Unless you're very ill, and we hope you're not, then this doesn't make too much sense. Even if you were gravely ill, it would make more sense to defer the purchase of the annuity until as late as possible. There are also some new with-profits and unit-linked annuities, which link your annuity income to stock market returns. This might sound appealing, right up to the point where you notice the charges on such schemes.

Anyway, if you've saved up through a pension then, as things stand at the moment, an annuity it is. They do give you certainty, but they don't give you much bang for your buck.

Gilts and cash

Outside of pensions, it's a question of finding the right assets to produce a decent and reliable income. The traditional method of doing this, as a Wise fund manager might say, is to 'increase your weighting in bonds and cash'. It's the easy option, because they do tend to have a higher yield than shares. So, while the income generated by the average company on the London Stock Exchange is about three per cent at the moment, you might get as much as 4 or 5 per cent from money in the bank or from gilts. You'll know us well enough by now to know what's coming, though, won't you?!

This gives us just the same problem as we had with annuities. The income from a gilt or a deposit account can look great to begin with, but over the years you'll watch everyone else's income go up, as prices rise, and your income could start to look a little feeble. It's tempting to think that you'll have less and less to spend your money on as you get older, but that doesn't really stand up. Walking sticks, carpet slippers and corn plasters all add up, not to mention nursing home bills. In any case, just because you might not necessarily need a decent income going into your eighties and nineties isn't a reason not to have it. Certainly any children you have will be grateful to you for investing your money as productively as possible.

The trouble is that the income from cash in the bank and from gilts doesn't stand up very well to inflation and increases in average earnings over the years. An indication of just how badly they keep up is the rate of interest that you can get from an inflation-proofed (aka index-linked) gilt, which is not much more than 2 per cent at the moment. So, to get a safe index-linked income from gilts, you actually end up only getting 2 per cent per year. To keep up with average earnings growth we'd have to take off 2 per cent, leaving us with, near enough, no return at all. This compares with a dividend yield from the average share on the London stock market of nearly 3 per cent per year at the moment. And that's a yield that we would expect to grow at least in line with average earnings. Of course, investing in shares also exposes you to risk on the capital value of your investments, but if your primary goal is income.... Hold that thought for a moment, while we have a quick look at corporate bonds.

Corporate Bonds

Corporate bonds are IOUs issued not by the Government, but by individual companies. Generally, they're split into lots of £1,000. So you lend a company the £1,000 and it agrees to pay you x% per year until the end of the loan, at which point you get your money back. These 'corporate bonds' are then tradeable on the stock market. The price of the debt will depend on how interest rates have moved since it was issued. So, if interest rates drop, then the bond will become relatively attractive and its price should move higher, because it's annual payment of interest, called the 'coupon', has stayed the same. If interest rates move higher, then the bond will be less attractive and its price should move lower, because the bond is only offering its original coupon, while the market is now expecting more.

The best way to flesh this out is with an example. Let's say you bought one £1,000 slice of "Tesco 7.5% 2007". Tesco would pay you the £75 (that is 7.5 per cent of £1,000) each year until 2007, when you'd get the £75 interest, plus your £1,000 back (on 30th July to be precise). The £75 payments are called the 'coupon'.

You might have noticed, though, that 7.5 per cent is a lot higher than base interest rates (4 per cent at the time of writing). That makes the bond more valuable than the face value of £1,000. Only a little bit more valuable, because there are only six more 'coupon' payments to come, but more valuable all the same. In fact, the market currently values these Tesco bonds at 107.89 per cent of their 'nominal' value, or £1,078.90 for each £1,000 nominal. (Nominal is just a fancy word for the face value of the bond, or what you stand to get back at the end.)

The fact that what you get back at the end is less than you pay up front means that annual return that you get on the bond is actually less than the 'coupon'. This annual return is called the 'yield to maturity' or the 'yield to redemption', or the 'redemption yield'. It works out the effective rate of interest that you're getting on all of the coupon payments, and the final £1,000 you get back at the end, given what you're paying for them now. It's the most important number since it tells you what your total annual return will be if you hold the bonds until the end (assuming that the company doesn't go bust). For these Tesco bonds, the redemption yield is 5.68 per cent. That compares to the redemption yield on a gilt maturing at around the same time of about 5.17 per cent.

So the question is, are you prepared to take on the risk of Tesco going bust in the next 5 years, for the sake of an extra 0.5% on your annual return? It can make sense, especially if you hedge your bets across the bonds of lots of different companies in different business sectors. The trouble is that the extra return you're getting is determined by how risky the market thinks the bonds are. The more return you go for, the more risky things will be. So, it can be a bit counter-productive. If what you're after is a rock solid income, with complete capital protection, then gilts, rather than corporate bonds are likely to make most sense.

There is an additional risk with bonds that comes if you don't hold them until they mature. As we saw above, the price of a bond will move around according to movements in interest rates. So if interest rates rise while you're holding the bond, then the price of the bond will fall. This problem applies to gilts as much as it does corporate bonds and the longer the time until maturity, the greater the risk. If you have a bond that redeems next year, then its value should be very close to the redemption money that you'll get back then and interest rates shouldn't make a whole heap of difference. If, on the other hand, you invest in a bond that still has 20 years to run, then the value of it will depend heavily on what other investors think will happen to interest rates over that period.

Another way of investing in corporate bonds instead of buying the bonds directly is to invest in a corporate bond fund. These funds have been very fashionable recently, with the stock market doing badly, but there are major problems. As ever, they start with costs. A typical bond fund might charge 1 to 1.25 per cent of your money each year. Now, if we think back to the Tesco bond we looked at a moment ago, it yielded a mere 0.5 per cent more than the comparable gilt. So, if your bond fund invested purely in bonds like Tesco, then you'd get a lower yield than you could get for a gilt (which you can buy for free at the post office) and you'd obviously be taking more risk. On any basis, that 1 per cent of charges will take a large chunk out of the extra return you're expecting from investing in more risky bonds. The balance is likely to be better if you'd have simply stuck with gilts, or perhaps a wide range of directly-held corporate bonds, in the first place.

Bond funds also suffer from increased risk because they will trade in and out of particular bonds, with little regard to when they mature. They therefore carry the risk of prices changing against them. Of course, the fund managers will tell you how carefully they select individual bonds and how they'll get into cheap ones and get out of expensive ones, but it's similar to what we saw in Chapter 7 about equity fund managers. If they're all doing it, how can they all be right? The answer is that they can't. If anything, given the more precise nature of bonds, the problems with charges and underperformance are magnified with a corporate bond fund. If you are minded to go down the route of bonds, then you're most likely to get the best balance of risk and reward with gilts. If you want to try for extra returns with a little more risk, then the better bet is to commit a portion of your investments to shares.

Shares

Shares are often dismissed as a source of income because their capital value can change so much over a short period. We Fools, however, would say that this is very woolly thinking. If the aim of your investing is to generate an income, why should you care if the capital value of your investments changes wildly? What you should be concerned about is the safety of your stream of income. In these terms, shares are far more stable than people would have you believe.

As we saw in Chapter 11, most companies provide their shareholders with an income by paying a 'dividend'. The idea is that this dividend rises over the years and the more investors expect the dividend to rise, the more expensive the shares will be relative to their dividend. Let's take the example of a slow but steady performer, Snoozeville Pillow, which made earnings per share of 8p per share last year and paid half of this, 4p, out as a dividend. The other 4p of earnings got kept back within the company to invest for the future and thereby, hopefully, increase the dividend in future years.

Just how much investors will pay for this share will depend on how much they expect the dividend to rise. If they think it could rise a lot, then they might be happy to pay 200p for the shares so that it has a 'dividend yield' of just 2 per cent (4p divided by 200p). If, however, investors don't think that the dividend will rise much, then they might pay just 100p for the shares, giving a 'dividend yield' of 4 per cent. If investors are really gloomy and actually think the dividend might fall next year, they may only be prepared to pay 50p, which would amount to a dividend yield of 8 per cent.

Is this making sense? Fantastic! So…the price of the shares, and therefore how much you get in income from the shares per pound that you put in, aka the 'dividend yield', will be determined by how much investors expect that dividend to grow. In other words, you think of the shares just like you would a bond, it's just that the interest, or rather dividends, you get varies according to how well the company does.

If you're investing to generate an income, then you need to find a basket of shares that deliver the sort of income you're looking for, but which have prospects to increase that income at least alongside the rate of average earnings growth in the economy. That way, you can expect your income to maintain its value alongside what everyone else is earning. Beyond that, the sort of qualities that you should look for are similar to those that we looked at in Chapter 12. You're looking for companies that have a strong and dependable business franchise that they're likely to maintain over many years. You want companies that seem almost certain to occupy at least the same slice of the wolrd's economy in the decades to come.

So, for starters, you might look though the Financial Times, or another newspaper's share section, to look for large, solid companies that deliver a dividend yield in the range you're looking for. Beware of anything that has a yield much above the redemption yield on long dated gilts: about 5% in June 2002. The reason why they have a yield this high is most likely that the market expects the dividend to be reduced in due course. A cursory glance at the newspaper, on 23rd May 2002, brings up the following companies:

Company	Dividend Yield (%)	Company	Dividend Yield (%)
EMI	5.9	Rolls Royce	4.4
Severn Trent	5.8	British American Tobacco	4.2
Royal & Sun Alliance	5.8	Gallaher	4.2
CGNU	5.7	Alliance & Leicester	4.1
Abbey National	4.8	Old Mutual	4.1
Powergen	4.8	Boots	3.9
Scottish & Newcastle	4.6	HSBC	3.9
Six Continents	4.6	Lattice Group	3.9
Lloyds TSB	4.5	Sainsbury	3.7
Tomkins	4.5	Standard Chartered	3.6

So there are twenty companies that you, or rather we, would expect to broadly maintain their share of the overall economy over the years, whilst paying a generous dividend. I've excluded several companies, including Invensys (with a yield of 6.7 per cent) and Scottish Power (7.1 per cent), because the yields are just a bit too high, suggesting that they're going to be reduced at some point. The average dividend yield on the selected companies is 4.6%. That's double the income that you'd get from an index-linked gilt. Yet the income from the index-linked gilt will only increase along with inflation, while the income from our group of solid companies, can be expected to increase with the rate of average earnings growth in the economy. After all, that's roughly the rate that you'd expect the companies profits to be growing at.

Of course, the companies that you might select will be different from ours. Perhaps you don't think EMI has a future because of music piracy over the Internet. Perhaps you wouldn't go near British American Tobacco or Gallaher for ethical reasons. As always, you need to look into the companies for yourself, but keep in mind that you're trying to find companies with a healthy dividend yield and which you expect to maintain their business over the years, relative to the rest of the economy.

The big stockbrokers produce dividend forecasts for the next couple of years and these can be very useful. The most useful figure is the 'consensus' forecast, which is an average of the different brokers. Try asking the company itself, through its investor relations department. Alternatively, you could try looking, or asking, on the relevant company discussion board at www.fool. co.uk. For the companies we looked at above, the dividend yields for this year, next year and the year after, based on the current price and consensus dividend forecasts are:

Company	Dividend Yield (%)		
	This Year	Next Year	Year After
EMI	5.9	3.0	3.0
Severn Trent	5.8	6.1	6.2
Royal & Sun Alliance	5.8	5.9	6.0
CGNU	5.7	3.4	3.6
Abbey National	4.8	5.1	5.4
Powergen	4.8	5.1	5.3
Scottish & Newcastle	4.6	4.7	4.9
Six Continents	4.6	4.8	5.0
Lloyds TSB	4.5	4.9	5.3
Tomkins	4.5	4.6	4.6
Rolls Royce	4.4	4.4	4.7
British American Tobacco	4.2	4.3	4.6
Gallaher	4.2	4.4	4.7
Alliance & Leicester	4.1	4.5	4.9
Old Mutual	4.1	4.4	4.6
Boots	3.9	4.2	4.4
HSBC	3.9	4.1	4.5
Lattice Group	3.9	4.3	4.4
Sainsbury	3.7	4.1	4.4
Standard Chartered	3.6	3.8	4.2
Average	4.6	4.5	4.7

The first thing to notice about this table is that the companies nearer the bottom, with the lower dividend yields to begin with, are generally expected to show better growth over the next two years. That's why investors value them more highly and that's what gives them the slightly lower yields to start with. As you get higher up the list, less growth is expected. In fact, near the top of the list are EMI and CGNU, which are committing the great sin of actually reducing their dividends this year. They're the prime reason why our dividend income from the entire 20 companies would fall, very slightly, to 4.5% next year. Not what we're aiming for, but it's hardly the stuff of nightmares and, besides, we're comfortably back on the growth track for the following year.

Of course, having noticed the expected reductions from EMI and CGNU, you'd probably strike them from your list of potential investments. That would then leave you with eighteen companies producing 4.4 per cent in dividend income this year, with 4.7 per cent expected for next year and 4.9 per cent for the year after. That amounts to dividend growth of 5.5 per cent, which is not far away from the average earnings growth that we're expecting our dividends to grow by. From time to time there might be a dividend cut from the odd company, but the impact on the overall portfolio should be limited. The normal rules about diversification apply, although they're a bit harder to apply here because you're restricting yourself to shares and sectors that are expected to be steady, while not setting the world on fire. As best you can, though, you'll want to find 15 or so companies that are exposed to different factors. What you want to avoid is several companies suddenly reducing their dividends at the same time.

Once you've put the portfolio of shares together, your focus should remain entirely on the income that they're producing for you. That is, after all, the prime reason that you're investing in them. Instead of being concerned if a share price has been sliding over the last year, be concerned if there's reason to suppose that its dividend might not grow. Instead of being concerned if the portfolio's value falls over a year, be concerned if there's reason to suppose that the overall dividend income might not increase. In diversification terms, you should start to worry if a share starts to account for too large a slice of your portfolio's income, rather than worrying that its capital value is now a large percentage.

So it's essentially a question of leaving the companies alone and letting the dividends flow in. Every now and again, you might find that a company fails to increase its dividend and this is where you have to make difficult decisions. If you think it's a sign of things to come, then you'll want to ditch the shares. But you might be happy to do nothing if you think that the dividend should now have better prospects for growth, as a result of the company being left with more of its profits to invest for the future.

You might also find that a company moves away from being the steady income generator that you thought you'd bought, rather as GEC changed into an altogether more flighty and growth oriented Marconi a couple of years ago. If a company no longer fits the reasons for buying it, then it's time to review that decision. There are no easy answers to this sort of thing, except that you need to keep a focus on what you're trying to achieve: a decent income that grows steadily along with the economy. There's an ongoing discussion about these types of issue on the appropriately-named High-Yield Portfolio discussion board on the Motley Fool website.

Income from investment trusts

Many people, however, are not keen on investing in direct shares. Unfortunately for them, the normal Foolish advice, to invest via an index tracker, doesn't really work when it's income you're after. The problem is that index trackers have a relatively low dividend yield, because more is expected by way of capital growth. That's fine while you want your investments to grow, but not so fine if you want them to generate an income.

The best funds for generating an income are probably investment trusts. These have several advantages over unit trusts, as we saw in Chapter 17, mostly relating to the fact that they are actually companies and have to do things for the long-term benefit of their shareholders (that's you, by the way, if you invest in an investment trust). Amongst other things, this means that they can't advertise and cost savings from this and elsewhere has meant that they've typically outperformed unit trusts over the years.

It gets better still for the really big (generally long-standing) investment trusts. Again because they're companies, they're obliged to pass to their shareholders the benefits of any economies of scale in the costs of managing them. So, the bigger they get, the smaller their charges tend to get as a percentage of your money. The largest investment trusts therefore tend to have 'total expense ratios' well below 1%, comparing favourably even with index trackers.

For income, however, investment trusts have a further string to their bow, and that comes from their 'discount'. Take an investment trust that has investments (less debts) of £500m (called its 'net asset value' or 'NAV') and 500m shares. That would give it NAV per share of 100p. However, the shares might typically trade at only 95p. That would give the trust a 'discount' of 5 per cent.

As far as the capital value of your investment is concerned, you should probably ignore the discount. You might buy your investment trust for a discount of 5%, but you should probably also work on the basis that the discount of 5% will still be there when the time comes to sell. Overall, that would have no effect on your expected rate of return.

Imagine, however, a basket of shares, worth £10,000, that provides a dividend yield of 5%. You could buy the shares directly yourself, paying £10,000, and collect your £500 per year income. Alternatively, you could buy the same basket of shares in an investment trust, at a discount of 5%. So you pay up £9,500, but still get your £500 income (we're ignoring costs for the time being). That amounts to a dividend yield of 5.26% – a useful improvement on buying the shares directly.

Of course, you then have to knock off the charges. On the whole, these will be greater than the 0.26% advantage that you get because of the discount. However, the fact that the discount at least wipes out a part of your (already low) charges might sneak them ahead of index trackers on the charges front and they're providing you with that nice yield that you wanted.

Choosing high yield investment trusts

To get the benefit of all this, then, you want an investment trust that:

(a)   has a nice dividend yield (but not too nice because, as with shares, much more than 5% would be an indication that the market doesn't think it's sustainable);

(b)   is nice and big, so that it has a low total expense ratio; and

(c)   has a decent discount.

The place to start for this information is the Association of Investment Trust Companies (AITC) Monthly Information Service, available on its website.

The sectors to look at are Global Growth and Income, Global High Income, UK Growth & Income and UK High Income sectors (although for the global funds, you should also think about the geographical weightings).

It's probably best to stick to the 'conventional and packaged units' segments for each sector. But ignore 'packaged units' which are created by combining the different segments of split capital trusts. They lack transparency and you'd expect them to have higher charges anyway. If you've followed the recent debacle with split-capital investment trusts and the supposedly safe zero-dividend preference shares, then you'll probably be delighted to steer clear of these anyway.

The AITC doesn't give figures for the total expense ratios, but you can get these from several websites, including the FT Fund Ratings service. In many cases, you'll also be able to get the information by phoning up the relevant investment trust. On the whole, as we saw above, the bigger the size of the investment trust, the lower its charges should be.

Once you've picked on a few likely candidates, you should investigate them in a similar fashion to how you'd look at any company, since that's exactly what they are. Start by calling them up and asking for a copy of their annual accounts. You might also find it useful to discuss selections with like-minded Fools on the Investment Trust and Unit Trusts discussion board at the Motley Fool.

Stick to the Foolish Basics

Investing for income, then, is little different from any other type of investing. It just has a slightly different focus. Just as with 'growth' investing, you're tying to find a cheap and efficient means of harnessing the long-term returns of the stock market. The only real difference is that you want a larger proportion of these returns to come to you by way of dividend rather than by way of share price growth. So, stay well diversified, keep your costs low and stick to strong, solid, dare we say 'obviously great' companies.

Six Lessons From the Technology Boom and Bust

"Those who do not learn from history are doomed to repeat the mistakes of history."

Santayana

The stock market will never move serenely upwards in a nice straight line. Times change, companies' prospects change and, perhaps most importantly, investors' views of prospects change. The last couple of years in the stock market have provided an unpleasant reminder of all this. The years 2000 and 2001 were the first two consecutive years that the stock market has given negative returns since 1973 and 1974, with an overall fall of 18%. Much worse than this, though, is the performance of the technology, media and telecoms companies which have seen an unravelling of the bubble that famously expanded in late 1999 and early 2000. Many of the companies in these sectors have seen their share prices fall by 90% or more. In fact, quite a few have simply gone bust or been wound up.

In investing terms, it's the stuff of nightmares and it's safe to say that we Fools don't care too much for bubbles. They're the enemy of the long-term value-based investor because they bring with them the risk of paying far too much for our shares. We'd much rather find some top quality companies and quietly sit on them while we wait for them to make us rich. Unfortunately, paying too much for them in the first place is not conducive to becoming very rich.

Unfortunately, too, there's not very much you can do to avoid bubbles.

As we'll see in a moment, they've come and gone throughout history and they'll continue to do so. So, instead of hoping to avoid them, we need to understand that they'll appear from time to time and adopt an investing strategy that can prevent us from being exposed to their worst effects. Thankfully, this doesn't involve any changes to what we've already been suggesting throughout this book. It does, however, serve up a useful opportunity for a few reminders. Before we get onto that, however, we first need to know our enemy.

A Brief History of Bubbles

Probably the most famous bubble of all was the 'South Sea Bubble', which began in 1711 when Britain was struggling under a pile of debt after too much fighting with the pesky French. The idea was that those people who had lent money to the Government could exchange those bonds for shares in the new South Sea Company. The company, in turn, was given an exclusive licence to trade with the Spanish colonies in South America, as well as an annual payment from the Government of about £600,000. For investors, who apparently thought that South America was one big lump of gold, it was all too much.

Even though trade had been slow to develop because of various squabbles with Spain, people were queuing up when it was decided to do another national debt for shares swap in 1720. The share price shot up from about £100 in January to a peak of nearly £1,000 in July, giving the company a value of about £200 million. That's a fair-sized company by today's standards, but in the money of 1711, it was almost the world.

It's not entirely clear what sparked the eventual collapse, but it may have had something to do with some South Sea shares subscribers needing to find actual money to pay for their shares and a realisation that the dreams of gold in South America were just that – dreams . It all happened quickly, though, and by October the share price had fallen back to about £120, equating to barely more than the value of the Government's annual payment to the company. Many people got themselves overexposed to the shares and lost a bundle. Sir Isaac Newton, said to have lost £20,000, commented "I can calculate the motions of heavenly bodies, but not the madness of people."

The South Seas investors clearly hadn't learned their lesson from the frenzy that had gripped Holland, nearly a hundred years earlier over, would you believe, tulip bulbs. The apparently innocent tulip bulb had first been introduced into Europe from Turkey in the mid to late 16th Century as something of a curiosity, but by the early 17th Century, they had become a status symbol of the rich and famous. If you didn't have the right tulip, you were nobody.

At the peak of the nonsense in the 1630s, many decent Dutch folk apparently gave up their day jobs to indulge in tulip trading. A single bulb of the highly-prized 'Semper Augustus' tulip is reported to have sold for as much as 5,000 guilders at the peak, which would have been enough to buy a posh house in central Amsterdam. Records show the bubble bursting in about 1637, though it's not clear what was the catalyst for the collapse.

Since then, we've had bubbles in railway shares in Great Britain and North America in the nineteenth century and a bubble in radio shares that ended with the stock market crash in 1929. No doubt there have been others and there will be more in future, because the roots of any bubble lie in human nature. The essential elements seem to be:

1. To have something the value of which is impossible to calculate and seemingly limitless.
2. For its price to start to rise quickly in value, catching the public imagination.
3. For investors to stop worrying about how much the thing is worth, but instead to focus on how much and how quickly it has risen in value.
4. For the fear of losing money to give way to the fear of missing out.
5. For something to happen to remind investors that they can lose money after all.
6. For the whole thing to implode on itself.

This is very much the pattern that the technology bubble has followed in recent years. It all starts with the information technology revolution and the Internet. All of a sudden, there was the potential for any company to reach a seemingly limitless market at the click of a button. The shares of any and every company involved with the Internet or information technology grew rapidly to a point where it seemed, for a time, that they could only go one way. More companies, with the flimsiest of business plans floated on the stock market to take advantage of the money that investors were prepared to throw at them.

People will argue about what set the eventual decline in motion back in March 2000, but, most likely, it was a slowing US economy combined with a fall in the advertising rates that were supporting so many Internet companies. Then there were the huge amounts paid by mobile phone companies to operate third generation (3G) networks across Europe. Anyway, the downwards spiral has been severe. With companies going bust and share prices falling, no one wanted to invest more money into technology companies. That meant that those companies weren't spending money with their suppliers, so they started to suffer too. So the downturn has spread through all technology and associated industries. It stands to reason that companies will have to start spending money again some time and that investors will give them more of it again, but there isn't much sign of anyone doing anything but lick their wounds at the moment. Perhaps the most positive sign is that it doesn't look like it can get much worse, but then it looked like that a year ago and it's been worse since.

So times and technology move on. We're now talking about 3G mobile phone networks and the like, where before we were talking about trading with the new world, tulip bulbs, railways and radio. Heavens knows what will kick-off the next bubble, but that's precisely why it should be hard to spot. In terms of dealing with it, however, it's the nature of bubbles that matters, rather than the actual subject matter. Here are some lessons which the most recent one has taught us. There's nothing new here, but the reminders are fresh and stinging and all the more valuable for that.

1. Don't Follow The Crowd

John D Rockefeller is famously said to have sold all his shares before the 1929 crash after he started getting share tips from his shoe-shine boy. After all, it stands to reason that if everyone is shouting something from the rooftops, then there's unlikely to be much value left in it for you.

This is backed up by figures from the Investment Management Association (IMA), showing monthly sales of unit trusts in the UK hitting £3.2 billion in March 2000, just three months after the stock market peaked.

That compares to £1.3 billion in March 2002. More revealing still is the fact that a whopping 23% of the March 2000 sales went into what they call 'specialist funds', 90 per cent of which are invested in technology companies. The crowd was clearly chasing technology funds egged on, it has to be said, by the investment industry's marketing machine. Sadly, as we now know, it was very definitely not the place to be.

Bubbles are driven by crowd behaviour, so if you want to avoid them, then you want to avoid the crowd as well. Unfortunately, this is a lot easier to say than it is to do. In fact, sales of unit trusts, and of technology funds in particular, had been on the increase for most of the 1990's. So it would have been next to impossible, at the right time, to say 'this time it's too much, Darling! I'm taking us out of equities until I see a sharp fall in unit trust sales'. You could, for example have said that back in 1996, when annual unit trust sales jumped 50% to £10 billion. Since then the stock market has risen around forty per cent, even after the last two years falls.

Unfortunately, this sort of data, like so many other things, only really tells us what has happened after the event. We can see now that the crowd was rushing into the stock market back in early 2000, but it's no different from noting that the FTSE All Share peaked back then. It's not something that we could have known at the time. So really, that leaves us with shoe shine boys and trying to judge the public mood and that's never easy at the best of times. The important thing, though, is to try to step back a bit and avoid getting swept up in a wave of hype.

2. *Throw Away The Rose-Tinted Spectacles*

Another factor linking most bubbles is that investors adopt what, with the benefit of hindsight at least, is an absurdly optimistic view of the future. Back in 2000, people seemed to assume that by now we'd all be using high-tech handheld computers to watch highlights of last night's football match while travelling to work. It might well be that this will happen eventually, but it seems obvious now that it's many years away. We don't even yet have the necessary third-generation (3G) mobile phone technology, despite the mobile phone companies spending billions of pounds buying licences to provide these services over two years ago.

This is probably the hardest lesson to take on board and the authors of this book are happy to admit to having let themselves get more than a little carried away at the height of the excitement. It's very hard not to. After all, the likes of Vodafone were coughing up £6,000,000,000 (we felt it important to write the noughts out) for the right to provide 3G services in the UK. They couldn't be wrong, could they? The trouble is, of course, that the management of Vodafone are just people and they were getting carried away as well. The reason they were getting carried away is precisely because the stock market was also getting carried away. At the time, Vodafone would not have been forgiven if it had walked away from the 3G auction without a licence. The hype and general over-excitement feeds itself. As Charles Mackay said in the preface to the 1852 edition of *Extraordinary Popular Delusions and the Madness of Crowds*:

> *Men, it has been well said, think in herds; it will be seen that they go mad in herds, while they only recover their senses slowly, and one by one.*

Some of the blame can be laid at the door of the investment analysts who perhaps should have known better. In fact, it appears in some cases that they privately did. Allegations are flying around that some analysts were promoting companies in public whilst privately dismissing them and indeed Merrill Lynch investment bank in New York has coughed up $100 million to settle proceedings which claimed that one of its analysts had done just this. In most cases, though, the analysts were probably just wearing the same rose-tinted spectacles as the rest of us. It was the investors who listened to them, bought the shares and made their share tips go up and that just gave them more confidence in their rosy view of the future.

The truth is that we should all take our share of the blame – apart, perhaps from the few that managed to stand back from it all. The trouble is that many of these apparently far-sighted ladies and gentlemen have been doom-mongering for years and will have missed out on much of the stock market growth that can genuinely be justified. Indeed, the 'bears' themselves can form a crowd and they've been getting pretty noisy lately. It must be too much honey. The reality is that it's incredibly difficult to find a sensible balance of optimism and scepticism. All we Fools can say is that you should try to think for yourself, do your own research and steer clear of group thinking and the madness of crowds.

3. *Stick To Quality, Not Meringues*

Even where investors do correctly diagnose a large and rapidly expanding market, they have a bad habit of thinking that any company involved in that particular area will prove vastly profitable. In reality, it is normally just a few companies that have the competitive advantages to make the most of it. The 'alternative' telecommunications carriers that have been springing up over the last few years are a good example of this. With the advent of the Internet and other data services, telephone useage has been on the increase and that will surely continue. Unfortunately, this encouraged so many companies into the market, that there is now a glut of telephone capacity. The result is intense competition and falling prices. Great for consumers, but not very good for profits. If you're going to depart from the basic Foolish index-tracking strategy and pick your own shares, you will want to avoid this type of situation.

We talked about some of the factors that can provide companies with a competitive edge back in Chapter 12, Obviously Great Investments. Essentially it involves having something unique that enables the company to add value in a way that its competitors can't. Not only that, but you'd ideally want a company that dominates and adds the value in its entire supply chain. In the process of bringing Premiership football to your television screen, who adds the most value? Whose position would be hardest to replicate – the players, the football clubs, the broadcasters or the manufacturers of TVs and set-top boxes.

In the excitement of a stock market bubble, investors seem to stop making these distinctions. Instead, it's just a case of buying anything and everything that appears to be going up a lot. To demonstrate this, our sister site in America, www.fool.com, came up with an inspired April Fool's day gag back in 2000. They kicked off the day by announcing, at 9.45am, that a new company, eMeringue.com, "the Internet's number 1 meringue delivery service", had been listed on the (fictitious) Halifax Canadian Exchange and that it represented the investment opportunity of a lifetime. "If you've been a veteran user of our site," they wrote, "you'll know that we think you should do your own research and make your own decisions. But on this one day, in this one hour, we at the Motley Fool have done your research for you. We believe in eMeringue so much that we have underwritten it, and at market open we have issued a Strong Buy recommendation on shares in eMeringue".

One of the Foolish techie experts had knocked up a website for it at www.emeringue.com (take a look and try the Eggulator, it's still there) and the Fool site was hooked up to provide a fake share price quote for the company all day long. The shares, offered at $22 each, were shown to open at $84 and quickly rush to $218 by noon. At which point, eMeringue announced that it was launching a hostile takeover for another made-up Internet company, Cyber Crust. Said CEO Larry McClosky: "This will be the first step toward our five-year goal of producing an entire pie."

Unfortunately, by mid-afternoon, the SEC was announcing that it had found accounting irregularities in the company's prospectus and the shares started to fall, helped along by a food poisoning scare. By the end of a busy day's trading, eMeringue closed at just 88 cents a share and McCloskey was arrested trying to hijack a Carnival Cruise line to Finland with a frosting gun. The game was up.

Astonishingly, our colleagues in America had brokers on the phone throughout the day trying to find out more about the company. Clients had been calling them up wanting to get in on the action. They were not inter-ested in the company's fundamentals, couldn't have cared less about competitive advantages, but were simply aware that something was going up and were frightened of missing out. People had forgotten to think about the underlying business they were buying into.

Unlike the would-be investors in eMeringue.com, be sure to take the time to research any investment you make. Try to work out what gives it a competitive advantage and if you can't find one, then start looking else-where. If you do think you've found something, then think about it some more. There is no rush! Of course, there are no guarantees that you'll be right about the apparent advantages, and the shares might still be overvalued, but by looking for a quality that sets the company apart, you'll have made a good start. At least it should have kept you out of the worst horror stories of the last couple of years.

4. Keep Investing Slowly And Steadily

No matter how much we've stood back from the crowd, kept our feet on the ground and maintained a focus on quality, any money invested near the peak of the stock market will probably have lost a large slice of its value –

especially if it went into technology companies. For most people, though, investing throughout their working lives, overpaying for shares from time to time should not be considered too great a disaster – because there will be many more times when the shares are bought at a fair, or cheap, price.

This is what we were talking about in Chapter 7, when we said 'Fear Not A Falling Market'. If you'd been investing steadily each month into an index tracker over the last 5 years, from May 1997, you'd have made a return of a little over 9 per cent per year. That's a touch below the long-term average, but it still comfortably beats cash in the bank. Even if you'd started contributing monthly to an index tracker at the peak of the FTSE All Share in December 1999, you'd have lost, on average, about seven per cent per year on your investments. That's clearly not great, but it puts all the talk of a market collapse into some kind of context.

The same applies to individual companies. Although you're less likely to invest in them on a steady, monthly basis, you should be aiming to add to your investments periodically. So you might have had the misfortune to put your 1999/2000 ISA allowance into some overvalued technology shares. Your 2000/2001 allowance might even have gone the same way. But there should be plenty of years before that, and in the future, which will turn out OK. The stock market has its ups and downs, and the speed with which it can move from one to the other can be hair-raising at times, but over time, investing steadily and sensibly over the long term will smooth out the wrinkles.

5. Diversify!

Not only should you spread your investments out over time, but you also need to spread them over a range of different companies and industry sectors. Opinion is divided over how many companies you need, but something in the region of 10 to 15 different shares is generally considered to give sufficient diversification. Fewer than 10 companies and you could start to find that your investing fortunes are too heavily tied to just a few companies and more than 15 and you're likely to find it hard to keep track of them all.

Of course, it's no good if you have 15 different investments, but 90% of your money is in just the one company. That would be almost like having a one share portfolio. Even having 50% of your money in one company would be not too far different from holding just two companies. It's important to keep an constant eye on the 'weighting' of different companies in your portfolio and we would suggest that it's time to think hard about pruning a holding in any one company if it reaches more than 25% or so of your portfolio. Even beyond the 20% mark, you should have a lot of confidence in your judgement about it.

Human beings, bless us, are notoriously overconfident. No doubt it's programmed into our genes, to help us go out and kill mammoths in the depths of winter when our cave families are starving, but it plays havoc with us in modern life. The following came from an article about overconfidence by Whitney Tilson on www.fool.com:

- 82% of people say they are in the top 30% of safe drivers;
- 68% of lawyers in civil cases believe that their side will prevail;
- 81% of new business owners think their business has at least a 70% chance of success, but only 39% think any business like theirs would be likely to succeed;
- Mutual fund managers, analysts, and business executives at a conference were asked to write down how much money they would have at retirement and how much the average person in the room would have. The average figures were $5 million and $2.6 million, respectively. The professor who asked the question said that, regardless of the audience, the ratio is always approximately 2:1.

We feel unusually confident in saying that individual investors are apt to display overconfidence in selecting and monitoring in their share investments. Even if investors had genuine grounds for confidence in their selections, things can always happen that we could not possibly have predicted. Sensible Fools will recognise their limitations and deal with them by having a broad spread of shares.

Even if you spread yourself nice and evenly across 15 companies, it won't do you much good if they're all in the same industry sector and exposed to the same risks. So you should aim to have a portfolio of shares from a wide range of businesses and sectors. The recent bubble is a perfect example of this. If your portfolio had been spread over telecommunications, technology and media companies over the last couple of years, you will, most likely, have suffered a severe roasting. On the other hand, you could have lived with a few of these, so long as the remainder of your portfolio was in more solid, and different, industry sectors. So you might decide to invest in a leading bank, or supermarket, or branded consumer goods company, or one of the big oil or drugs companies. If you're spread across the stock market, then the individual shocks that arrive from time to time shouldn't do too much damage to your portfolio.

By taking this argument to its extremes, we find ourselves squarely back with that most Foolish of investments, the index tracker. By buying an index tracker, you buy a small representative sample of the entire stock market, giving you a representative slice of every company and sector. Your performance is tied to the market overall and you minimise the risks of being in the wrong bit of the market at the wrong time. So, not only do index trackers tend to do best over the long term, as we saw in Chapter 7, they do it with less risk than other types of equity investing. No wonder we like them so much!

6. Don't be put off investing!

Perhaps the most worrying aspect of a stock market slump is that it tends to scare investors away from the stock market. Investors see the stock market fall and run away from it, despite all the evidence that shows it's the best place for their money over the long term. In fact, this sort of behaviour might be precisely why the stock market does so well over the long term. If people are scared of it, then that's what should keep prices cheap (and long-term returns high). To take advantage of this, however, you need to make sure that you're not one of the people that are scared away. So steer clear of the crowd mentality and stick to building a diversified portfolio of shares steadily over the long term.

Where *Else* to Invest

They change their clime, not their frame of mind, who rush across the sea.

Horace, *Epistles*

In his excellent book *Mother Tongue – The English Language* Bill Bryson reveals that in the 1920s a US novel published in Britain required a glossary to apprise readers of the meaning of words like *grapevine, fan* (in the sense of a sports enthusiast), *gimmick* and *phoney*. In the 1940s an article in the *Daily Mail* proposed that British readers would be confounded by the use of words such as *commuter, seafood, rare* (as applied to meat), *mean* (in the sense of nasty), *dumb* (in the sense of stupid), *dirt road* and *living room*. As Bryson points out, it does seem an unjustified slight on *Daily Mail* readers that they would not be able to deduce the meaning of at least some of these words, but it does show just how close our countries have become in the last fifty years. There are still major, major differences, as both sides would admit, but in investment terms – and let's pinch ourselves to remind us that we are meant to be talking about investing here – there are many more similarities than differences.

The fact is that what happens on the US markets, on Wall Street, is very shortly mirrored in the UK market and others around the world. We don't believe in monitoring short-term market hiccups as a route to successful investing, but it is extraordinary the way the UK market will hang on news of the decision of the US Federal Reserve Board (their equivalent of the Bank of England) chairman on US interest rates, or be propelled upwards by confidence in US stocks. The one does not move without the other. Or rather, the UK market mirrors its transatlantic partner.

According to the 2001 Interbrand survey, 60 of the world's 100 most valuable brands are associated with American companies, including nine out of the top ten. We're pleased (and a little surprised) to say that the UK makes the second largest contribution to the list, tied with Germany with a total of eight brands, even though the biggest of these, Reuters, only makes it in at 52nd on the list. The two tables below list the world's top ten brands (because that's what we're talking about) and the eight from the UK that make it into the list (because we knew you wanted to know):

THE TEN MOST VALUABLE BRANDS IN THE WORLD

Global rank	Brand	Value($bn)	Country	Annual share price growth over last ten years
1	Coca-Cola	68.9	US	9.7%
2	Microsoft	65.0	US	26.0%
3	IBM	52.8	US	13.5%
4	General Electric	42.4	US	17.2%
5	Nokia	35.0	Finland	30.1%
6	Intel	34.7	US	33.3%
7	Disney	32.6	US	6.1%
8	Ford	30.1	US	8.1%
9	McDonald's	25.3	US	9.8%
10	AT&T	22.8	US	−2.3%

THE EIGHT MOST VALUABLE BRANDS FROM THE UK

Global rank	Brand	Value($bn)
52	Reuters	5.2
74	BP	3.2
77	Shell	2.8
78	Smirnoff	2.6
80	Burger King	2.4
89	Johnnie Walker	1.6
95	Financial Times	1.3
96	Hilton	1.2

Source: Interbrand Annual Survey 2001

We've seen three of these top UK brands before, when we discussed Diageo in Chapter 12. But even if Diageo helps the UK to sneak eight companies into the list, there really is no contest. However you look at it, if you want to invest in the biggest and most powerful brands in the world, then you can't ignore America. What's more, many, many of the companies over there are just as familiar to us, or more so, than our own. Going beyond the table that we showed above, have you ever heard of Marlboro, Hewlett-Packard, Gillette, American Express, Kodak, Nike, Kelloggs, Wrigley's? OK, we're boring you now, but it's hard to imagine that British consumers are much less familiar with the products of these worldwide giants than are their US cousins.

It's no surprise, then, that many investors like to wander across the pond in their search for great investments. You can see from the first table that these powerful US brands have performed well in share price terms over the last ten years as well (compared to the S&P 500 index which has risen at a rate of 9.9% per year) – and it's not as if most of them weren't great brands for a long time before that. Companies like these have made the US stock market one of the strongest performers in the world over the years. Take a look at this graph, which shows the progress of the Dow-Jones Industrial Average (a US index of thirty of the most important industrial stocks) since 1896:

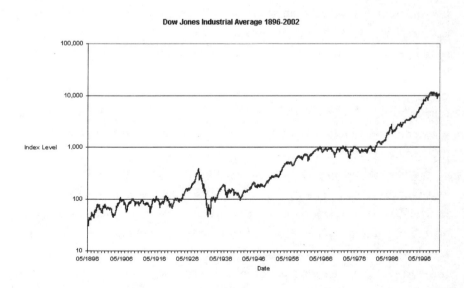

Dow Jones Industrial Average 1896-2002

Looks suspiciously familiar, doesn't it? That's because you saw almost exactly the same thing when you looked at the performance graph of shares on the London Stock Exchange earlier in this Foolish tome. Where they dip, we dip, where they peak, we peak and just as ours does, their graph zigs more than it zags and soars more than it sags. Although the shape is very similar, in absolute terms, the Dow Jones doesn't really show a fair comparison with the earlier graph, since it does not include re-invested dividends and therefore does not reflect *total* returns. The best comparison of the underlying picture that we can find is our old friend the CSFB Equity-Gilt Study. This finds that, since 1920, the US total real returns from equities has averaged 8.5%, whereas bonds have achieved only 2.7%. In the UK, these figures are remarkably similar at 8.6% and 2.8% respectively.

The regulatory environment in the United States has been firmly under the spotlight recently following 'accounting irregularities' at Enron, Worldcom and a few other companies. It seems to have shaken people's faith in the American economy but, in many ways, the shock waves that have reverberated out from these events are cause for comfort. In plenty of places around the world, frauds are conducted daily without anyone showing much sign of caring. Yet, in America, a few sets of dodgy accounts send the entire country into fits of hysterical navel-gazing. The fact is that there will always be companies with dodgy accounts. What matters most, though, is that this sort of thing is taken so seriously. With the witch-hunt that's sprung up, it certainly looks like the Americans are doing that. As always, you need to understand what you're investing in and understand how it makes its money. If it looks like a company is magicking money out of thin air, then forget it however much its accounts say it's making. You'll still get your fingers burnt by some dodgy goings on every now and again, but we're willing to bet you a dollar that you'll see less of it in America than most other parts of the world.

Buying and selling US shares over the Internet from the UK is as easy and cheaper than buying and selling UK shares. Using a US-based (or indeed UK-based), Internet 'deep discount' broker, you can expect to be able to buy and sell shares for as little as a flat rate charge of £6, no matter how large the transaction. And you can expect the trade to be carried through within under a minute, too. Some people get a little anxious at the thought of sending their money across the world and then trading it via the Internet. Just a few years ago this was science fiction and so it's not surprising that we feel wary. However, the Internet really has shrunk the world and with the opportunities that exist on the US market it seems perverse not to take advantage of them just because you're dealing with something new.

As we've just seen, the financial regulations concerning public companies are stricter than any in the UK – including four times a year company reporting – and any broker you choose should be indemnified up to at least $500,000 by the Securities Investor Protection Corporation (SIPC). Many carry far higher indemnity provisions than this (this is the US, land of litigation, remember) and one we know of carries provision as high as $57 *million*. Your friends and neighbours might look at you a little strangely because you're now buying a stake in some of the world's greatest businesses via your computer, but let them! You're a Fool now, you're making use of the communication revolution to invest sensibly and profitably for your long-term future and nothing's going to stop you.

The first step is often the most difficult. Good places to start are with the US book by David and Tom Gardner, *Rule Breakers, Rule Makers* and Warren Buffett's Shareholder letters on www.berkshirehathaway.com. Actually, what we really suggest is that you don't go out and start spending more money right away. Spend some time at the Motley Fool US site before you make any decisions about whether or not you want to invest in the US. There are some terrific investment ideas over there and first-time investors might want to pay particular attention to the Rule Maker and DRiP portfolios, which focus on investments in great American companies. The possibilities are limitless, links to resources for further research are easily accessible and help is readily at hand on the discussion boards.

If you do make the decision that you want to invest in the United States, then you have a number of options, including:

1. Doing so via a UK-based stockbroker. You'll find there are a number now that offer cheap, efficient Internet-based trading in US stocks. The basic series of steps to go through is the same as in Option 2 below.
2. Setting up a US Internet 'deep discount' brokerage account. Simply stop

by the Fool's deep discount brokerage centre (www.fool.com/dbc/ dbc2.htm), then:

- Fire off a series of e-mails to likely candidates asking whether it's possible to open an account from the UK;
- Ask your selected broker to mail you an application form and US W8 tax form. They use the normal post to send you the forms to make sure you're who you say you are, living where you say you do;
- Count off the days until they arrive and then fill out the forms and send them back;
- Await e-mail confirmation that your account is open;
- Transfer your pile of Foolishly saved cash by bank transfer to your new brokerage account;
- Await the e-mail saying that your money has arrived;
- Reflect that you are now an international Internet tycoon and investor, surfing the crest of the global investment wave. Feel good? You should!

3. Doing so via your Individual Savings Account. The details of how this works will vary and although there will be an obvious tax advantage, transaction charges may be hefty.

By logging onto the site using your username and password, you will be able to access the details of your portfolio, updated in real time according to the latest share prices, as well as buying and selling shares with the utmost ease. Of course, you're not going to let the ease and cheapness of the service tempt you into becoming a day trader, are you? As you do with your UK investments, you buy and hold quality companies on the basis of their fundamental performance, not on the whims of the marketplace or the hype of a hypester.

What about currency fluctuations over the years? Currently, the pound is strong, meaning it will buy plenty of US dollars. What if it gets even stronger in thirty years' time when you want to bring your dollars back to live in the UK? It might happen that way, yes, or the pound may be weaker then than it is now. In our opinion, there is risk inherent in any enterprise, but there's idiotic risk and there's Foolish risk. With the kinds of returns that great American companies have provided over decades and with the general strength of both our economies, this is a Foolish risk and not one which we think will figure hugely in your financial equations a few decades from now. In any event, many of the best US investment opportunites, like their UK counterparts, are dominant *global* companies, which earn their money all over the world in many different currencies. Although their shares are quoted in dollars and their dividends are paid in dollars, their fortunes are not solely linked to the fortunes of that currency.

Where *Else* to Invest: EuroFool

So that's it, is it? America and Britain. There are no other countries in the world worth investing in. The 300 million or so people on the other side of the English Channel are all living in an economic and investment wasteland where mangy dogs roam the streets and the occasional burst of gunfire breaks the tense silence of a sultry afternoon.

Er, no. There are many great investment opportunities in Europe, but to be honest most of us don't know a huge amount about them. We don't like to speak foreign languages when it comes to investing and we mean that in the nicest possible way. Actually, we love to speak foreign languages, but like to know what we're investing in. If we don't understand an investment, or don't feel comfortable with it, we don't invest. Our lack of familiarity, though, with Europe and the European markets is something that is going to change rapidly with the advent of the euro and the Internet.

However, the ease with which the new currency, the euro, will allow trading across borders is likely to open up the stock markets of Europe to such an extent that this book, largely confined as it is to dealing with investment in the UK, might seem like a laughable anachronism in just a few years. Whereas today we talk about the FTSE 100, tomorrow we'll almost certainly be talking about the Euro 100 or something similar. If what we're primarily worried about in investment is total return on our money, then we wish to invest in the best businesses we can, whether they're French, Dutch, British, American or Italian and, so long as there's no serious currency hit to be reckoned with, it seems ludicrous not to invest in a company simply because it's foreign. In a very few years, you will likely be able to trade almost instantaneously via the Internet on any of the exchanges of Europe, using your single pan-European stockbroker, and frankly we think this is going to be one hell of a market. Currently the US – the largest market in the world – has companies adding up to a market capitalization of $8.7 trilllion. The Bloomberg Europe 500 companies are currently worth $5.4 trillion (EUR5.5 billion).

Of course, if the standards of financial regulation aren't up to scratch in the country in which a company is listed, then that isn't much good, no matter what you think of the company itself. That's why we're so attracted to the soon-to-be-united countries of Western Europe with their high standards of financial reporting and some very well-known brand name companies. What would make us drown our grandmothers before investing in some of the other countries of Europe is precisely the lack of any of those things. Entry into some of the emerging markets of Eastern Europe, or indeed emerging economies anywhere else in the world, is to lay yourself open to precisely the kinds of currency fluctuations that could prove disastrous to your investments and to the possibility of outrageous scams or accounting 'irregularities' over which neither you nor anyone else has any control. There is real money to be made in the stable economies of the Western world. Don't spoil your investment returns by throwing money into a cauldron of economic turmoil.

The Ethical Fool

A custom loathsome to the eye, hateful to the nose, harmful to the brain, dangerous to the lungs, and in the black, stinking fume thereof, nearest resembling the horrible Stygian smoke of the pit that is bottomless.

James I (James VI of Scotland), *A Counterblast to Tobacco*

Agree or disagree with him, King James certainly had one or two strong thoughts on the smoking weed that had so recently been introduced from the Americas. So, certainly, will many of the people reading this. Whether you're pro or anti the free marketing of tobacco, there is no escaping the issue that there is an issue here, as there is with many other activities in the business world. What about arms manufacturing, or mining, or paper manufacturing and its consequent effect on deforestation? Depending on your outlook, this stuff can be tricky.

So what are we going to call this subject, about which the passions run so high? 'Socially responsible investing'? 'Ethical investing'? 'Green investing', even? The choice, ultimately, is yours, but what we're trying to get at is a self-imposed, selective approach to investing, one which has ultimately kept millions of potential investors around the globe from buying into certain public companies, whose corporate activities they deem immoral, damaging or exploitative.

If we lived in Utopia (from the ancient Greek *ou topos* meaning 'no place'), we could simply tell you to invest without concern. You'd be living in a perfect society with perfect laws and no need for regulatory bodies. You would know, in every moment you spent investing, that your company was maximizing the growth of well-being for every constituency: customers, employees, shareholders, management and society. If ever one group was temporarily over- or under-compensated, the whole structure would tilt immediately to correct it (probably slightly too far in the other direction, briefly, to create total equity). Doesn't it sound great?

Look at the name again. *Ou topos* – no place.

No such world has ever yet existed, unless Thomas More's legendary traveller was telling the truth. And most importantly, no single life has ever been continually, uncompromisingly painless. With no Utopia in our personal or professional lives, we certainly shouldn't expect one in our investing life. At the most basic level, we all just have to make the best of things.

The whole concept of ethics in investing has had much ink spilled over it, with many zealots beating each other around the head with their own moral codes and a number of very bad and highly-charging unit trusts springing up to meet the need for people to feel wholesome about their investing endeavours. It's a deadly serious issue and that's why we're touching on it here. Our approach is very simple, so simple in fact that we're in danger of being called naive:

*Buy what you are; buy **only** what you are.*

If you don't like British American Tobacco, don't invest in it. If you think companies that manufacture and export arms are immoral, don't invest in them. Never lose sleep over an investment that you made tentatively in an enterprise you don't wholeheartedly support. Flog it. Buy something else. Ultimately, when you buy a share in a business, you are providing it with capital so that it can further what it does. If you buy a share in a uranium mining company, then you are providing capital so that it can mine more uranium. If you don't approve of the mining of uranium, then you shouldn't be doing that, should you?! In fact, if enough people thought like this, it would be much harder for the companies doing things that people don't approve of to raise funds for what they do. Perhaps you can think of it as a grand global economic democracy. If everyone does their bit according to their values, then the world may become a better place. We can dream, can't we?

Buying what you are, what informs your daily life, what sits snugly with your beliefs and values about the world is the only way to feel comfortable with the investments you hold. No one else can tell you what you are and especially not the fund manager of an 'ethical' unit trust. When you buy one of these – and why would you, because their long-term returns have been abysmal – are you buying what you are or what someone else is? When you buy a unit trust, you're consigning the destiny of your money to a stranger you'll most likely never meet. Social responsibility? If you take ethics in investing at all seriously, then we fervently argue that you're being most *irresponsible* by saying, 'I'll buy that pleasingly-named unit trust.'

Let's go a little further. You don't like Hilton Group because you don't approve of gambling (and Hilton owns Ladbrokes and a string of casinos), but you stay in a Hilton hotel from time to time when on holiday. Whoops! Let's say you avoid investing in GlaxoSmithKline because you don't like animal testing. Then you fall ill and are prescribed a medicine by your doctor. Three days later, you look at the name on the packet ... If you're going to avoid investing in a particular company, then make sure you're not helping them more directly by buying their products. Make your investment pounds work in harmony with your consumption pounds and you'll feel right about what you're doing. You'll be in sync. You'll be a Fool.

The Active Shareholder

There's no way we can dictate the moral choices that you alone must decide for yourself. The history of the world is full to busting with people moralizing to others and we have no intention of joining their ranks. Decide for yourself what is acceptable, decide if your investing philosophy sits easily with your life philosophy and if it does, then that's fine. There may well come a time, though, when a company you bought into, and which you thought you knew well, goes off on a tangent with which you don't feel comfortable. Alternatively, perhaps you disapprove only mildly of the activities of a company and would like to invest in it, but at the same time would like to do what you can to modify their behaviour. The answer is to become an active shareholder.

Quite apart from the purely financial reasons not to own more than ten to fifteen companies at a time, there are good reasons from an ethical point of view not to hold more than this number. Not only can you not follow the details of their business if you own many more than this, but you can't follow their ethical activities either. As an active shareholder – a part-owner, remember – of whatever business you're invested in, you are uniquely placed to make your views heard. You can attend shareholder meetings, bombard who you like with letters, faxes and e-mails and generally make a nuisance of yourself (politely of course) and at all times your views will have to be heard. Working from the inside to change the face of business is likely to be much more effective than standing on the outside knocking on a large smoked glass door.

Investing in this way in a company whose business you essentially deem worthy of respect, but which has one or two practices of which you disapprove, can be very positive. What about the business, though, that you think is an absolute shocker? How can you justify to yourself making money out of that company and using it for your own personal gain? That, we're afraid, is an issue between you and your bathroom mirror. However, one rather elegant line of approach that you might want to consider is to only invest the money in Evil Activities PLC that you would otherwise donate to charity. Then, as an active shareholder you keep up your barrage from the side of morality and probity, but channel the profits from your investment – it's a sad fact that 'nasty' companies are often very profitable – into activities or charities that seek to counteract the damaging effects of the actions of your evil company. It's quite a neat way of changing the world, but won't do anything for your investment returns. Don't, therefore, take this money from the funds you are allocating for your retirement nest egg. This is strictly hobby money, but using part of your investment life to try and put things right can be an attractive idea for many people who are turned off the very idea of stock market investing by the dirty corporate world they feel they're buying into. Bear in mind, though, that simply by holding the shares, you are effectively providing the company with the capital it needs to pursue its activities.

One thing to note is that it is worth asking your stockbroker just what shareholder rights you are entitled to if you are holding your shares in a nominee account. (These are the types of accounts that many execution-only stockbrokers use to hold clients' shares communally, thus making dealing easier.) It's no good planning to be an active shareholder if you then find you don't have an easily exercisable voting right at meetings.

Conclusion

We live in a dirty world. (You didn't need us to tell you that.) As an investor – if you wish to use this opportunity – you have much scope to shape that world for the better. Do debate and discuss this issue with others, for down that path lies greater understanding and tolerance. Don't, however, let others bully you into a course of action with which you feel uncomfortable: you won't stick with it and the sum of resentment and ill-feeling will have been increased in the world, surely the very opposite of what we all hope will occur.

Rounding Up

Welcome to the End of the Beginning!

Now this is not the end. It is not even the beginning of the end. But it is, perhaps, the end of the beginning.

Winston Churchill, Mansion House speech following
the first major German defeat of the war at El Alamein, 1942

Congratulations. If this is the first time you have dipped your toe in the murky waters of investment, you have now reached the end of the very beginning of your life as a Foolish, savvy, active investor. From now on, you can start to put your critical skills to good use in building for your financial future. To celebrate this new phase, we're going to take the opportunity to have one last shot at the world of Wisdom, and believe us, it's a real cracker.

When the Motley Fool UK was launched in September 1997, we started off by sending one or two (250, actually) press releases out to the great and the good of the world of British financial journalism. In it we made one or two Foolish observations including the fact that, according to research from the *Investor's Chronicle* in March 1996, more than 90 per cent of managed unit trusts had underperformed their index over the preceding five- and ten-year periods. We believe that most of these press releases were filed straight into the paper shredder but just a few elicited some interest. In fact, David B. received a phone call from one of the worthies of financial writing at one of the UK's most respected newspapers. The encounter was so remarkable that he wrote about it later that day in an article on our Web site. Here's an extract:

*This afternoon, I found myself talking on the telephone to a senior City jour-
nalist on one of the national newspapers. It was an education in Wisdom and
went something like this.*

ME (SQUEAKILY). Erm, hello, it's David Berger of the Motley Fool UK
here.

HE (FOR HE IT WAS). Ah yes. I'm most concerned about this little scheme
of yours.

ME. Oh yes?

HE. Yes, all this guff about index trackers. I've written a lot about them
myself and I don't know where you get this figure of 90 per cent
underperforming the market. I am very concerned [that word
again] about this. It's not true, you know.

ME. Oh. It does come from a reputable source. In fact, I've read a lot
about index trackers in your newspaper, I'm sure. Although I think
this is from a different source.

HE (BREAST PUFFING AUDIBLY OVER THE PHONE). Yes, what you've read in
my paper was almost certainly written by me. I write a lot about
them and I'm very concerned [again] about this 90 per cent figure.
(D.B. flicks through past copies of the *Investor's Chronicle*.)

ME. Here we are, March 22nd, 1996, page 16. Of 203 UK unit trusts in
existence for ten years, only fifteen outperformed the market over
that period and that is even giving them an unfair advantage by
disregarding initial charges. The source of the data is Micropal.

HE (FOLLOWING A SHORT SILENCE). Good God!
(I kid you not, he really said 'Good God!' I have filed this as one of
my lifetime Golden Moments.)

HE (SLIGHTLY OFF BALANCE, BUT RECOVERING QUICKLY). Yes, well, I can
see what they've done. But I'm very concerned about these
message boards of yours. Won't people be able to cause a buying
panic by posting un-founded rumours on your message boards?
What's to stop that happening?

ME. Nothing, but we don't advocate buying on the basis of a single,
hysterical tip. We stress buying on the basis of a sound analysis of
a company's fundamentals. And anyway, anyone who believes an
outrageous story on the basis of no obvious evidence merely

because they want to, deserves everything they get. That's just stupid!

HE. Still, I am very concerned about this.

ME. Well, why don't you come and visit the site, or even better the American site where they have over 2000 message boards ... ?

HE (INTERJECTING, A TRIFLE IRRITADO NOW). Oh, don't talk to me about computers. I don't know anything about computers!

ME. More Foolish stuff.

HE. More Wise stuff.

ME. More Foolish stuff.

HE. Etc., etc.

And so it went on for a few more desultory minutes. Later, he talked to a fellow Fool in the USA and came out with this:

HE. But your information is quite simple, isn't it? It's not very sophisticated.

THE FELLOW FOOL. Exactly.

It's hard to imagine a more succinct illustration than this snapshot for why there is a need for a sane, understandable alternative to the stuffy blather you so often find being purveyed as financial information these days. Of course, we hope that this book and the daily to-ings and fro-ings at our website go some way to meeting this need, but as of now it's in your hands, those of the reader, to judge.

Our aspiration is that even if you don't agree with everything written here and even if some of it seems incomprehensible – for which we blame no one but ourselves – you will at least put the book down with the belief that it is *possible* for you to understand enough about investment to manage your own financial affairs. We don't expect everyone to rush off and suddenly become self-sufficient amateur stock market investors. The process of learning and understanding simply doesn't work like that. We do hope, though, that with a small chink of light showing at the end of a long black tunnel you may now be starting to question any and everything that is being sold to you in the financial world and scheming about how *you* can do it better.

Hurry Up and Slow Down

Inspiration and panic make dangerous bedfellows and it's quite possible that by turns both of these will have accompanied you on your journey through these pages. Talk of endowments and other Wise investment plans may have caused you to fear that your best years are behind you, squandered on wastrel investments with huge charges and underperformance by way of return. Combine this with the exciting possibilities open to you in the stock market – from index trackers to the Obviously Great Investments and beyond – and you may be inspired to rush out and transform all your investments into Foolish ones. Now. Right now.

But stop!

Go back.

Don't do it.

Precipitate, unthinking action is not the way to set yourself up for a lifetime of secure, profitable investment. Similarly, precipitate, unthinking *inaction* is not the right way either. Interestingly, one evening in May 1998 we asked a selection of visiting Fools, at our Fool UK focus group meeting/Pizza Express field study trip, what the hardest thing had been about starting in investment. Simultaneously, two answers were shot back. The first was: 'The hardest thing was buying my first share.' The second was: 'The hardest thing was *not* buying my first share.' Whichever of these categories you fall into, you need to think incrementally.

The only way you will be able to set up the habits of a lifetime of sensible investment is by approaching the whole subject cautiously, yet steadily. Don't rush out and cancel your endowment policy, AVC or Personal Pension Plan. It is entirely possible that you will have passed the point where you were paying 80 per cent or more of your contributions in charges and it may make more sense to hold onto it. You may decide not to increase the amount you put into it and instead divert those extra savings elsewhere, but that's another story entirely.

We suggest that the first thing you do is put down this book and have a good old think about your investment goals, the amount you can realistically save and where your interests lie. Where they really lie. It is easy to be inspired (which is a good thing) but inspiration alone is not going to carry you through a lifetime of investing. It requires persistence, too. Ask yourself if you're going to want to be the type of person who keeps an eye on their shares every few weeks and is prepared to put in a fair amount of graft to choose them in the first place. No? You're not? Then you don't want to be investing in a relatively small company like Pizza Express, or an up-and-coming chip designer (the silicon variety). Some more reliable investments are likely to suit. If you think you'll just be able to muster enough interest to read this book and then forget about investment for the next twenty or so years, then an index tracker is most likely what you're after. Take a good hard look, too, at the investments you already have. Learn about them, about how well they've done for you and how much they might have cost you. If you decide to ditch one or any of them, make sure you do so after having weighed up the pros and cons carefully. From now on, you have no one to blame but yourself. Similarly, when things go well, as they most assuredly should, if you approach investment sensibly and realistically, then no one else will be standing in line to take the credit which will rightly fall to you.

Oh yes, debt. Almost forgot about that. That comes before any of the above. Pay off any non-mortgage debt as quickly as you can before you start investing, and also aim to refinance any large chunks of credit card debt with a personal loan from your bank at a lower rate as quickly as you can. You knew that anyway.

When you've decided what strategy you might like to follow, then immediately do nothing. Nothing, that is, except track the progress of your strategy on paper, or on a Web site with portfolio tracking facilities. After three months, six months, a year – yes, as long as that, or even longer – think about committing a small amount of your funds to your chosen strategy. Start with 5 per cent and work up as you feel comfortable. You're in it for the long haul and there's no sense in rushing into something you don't feel comfortable with and which you're going to bail out of at the first sign of market volatility. If you get yourself bitten badly in the stock market at the start, it'll be a long time, if ever, before you're back.

The Bottom Line

Several years ago, one of us (D.B.) spent a year working with a Frenchman: '*Mais*, Daveed, explain once more, what ees ze "Bottom Line"?' It does seem as if there is no equivalent expression in French (if you're a French scholar and you think there is, then you know where to e-mail us) and he never quite grasped the concept to his satisfaction. Of course, we know what it means and the expression we use in our daily lives ('Yeah, Snodbury United may have played well, but the bottom line is they lost twelve-nil') probably comes from company accounting, where the bottom line means after-tax profits. This is the money that remains to be divvied up between the company and its shareholders after all the froth and fury of the annual accounts has been played out. Often, it's the whole reason that investors have bought into the company and some would say the whole reason a public company exists.

'What's the bottom line?' is a question we should always ask, whatever endeavour we're about to embark upon. Of course, we hope that the process of reading this Foolish volume has encouraged you, nay, converted you, into a fanatical devotee of the bottom line when it comes to your investments and your financial future, but since you've now come to the end of it, it seems reasonable to ask what's the bottom line of the book itself and the Motley Fool as a whole? What have we been trying to say here? What are the crucial points we hope you'll take away from this book and which, in our opinion anyway, make it worth the purchase price? Okay, we think it's all pretty well encapsulated like this:

- Investment is not inherently difficult to understand.
- The average person is not as stupid as they are made out to be.
- Many types of investment on sale today overcharge and underper-form.
- The people selling you those investments have interests diametrically opposed to your own.
- Investors should understand and have faith in the supremacy of shares as the long-term route to growing wealth.
- An understanding of the awesome power of compound interest is a prerequisite for any successful investor.
- The application of simple, common-sense rules and a small amount of knowledge can produce returns far exceeding those of the professionals.

- The Internet facilitates the spread of knowledge and information in a revolutionary and unprecedented fashion.
- Shareholders are uniquely placed to play an active role in modifying corporate behaviour for the greater good of society and of the world as a whole.
- Taking responsibility for your own investments and financial future need not be onerous and is one of the most lucrative, enjoyable and fulfilling activities open to you.
- The emphasis is on enjoyable.

That's it. That's our bottom line. The end of the beginning. We hope it pleaseth you.

Be Foolish, one and all!

DAVID BERGER
JAMES CARLISLE

Acknowledgements

In most of mankind, gratitude is merely a secret hope for greater favours.
Duc de la Rochefoucauld, *Maximes*

Permission Acknowledgements

Permission to use existing material

We thank PanMacmillan for permission to quote from *The Hitch Hiker's Guide to the Galaxy*. And we are very grateful to CSFB for permission to use that marvellously sloped graph, along with incredibly compelling numbers from the CSFB Equity Gilt Study. And finally, thanks to Gartmore for the data on their UK Index fund.

Acknowledgements for the second edition

Thanks go to David and Tom Gardner, founders of the Motley Fool and co-authors for two things. Firstly, the cerebral short circuit you both possess which came up with an idea as crazy as the Fool in the first place. Secondly, for having the vision, passion and humanity to have steered it thus far and thus well.

David's thanks also go particularly to his long-suffering wife Carol, their two impish boys Max and Tom and his irreplaceable parents Gerry and Maurice. Also, to Benoit and Otti Zurkinden, good friends, for the loan of their apartment in the Swiss Alps to complete the manuscript.

James is particularly grateful to his wife Sara, for taking him on and looking after him through a series of tight book deadlines and coping with the mess they create at home. Also to his parents for teaching him to think for himself and apologies for any irritation this may have caused over the years.

Finally, a word to the staff of the Motley Fool U.K., particularly those whose jobs disappeared in the necessary cost cutting last year. Special thanks also go to the ever-increasing number of users on our website who sent in feedback on the first and second editions of this book. Thanks to everyone, in fact, who has contributed to this tremendous endeavour and who keep it moving inexorably on the right course, that of a path to greater financial freedom for the ordinary people of the UK.

DAVID BERGER

JAMES CARLISLE

Foolish Glossary of Investment Terms

'When I use a word,' Humpty Dumpty said in a rather scornful tone, 'it means just what I choose it to mean – neither more nor less.'

Lewis Carroll, *Through the Looking Glass*

None of us likes complicated words and many of us are distinctly allergic to them. Often it seems as if they are bandied about simply to confuse. However, like most things in life, it's not quite that simple. Using specialist terminology can be a useful aid to communication and means that you don't have to go into long-winded explanations every time you want to explain a particular concept.

But don't take it from us, take it from Sir David Attenborough:

The first time I travelled in the forests of Borneo, I knew no Malay. My guide, a Dyak hunter who, with his blowpipe, regularly collected birds for the local museum, knew no English. So, to begin with, we had some difficulty – to put it mildly – in sorting out where we should go and what we should do. On our first day out together, we were paddling up a river in a canoe, when I heard a sonorous tok-tok-tok-tok call echoing through the trees. I cupped my hand round my ear and raised my eyebrows towards my guide. He then, for the very first time in our acquaintance, spoke words that I precisely understood. 'Caprimulgus macrurus,' he said and I knew immediately that I was listening to the voice of the long-tailed nightjar. It was a nice demonstration that those cumbersome Latin names, sometimes mocked by the ignorant as pretentious obfuscations invented by scientists to prevent others understanding what they are talking about, do indeed constitute a truly international lingua franca.

(Foreword, *Oxford Dictionary of Natural History*)

To the accompaniment of a gentle 'lap, lap, lapping' along the side of the canoe, the ever-present 'drip, drip, dripping' of huge droplets from the dark, forest canopy overhead, eerie shrieks from the impenetrable green tangle on the banks and the occasional 'Thwoop!' as your Dyak guide spits another wad of betel nut into the river, please feel free to consult our Foolish glossary of investment terms.

Additional Voluntary Contributions (AVCs) Many try and enhance their OCCUPA-TIONAL PENSION schemes by paying into one of these plans. Watch out for the hefty charges and dismal underperformance, though. Like PERSONAL PENSIONS, they attract tax relief.

Advisory Stockbroker Stockbrokers who offer advice on which shares to buy and sell. We don't favour using them. See EXECUTION-ONLY STOCKBROKER and CHURNING.

Alternative Investment Market (AIM) AIM opened in 1995 for small, growing companies. It's less difficult to be listed here than on the LONDON STOCK EXCHANGE and shares are higher risk and more likely to be difficult to buy and sell. See LIQUIDITY.

Analyst A financial professional who analyses securities to determine their 'fair' or 'intrinsic' value. The term is generally applied to almost any professional investor who does research of some kind.

Annualize To take an item measured over a certain period and restate it on an annual basis. For instance, if it costs £10 million every month to run a factory, the annualized cost is £10 million x 12, or £120 million, since there are twelve months in a year.

Annual Percentage Rate (APR) When you borrow money, this rate should always be quoted to you. It's the percentage rate that your loan will cost you each year, including all charges. Incredibly, APRs for credit cards can reach around 20 per cent.

Annual Report A yearly statement of a company's operating and financial performance punctuated by pictures of families enjoying the firm's products and/or services.

Annuity The investment you purchase with your pension fund, which will provide you with a regular income in your retirement. They are intrinsically poor investments.

Appreciation Increase in the price (or value) of a share or other asset. Appreciation is one component of total return.

Balance Sheet Part of the ANNUAL REPORT. It provides a look at a company's assets, debts and shareholder equity at one particular point in time. See also CASH FLOW STATEMENT and PROFIT AND LOSS ACCOUNT.

Bank of England Set up in 1649, the 'Old Lady of Threadneedle Street' is the 'lender of last resort', which means that it shores up the banking system if there is a liquidity crisis. To put it another way, it lends us money when everyone else has run out. At a more mundane level, it sets interest rates to help the Government meet its inflation targets. The stock market often gets very excited about these short-term interest rate movements.

Bankruptcy When a company owes more than it can pay, or when its debts exceed its assets, it's bankrupt.

Bear So you think that the market is headed south? You're bracing yourself for a crash or correction? You feel that share XYZ will soon be taking a tumble? Guess what – you're a bear! Bears are investors with pessimistic outlooks, as opposed to BULLS.

Bid-offer Spread The difference between the bid price (at which the holder can sell shares) and the offer price (at which the holder can buy shares). On occasion this can be quite large and depends on the equity's underlying price, LIQUIDITY, volatility and a number of other factors. Many UNIT TRUSTS also have a bid-offer spread and effectively this amounts to an EXIT CHARGE when the investor sells.

Big Bang The first big shake-up of the stock market in October 1986, when computers were introduced into the trading process for the first time. This was followed in 1996 by the introduction of CREST and then in 1997 by BIG BANG II.

Big Bang II 20 October 1997. The use of a computer-driven trading system to cut out the middlemen in share trading, who match buyers and sellers. Initially, this was just for FTSE 100 shares, but is likely to be extended.

Blue Chip A share in a large, safe, prestigious company. Unilever is a blue chip, so is Lloyds TSB and so is Tesco. Many of the other shares making up the FTSE 100 would also be considered blue chips. The small mining company Minmet is not a blue chip. Neither is Fortune Oil.

Bond A bond is essentially a loan. Bondholders lend money to governments or companies and are promised a certain rate of interest in return. Interest rates vary depending on the quality or reliability of the bond issuer. UK Government bonds, or gilts, for example, carry no risk and thus offer the lowest sterling interest rates. Company bonds offer higher interest rates, with the riskiest companies' bonds offering the highest of all and being called junk bonds.

Bonus Issue Not to be confused with a SHARE SPLIT. If a company believes that its share price has risen to a point where it might affect liquidity, they may have a bonus issue or a share split. This reduces the share price but increases the number of shares outstanding. With a bonus issue, you get issued with new shares on top of your existing shares. By contrast, with a share split, your shares actually get split into smaller chunks. So, if you start with ten shares and the company does a 3 for 1 bonus issue, you'd be given three more shares for each share that you already hold. You'd therefore end up with forty shares. This would be equivalent to a 4 for 1 share split, in which each of your ten shares gets split into four. The difference between the two approaches means something to accountants but not to anyone else.

Broker One who sells financial products. Be it in insurance, pensions or shares, most brokers work under compensation structures that are at direct odds with the greatest good of their clients. (Also see INDEPENDENT FINANCIAL ADVISER, EXECUTION-ONLY STOCKBROKER, ADVISORY STOCKBROKER, STOCK-BROKER.)

Building Society A mutual organization, owned by the people saving money in it and borrowing money from it. Increasing numbers have converted to banks in recent years, paying windfall profits to the owners. See DEMUTUALIZATION.

Bull Are your glasses rose-coloured? Do you see nothing but blue skies ahead for the stock market or a particular share? Then you're a bull – an optimistic investor – as opposed to a BEAR.

CAC 40 French INDEX of – wait for it – the 40 major French companies.

Capital The overall pile of assets which a company uses to carry on its business, or an investor's pot of cash and investments.

Capital Gain You bought a share and later sold it. If you made a profit, then you'll have a capital gain. If you lost money, you'll have a capital loss. Too much in the way of capital gains and you might have to pay capital gains tax.

Capped Rate Mortgage The mortgage interest rate cannot go above a certain level if mortgage rates rise, but can fall as rates drop. Ain't no free lunches, though, and, for various reasons, the interest rate may fall more slowly than otherwise.

Cash Flow Statement The part of a company's ANNUAL REPORT that tells you how much money a company really is making, rather than what an accountant thinks the company is making (as in the PROFIT AND LOSS ACCOUNT). See also BALANCE SHEET.

Chief Executive The Chief Executive is the highest executive officer in a company, rather like the captain of a ship. He or she is accountable to the company's Board of Directors and will be a member of that Board. The Chief Executive participates in setting strategy with the Board and other officers and is responsible for developing strategies to meet the company's goals.

Churning The unconscious or conscious overtrading by a STOCKBROKER in a customer's account. Since stockbrokers are generally compensated by the number of transactions made on a customer's behalf, there is a temptation to trade for the sake of it. It's illegal, but hard to prove.

The City London's financial district, which encompasses the square mile of the old City of London, bounded to the south by the Thames, to the west by the Law

Courts, to the east by the Tower of London and to the north by Billingsgate Market. It's full of banks, sandwich shops and wine bars.

Commission The way a STOCKBROKER or an INDEPENDENT FINANCIAL ADVISER is compensated. When he or she makes a transaction for a customer, the customer pays a commission.

Common Stock A US term for SHARES.

Compound Interest The investor's best friend. One hundred pounds invested in the stock market in 1869 would be worth about £15,000,000 today. Now, *that's* compound interest!

Correction A decline, usually short and steep, in the prevailing price of shares traded in the market or in an individual share. Any time that commentators cannot find a reason for an individual stock or the entire market falling, they call it a correction. A really big correction gets called a CRASH.

Coupon The interest paid by a bond or gilt as a percentage of the nominal value.

Crash A really big CORRECTION. The worst crashes in modern times were in 1929 and 1974. The last couple of years have been no picnic but probably not quite a crash (yet).

CREST Introduced in 1996, this is a computerized system to settle up share purchases. No more bits of paper changing hands.

Cum-dividend *Cum* means 'with' in Latin. If you buy shares cum-dividend, you are buying them at a time when you will be entitled to receive the next dividend. This is as opposed to EX-DIVIDEND, where you buy the share without that entitlement.

Current Account Mortgage A type of mortgage in which your debt is effectively held in a current account. Interest due is calculated daily as opposed to yearly, which can make a significant difference to the cost for those on a REPAYMENT MORT-GAGE. Also more flexible and allows periods of both under- and overpayment of the mortgage to suit the borrower's changing financial circumstances.

Dax An index of major German companies.

Day Trader Day traders are in and out of the market many times during the course of one trading session and may not even hold a position in any securities overnight. This approach tends to make your broker rich at your expense. By losing so much of your returns in trading costs, day traders deny themselves the opportunity of participating in the long-term creation of wealth generated by business over the long term.

Defined Benefit Scheme A type of pension. See FINAL SALARY SCHEME.

Defined Contribution Scheme Another type of pension. See MONEY PURCHASE SCHEME.

Demutualization The process building societies go through when they convert to banks and thus go from being owned by their members (the borrowers and savers of the society) to being a PUBLIC LIMITED COMPANY owned by shareholders. There are pros and cons and the arguments rage on...

Derivatives Derivatives represent contracts conferring rights and obligations to do something with a security at a particular point in time. OPTIONS and FUTURES are derivatives. They can be used to lessen investment risk, but often their main attraction is that they are highly geared (see GEARING) and can thus offer spectacular profits ... and spectacular losses. They generally have substantial associated costs and we do not advocate their use.

Disclosure Since 1995 INDEPENDENT FINANCIAL ADVISERS and TIED AGENTS have been forced to disclose the level of commission they will earn from selling financial products to clients. It's a good thing, but the investor still isn't able to compare the levels of commission between investments. STOCKBROKERS also have to tell you of any financial interests they have in SECURITIES they are recommending.

Discount Broker The US term for EXECUTION-ONLY BROKER.

Discounted Rate Mortgage A mortgage with a guaranteed reduction in the variable mortgage rate (say, 2 per cent below the variable, whatever it may be). Generally the variable rate that you'll switch to when the discount ends will be higher than otherwise so that the bank can afford all the enticing discounts in the first place. Even if you're not tied into the variable rate by a REDEMPTION PENALTY, borrowers often forget to switch to a better rate. We'd generally suggest finding a cheap, non-discounted rate in the first place.

Dividend A distribution from a company to a shareholder in the form of cash, shares, or other assets. The most common kind of dividend is a distribution of cash out of a company's earnings. See DIVIDEND YIELD.

Dividend Yield The dividend divided by the current share price, expressed as a percentage. Different companies have different policies on the size of their dividend payouts.

Dow-Jones Industrial Average The thirty companies chosen by editors of Dow-Jones & Company that are supposed to epitomize the very best American corporations and reflect the landscape of corporate America.

Earnings The after-tax profit that a company makes after all costs of delivering a product or service have been accounted for. See EARNINGS PER SHARE.

Earnings Per Share (EPS) EARNINGS divided by the current number of shares outstanding. This is one of the principal elements used in determining at what value the shares should trade. See also PRICE/EARNINGS RATIO.

Endowment A life assurance and savings and investment policy, classically sold to back an INTEREST-ONLY MORTGAGE. The key word here is 'sold'. No one in their right minds would 'buy' one of these overcharging and underperforming abominations these days. See WITH-PROFITS INSURANCE and SURRENDER VALUE.

EPIC Stands for Electronic Price Information Code. Also known as 'Ticker Symbol', it is an abbreviation for a company's name that is used as shorthand by share quote reporting services and various online sites.

Equities A concept that comes from 'equitable claims'. Equities are essentially shares in a company. Because they represent a proportional share in the business, they are equitable claims on the business itself.

Exchange Traded Fund (ETF) A form of INDEX TRACKER that's essentially a cross between UNIT TRUSTS and INVESTMENT TRUSTS. There's more about them in Chapter 17.

Ex-dividend A share sold without the right to receive the dividend payment which is marked as due to those shareholders who are on the share register at a pre-announced date. These shares have 'xd' next to their price listings in the *Financial Times*.

Execution-only Stockbroker Stockbrokers who offer fewer of the services championed by ADVISORY STOCKBROKERS, but charge cheaper transaction fees. Basically, you tell them to buy or sell a particular share and they get on and do it with no frills and no hassles. Often they hold your shares in a NOMINEE ACCOUNT. Execution-only brokers are ideal for do-it-yourself investors – that's you. They are called discount brokers in the USA.

Exit Charge A sales charge paid for redeeming a unit trust or other investment. See FRONT-END LOADING.

Final Salary Scheme An occupational pension scheme where the benefits are calculated as a percentage of final salary (maximum $^{40}\!/_{60}$ ths). Also known as a DEFINED BENEFIT scheme, they mean that the employer takes the risk of things not working out on the investment front. Employers don't like this very much and are stampeding to change to MONEY PURCHASE SCHEMES.

Financial Services Authority (FSA) The top investment watchdog. If you have a problem with a financial adviser, stockbroker, bank or other financial institution, contact them on 0845 606 1234 and they should be able to tell you what to do.

Fixed Rate Mortgage The interest rate on the mortgage is pegged at a set level for an agreed number of months or years. Pull out before the end of that period and you'll end up paying a REDEMPTION PENALTY.

Flotation See NEW ISSUE.

Fool One who exhibits a high degree of FOOLISHNESS.

Foolishness The state of being wry, contrary, canny and capable of looking after your own investments. Fools believe in shares as the long-term path to wealth creation and believe that this is best achieved by investing in INDEX TRACKERs and buying and holding good companies for the long haul based on their fundamental financial and business strengths. This sort of behaviour does little to support the salaries of those in the financial services industry. See WISDOM.

Front-end Loading A sales charge paid when a PERSONAL PENSION, AVC, ENDOWMENT or other investment is purchased. It can amount to the bulk of the first few years' contributions. The sellers of financial products are very keen on it. We're not.

FTSE All Share Index An INDEX containing around 800 of the largest companies on the LONDON STOCK EXCHANGE. The FTSE All Share Index (also known as the

FTSE-ASI or, simply, the All Share) and the FTSE 100 are the indices generally tracked by index trackers (see INDEX TRACKER).

FTSE 100 An INDEX containing the 100 largest companies by MARKET CAPITAL-IZATION on the LONDON STOCK EXCHANGE. Came into being in 1984 and largely superseded the FT 30.

FTSE 250 An INDEX containing the next 250 largest companies, after the FTSE 100, by MARKET CAPITALIZATION on the London Stock Exchange, created in 1992.

FT 30 For many years, the FT 30 was the INDEX most often quoted in relation to the LONDON STOCK EXCHANGE. It was originally conceived as being the UK equivalent to the DOW-JONES INDUSTRIAL AVERAGE, but is little quoted now.

Full-service Broker The US name for an ADVISORY STOCKBROKER.

Futures A type of DERIVATIVE that allows people to buy or sell, for a price today, securities to be delivered some time in the future. Futures are a great way to lose your money because, for instance, if the security rises in value before you must deliver it, you might not be able to buy enough to fulfil your part of the bargain.

Gearing Buy a house for £100,000 with a deposit of £10,000 and the rest as a mortgage. Six months later, sell it for £150,000 and you've made 500 per cent profit on your original deposit – that's gearing. Of course, it can work the other way too (see NEGATIVE EQUITY). Gearing can be expressed as the ratio of debt to assets and is used by companies and investing individuals to enhance their profits, as well as homeowners to allow them to buy a home.

Gilts When the Government needs to borrow money, it sells you these. They are very safe and their US equivalent is the Treasury bill, or 'T-Bill'.

Gross The payment of any form of taxable income without the prior deduction of tax.

Independent Financial Adviser A financial adviser who is not employed by a particular company to market their products. They may be paid by COMMIS-SION, which in our view amounts to a conflict of interest, or else by agreed fee. We prefer to call these people Financial Advisers (salespeople).

Index Groups of shares mathematically reworked to be representative of the current level of the market or of different subgroups of companies within the market. See FTSE 100, FTSE-ASI, FTSE 250, FT 30.

Index-linking Something that increases at the rate of inflation is index-linked.

Index Tracker The only type of unit trust that makes sense to us. While most unit trusts are actively (mis-) managed, index trackers are computer-driven and designed to mimic the performance of a given stock market index such as the FTSE 100 or the FTSE ALL SHARE INDEX. Over the long term, they outperform the vast majority of actively managed unit trusts.

Individual Savings Account (ISA) ISAs started in April 1999 and have replaced PEPs and TESSAs. You can invest £7000 per year into a wide variety of investments. They are very attractive to FOOLs.

Inflation The process by which the real value of money is eroded over time. Inflation rates vary over the years and indirectly cause the direction of interest rate movements. The worst rate of inflation in modern times was in Hungary in the 1930s and 40s. By 1946, the 1931 gold pengo was valued at 130 million trillion paper pengos. You would not have wanted to retire in 1931 on an annuity of 100 pengos a month.

Initial Public Offering (IPO) The US name for a company's first sale of SHAREs to the public. In the UK we call it a NEW ISSUE or FLOTATION.

Inland Revenue Come on, you know who these people are! You probably don't know their very helpful Web site, though, which is at www.inlandrevenue.gov.uk/

Insider Dealing This is when you buy or sell a share and at the same time possess privileged information that would move the price if it were widely known. It's illegal, but is also widespread and there are few prosecutions for it.

Institutions Institutional investors include pension funds and unit trusts. These are the big players in the stock market as they have a lot of money to invest. As major shareholders, they often have a say in company decisions.

Interest-only Mortgage Monthly payments to the lender are made up simply of interest. You don't pay off any of the CAPITAL of the mortgage during the term of the mortgage, but do so at the end, having – hopefully! – accrued a large enough amount of money in an investment fund. In the past, ENDOWMENTS were sold to back this type of mortgage. They didn't do it very well and we're pleased to say that INDIVIDUAL SAVINGS ACCOUNTs are more commonly used for this purpose these days.

Investment Club Group of investors that meets regularly to discuss which shares to buy and sell out of a common fund. See PROSHARE.

Investment Trust A public limited company that makes investments into a variety of other companies. Like actively managed UNIT TRUSTs, these are pooled investment funds and they tend to underperform the stock market average. However, investment trusts (particularly the very large ones) tend to do better than unit trusts since they tend to have lower charges.

ISEQ The Irish stock market INDEX.

Large-cap See MARKET CAPITALIZATION.

Leverage The US term for GEARING.

Life Insurance See TERM LIFE INSURANCE and WHOLE OF LIFE INSURANCE. (By the way, life *in*surance is used to mean the same as life *as*surance these days.)

Liquidity The easier it is to turn an asset into cash, the more liquid it is. Shares in LISTED COMPANIES are very liquid as they can be sold at any time during normal market hours. Works of art and homes are not nearly as liquid because you need to find an interested buyer. Since every buyer needs a seller and vice versa, PENNY SHARES, which are very thinly traded, are more *illiquid* than larger capitalization shares.

Listed Company A company whose shares are listed on a STOCK EXCHANGE.

London Stock Exchange The place where shares in the 2000 or so UK public companies are bought and sold. It is in the CITY.

Margin 1. Borrowing money to use specifically for buying securities of any kind in a broking account. Buying shares on margin is very risky. 2. A measure of profitability of a company, like profit margin, operating margin or gross margin.

Market Capitalization The total market value of all of a firm's outstanding shares. Market capitalization is calculated by multiplying a firm's share price by the number of shares outstanding. Large-cap., medium-cap., small-cap. refer to companies in decreasing order of market capitalization.

Medium-cap See MARKET CAPITALIZATION.

MIG Mortgage Indemnity Guarantee. If you borrow more than 75 per cent of the value of your house, you may get stung with one of these. It insures the lender against you being unable to pay. Even though it's you that pays this premium, it still won't stop you ending up at the Salvation Army soup kitchen. Do your best to avoid them, they're a rip-off.

Money Purchase Scheme Pension schemes where you build up a pot of cash, out of which your pension will be generated, also known as a DEFINED CONTRIBUTION scheme. The effect is that you take the risk of the investments not doing their job. Personal pensions and AVCs work on this kind of system, as do an increasing number of OCCUPATIONAL PENSION SCHEMES.

Mortgage A loan to buy a home, where you put up the property as a security against your paying back the loan.

Mutual Fund The US equivalent of a UNIT TRUST.

Nasdaq A national US stock market where trades are made exclusively via computers. The second largest market in the country, the Nasdaq is home to many high-tech and newer firms, including Microsoft. It hasn't done very well over the last couple of years, but that's a very short time for a stock market.

Negative Equity Bought a house for £80,000 and now it's only worth £60,000? Bad luck – that's £20k of negative equity you're sitting on there. See GEARING.

New Issue The first time a company is floated on the stock market. Selling your company, or a part of it, to outside investors is a way to raise money for expansion plans.

New York Stock Exchange (NYSE) The largest and oldest stock exchange in the United States, this Wall Street haunt is the one frequently featured on television, with hundreds of traders on the floor staring up at screens and answering phones, ready to trade stocks upon command from their firms.

Nil-paid Rights See RIGHTS ISSUE.

Nominee Account A type of account in which STOCKBROKERS tend to hold shares belonging to clients, to make buying and selling those shares easier. It does mean, however, that it might be difficult to get the benefit of any shareholders' perks.

Occupational Pension Scheme A form of pension scheme set up by employers. See FINAL SALARY SCHEME and MONEY PURCHASE SCHEME.

OEIC See OPEN ENDED INVESTMENT COMPANY.

Open Ended Investment Company These are similar to unit trusts. In fact, many UNIT TRUSTS are already converting to them. Ostensibly, they will be simpler for investors to understand and the charges will be lower as there will not be a BID-OFFER SPREAD between the buying and selling prices. In practice this will likely be replaced by a 'Dilution levy'. *Plus ça change ...*

Options Contracts that give a person the right to buy or sell an underlying share or commodity at a set price within a set amount of time. They're a risky and expensive way of investing in shares. The majority of options expire worthless.

Paid-up Value If you stop paying into your AVC or Personal Pension, but leave the money where it is, this is the amount of money that will be left to grow in the investment fund. In the first years of the plan, this is generally much less than the amount you have put in. See TRANSFER VALUE.

Penny Share A share of very low MARKET CAPITALIZATION (often a few million pounds) trading in multiples of just a few pence. They are very volatile, subject to extreme price fluctuations on the flimsiest of rumours and not at all the thing for the long-distance FOOL. See LIQUIDITY.

Personal Equity Plan (PEP) Started in 1987. They've been superseded by ISAs and you can no longer pay money into them. Existing PEPs, though, are still sitting there, growing away free of tax.

Personal Pension A private (i.e. non-state, non-occupational) pension. Charges can eat dramatically into what is often, in any case, poor investment performance and we prefer STAKEHOLDER PENSIONS which limit the damage on the charges front. You then have to spend the bulk of your fund on an annuity. Personal Pensions receive tax relief on contributions. See also AVC.

Portfolio Management Give all your money over to the STOCKBROKER and say, 'Here, go manage this.' It's one step up even from an advisory service. See ADVISORY STOCKBROKER.

Price/Earnings Ratio (P/E) A measure of a company's share price calculated by dividing the share price by the EARNINGS PER SHARE. Generally, the more future growth investors expect from a company, the higher its price/earnings ratio.

Profit and Loss Account Part of a company's ANNUAL REPORT, in which accountants try to explain to investors how much money the company is making. See also BALANCE SHEET and CASH FLOW STATEMENT.

ProShare A pressure group representing the interests of the private investor. They publish a magazine called The Investor, and also have a useful information pack on how to set up an INVESTMENT CLUB. Contact them on 020 7220 1750 or at their Web site – www.proshare.org.uk/

Public Limited Company (PLC) As opposed to private (ltd.) companies, PLCs have a few extra legal requirements to go through to demonstrate, amongst other things, their creditworthiness. Only PLCs can be listed on the LONDON STOCK EXCHANGE or the ALTERNATIVE INVESTMENT MARKET.

Quarterly Reporting In the US after each quarter-year a company is required to file a report providing investors with juicy details on how the company is doing. In the UK equivalent reports are generally seen only every six months.

Redemption Penalty If you try and bow out of a CAPPED RATE, DISCOUNTED RATE or FIXED RATE MORTGAGE early, you may well be liable for one of these.

Repayment Mortgage As well as paying the interest, the monthly repayments on this type of mortgage repay part of the CAPITAL. Early on, the majority of the monthly payment goes towards the interest. See also CURRENT ACCOUNT MORTGAGE and INTEREST-ONLY MORTGAGE.

Revenue See SALES.

Rights Issue When a company raises money from SHAREHOLDERS by issuing new shares. Existing shareholders are given the right to purchase a certain number of new shares for each existing share that they hold at a discount to the market value. Each shareholder can either take up this right to buy the discounted shares or sell the right (known as NIL-PAID RIGHTS) to others.

Sales The money a company collects from a customer for a product or service. It generally forms the top line in a company's profit and loss account. Also known as TURNOVER or (in the US) REVENUE.

Securities Securities is just a blanket way to refer to any kind of financial asset that can be traded.

Security & Exchange Commission (SEC) The United States agency charged with ensuring that the US stock market is a free and open market. All companies with stock registered in the United States must comply with SEC rules and regulations, which include filing quarterly reports on how well the company is doing.

Share A SECURITY that represents part ownership of a company.

Shareholder If you buy even one SHARE in a company, you can proudly call yourself a shareholder. As a shareholder you get an invitation to the company's annual meeting, and you have the right to vote on the members of the Board of Directors and other company matters.

Share Split See BONUS ISSUE.

SIPP Self Invested Personal Pension. A form of PERSONAL PENSION, but the plan holder calls the shots in terms of which investments fill the plan.

Small-cap See MARKET CAPITALIZATION.

Stakeholder Pension A new form of PERSONAL PENSION. They are designed for people who do not have access to OCCUPATIONAL PENSION SCHEMES and will have lower costs than most PERSONAL PENSIONS. You will still have to spend the bulk of your investment fund on an ANNUITY, but the enforced low charges are a step in the right direction.

Stamp Duty A tax you pay on buying shares (0.5 per cent). For property, it starts at 1 per cent for properties worth over £60,000, increasing to 4 per cent for properties worth £500,000 or more.

Standard and Poor 's 500 Stock Index (S&P 500) An index of 500 of the biggest and bestest companies in American industry.

Stock The same as a SHARE and used more commonly in the US. A share of stock (confusing, yes – just use the two interchangeably; everyone else does) represents a proportional ownership stake in a corporation. Investors purchase stock as a way to own a part of a publicly traded business.

Stockbroker A middleman who buys and sells shares on your behalf and earns commission on the transactions. Considered by many to be the fifth-oldest profession after prostitutes, pimps, tax collectors and accountants. See ADVISORY STOCKBROKER, EXECUTION-ONLY STOCKBROKER and PORTFOLIO MANAGEMENT.

Stock Exchange A place where stocks and shares are bought and sold. The LONDON STOCK EXCHANGE serves this function in the UK.

Surrender Value If you cash in your ENDOWMENT before its time, this is what you'll get. On average, it takes more than seven years for the surrender value to equal the money you've put in. Generally, you'll do better to try and sell it.

Tax-deferred When you invest in something like an AVC or PERSONAL PENSION, you receive an initial tax refund from the Government and are then deferring taxes until you withdraw money in the form of ANNUITY payments, when you will be liable to income tax.

Tax-efficient AVCs, PERSONAL PENSIONS, ISAs – we have many, many ways in this country to invest with a minimum tax penalty. Some are far better than others.

Term Life Insurance A no-nonsense life insurance plan where you pay low annual payments (premiums) in return for a payment to be paid to your dependents if you die during the term. See WHOLE OF LIFE INSURANCE.

Ticker symbol See EPIC.

Tied Agent Less independent even than an INDEPENDENT FINANCIAL ADVISER. These are company salespersons, trying to sell you the products of the company they work for. Buying from them is a fool's, not a FOOL's game.

Transfer Value If you stop paying into your AVC or PERSONAL PENSION, and decide to take the money out, this is what you'll be left with. In the first years of the plan, this is generally much less than the amount you have put in. See PAID-UP VALUE.

Treasury The Government's finance department. They have a natty little Web site: www.hm-treasury.gov.uk/

Turnover See SALES.

Underwriters The STOCKBROKERS who help a company raise money by issuing new shares. They get paid a fee in return for promising to take up the shares if others don't. There is generally a let-out if the market is going haywire, so most people regard it as money for old rope.

Unit Trust Your money is invested with thousands of others in one pooled fund. Presiding over the fund is a manager or managers responsible for achieving the fund's stated investment objective. Most unit trusts under-perform the INDEX and have high charges. INDEX TRACKERS are the only form of unit trusts we advocate.

Valuation The determination of a fair value for a security. If you don't use some reasonable method, then you have what is technically called a 'guess' or a 'hope'.

Wall Street Also known as 'The Street' in US cocktail-party patter, this is the main drag in New York City's financial district.

Whole of Life Insurance This will cover you until you die, whenever that may be, unlike TERM LIFE INSURANCE. Don't think, though, that you'll pay the same premiums for the rest of your life – they'll be revised upwards every ten years or so!

Wisdom The state of being Wise. These are the people who seek to sell you inherently underperforming investments, hobbled even further by heavy charges. See ENDOWMENTS, FOOLISHNESS, INDEPENDENT FINANCIAL ADVISER and TIED AGENT.

With-profits Insurance Insurance policies that have both an insurance cover element and an investment element. Some ENDOWMENTS are 'with-profits' insurance policies. Remember that quote in the pensions chapter from the *Daily Telegraph* about endowment mortgages? It goes well here: 'It cannot be said too often that the advantages to the householder of an endowment mortgage are as nothing compared to the gain to the policy salesperson, that life assurance has nothing to do with house purchase, and that savings-related life assurance is a waste of money.'

Yield See DIVIDEND YIELD.

Zymurgy The pre-epileptic state a non-Foolish investor enters when the market drops 10 per cent in a day.

Appendices

Appendix 1
Coping with Compound
Interest: The Mathematics

I shall light a candle of understanding in thine heart, which shall not be put out.

2 Esdras 14: 25

In Chapter 2, we looked at the awesome power of compound interest and, in the first edition of this book, we left it at that. It turned out, though, that this was not enough for some people. 'Tell us more about this compound interest,' some Fools cried. 'How does it actually work? Remove this cloak of magic and give it to us straight.'

This is what we shall be attempting to do in this appendix. We hope the first bit, which is the important bit, is relatively easy to follow. Unfortunately, the sums get a little hairy towards the end but it certainly looks pretty fancy on paper. If you don't follow it all, don't worry. This is about as hard as the sums ever get in investment (actually no harder than GCSE mathematics) and, anyway, to be a successful investor you don't need to understand all this stuff. It's strictly for those who are interested. People who want to know how to compound regular payments, however, but don't want to go through all the derivation of the formula can skip to the section 'The Magic Formula' on page 334. Alternatively, you could try our natty little online calculator at www.fool.co.uk/school/compound.htm.

Let's start with some good news. Compound interest is not really mathematics, it's just arithmetic and, for us anyway, arithmetic is a lot less scary. Arithmetic just involves adding things together and taking them away. If you add a lot of the same thing together it becomes multiplication, it's just like addition gone a bit mad. Compound interest is just like multiplication gone mad. It's like adding a lot of things together and then adding all those together lots of times. Because there are a lot of sums to do, a calculator will come in very handy, but don't worry too much about this – the most important thing is to follow along and get a feeling for how it all works.

Compound Interest on Lump Sums

Let's start with a simple example. Imagine that you lend someone £100 and they agree to pay you an annual rate of interest of 10 per cent.

After one year

How much will they owe you after one year? Well, first of all, they still owe you the original £100. Then, on top of this, they owe you 10 per cent of £100 in interest. For anyone who has difficulty with percentages, 10 per cent can be thought of as 'ten hundredths', so 10 per cent of £100 is '£100 divided by 100 and multiplied by 10', which equals £10. So you are owed £100 plus £10, which equals £110.

After two years

At the beginning of year two (that is, the end of year one), you are owed £110. So, at the end of the second year, you are still owed the £110 but, on top of this, you are owed your interest for year two. This interest amounts to 10 per cent of £110 or '£110 divided by 100 and times 10', which equals £11. So, at the end of year two, you are owed £110 plus £11, which equals £121.

After three years

At the beginning of year three (that is, the end of year two), you are owed £121. So, at the end of the third year, you are still owed the £121 but, on top of this, you are also owed your interest for year three. This interest amounts to 10 per cent of £121 or '£121 divided by 100 and times 10', which equals £12.10. So, at the end of year three, you are owed £121 plus £12.10, which equals £133.10.

All three years together

Below is a table that breaks it all down into its components.

Don't worry if the table doesn't make sense. We just thought that it might help for some people. What we're trying to get across is that, after year one, you have your original sum (the £100), plus your interest (the £10). After year two, you have your original sum (the £100), plus your interest (the two £10s), plus your interest on your interest (the £1). By the time we get to year three, we have your original sum (the £100), plus your interest (the three £10s), plus your interest on your interest (the £1s), plus your interest on your interest on your interest (the 10p). Phew.

	Year 1		Year 2		Year 3	
	Start	Int.	Start	Int.	Start	Int.
	100	10	100	10	100	10
			10	1	10	1
					10	1
					1	0.1
Total	100	10	110	11	121	12.1
End Yr Total	**110**		**121**		**133.1**	
Int. = interest						

It is because you are getting interest on your interest (and interest on your interest on your interest …), that it is described as 'compound interest' and this is what causes the seemingly miraculous results.

A quicker way to work it out

If we want to say, 'Keep what you had and add another 10 per cent,' it's the same as saying, 'Multiply what you had by 1.10 (or, simply, 1.1).' The 0.1 is equivalent to the 10 per cent and the 1 is there so you keep what you had. Now, remember that each year we want to 'keep what we had and add another 10 per cent'. So, each year we want to multiply by 1.1. After each year we end up with the following amounts:

After Year 1	£100 x 1.1	which equals £110
After Year 2	£100 x 1.1 x 1.1	which equals £121
After Year 3	£100 x 1.1 x 1.1 x 1.1	which equals £133.10

So, if we put £1000 in a bank and it earns annual interest of 10 per cent, how much will we have after three years? The answer is

£1000 x 1.1 x 1.1 x 1.1 (which comes to £1331).

If our £1000 was only earning 8 per cent in interest but we had it for four years, we would have

£1000 x 1.08 x 1.08 x 1.08 x 1.08 (which comes to £1360.49).

Now, hopefully this is all clear. If it's not, then go back and re-read it up to here, because now things are going to get a little bit more tricky.

The shorthand approach

Well, it's not that hard really. And in fact the only reason this bit is here is to save you a bit of wear and tear on your keyboard or calculator.

We can reduce the number of buttons that you need to push by thinking of '1.1 x 1.1 x 1.1' as '1.1 to the power of 3'. So, '1.1 to the power of 3' means three 1.1s multiplied together.

If we have £1000 earning interest at 10 per cent for three years, we have '£1000 times 1.1 to the power of 3', which is equivalent to '£1000 times 1.1 x 1.1 x 1.1', which equals £1331.

If we had £1000 earning interest at 8 per cent for four years, we would end up with '£1000 times 1.08 to the power of 4', which is equivalent to '£1000 x 1.08 x 1.08 x 1.08 x 1.08', which equals £1360,49.

The words '1.1 to the power of 3' can also be written in shorthand as 1.1, with a little 3 slightly above and to the right of it – like this: 1.1^3. Computers aren't very good at putting in the little 3 so you may sometimes see it written as '1.1^3'. 1.1^3 is the same as 1.1^3.

Doing the sums

There are several ways of doing '1.1 to the power of 3' on a calculator. The first and simplest way is just to do 1.1 x 1.1 x 1.1. This is nice and easy and simple enough to get your head around. The trouble is that when the sums get a bit bigger it becomes a little bit boring. Imagine doing 1.0835 to the power of 30.

The second and third ways depend (very slightly) on what sort of calculator you have. So, if your numbers are coming out a bit funny, it might be that you need to get your calculator's instruction booklet out. What? Of course you kept it. It's in the bottom of THAT drawer (or maybe that other one).

Anyway, the second way is to type in 1.1, then hit the multiplication button (marked with an X) TWICE. A little 'k' (or something) should come up on the calculator's screen. This has told the calculator to multiply the number you put in (in this case 1.1) by itself every time you press 'equals'. So, the first time you press 'equals', it comes up with 1.21 (that is, 1.1 times 1.1). The second time you press 'equals', it should come up with 1.331 (that is, 1.1 times 1.1 times 1.1). Notice that you are actually pressing the equals sign one less time than the number you are going to the power of. This is because you had already put the number in to the calculator (representing the first power in the process). So, if you start with £1000 and earn interest at 8 per cent for four years, you could type 1.08 into your calculator, press 'X' twice and press 'equals' three times. The screen should now show 1.36048896. You now multiply this by the £1000 that you started with and you get the answer – £1360.49 (I know, it's actually £1360.48896 but I'm rounding to the nearest penny, OK?).

The third way to work it out involves using the 'X to the power of Y' button. Basically this means using a 'scientific calculator'. The button you want will be marked with an X, with a little Y slightly above and to the right of it – like this: χ^Y. On the calculator on a computer, it will probably be marked 'X^Y'. To work out '1.1 to the power of 3' on a typical scientific calculator, what you do is this. Put in the 1.1, then press the χ^Y button, then press 3, then press = and, hey presto, it comes up with 1.331. If you start with £1000 and it earns interest at 8 per cent per year for four years and you want to know what you end up with, you do this. Put in the 1.08, then press the χ^Y

button, then press 4, then press 'equals'. The screen should now show 1.36048896. You now multiply this by the £1000 that you started with and you get the answer – £1360.49.

Now try doing it backwards

If you've got a calculator with an χ^γ button, we can have a go at doing it backwards. For instance, if we know that we want £1500 in five years' time and we have £1000 now, how do we work out the annual return that we need to achieve? Well, to get to £1500 from £1000 means we need to multiply our money by 1.5 times. This is calculated by dividing the end money by the start money (that is, £1500 divided by £1000). What we need, then, is a number which, when we 'put it to the power of 5' gives us 1.5. We get this by using the same χ^γ button on the calculator. But, this time, we have to press 'inv' or 'shift' beforehand so that the calculator knows we are doing it backwards.

So, we put 1.5 into the calculator, press 'inv' or 'shift', then press the χ^γ button, then press 5, then press = and we get 1.08447. What this basically means is that £1000 x 1.08447 x 1.08447 x 1.08447 x 1.08447 x 1.08447 equals £1500.

You can check the answer by 'putting it to the power of 5' and making sure that it comes out as 1.5 again.

So, what does the number 1.08447 mean? It is a growth rate in disguise. Remember that when we wanted to 'keep what we had and add another 10 per cent', we had to multiply by 1.10? So, 1.08447 is the number that we would multiply by if we wanted to 'keep what we had and add another 8.447 per cent'. To turn £1000 into £1500 over five years, we would therefore need an annual rate of return (or, growth) of 8.447 per cent.

Compound Interest – Regular Payments

OK, did you manage to follow all that stuff on lump sums? If not, you might want to go through it again, because now things are going to get a little harder still. We are now going to look at compound interest on regular payments. In normal language, this means answering the following question. If I save £100 per month for ten years and my annual rate of growth is 12.6825 per cent, how much money will I have?

First of all, we should issue a maths warning. This is going to be a bit more complicated than basic compound interest and will even involve a bit of mathematical smoke and mirrors. But the smoke is quite fine and the mirrors are quite shiny and hopefully you will at least sort of follow what we're saying. It has been said before and it will be said again but – DON'T PANIC.

Undressing regular payments

At the beginning of this appendix, we said that compound interest was just an example of addition gone mad. It is a matter of adding a lot of things together and then adding all those together a lot of times. The good news is that regular payments are no different. Regular, let's say monthly, payments are just a series of lump sums. We just have to work out what each monthly lump sum is worth at the end and add them all up. This is the key to understanding it. Unfortunately, it can also lead to an awful, awful lot of adding up. This is what all the smoke and mirrors are about. They're just a way of condensing all the adding up so that it can be done in a matter of minutes. If you don't follow everything in this section, then it doesn't really matter, because the formula is at the end. The reason for going through it all is just that Fools never like putting their faith in mystery and it is nice to have at least a vague grasp of where the numbers are coming from.

A simple example

Imagine that you save £100 at the beginning of each month with a monthly rate of interest of 1 per cent. At the end of three months, you have invested three lump sums. One has been invested for three months, one for two months and the last one for only one month.

The first lump sum is now worth £100 x 1.01 x 1.01 x 1.01. That is, £100 x 1.01³. This comes out as £103.0301. To the nearest penny, it's £103.03.

The second lump sum is now worth £100 x 1.01 x 1.01. That is, £100 x 1.01². This comes out as £102.01.

The third lump sum is now worth £100 x 1.01. This comes out as £101.

Adding these together, after three months we would have

£103.03 + £102.01 + £101 = £306.04

So, if after three months we have

£100 x 1.01^3 + £100 x 1.01^2 + £100 x 1.01,

what do you reckon we'll have after, say, five months? How about

£100 x 1.01^5 + £100 x 1.01^4 + £100 x 1.01^3 + £100 x 1.01^2 + £100 x 1.01

This comes out as

£105.10 + £104.06 + £103.03 + £102.01 + £101 = £515.20

If we saved like this for ten years (that is, 120 months), we would end up with

£100 x 1.01^{120} + £100 x 1.01^{119} + … + £100 x 1.01^2 + £100 x 1.01

The problem we have is that, without the aid of a spreadsheet or a special calculator, working this out involves doing 120 separate sums and then adding them all up. Unless you're Carol Vorderman, that's not going to be much fun! What we need is a way of condensing the sum. This is where the smoke and mirrors come in.

Here's the smoke

Let's start by adding some mathematical smoke. We will call the amount of each monthly payment 'a' and our monthly rate of interest will be called 'r'. After three months, we have

$a(1+r)^3$ + $a(1+r)^2$ + $a(1+r)$

DON'T PANIC! We know there are some multiplication signs missing. You're allowed to do that. By putting a number immediately in front of brackets, you are saying that you are multiplying everything in the brackets by that number. It's just mathematical shorthand. We're going to have some big sums to do and we're not going to make them look messy (and even more confusing) by putting in Xs everywhere. They're surplus to requirements because we know what we mean.

Another point to make is about the order you do the sums in. That's why we need brackets in the first place. Brackets come first so, before doing anything else, we have to do the sums that are inside the brackets (that is add the 1 and the 'r' together). After brackets come indices ('indices' is just a posh way of saying 'to the power of'), so the next thing we do is put the contents of the brackets to the power of whatever. Next comes multiplication (so we multiply by the 'a') and, finally, we have addition, so we add the three separate sums together. In fact you can remember the full list by the mnemonic 'BIODMAS'. It stands for 'brackets', 'indices', 'of', 'division', 'multiplication', 'addition', 'subtraction'. If you don't believe that the order you do things in makes a big difference, then write down some sums and try doing them in different orders. You'll soon get the point.

There is nothing sneaky about this order thing. It is just a convention, whereby mathematicians can explain to people reading what order they should do the sums in. If you want to move something to the top of the list, you just put it in brackets (as we have with the '1+r').

Still with us? OK, the next thing to notice is that each of the bits of the equation is multiplied by 'a'. So, we can put it all in brackets and multiply the contents of the brackets by 'a'. What we mean is that

$a(1+r)^3 + a(1+r)^2 + a(1+r)$

is the same as

$a((1+r)^3 + (1+r)^2 + (1+r))$

In fact, each of the bits is also multiplied by a '1+r', so we can take one of these outside the brackets too. Don't forget that $(1+r)^3$ is the same as $(1+r)(1+r)(1+r)$, which is the same as $(1+r)(1+r)^2$. So:

$a((1+r)^3 + (1+r)^2 + (1+r))$

is the same as

$a(1+r)((1+r)^2 + (1+r) + 1)$

And now come the mirrors

There was an article about all this that went up in the personal finance section of the Motley Fool's UK Web site in January 2000. This part of it was unbearably confusing and it is a testament to the power of the Motley Fool community that it is now a lot simpler. You see, a kind Fool sent in an e-mail explaining how it could be done so much more simply. He really buffed up the mirrors, if you like. So, if you think this is bad, just be glad you weren't exposed to the murky mirrors from before. Anyway … We were trying to find the answer to the following sum without actually having to add it all up.

$$£100 \times 1.01^{120} + £100 \times 1.01^{119} + \ldots + £100 \times 1.01^2 + £100 \times 1.01$$

As we have seen, this can be written as

$$100(1.01)(1.01^{119} + 1.01^{118} + \ldots + 1.01 + 1)$$

If we replace the hundreds and the 0.01s by 'a' and 'r', we get

$$a(1+r)((1+r)^{119} + (1+r)^{118} + \ldots + (1+r) + 1)$$

In fact, if we replace the 120 by 'n', we get

$$a(1+r)((1+r)^{n-1} + (1+r)^{n-2} + \ldots + (1+r) + 1)$$

It makes sense to reduce the sum to this, because then we can use the compressed formula for any periodic amount, for any periodic rate of growth and for any number of periods. What we need to do now is to compress this unwieldy sum. To do this, we need to get rid of the + … + bit.

For the moment, let's leave the a(1+r) to one side and just concentrate on adding up what's in the big bracket, since this is where the problems are. We can come back and multiply by a(1+r) at the end. We're also going to replace all the other (1+r)s with 'R', to make things look a little nicer. Again, don't worry, we can put the (1+r)s back in at the end. So, we're trying to compress the following (V just stands for 'Value' – that is, the answer we're trying to get):

$$V = R^{n-1} + R^{n-2} + \dots + R + 1$$

Are you ready for this? What you do is multiply both sides of the sum by R. We can do this because, if one thing equals another, then that thing multiplied by R will equal the other thing also multiplied by R. That's what equals signs are all about. So long as you do the same to both sides, then they're both still equal (just a bit different to what they were before). So, you get

$$VR = R(R^{n-1} + R^{n-2} + \dots + R + 1)$$

Multiplying what's in the big bracket by the R outside, we get

$$VR = R^n + R^{n-1} + \dots + R^2 + R$$

Notice that R^n is R^{n-1} times R in just the same way as 1.01^{120} is 1.01^{119} times another 1.01.

Now, we can subtract V from the left-hand side of the equation and $R^{n-1} + R^{n-2} + \dots + R + 1$ from the right-hand side. Remember that, since these two things are equal, we are taking the same amount from each side which is therefore allowed. This leaves us with

$$VR-V = R^n + \mathbf{R^{n-1} + R^{n-2} + \dots + R^2 + R}$$
$$\text{Minus}$$
$$\mathbf{R^{n-1} + R^{n-2} + \dots + R^2 + R} + 1$$

To make it a bit easier to spot what's about to happen, we've pulled some bits out of the + … + bit and put some of them in **bold**. You see the classy thing is that all the stuff in the middle cancels out. For instance, we're taking R^{n-1} away from R^{n-1} and this gives us, you've guessed it, nought – not a thing. So, after all the dust settles, all we're left with is

$$VR-V = R^n - 1$$

How about that!! Of course, that's not quite what we want (we're after V), but we're nearly there. We can put a bracket in the left-hand side so it looks like this:

$$V(R-1) = R^n - 1$$

And then we just divide both sides by (R–1) and we get

$$V = \frac{(R^n - 1)}{(R - 1)}$$

Now, we've got our V, but we need to replace our R's with (1+r)s and multiply everything by a(1+r) and this gives us

$$V = \frac{a(1+r)((1+r)^n - 1)}{r}$$

We can now work out the answer to our original question. It seems a long time ago now, so I'll repeat it. If you save £100 per month for ten years with a monthly rate of interest of 1 per cent (which is the same as an annual rate of 12.6825 per cent), you will end up with

$$\frac{(£100 \,(1.01)(1.01^{120} - 1))}{0.01}$$

Remember that you have to do everything in the right order. To start off with, work out what's in the big bracket on the top. Within that bracket, you must do the smaller brackets first. So, do 1.01^{120} first, take the 1 away (giving you 2.300387 on your calculator screen) before multiplying by 100 and 1.01 (giving you 232.3391). Finally, you can divide this by 0.01 and you get £23,233.91 and that's the answer. Not bad for ten years' saving.

Of course, we know from the Miracle of Compound Interest that the longer you save for, the more it takes off. If we were saving £100 per month for twenty years, we'd have:

$$\frac{(£100 \,(1.01)(1.01^{240} - 1))}{0.01}$$

Now we're really talking. This comes to £99,914.79. If we did it for thirty years, we'd have £352,991.38 and after forty years, we'd have £1,188,242.02.

The magic formula

So the magic formula for compounding regular payments is this:

$$V = \frac{a\,(1+r)((1+r)^n - 1)}{r}$$

Where V = future value

a = periodic amount

r = interest rate for a period

n = the total number of periods

Remember that if you are saving monthly, your monthly rate on interest (or growth) is the number (less 1) which, when you put it to the power of 12, gives you your annual rate of return (plus 1). Similarly, the daily rate of interest is the number (less 1) which, when you put it to the power of 30 (in fact, more like 30.4375: that is, the average month), gives you your monthly rate and when you put it to the power of 365 (or rather 365.24: that is, the average year) gives you your annual rate.

So, imagine that you are saving £200 per month in an index tracker. The tracker has costs of 0.5 per cent (charged annually) and you expect the index to rise by 10 per cent per annum. How much will you have after twenty-five years? Since our annual costs are 0.5 per cent, our actual annual return is only 9.5 per cent (10 per cent less 0.5 per cent). To get the monthly rate of growth, we need to find the number which, when we put it to the power of 12, gives us 1.095. In other words, the monthly interest rate is $1.115^{1/12} - 1$. This comes to 0.007591534 and is our 'r'. Our monthly amount, or 'a', is £200. The number of periods is 'n' and comes to 25 x 12, or 300. So, we get,

$$V = \frac{£200(1.007591534)(1.007591534^{300} - 1)}{0.007591534}$$

This comes to £230,103 to the nearest pound.

So, there it is, Fools, it's as simple as that – we wish. Anyway, if you want to save yourself a lot of trouble, you could simply use our online calculator to work these things out, at www.fool.co.uk/school/compound.htm.

Appendix 2
What Makes a
Good Index Tracker?

Give a man horse he can ride, Give a man a boat he can sail.
James Thompson, *Sunday up the River*

As you may have gathered from our various mutterings in this book, there are few subjects as close to a Fool's heart as index trackers. It seems only fair, then, that we put these creatures under the microscope and see what makes them tick. In fact, we'll try and go a step further than this and see what goes into making a good one. It's worth noting, though, that you don't have to read this appendix to invest in index trackers. What we've written elsewhere in the book is enough. This appendix is strictly for the interested, which is why it's just an appendix. Anyway, let's start at the beginning.

What Is an Index Tracker?

An index tracker attempts to match the performance of a particular 'index' of shares. In other words, it attempts to grow as closely as possible to the growth rate of that index of shares. It does this by exposing itself to the performance of the shares in that index. To keep things simple, let's imagine that the table on page 336 shows the biggest five companies on a theoretical stock market and that we want to create an index of them.

The *market cap* or *market capitalization* is the figure for the total value of all the shares in each company. It is therefore the sum of the value of every shareholder's shareholdings, the sum total of every pound invested in each company. £400 billion is therefore the sum total of every pound invested in these five companies.

Company	Share price	Shares in issue (millions)	Market capitalization (£m)
Allied Pharma	1600p	10,000	160,000
British Banking	500p	20,000	100,000
Cable Telecoms	800p	10,000	80,000
Deep Hole Mining	100p	40,000	40,000
Exploration Oil	1000p	2,000	20,000
Total			400,000

There are basically two types of index that people might try to make out of this: *weighted* and *unweighted*. An unweighted index would give equal weight to the movements of each company. Each company would make up one fifth of the index. So, one fifth of the index's percentage movement is accounted for by each share. If Allied Pharma goes up 10 per cent, then the index will rise 2 per cent. If Exploration Oil moves up 10 per cent, then the index will also rise 2 per cent. If both Allied and Exploration rise 10 per cent, then the index will rise 4 per cent. If one rises 10 per cent and the other falls 10 per cent, then the index will be unchanged. Of course, if all the shares in the index rose 10 per cent, then the index would rise 10 per cent.

A weighted index gives different weights to the effect of each share's movement on the index according to how big the company is (by market cap. or total money invested). Allied Pharma, with a market cap. of £160 billion, makes up 40 per cent of the index (that is, 160 divided by 400). So, if its shares rise 10 per cent, the index will rise by 4 per cent. Exploration Oil, on the other hand, only accounts for 5 per cent of the index. A 10 per cent rise by Exploration therefore only has a 0.5 per cent effect on the index. In other words, movements in Exploration Oil's share price only have an eighth of the effect on the index that movements in Allied Pharma's have. This is because Exploration is only an eighth of the size, and only has an eighth as much money invested in it.

The important thing about weighted indices is that they reflect the average performance of every pound in the index. You can think of a weighted index as being like a portfolio which owns all the shares in all the companies. Whatever happens to the share price of the companies in the index, a weighted index matches the performance of the average pound invested in it.

Anyway, the point of all this is that if we want a tracker that gives us the average performance of the market as a whole (which we do) then, for starters, we need to be tracking a weighted index. For this reason, the majority of indices are weighted. Examples from the UK include the FTSE 100, the FTSE 250, the FTSE 350 and the FTSE All Share. In the US, there is the S&P 500. Perhaps the most famous index in the world, the Dow-Jones Industrial Average, is an unweighted index. Other unweighted indices are the FT 30 in the UK and the Nikkei 225 in Japan. Tracking these (unweighted) indices would not (necessarily) give you the average performance of the US, UK and Japanese stock markets and would therefore be a fairly pointless exercise.

Going back to the weighted indices, the good news is that there are plenty of these to track. However, before trying to work out which one is best, we need to consider how trackers actually go about tracking their various indices.

How Does a Tracker Track?

There are three basic ways that a tracker tracks an index: **Full Replication, Statistical Sampling** and **Use of Derivatives** .

Full replication

This is the most straightforward method of tracking an index. It involves simply creating a portfolio including all the shares in the index at their relevant weights. So, if you were setting up a tracker fund with £4 million to track the performance of the theoretical weighted index that we looked at above (which we'll call the TMF 5, standing for 'The Motley Fool 5'), then we would need to buy 0.001 per cent of each company (that is, our fund of £4 million divided by the total value of the index of £400 billion). So, we'd buy the following:

Company	Share price	Shares purchased	Value
Allied Pharma	1600p	100,000	£1,600,000
British Banking	500p	200,000	£1,000,000
Cable Telecoms	800p	100,000	£800,000
Deep Hole Mining	100p	400,000	£400,000
Exploration Oil	500p	20,000	£200,000
Total			**£4,000,000**

Once we've bought these shares, then all things being equal, we can just leave the tracker to do its job. We basically only have to buy and sell the shares in three situations.

Index changes

The TMF 5 is designed to follow the performance of the average pound invested in the five biggest companies on our theoretical stock market. So, if Exploration Oil shares did badly and it was overtaken, in terms of market capitalization, by Future Technologies plc whose shares have recently been doing well, then Future Technologies would replace it in the TMF 5 Index. We would therefore have to sell all our shares in Exploration Oil and buy, instead, shares in Future Technologies (we might also have to tinker with the overall weightings of all the stocks if our correctly weighted stake in Future costs more than we get for our Exploration shares).

Share capital changes

This is when the member companies issue new shares or cancel any of their existing shares. Imagine that Deep Hole Mining issued one new share for every four of its existing shares to buy the Australian company Gold Diggers Pty Ltd. The TMF 5 would have to reconstitute itself to take account of this. Assuming that the market was ambivalent towards the deal and the share price of Deep Hole didn't move, the new index would look like this:

Company	Share price	Shares in issue (millions)	Market capitalization (£m)
Allied Pharma	1600p	10,000	160,000
British Banking	500p	20,000	100,000
Cable Telecoms	800p	10,000	80,000
Deep Hole Mining	100p	50,000	50,000
Exploration Oil	500p	2,000	20,000
Total			410,000

So all the other companies' weightings have fallen. Allied Pharma's weighting has fallen from 40 per cent (160/400) to 39.0 per cent (160/410), while Deep Hole's weighting has increased from 10 per cent (40/400) to 12.2 per cent (50/410). As a result, a little of each of the other companies will need to be sold and the money used to buy extra shares in Deep Hole.

New money from investors
The third reason for buying and selling would be if a new investor came along and asked to invest £100,000 in the tracker fund (or if an existing investor decided to withdraw £100,000 from the tracker). In this case, we would have to add 2.5 per cent to (or sell 2.5 per cent of) the value of each of our holdings.

This is what is happening all the time with unit trusts. Every day, people are coming along to put more money in or to take money out. If there is a pound put in for every pound that gets taken out, the balance is maintained. However, if, overall, money is flowing into the fund, then it will need to be buying shares in each company each day to maintain its correct exposures. If there is net money flowing out, then it needs to be selling shares in each company each day to maintain the balance. All this buying and selling costs money and it is mostly borne by the new or departing investors.

The main advantage of the full replication tracking approach is that you can expect to match the index very closely. The disadvantage is that it can be expensive and it is only really very practical where you have a small number of shares in an index. The FTSE 100, with its 100 member companies, lends itself reasonably well to this.

Statistical sampling

With an index like the FTSE All Share (which has around 700 member companies), full replication is likely to be extremely costly to achieve. To track these larger indices, most fund management companies will therefore use a process called statistical sampling. The fund doesn't try to hold every share in the index, but it analyses the index and works out its investments so that it is very confident of achieving a performance very close to it.

So, at a basic level with the TMF 5 we might decide that since Exploration Oil only accounts for 5 per cent of the index's value, then we don't actually need to hold it to ensure a performance very close to the index. We do, though, have to keep a close eye on it. If it increases by 20 per cent relative to the rest of the index, then we will underperform by 1 per cent and we don't want to risk underperforming by more than that. We might therefore decide that we can afford to save costs by not holding Exploration unless and until it increases to a level where it accounts for 6 per cent of the index. Of course, if Exploration underperformed the rest of the index then we would benefit from not holding it.

Statistical sampling is a bit of a fudge. If money flows into the fund from new investors, shares of one sort or another will certainly have to be bought, but we might be able to save a bit on costs by not sticking rigidly to buying exactly the right amount of every single company. With a large index such as the FTSE All Share, the relationships between the different shares will be examined, so that the tracker's manager can be very confident of not departing very far from the index. Of course, some companies will be good at this and others bad. To have the same range of likely performance compared to the index, it might cost one company less than another. Unfortunately, few trackers have a long enough track record for us to work out who's good and who's bad. It's probably not a bad idea, then, to stick with the more established fund management companies who have good experience of this sort of thing. Pound for pound, it is also probably cheaper for the larger funds to do all the sums needed for this method.

Use of derivatives

Finally, a tracker might use things called 'derivatives' to match the performance of an index. For instance, it might leave all its investors' cash in the bank and use it as the collateral for a futures contract on the performance on the relevant index. By buying the right derivatives, a fund can organize things so that its performance will reflect the performance of an index very closely.

One advantage of doing things this way is that money coming into the fund just goes into the bank. In the same way, when people take their cash out, it can simply be paid out of the bank. This might be a lot simpler than having to buy or sell all of the shares every day (or a representative sample of them). However, the fund manager would still need to increase or reduce the level of exposure the fund has to the index each day, and there will be costs associated with this.

A fund might combine using derivatives with some form of statistical sampling. By buying an underlying level of derivatives exposure, the fund might be able to reduce costs in the buying and selling of the actual stocks that it needs to top up its exposure.

Call us old fashioned but, despite some potential for cost savings, we Fools don't really like the sound of trackers using derivatives. We're sure they're all very careful, but everyone was sure that Barings Bank was very careful until it went bust. Insuring against problems would just increase costs and, to us, it looks like yet another case of it being best to keep things simple.

Which Index?

Choosing the market or index that you want to track is obviously of primary importance. Fools living in the UK are most likely to want to be exposed to the UK stock market. On the whole, this means choosing between the FTSE 100 and the FTSE All Share. We're therefore going to limit the comments here to these two indices. However, it should generally be pretty relevant to choices between other indices.

The FTSE 100 is an index of the UK's biggest 100 companies. The FTSE All Share is designed to follow the whole of the stock market. To do this it contains about 800 companies. These are mostly, but not necessarily, the 800 biggest companies. However, even the FTSE All Share avoids around a thousand or so of the real tiddlers. Still, as soon as the tiddlers start getting big, they tend to get included, so the FTSE All Share should never be far away from the average performance of the whole market (to a lesser extent, the same can be said about the FTSE 100). The FTSE 100 companies make up about 80 per cent by value of the FTSE All Share so the differences between them are fairly small. Even so, the FTSE All Share has a slightly better spread of investments than the FTSE 100 and it therefore represents the overall UK market that little bit better.

As far as the returns from the FTSE 100 and the FTSE All Share themselves (that is, not necessarily the trackers) are concerned, history has things very slightly in favour of the FTSE All Share. The argument goes that smaller companies are more risky and, over the long term, the market prices them to compensate you for taking this risk on. However, recent history (perhaps the last ten years or so) has things on the side of the FTSE 100. The argument for this is that, in the modern globalizing economy, big is best (because of things like 'economies of scale'). If any threat is posed by the smaller companies then, the story goes, they just get taken over or crushed by the big boys.

All in all, there is probably not much to choose between the two indices (although this is not necessarily so for the trackers following them). Other factors are more likely to make a difference.

Deviating from the Index

On top of the performance of the underlying index, you also need to consider the amount by which a tracker misses its index. Tracking an index is not as straightforward as it sounds (or, rather, tracking an index cheaply isn't very easy). So, we need to look at the reasons why certain types of tracker might deviate from the index they're tracking.

One reason for a deviation is dividends. Most indices, including the FTSE 100 and the FTSE All Share, do not include reinvested dividends. As a result, any tracker that includes reinvested income (often called 'accumulation units') will look better than its index (or it should do anyway) because it's getting an extra couple of per cent or so per year. This difference is purely artificial and, as long as you are comparing like with like, it can be ignored.

When companies describe other deviations in the performance of their trackers, they seem to use the words 'tracking error' to describe any departure from the performance of the underlying index. However, to get to the bottom of things, we need to look at things a little more closely.

Charges

The number one reason for a tracker not performing in line with its index is its charges. It's the number one reason because it is easily quantifiable, operates in one direction (that is, downwards) and is relatively visible. If the index manages an annual rise of 12 per cent and your tracker charges 1 per cent per annum then, all other things being equal, your return will only be 11 per cent. It's as simple as that.

Well, not quite. You have to be careful that you've picked up all the charges. First of all, there is the annual management fee, which is frequently described (incorrectly) as the total charges. In addition, there will generally be some 'admin and trustees fees' or something like that.

Also, don't forget the effect of any 'initial charge' and/or 'bid-offer spread'. On the whole, very few trackers have an initial charge these days and it therefore makes sense just to avoid any that do. The bid-offer spread reflects the tracker's costs in buying (or selling) the underlying shares in the particular index when you put money in (or finally take it out). The difference between the bid and offer price of units should be a very small percentage (certainly less than 1 per cent and probably less than 0.5 per cent) of the actual cost of the units.

On top of all this, there are the dealing charges involved in buying and selling shares to keep the tracker in line with its index. Generally, the dealing charges that relate to new money coming into the fund (or old money leaving) will come through in the 'bid-offer spread'. Where there is no bid-offer spread, the costs will be reflected in the annual fees. Overall it probably makes little difference how it is done, except that you need to be aware of it and include it in any comparison.

There will also be the costs of buying and selling shares to keep the tracker properly weighted. All trackers will suffer a little from this, but statistical samplers will suffer less, since they have more flexibility about which shares they buy and in what volume. This should enable them to save on dealing costs.

Tracking error

There are basically two types of tracking error. In the first type, the error is as likely to be towards the up side as the down side, whereas in the second it is weighted in one particular direction. For want of better expressions, we'll call these unbiased error and biased error. Not surprisingly, an error biased to the down side is much worse than an unbiased error of the same amount, since it has definitely gone against you.

Biased tracking error

Biased tracking error has a tendency to be in one particular direction. In this way, it actually tends to make the tracker perform above or below its index. Unfortunately, biased tracking error will tend to be towards the down side (otherwise everybody would be doing it). Charges, which are so important that they got their own little section above, are the most obvious form of down side weighted tracking error.

Other forms of biased tracking error should have a much smaller effect. All the time, a unit trust tracker has people putting money into it and taking money out. It therefore has to buy and sell shares to maintain its weightings in the index. However, in amongst all this buying and selling, the fund may, for instance, tend to have a very small permanent cash balance. In a rising market, this will tend to cause the tracker to fall behind its index whereas, in a falling market, it would tend to cause the tracker to beat its index. Since, as we saw in Chapter 4, markets tend to go up over the longer term, then this would be an error biased towards the down side. This type of error is a problem for unit trust trackers since these are the ones that accept new money into the fund and let old money leave, but we needn't worry about it too much, since the effects should be pretty small. Investment trust trackers avoid this problem because they are structured so that they don't have money flowing into and out of them. Unfortunately, partly as a result of this, it can make it more expensive to put investment trust trackers into an ISA.

Unbiased tracking error

There are two main sources of unbiased tracking error. The first is when new companies come into and leave the index. The tracker generally has some flexibility to decide when to sell the old companies and buy the new ones.

Sometimes it will get it right, sometimes it will get it wrong. On the whole it won't make much difference over the long term. Having said that, it could be argued that shares that are about to join the index are heavily in demand and that trackers always have to pay too much for them. This would turn part of this error into an error biased to the down side. However, since we are talking about the shares joining the index, we are generally talking about very small weightings and the effect should be small. This will mainly be a problem for the FTSE 100 trackers, since the relative weighting of the shares coming into and leaving the index is much greater for the FTSE 100 than for the FTSE All Share. It will also be more of a problem for full replication trackers than statistical sampling trackers, since the latter have much more flexibility about when to buy the new entries.

A second form of unbiased tracking error is almost entirely a problem for the statistical samplers. This makes it more of a problem for the more widely-spread indices like the FTSE All Share (which are more likely to use this approach). It simply comes down to the fact that they do not actually own (or attempt to own) all the shares in the relevant index. So, if the shares they don't own happen to do very well, then the tracker will do a bit worse than its index. Of course, it works both ways and if the shares that the tracker doesn't own do relatively badly, then the tracker will beat its index. The effects should be fairly small and, over many years, they should all even out.

How big a variation you might get from year to year depends on the index tracked, how good the manager is at tracking it and how much (of your) money the manager throws at the problem. If you were prepared to pay the extra, then you could fully replicate the FTSE All Share index. However, it almost certainly wouldn't be worth it because the extra charges would drag the performance down. It would be a self-defeating strategy because, by paying more to try to reduce a small error that might as easily work in your favour as work against you, you turn it into an error, in the form of charges, which you know will work against you. In the end, it will always be a bit of a balance but, the longer you are invested for, the more likely the cheapest method of tracking is to come out on top.

The Moral of the Tale

The trouble with all this tracking error stuff is that you need a very long performance history to have any real confidence about the level of overall tracking error. You'd need longer still to have any confidence about how much of this was simple error and how much was biased against you. Of course, the beauty of investing in trackers is that so long as you follow a few fairly obvious fundamentals it isn't going to make a great deal of difference which one you go for.

First and foremost, as with all investments, you want to avoid high (apparent and hidden) charges. Secondly, you want something that isn't likely to vary too far from the index (within reason). Finally, if there is to be any variation, then you'd obviously prefer it to be even-handed. The second and third points are likely to come down to thinking about the index that you're tracking, thinking about how it is being tracked and thinking about the reputation of the company doing the tracking. As trackers get a longer and longer history (they're a relatively new breed), we'll be able to make better and better judgments about who's any good at making them work. For the time being we'll have to feel our way a bit. Still, we can be sure that, over the long term, our performance is going to be better than the vast majority of actively managed funds.

Appendix 3
Major UK Index Trackers

Acquaintance I would have, but when't depends
Not on the number, but the choice of friends.

Abraham Cowley, *Of Myself*

(Information as of April 2002)
N.B. None of the following tracker funds levies an initial charge.

Dresdner RCM UK Index
Index: FTSE All Share
Annual charges: 0.6% (0.5% management plus 0.1% trustee fees etc)
Bid/offer spread: 0.5%
Minimum investments: £500 lump sum, or £25 per month
Website: www.dresdnerrcm.co.uk
Tel: 0800 317573

Fidelity Moneybuilder
Index: FTSE All Share
Annual charges: 0.72% (0.5% management charge + 0.22%)
Bid/offer spread: 0%
Minimum investments: £500 lump sum or £50 per month
Website: www.fidelity.co.uk
Tel: 0800 414161

Edinburgh UK Tracker Trust
Index: FTSE All Share
Annual charges: 0.25%
Bid/offer spread: 1.3% (estimated)
Minimum investments: £250 lump sum or £30 per month
Website: www.edfd.com
Tel: 0131 313 1000

Gartmore UK Index
Index: FTSE All Share
Annual charges: 0.75%
Bid/offer spread: 0.5% (estimated)
Minimum investments: £1,000 lump sum or £100 a month
Website: www.gartmore.co.uk
Tel: 0800 289336

HSBC FTSE All-Share Fund
Index: FTSE All Share
Annual charges: 0.5%
Bid/offer spread: 0%
Minimum investments: £500 lump
sum or £25 a month
Website: www.hsbc.co.uk
Tel: 0800 289505

iShares FTSE 100
Index: FTSE 100
Annual charges: 0.4% (0.35%
management plus 0.05% other)
Bid/offer spread: 0.5%
Minimum investments:
Website: www.ishares.net
Tel: 020 7668 8000

Legal & General UK Index
Index: FTSE All Share
Annual charges: 0.53% (0.5%
management plus custodian and
registrar fee)
Bid/offer spread: 0%
Minimum investments: £500 lump
sum, £25 monthly.
Website: www.legalandgeneral.com
Tel: 0800 0920092

M&G Index Tracker
Index: FTSE All Share
Annual charges:0.439% (0.3%
management plus custodian and
registrar fees)
Bid/offer spread: none
Minimum investments: £500 lump
sum, £10 monthly investment
Website: www.mandg.co.uk
Tel: 0800 390390

Scottish Widows UK Tracker
Index: FTSE 100
Annual charges: 0.5%
Bid/offer spread: 0%
Minimum investments: £500 lump
sum or £50 monthly
Website: www.scottishwidows.co.uk
Tel: 08457 678910

Virgin UK Index Tracker
Index: FTSE All Share
Annual charges: 1%
Bid/offer spread: 0%
Minimum investments: £1 for lump
sums or monthly investments
Website: www.virginmoney.com
Tel: 08456 101020

Appendix 4
Useful Web Sites

With as little a web as this I will ensnare as great a fly as Cassio.
William Shakespeare, *Othello* (I, i)

As we've already pointed out on a number of occasions, the Internet represents a fantastic resource for the private investor. So much so that it's hard to make a case for not getting on the Internet and making use of it. We wouldn't really be doing our duty if we didn't give you a list of the addresses of a few Web sites to get you started. The only problem with lists like this is that they can be a real pain to use. Things change and they change very rapidly. All of these links were valid at the time of writing, but some of them will have ceased to exist by the time it reaches the bookshops. Don't worry, because we have created a Foolish Resources section at **www.fool.co.uk/community/resource/**where you can find all these links online. Most of them refer to sites beyond the Motley Fool, for which we can take no responsibility.

Government and regulation
Association of British Insurers – **www.abi.org.uk**
Bank of England – **www.bankofengland.co.uk**
Companies House – **www.companieshouse.gov.uk**
Department of Trade and Industry – **www.dti.gov.uk**
Department for Work and Pensions – **www.dwp.gov.uk**
Financial Services Authority – **www.fsa.gov.uk**
Government Impartial Pension Guide – **www.pensionguide.gov.uk**
HM Treasury – **www.hm-treasury.gov.uk**
Inland Revenue – **www.inlandrevenue.gov.uk**

Occupational Pensions Advisory Service – **www.opas.org.uk**
Occupational Pensions Regulatory Authority – **www.opra.gov.uk**
Office for National Statistics – **www.statistics.gov.uk**
Office of Fair Trading – **www.oft.gov.uk**

News and weather
BBC News – **news.bbc.co.uk**
BBC Weather Centre – **www.bbc.co.uk/weather**
Bloomberg UK – **www.bloomberg.co.uk**
Daily Express – **www.express.co.uk**
The Economist – **www.economist.com**
Financial Times – **www.ft.com**
The Guardian – **www.guardianunlimited.co.uk**
The Independent – **www.independent.co.uk**
Met Office – **www.met-office.gov.uk**
The Mirror – **www.mirror.co.uk**
Reuters – **www.reuters.co.uk**
Sky News – **www.sky.com/news**
The Sun – **www.the-sun.co.uk**
The Telegraph – **www.telegraph.co.uk**
The Times – **www.timesonline.co.uk**

Personal finance
Association of Investment Trust Companies – **www.aitc.co.uk**
Association of Unit Trusts and Investment Funds – **www.investment funds.org.uk**
Motley Fool UK – **www.fool.co.uk**
Motley Fool US – **www.fool.com**
FT Your Money – **www.ftyourmoney.com**
This is Money – **www.thisismoney.com**
Trustnet – **www.trustnet.com**

Search engines
Google – **www.google.com**

Stocks and shares
Company Annual Reports Online – **www.carol.co.uk**
FTSE International – **www.ftse.com**
Motley Fool UK – **www.fool.co.uk**
Motley Fool US – **www.fool.com**
ProShare – **www.proshare.org.uk**
UK-Wire – **www.uk-wire.co.uk**

Appendix 5
The Pan-galactic
Gargle Blaster

For those of you who are wondering just what is in the Pan-galactic Gargle Blaster, the 'best drink in existence' to which we alluded in the Introduction, then read on:

Here's what the Encyclopaedia Galactica *has to say about alcohol. It says that alcohol is a colourless volatile liquid formed by the fermentation of sugars and also notes its intoxicating effect on certain carbon-based life forms.*

The Hitch Hiker's Guide to the Galaxy *also mentions alcohol. It says that the best drink in existence is the Pan-galactic Gargle Blaster.*

It says that the effect of drinking a Pan-galactic Gargle Blaster is like having your brains smashed out by a slice of lemon wrapped around a large gold brick.

The Guide *also tells you on which planets the best Pan-galactic Gargle Blasters are mixed, how much you can expect to pay for one and what voluntary organisations exist to help you rehabilitate afterwards.*

The Guide *even tells you how you can mix one yourself.*

Take the juice from one bottle of that Ol' Janx Spirit, it says.

Pour into it one measure of water from the seas of Santraginous V – Oh, that Santraginean sea water, it says. Oh, those Santraginean fish!!!

Allow three cubes of Arcturan Mega-gin to melt into the mixture (it must be properly iced or the benzine is lost).

Allow four litres of Fallian marsh gas to bubble through it, in memory of all those happy Hikers who have died of pleasure in the Marshes of Fallia.

Over the back of a silver spoon float a measure of Qualactin Hypermint extract, redolent of all the heady odours of the dark Qualactin Zones, subtle, sweet and mystic.

Drop in a tooth of an Algolian Suntiger. Watch it dissolve, spreading the fires of the Algolian Suns deep into the heart of the drink.

Sprinkle Zamphuor.

Add an olive.

Drink...but...very carefully ...

The Hitch Hiker's Guide to the Galaxy *sells rather better than the* Encyclopaedia Galactica.

From The Hitch Hiker's Guide to the Galaxy

by Douglas Adams (Pan, 1979).

The Motley Fool UK would like to add that it accepts no liability for anyone following the directions above. All claims to be addressed to Douglas Adams.

Index

The following Motley Fool books are also published by Boxtree:

The Motley Fool UK Investment Workbook

The Fool 's Guide to Investment Clubs

The Fool 's Guide to Online Investing

How to Invest When You Don 't Have Any Money:The Fool 's Guide

Rule Breakers, Rule Makers:The Foolish Guide to Picking Shares

Make Your Child a Millionaire:The Fool 's Guide

The Old Fool 's Retirement Guide

A Girl's Best Friend Is Her Money

These are available from all good bookshops, or can be ordered direct from:

Book Services by Post
PO Box 29
Douglas
Isle of Man
IM99 1BQ

Credit card fotline +44 (0) 1624 67513
Postage and packing free in the UK